Diary from the Years of Occupation, 1939-44

Polish army captain Dr. Zygmunt Klukowski and his son George, 1920.

Diary from the Years of Occupation 1939–44

Zygmunt Klukowski

Translated from Polish by
George Klukowski

Edited by
**Andrew Klukowski and
Helen Klukowski May**

Foreword by
Monty Noam Penkower

University of Illinois Press
Urbana and Chicago

© 1993 by the Board of Trustees of the University of Illinois
Manufactured in the United States of America
C 5 4 3 2 1

This book is printed on acid-free paper.

Library of Congress Cataloging-in-Publication Data

Klukowski, Zygmunt, 1885–1959.
 [Dziennik z lat okupacji zamojszczyzny, 1939–1944. English]
 Diary from the years of occupation, 1939–1944 / Zygmunt Klukowski ;
translated by George Klukowski ; edited by Andrew Klukowski and
Helen Klukowski May ; foreword by Monty Noam Penkower.
  p. cm.
 Translation of: Dziennik z lat okupacji zamojszczyzny, 1939–1944.
 Includes index.
 ISBN 0-252-01960-1 (acid-free paper)
 1. World War, 1939–1945—Poland—Zamość (Voivodeship)
2. Klukowski, Zygmunt, 1885–1959—Diaries. 3. World War, 1939–1945—
Personal narratives, Polish. 4. Zamość (Poland: Voivodeship)—
History. I. Title.
D802.P62Z3413 1993
940.53'4384'092—dc20
 [B]   92-11032
                                                 CIP

Contents

Illustrations follow page 2

Foreword:
The Klukowski Chronicle

Monty Noam Penkower

The invasion of Poland by sixty German divisions on September 1, 1939, signaled but the first step in Adolf Hitler's quest for *Lebensraum*. According to the Nazi dictator's geopolitical-racist view, "living space" in eastern Europe would provide food and raw materials, achieve territorial continuity, and infuse the nation's body with new blood. While unleashing World War II, implementation of this policy in the occupied territories ultimately included the killing of their political and intellectual leadership, the annihilation of the Jews, the exploitation of the masses through slave labor, and the transfer to Germany of Polish and Slav children who would improve the "Aryan" race.

In the mind of Berlin, Poland as a nation had ceased to exist. Quickly annexing parts of western and northern Poland, the Third Reich organized a civil administration, the General Government, in the remaining area allotted it under the secret Nazi-Soviet pact of August 1939. (The Soviets seized eastern Poland up to the Bug and San rivers. Following Germany's June 1941 invasion of Stalin's imperium, the district of Galicia was formed and incorporated into the General Government. Expressly marked for murder were Poland's 3.3 million Jews, 90 percent of whom perished in ghettos, concentration camps, and the death centers of Chelmno, Belzec, Sobibor, Treblinka, Majdanek, and Auschwitz-Birkenau. Three million other Poles, 10 percent of the nation's prewar population, died under the swastika. According to official estimates, 2.4 million Polish citizens went through forced labor and deportation to Germany and other occupied countries; 863,000 faced detention in prisons and concentration camps; more than 2.4 million were forced to leave their homes.

This Germanization proved exceptionally harsh for the Zamosc province in eastern Poland. The southern part of the Lublin district, a predominantly agricultural area divided before the war among the four districts of Zamosc, Tomaszow Lubelski, Hrubieszow, and Bilgoraz, boasted of some 340,000 Poles, 110,000 Ukrainians, and 60,000 Jews. Beginning in May 1940, several thousand Poles suspected of potential resistance fell victim to the *AB-Aktion*. Two years later the Jews of the region were deported with horrendous efficiency to the death chambers of Belzec. Then, on November 12, 1942, SS *Reichsführer* Heinrich Himmler, *Reich* Commissioner for the Strengthening of German Nationhood and, concurrently, in charge of the "Final Solution" of the "Jewish question," agreed with General Government director Hans Frank to have this province declared the first resettlement area. Preliminary preparations included the destruction of six villages and the removal of 2,000 people.

The pacification of Zamosc officially began on November 27, 1942, under the command of Odilo Globocnik, who had almost completed his supervisory task of murdering the General Government's Jews in *Aktion Reinhard*. Some 300 villages were emptied of their population of 110,000. Ten thousand people died in the course of the forced evictions. The survivors were transported to Germany for slave labor, dispatched to concentration camps, shot, or sent to villages in the Lublin and Warsaw districts. More than 30,000 children were handed over to strangers. Some died in Auschwitz or during the deportations, and some were designated for Germanization in the *Reich;* German sources list a total of 4,454 such children in foster homes. Four-hundred additional villages escaped the evacuation pilot project, which ended in August 1943, because the SS lacked the requisite manpower.

These events strengthened the Polish resistance movement, operating as an underground state with ties to a government-in-exile in London. The singular killing of Zamosc's Jews and the expulsions of its peasantry led partisan commanders to suspect that the Poles might be next in line for systematic death. Struggling for sheer survival, partisans engaged Germans in numerous clashes. The Nazis retaliated by wiping out entire villages as examples of collective punishment. *Aktion Sturmwind* alone deployed three *Wehrmacht* divisions in June 1944 against 1,100 men from the *Armia Kra-*

jowa (Home Army) and the National Democratic party and another 1,000 from the left-wing Peasant party's PPR and Soviet partisan units. Heavy fighting that same spring between the Ukrainian Insurgent Army and the Polish resistance resulted in great losses to both sides, and the districts of Hrubieszow and Tomaszow Lubelski were cleared of their inhabitants. The agony of Zamosc ended with the arrival of the Red Army in July 1944, only to be succeeded by another arduous, far longer occupation.

Fortunately for the historical record, the tribulations of the Zamosc region had their chronicler in Dr. Zygmunt Klukowski. Born the youngest of three children to Dr. Jordan and Felicia (Podwinski) Klukowski in Odessa on January 23, 1885, Zygmunt completed his high school studies in Moscow. Enrolling in that city's University Medical School, he spent a few months in prison for activity in Polish underground organizations during the First Russian Revolution of 1905. After release from jail, Zygmunt moved to Crakow, able to attend its Jagiellionium University School of Medicine. With his degree awarded in 1911, Klukowski secured employment as a physician at the Radziwill estate in Nieswierz, where he met his future wife, Dr. Helena Wojciechowski.

The next few years regularly found Klukowski in uniform. Drafted into the Russian army in September 1914 as a surgeon, he worked briefly in a medical evacuation unit and then in a Moscow military hospital. His wife joined him there in 1915, where their son, Jerzy (George), was born a year later. Moving all about the country during the Russian revolution, the family finally returned in 1918 to a free Poland. During the Polish-Russian war, Klukowski served as military surgeon in the Polish army, discharged as a captain in 1921 with the Cross of Valor.

In October 1919 Zygmunt Klukowski was appointed superintendent of the Zamosc county hospital in Szczebrzeszyn, a post he would hold for almost thirty years. Aside from administrative and medical duties, he taught in the training colleges of Szczebrzeszyn and Zamosc and at the University of Crakow. A passion for Polish history and biography resulted in a unique collection of more than fourteen thousand volumes, which, with a collection of ex libris, he willed to the Catholic University in Lublin. Ever energetic, Klukowski also served as chief of the town's volunteer fire department, taught history in the local high school for a time, and helped organize the Zamosc city library. In 1930 he obtained a divorce from his wife; a second marriage, to Zofia Szymanski, in 1933, resulted in a son, Tadeusz.

The outbreak of World War II brought the fifty-five-year-old doctor back to active duty for the White Eagle on a Red Field. Discharged after one month's work with a military hospital in retreat to the Rumanian border, he returned to his former post. During the entire German occupation

Klukowski served the *Armia Krajowa* under the code name "Podwinski." His secret tasks included writing down for its information service all that occurred in a 75-100-mile radius and passing along reports from partisan unit to unit. Obsessed by an urge to record notes for a future history of the war in Zamosc and in Poland, he also kept a diary almost on a daily basis, hiding it from the Germans at great risk amid the hospital's old buildings. Gestapo arrests on more than one occasion, even imprisonment in Zamosc's Rotunda prison, did not dampen his resolve.

Grim, indeed, for Klukowski was the Soviet occupation that followed the war. Under the code name "Satyr," he served in the Polish underground and kept a diary of the Communist terror. Arrests by the NKVD, before and after he testified in case 8 of the International Military Tribunal trials in Nuremberg, led to Klukowski's demotion to ward physician. Yet he managed to publish five volumes on the German occupation of the Zamosc region and prepared three other manuscripts, subsequently given to the Catholic University of Lublin. In July 1952, while unsuccessfully seeking to defend his son Tadeusz from execution for partisan activity linked to Operation Martyka, Klukowski himself was sentenced to a ten-year incarceration term. After four years in Wronki prison, the doctor was pardoned and "rehabilitated."

In June 1956 Klukowski decided to relocate to Lublin, where he spent the remaining years of his life. A first edition of *Diary from the Years of Occupation* was published in Poland in 1958, with a second edition the following year. The book earned him the country's literary award for the best World War II memoir. This joined the company of other past honors, including the Order of the White Crow from the Polish Bibliographical Society, the Cavalier Cross of *Polonia Restituta* for lifelong devotion to the cause of Polish freedom, and the twice-received Gold Cross of Merit.

Dr. Zygmunt Klukowski died on November 23, 1959, after a long struggle against cancer. Buried in the Szczebrzeszyn cemetery's special section dedicated to the soldiers of the Home Army, he has not since been entirely forgotten. His name adorns the street passing the hospital he served so faithfully, and in 1986 the townspeople erected a monument in his honor. Its plaque, located in the town square, reads:

> Dr. Zygmunt Klukowski
> 1885–1959
> Physician, Bibliophile, Historian,
> Writer, and Civic Leader
> Citizens of Szczebrzeszyn

Zygmunt Klukowski's dream that his diary would be translated into both English and French never materialized. Now, more than thirty years after his death, this abridged American edition appears thanks to a family effort. His son George, who spent almost six years of World War II in German POW camps, translated from the original volume. His grandson Andrew edited the manuscript, and his granddaughter Helen Klukowski May contributed the typing; his great-granddaughter Hayden May prepared photographs and enlargements. The work, concluded George, "reflects the pride of four generations of the Klukowski family."

For readers of the diary, its publication is indispensable for an understanding of Poland's fate under Third Reich rule. German looting, a brief Soviet occupation, specific Nazi attacks against Catholic clergy and the professional classes, forced evacuations—all find their place here. Ukrainian brutality, gestapo arrests, rape, and incessant killings are vividly described. Personal peril, the spread of typhus, limited hospital supplies, and a serious heart condition notwithstanding, Zygmunt Klukowski remained at his post, treating the sick and the wounded without discrimination.

Nazi descent into the primordial barbarism since known as the Holocaust also receives its due. Already in October 1939 Jews were being singled out to clean the public latrines and city streets; they were whipped and forced to pay exorbitant fines. Food supplies, medical attention, and library access were officially denied them. Some refused to wear the Star of David on arm bands; others walked in restricted areas and even bought weapons and ammunition—to scant avail. In August 1940 Jews' stores were put up for auction; that October all Jewish males were arrested to build an airfield for the *Luftwaffe;* one year later any clothing made of fur was surrendered under penalty of death.

In March 1942 the first transports of Jews from western Europe passed through to Belzec, followed by mass deportations across the Zamosc region. Klukowski laconically recorded their end: "Some are killed with electricity, some with poison gas, and the bodies are burned" (April 8, 1942). Passive resistance could not stem the design of death. Those not yet taken were shipped to German labor camps or fell prey to execution, with the Nazi-appointed Jewish Council ordered to pay for any ammunition expended. By November, Zamosc and Szczebrzeszyn were *Judenrein,* several hundred Jews escaping to the surrounding forests and a life of partisan warfare. (On occasion such fugitives subsequently faced deadly assault from *Armia Krajowa* ranks, especially beyond the Zamosc region.) The small remnant fled the Klemensow airfield in May 1944, seizing a last chance before liquidation.

Most informative is Klukowski's eloquent testimony to the perseverance of the Polish resistance. Religious services continued, a confiscated wall-size painting of Prussian tribute to the Polish king Sigismund was clandestinely retrieved, machine guns were buried for future use. Gendarmes and informers were killed, funds stolen for the underground, illegal newspapers printed, trains derailed. In response to the initial Germanization of Zamosc County in November 1942, peasant battalions and other units confronted the enemy in battle. Flour mills, sugar refineries, railroad stations, and bridges were blown up and the exploits reported in the information bulletins of the Home Army. Eventually, increasing Soviet liberation of villages augmented these attacks from the forests, so that a jubilant Klukowski could celebrate Polish National Holiday and the second day of Pentecost in May 1944 with impressive gatherings of comrades-in-arms. Two months later the Polish flag hidden by Klukowski for almost five years was unfurled aloft the hospital in Szczebrzeszyn.

The power of this lengthy narrative is heightened by a pervasive scrupulousness. Polish collaborators—some named here—surface alongside patriots. Denunciations of underground members and arms caches occur regularly. Some natives freely sign *Volksdeutsche* lists to obtain sundry benefits. Robberies for individual gain, female fraternization with German soldiers, "blue police" help in the beatings and murder of Jews—these actions also merit Klukowski's painstaking attention. Deportations of Jews were watched impassively, on occasion with laughter, by some members of the populace. Poles then looted former Jewish homes and even helped gendarmes hunt for Jews avoiding mass roundups. Many of his countrymen Klukowski sadly concluded on November 26, 1942, saw the Jews "not as human beings but as animals that must be destroyed." The author, who administered to Jews as generously as to others under his professional care, cites two Poles who hid Jews then paid for heroic decency with their lives (January 6 and March 22, 1943).

The diary and related activities played a large role in sustaining Klukowski's spirits. Exactitude his lodestar, he noted discrepancy and rumor for future objective assessments. Klukowski took pride in illegal publications and future plans shared with him by fellow intellectuals in Warsaw and made a concerted effort to collect invaluable documentation, in different languages, about the war. He also began a reference work devoted to Polish physicians, penned an autobiographical memoir covering the years 1918–39, and persisted in further research for a history of the Zamosc region. Shortly before Szczebrzeszyn's liberation, the doctor even completed a book-length manuscript on the history of medicine at the Zamoyski estate.

"In spite of the arrests, torture, evacuations, and murders, we survived." With these words the Klukowski chronicle comes to a close. Yet its author did far more than live to witness the Third Reich's *Götterdämmerung*. The unparalleled *Diary from the Years of Occupation*, which he kept so assiduously, is an essential primary source for Poland's plight in the World War II years. Honestly capturing myriad facets of that bloody torment, its detailed exposition, together with Klukowski's other literary work, rescues individuals and significant experiences from likely oblivion. Dr. Zygmunt Klukowski's steadfast commitment to the Hippocratic Oath and to his country's independence inspires and instructs, as well, about the nature of moral courage. His rare, principled behavior, joined by similar models of humanity in that inhuman time, indicates the only possible counterweight to nihilism and destruction—the fortitude and dignity of humankind.

Translator's Note

It is very difficult to write about one's own father. One tends to concentrate on daily routines, life at home, and maybe even some vacation trips. These memories are very important to me personally, but here, for future historians, I will address Dr. Zygmunt Klukowski's own inclinations and skills as a historian and the experiences that prepared him to chronicle the momentous events recorded in his *Diary from the Years of Occupation, 1939–44.*

Until 1939 I was able to be a witness to his life. The onset of World War II separated us, and it was not until 1947 that I was able to once more see my father, when he was a witness at the Nuremberg war trials. Much of my information is based on conversations with and correspondence from my first cousin, Antoni Klukowski. During my 1987 visit to Poland I was able to visit Antoni and also to research my father's private memoirs, which he bequeathed to the library of the Catholic University in Lublin. Some early material appeared in the article "Recollections from Moscow, 1896–1912," in the *Archives of the History of Medicine*, published in Poland in 1957.

My father came from a learned family from the Podole region of Poland. His father, Jordan Klukowski, had a doctorate in pharmacy. My father's older brother, Juljan, eventually became a lawyer, and his sister, Zofia, entered the teaching profession. When my father was of high school age the family moved to Moscow, where Jordan Klukowski had been appointed professor of pharmacy at the university. The local high schools taught all subjects in Russian. Polish language, history, and literature were taught at home by the family. My grandmother ran a very proper Polish household, where only Polish and some French were permitted. My father once mentioned to me that occasionally this was slightly embarrassing. My grandmother, who knew Russian but was not very proud of it, sometimes spoke it in a very primitive style, not at all conducive to her position as the wife of a professor at a Russian university.

My uncle Juljan became very active in various Polish philanthropic activities and organized the first Polish library in Moscow. Within a short time this library grew in size to the point that it was necessary to build an enclosure, which came to be known as the Polish Club. The entire cost of construction was paid by a retired Russian general of Polish ancestry, Alfons Szaniewski. Just before the grand opening of the library, called the Szaniewski Polish Library, the general ordered a large sign erected reading "*Wiedza To Potega*" (knowledge is power).

Those words became my father's future motto. As he points out in his early writings, during the first years of high school he learned only enough to be moved from one grade to another. Once he joined the Polish library, however, and came under the educational guidance of his older brother, his grades improved dramatically. His best subjects were history and literature, and his Latin and French achievements were admirable. (I recall, sometime in the late 1930s, my father having a philosophical discussion with a German professor in Latin.) During high school he also became involved in the activities of various Polish youth organizations that had as a central theme the reorganization of a free Polish state.

In 1904 my father enrolled in the medical school at Moscow University, but when the tsarist government closed all the universities following the Russian revolution in 1905, many Polish students in Moscow decided to leave. My father went to Warsaw, which was under Russian occupation and rule. After a short while he was arrested by the Russian secret police, interred for several weeks, and barred from attending any other Russian university. He then moved to Cracow, which was under Austrian occupation. He enrolled in the medical school at Jagiellonium University, where he studied history as diligently as medicine. During his university years he again became active in many Polish organizations, concentrating especially on printing and distributing materials designed for Polish students and workers under Russian occupation. He received his degree in 1911 and a license to practice medicine in Russia in 1912.

After various civilian and military positions my father became superintendent of the new county hospital in Szczebrzeszyn in the Zamosc region, on October 20, 1919. Since this is the hospital that later became the central setting of his *Diary from the Years of Occupation*, his description of it, from his unpublished notes, is worth quoting:

The hospital was in very poor shape when I arrived. The previous superintendent came to the hospital for only a few hours a day. Briefly, after his
death, the administration was in the hands of a Mr. Dunin-Rzuchowski, an
old man. He was a very dedicated man who died in 1926.

The hospital service was in the hands of an old nurse, an Orthodox nun
from the convent in Radecznica, Zofia Klimczuk. She was in charge of a
group of dedicated, but untrained women, who tried to do their best for
the patients.

At the beginning, the hospital had fifty beds. A physician from Zamosc,
Dr. Bogucki, visited the hospital only three times a week. The situation
was chaotic. Because of the lack of electrical power, lighting was supplied
by petroleum lamps or candles. It was especially bad during night emer-
gencies. The plumbing was in poor shape also. Heating was another problem. Wood stoves supplied the only heat to the hospital wards. At the time
of admittance, patients were suppose to supply their own bedding, including
pillows.

Once his hospital duties and his personal life stabilized, my father began
working at some of his hobbies, namely, collecting books and studying the
history of medicine. He decided to assign a quarter of his earnings to the
purchase of books, including Polish biographies, autobiographies, and historical works. He kept an open account with some of the largest publishers.
At the time of his death his library numbered more than fourteen thousand
volumes, of which about eight thousand were biographies. This was one of
the largest privately owned libraries in Poland. He willed it to the Catholic
University in Lublin.

My father was very strict in one sense: he never lent any of his books,
the only exception being to his best friend, the notary Henryk Rosinski.
Yet he was not selfish about his books. Anyone who wished to study was
welcome into his house. He had special guest quarters where scholars
could spend their time. The only request he made of the guests was to sign
a guest book, ideally with some comments. Over the years this "book"
grew to several volumes, which are now deposited in Lublin along with his
vast collection of books.

From the first days of his stay in Szczebrzeszyn my father was involved
in education. He agreed to teach at the teacher training colleges in Szczebrzeszyn and Zamosc. He promoted the establishment of a high school in
Szczebrzeszyn and even taught Polish history until a full-time teacher could
be hired. Along with Dr. Bogucki and a few others he organized an unusual club, the Klub Zonatych Kawalerow (Married Bachelor's Society).
This very exclusive club was involved in the printing of special high-
standard biographical sketches. Beginning in 1927 my father was instru-
mental in the organization known as the Kolo Milosnikow Kziazki (KMK),
Zamosc's Book Fun Club. Along with Rosinski he organized the Zamosc

city library, which grew to approximately ten thousand volumes and a membership of one thousand.

As another hobby my father began an ex libris collection. Eventually this became one of the largest in Poland, and its fame spread as far as Germany. His nephew, the architect Jan Klukowski, designed for him seven personal ex libria, the most famous of which showed the initials Z.K. on either side of his caricature and an inscription below reading (in Polish) "I don't lend books."

During 1923–39 my father published numerous papers, most of them concerned with the history of medicine in Poland. In 1925, one of his first books was published, *Medical Services at the Radziwill Estate during the Nineteenth Century.* He was elected to the Polish Academy of Sciences and Letters and in 1938 received its second highest award, the Silver Laurel Wreath.

My father was a very popular and well-liked physician. After spending several hours each day at the hospital he still found time to make house calls to other patients. At first his practice was limited because he traveled by horse and buggy, but after he purchased his first car in 1932 his practice tripled. The local peasants were very poor but possessed an extraordinary amount of Polish pride, almost stubbornness. On one occasion my father delivered a baby and accepted a dozen eggs in payment so as to make the family feel that they had not received charity. On many other occasions when special consultations were required the honoraria could be quite high. In 1932 he was called to Tel Aviv and received an honorarium in British pounds in addition to having all his expenses paid.

During World War II, after a brief tour of duty with the Polish medical corps, my father returned to Szczebrzeszyn, once again to serve as superintendent of the county hospital, but now under German occupation. He ministered to the sick and wounded, be they Polish, Jewish, or German. Practically from the first day of occupation he was involved with partisan organizations, especially with their information services. He also began keeping a detailed diary, precariously staying one step ahead of the Germans by hiding it daily in different places.

After the German army withdrew in 1944 the Soviet troops disarmed the Polish Home Army and the movement again went underground. In 1944–45 my father kept another diary, this time documenting events occurring under Soviet occupation. He began organizing his notes, diary, and other materials dealing with the German occupation. *German War Crimes in the Region of Zamosc* was published in early 1946; four other volumes followed: *German Terrors in Zamosc Region, Zamosc Region's Fight against the Germans, Germany and the Zamosc Region,* and *Underground Activities in the Zamosc*

Region. He also published several articles in various magazines, including two in the bulletin of the Jewish Historical Institute. On the reputation of his powers as witness and his respect for historical detail, my father was called in 1947 to testify at the war crimes trials in Nuremberg. This gave him enough time to visit my home in Germany and afforded him his only opportunity to spend some time with my wife, Wanda, and his recently born grandson, Andrew.

After he returned to Poland he spent some time each day, after completing his professional duties, organizing his notes and preparing the typewritten material for publication. The resulting manuscripts, which he later deposited in the library of the Catholic University in Lublin, include "Memoirs from the Zamosc Region," "Diary from the Years of Occupation, Volume II: The Soviets" (now being prepared for publication by our family), and "History of the Zamosc Estate." Approximately twenty-five hundred pages of miscellaneous notes relating to the German and Soviet occupations are also on file at the university. The exact whereabouts of the "History of the Szczebrzeszyn Hospital" are unknown, but it is thought that the manuscript was given to a physician in the area for safekeeping.

In July 1952 my father suffered a terrible blow when his other son, Tadeusz, was arrested, sentenced to death, and executed at age twenty-one for his involvement with a partisan operation known as "Martyka" (named after the commandant of the underground operation). When my father arrived in Warsaw in a futile attempt to defend Tadeusz, he too was arrested and served four years in Wronki prison. Characteristically, he kept a diary of his experiences there. (This diary is currently missing, but my son and I have begun a search for it.) After his release, my father returned to Szczebrzeszyn but then moved on to Lublin, where he rented an apartment across from the Catholic University library. The governor of the Lublin region assigned him a secretary, who was a big help in organizing his manuscripts.

By the time the first edition of *Diary from the Years of Occupation* was published in Poland, in 1958, my father was too ill to supervise personally the editing and printing of his work, so he had to rely on other people. Some changes were made, such as in wording and the omission of weekday names; I have restored those aspects of his original version that I believe best represent his intention. Before the work of translation began, my son and I decided that it would be best to abridge the translation to make it easier to keep the Polish feeling of the sentences. Because Polish has a completely different sentence structure from English, editorial work was also needed, which included breaking up overly long sentences and combining very short paragraphs that were clearly related. Punctuation and spelling were regularized somewhat. Thus, this translation is about 8 percent shorter than the Polish first edition. But the historical integrity of the diary has been kept intact. Never did we omit any historical or personal reference that might be considered relevant.

George Klukowski

Editor's Note

George Klukowski died on the morning on June 30, 1991, in Cracow. He had returned to his beloved country once again to learn as much as he could of his father's life before and after World War II. The trip was fruitful; his intrepid detective work turned up volumes of manuscripts written by Zygmunt Klukowski covering the years 1919–39 and 1945–56. When illness struck my father, he was in the bell tower of Wawel Cathedral, the most politically symbolic spot in all of Poland. Scores of Polish kings and heroes are buried there. My father died knowing that his father's *Diary from the Years of Occupation* would be published soon in English.

Andrew Klukowski

Preface to the First Polish Edition

A few months before the outbreak of World War II, in September 1939, when it was completely clear that war was unavoidable and the military encounter with Germany could start at any time, I started to write this diary.

I was aware that the fight would be very hard and that we had to survive through very difficult times. Later I found out that it was much worse that I ever expected.

All my observations and experiences were written day after day. Normally, every evening before going to bed, I made short notes of all the events of the day. But when, especially toward the end of the occupation, the tempo of our lives became more and more hectic, and when the important events were coming one after another, I made notes several times a day. I was obsessed by an urge to put all the details of daily events on paper, hoping that in the future they would help in writing the history of the war, in not only the Zamosc region but also in Poland. During that time I completely overlooked my personal safety in case those notes fell into German hands. All my notes were written on loose sheets and stored in places known only to me.

At that time I was living in the superintendent's quarters of the county hospital in Szczebrzeszyn. The hospital facilities were converted from an old monastery built in 1680. In those old buildings there were many secret hideouts known only to me. The Germans, even after several very detailed searches through my quarters and through the entire hospital, were unable to find anything.

It was very difficult to describe all the aspects of the underground activities that became more active every day, and my own involvement in them. I was constantly aware that some day, some of my notes might fall into German hands, so I had to be very careful in the use of names and locations. I used my own reference system so as not to endanger other people, but in time, when my hideouts proved to be secure, I started compiling more detailed information. I tried to write objectively, but it was difficult because we were without any sources of information like radio or free press. The only newspapers that were permitted were German, edited in the Polish language.

As I noted previously, I wrote my diary on the spot without any literary workout and without hope that it would be printed in book form. All my notes are printed as were originally written without any special editing.

Zygmunt Klukowski, M.D.
Szczebrzeszyn, April 1958

Zygmunt Klukowski as a student at Moscow University, 1905.

Zygmunt Klukowski's future wife, Dr. Helena Woyciechowska, 1905.

Dr. Zygmunt Klukowski (*center*) with his uncle Juljan Klukowski and his cousin Eryk Lipinski, circa 1910.

Russian army captain Dr. Zygmunt Klukowski, 1915.

Dr. Zygmunt Klukowski, 1940.

Dr. Zygmunt Klukowski ex libris created by his nephew Jan Klukowski.

"Sigismundus—King of Szczebrze-szyn," a caricature of Dr. Zygmunt Klukowski created by his nephew Jan Klukowski, April 10, 1941.

P i e ś n i

Oddziałów Partyzanckich

Zamojszczyzny.

1944

The front cover of the soldiers' song-book from the Zamosc region, compiled by Dr. Zygmunt Klukowski.

The monument, with a close-up of the plaque, dedicated to Dr. Zygmunt Klukowski in Szczebrzeszyn. Photographs by Dr. Klukowski's nephew Antoni Klukowski.

Dr. Zygmunt Klukowski's tomb in the military A.K. (Home Army) section of the Szczebrzeszyn cemetery.

Dr. Zygmunt Klukowski Street in Szczebrzeszyn.

St. Catherine's Church and the county hospital in Szczebrzeszyn, 1991.

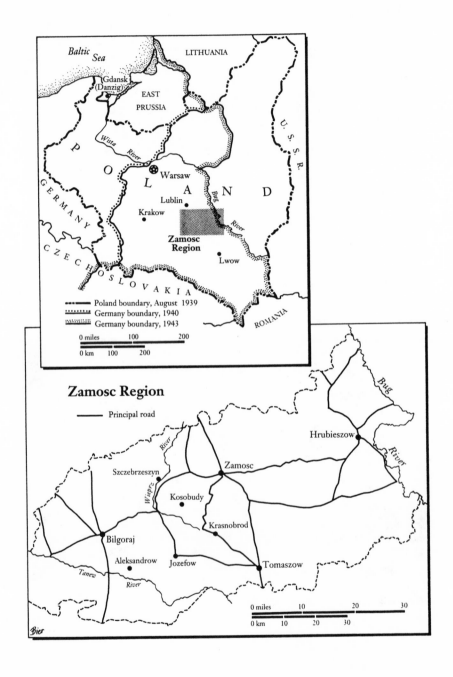

Zamosc Region

—— Principal road

Bier

The Shock of Defeat

June

June 19 In the last few months we are living in suspense. Will it be war or not? And when? Just yesterday in Zamosc for the first time I felt that war is close. I met Count Tarnowski from the Sucha estate. He was looking for a safe place to move his library. He said that after talking with military officials he decided to evacuate his castle in Sucha, only 25 km from the Slovakian border. (At this time Slovakia was occupied by Germany.) He finally decided to move his books someplace close to Lublin, but he still was looking for a place to hide the collections of old armor of the Archduke of Habsburg from Zywiec. Finally Wazowski, the mayor of Zamosc, assigned for this project a room next to his office.

Some banks and savings and loans from Katowice rented two large basements in an old building, beneath the movie theater Stylowy in Zamosc in order to move in all of their files. In a word, a foretaste of war, so well known to me from the past.

August

August 12 In July I spent four weeks vacationing in Iwonicz. Now in August we know that war with Germany is inevitable. Nervous tension is increasing from day to day. Today, without any previous notice, the Ninth Infantry Regiment was called up for field exercises in the Szczebrzeszyn and Klemensow area.

This afternoon I visited the county office in Zamosc. I received instructions to call back every hospital employee from vacation.

August 14   During the night in Szczebrzeszyn they called forty people to active duty, including Dr. Jozwiakowski and Judge Sokolowski. Everybody went to the railroad station to see the departing men. The spirit of the draftees is very high.

I am completely thrown off balance. It is difficult for me to do my daily chores.

August 25   We are living in unusual tension. I am waiting for the call to active duty any time. I am afraid that maybe I will have to stay in my hospital. Everywhere people are talking about men who have already been called. So far as I know, the army called for duty physicians even older than me.

I know that war will start soon. People are anxious; you can hear that everybody wants it to start now. But you can see some unusual happenings, like shortness of small change. People are holding on to small coins. Everybody is handing over 20-zloty bills and asking for change. Some people are giving 15 zloty in coins for a 20-zloty bill.

More and more official files are being moved from Katowice Bydgoszcz and other cities on the western border to Zamosc and Lublin. Many people are leaving Warsaw to get away from the capital in the event of war. Officially, the beginning of the school year was postponed indefinitely. It is being said that this will be for only a few days.

All vacations were canceled. Everybody is listening to radio news. Yesterday they called another 200 men to active duty. Today the Ninth Infantry Regiment moved out of their quarters, but where are they going? It is unknown.

August 28   Today is the 350-year anniversary of the establishment of the Zamoyski estate. A very good speech was presented by Prof. Kolankowski and a very dull one by Mr. Golinski. Everyone there tried to please young Zamoyski. It was very unpleasant to hear a speech by Prof. Rev. Kruszynski, from Lublin University, who by the way is a very good speaker, addressing this young man, who as of yet had not shown any ability for administration, as "distinguished and revered." There was a very small audience. No one from the county or state administration was present.

August 30   Yesterday afternoon the general mood was nervous as never before. Everybody is waiting for some important news. We hear rumors that today a general mobilization will be ordered. Today in the morning the same. Around 3 P.M. I received a call that posters with announcements of a general mobilization were hung in the city. In the streets I saw many people. Some women were crying, but there was no panic.

I ran as fast as I could to city hall to find out if I am finally called to active duty. After that I drove to the city of Zamosc to find out the future of my hospital. I was told to turn hospital administration over to Dr. Warchalowska. The general atmosphere in the city is more calm now. People know about the general mobilization and are trying to organize their own lives. I visited Zamosc twice.

After returning to Szczebrzeszyn I went to my tailor to check on my uniform and to order a new pair of boots.

On all the city streets there is unusual traffic.

August 31   First day of mobilization. The traffic increased. In the morning I turned all my hospital functions over to Dr. Warchalowska.

In the evening, in all surrounding cities and villages, the military called for anti-aircraft drills, with little success.

September

September 1   Second day of mobilization. The early morning traffic was very heavy. From the radio we obtained some news about the German attack on our soil, about the air bombardment of Gdynia and Cracow. I was very upset after hearing of the air attack on Cracow. I remember clearly how in World War I the Russians were planning to destroy the city.

Around noon I drove to Zamosc. Everybody is talking about war, and everybody is sure that we will win. The unfounded rumor about Polish troops taking Gdansk boosted the general morale. This afternoon I went to Zwierzyniec. There the situation is the same. People have begun preparing themselves for air defense. Also in my hospital the personnel are working on blacking out all windows. No one had done this before. Even the county was giving detailed instructions on how to prepare the buildings against air attacks. But already the stores were out of black paper, tacks, and tape. Within a few days all the stores were sold out of items such as matches, candles, kerosene, salt, and cigarettes—typical black market items.

The area is crowded with people moving from the west. The police are preparing buildings for offices to be moved from western cities.

September 2   Third day of mobilization. Radio news: 100 German tanks and 37 aircrafts were destroyed, and later 12 of our own planes lost. German air raids are closer and closer. Lublin, Lwow, people have said even Zamosc. Everybody is preparing themselves in case of raids. The hospital personnel are digging trenches. The war atmosphere can be felt everywhere.

September 4   Yesterday at 7 A.M. I left the hospital with my wife and son Tadeusz and drove to Lublin. All of the hospital personnel were at my departure with flowers, speeches, and tears.

On the highway, even though it was Sunday, there was heavy traffic. Closer to Lublin we encountered more and more horse-drawn wagons going in all directions. The buses were full of people trying to escape from the city. People were leaving, remembering the air strike of September 2. Just outside Lublin, next to the buildings of the Plage-Loskiewicz plant, I noticed the first devastation of the war: three completely destroyed apartment buildings. Many houses had broken windows and collapsed roofs. Witnesses said that several people had been killed or wounded. At first those casualties made a big impression on the people, but now that is subsiding. All the streets are full of people. Everyone is waiting for England and France to declare war against Germany. But when?

I registered my arrival in the military hospital of District 2, and from Lt. Col. Tabidze I received instructions to start an X-ray unit in Field Hospital No. 204. I tried to explain to Lt. Col. Tabidze that I had no experience in running an X-ray unit, but his answer was simple: "No one can change assignments worked out by the higher command." After this response, there was nothing to say.

I received the newest cannister gas mask, weighing 8 lbs., and went out to lunch. During lunch I heard a radio communiqué that England had already declared war against Germany and that France would follow in a few hours. This announcement was followed by the playing of the three national anthems, British, French, and Polish. It was received by everybody with enthusiasm. In a few minutes all the streets were decorated by flags of the three nations.

Everywhere you looked there were many soldiers and many uniformed physicians who seemed to have a special urge to salute everybody.

In Lublin I was told to go to Glusk, about 4 km away, where the headquarters of Field Hospital No. 204 was supposed to be. When I reached Glusk I was told to move to another village, Wilczopole, another 4 km of very poor dirt road, which my small Opel barely made.

Finally, I arrived at the large village of Wilczopole, and after signing in at the hospital office, I received quarters in a small peasant house, together with Maj. Boleslaw Modzelewski, a physician known to me from Zamosc.

After moving in all of my belongings, I reported in person to the hospital commandant, Maj. Stanislaw Wszelaki. Walking through the area I noticed complete disorganization. No one paid any attention to the several physicians and surgeons, which made us feel unimportant.

The village seemed completely silent; the street traffic was minor. One saw only a few enlisted personnel moving slowly about. No radios or newspapers; the news came only from people who had overheard others. Without doing any work, I decided to retire at 7 P.M. and slept the entire night.

At 6 A.M. the next day I went with Dr. Modzelewski to the village to search out any news. I went to Maj. Wszelaki asking for something to do. He told me that in a few days we would all be very busy so it would be a good idea to rest now. He was supposed to be working on new assignments. This afternoon we were to have a briefing.

I went looking for the enlisted personnel assigned to the hospital. All the men were of different ages, from twenty-one to over fifty, and from completely different backgrounds, and almost no one had any hospital experience. I noticed two high school teachers, one known to me from Szczebrzeszyn, Piotr Bohun.

The commandant seemed very pleased by today's revue. Yesterday he complained that the reservists had no training. He also complained that many Ukrainians showed up for service before any others. He expects more than twenty physicians. As we walked with Dr. Modzelewski I became very upset about having nothing to do.

Here was the second day, with much of the work to do, even in my own hospital in Szczebrzeszyn, and the only recreation in our lives were air raids. Every few hours when a German airplane approached, the lookout on the church tower sounded the alarm and all the traffic stopped. People went to the trenches and laid down while others stood still around the buildings and watched, but so far no one is really excited.

I am having a difficult time getting used to the tight uniform and boots, and the gas mask's heavy cannister made walking hard. I am not too disturbed about that, but I would like to have something to do. After organization, we are supposed to go to Wlodzimierz and start operations. The general mood is very high. Everyone is sure that we will win. No one accepts the possibility of defeat, especially now that England and France are at war.

September 5   In the morning we went with Maj. Wszelaki to Lublin, where I stayed approximately three hours. During this time we experienced an air raid on Lublin by German bombers. With the alarm sounding, all the streets became deserted. Everyone went to some shelter. Only men wearing civil defense arm bands could be seen on the streets. The entire alarm lasted about forty minutes. Two aircraft were shot down. I saw several wounded being taken to the hospital.

Generally, traffic was heavy. There were a lot of people new to the town. Many passenger cars were full of people and their luggage; most were women and children. I met many friends. I talked briefly with Gen. Kollataj-Strzednicki, with whom I had attended Moscow University. The radios and newspapers brought us the bad news that Czestochowa, Bydgoszcz, and Grudziadz were taken by the German army, but public spirit is still high. Everyone still talks about victory.

September 6   German aircraft have been flying since early morning, particularly above Swidnik and Lublin. Today we received a shipment of uniforms for the enlisted men, very good quality but the wrong sizes. I have blisters on my right foot and can barely walk. We have nothing to do. We are awaiting instructions from our commandant. I hope to move to Wlodzimierz soon and finally begin work. This evening another briefing. Tomorrow I go to Lublin for some new fumigating equipment. So far today is another nonproductive, dull day. In two days we are supposed to move to Wlodzimierz.

September 7   This morning I went to Lublin. I came back around 7 P.M. very tired because the whole day I was on my feet without even any time for lunch.

Lublin looked very depressing. The streets were full of cars of all types and makes. Luggage was on the roof of the cars and was hanging from fenders and bumpers. The gas stations were full of people but no more gasoline. Military stations were given gas only for military purposes. Around those stations I observed long lines of vehicles coming from both directions. Sometimes traffic is so heavy that no one can move. Some cars without gas are abandoned; others are being pulled by horses. More and more people are using horse-drawn wagons, but most are still using cars.

From Warsaw the evacuation of government offices has just begun. You can identify high-ranking officials, ministers, and members of the diplomatic corps by the official banners on many of the cars. This exodus is creating a panic that is spreading quickly. Some people are leaving without any plans, just to go.

In a coffee shop I met a woman with two children whom I know from Iwonicz. She is fleeing from Poznan. She stopped at one hotel in Lublin but was thrown out in a few minutes because the room was needed for a dignitary from Warsaw. She was in shock, not knowing what to do. All the hotels are reserved for the dignitaries. Above the city you can see more and more German aircraft.

The news is terribly bad. Besides Czestochowa, Grudziadz, and Bydgoszcz, the following cities have fallen into German hands: Cracow, Zakopane, and Lodz. German armies are rushing toward Warsaw, the capital.

The local population is holding up relatively well. All the panic comes from the outsiders. Many products in the shops are sold out, especially camping equipment, luggage, and soap. The restaurants are full. Food can be obtained, but you must wait a long time.

I returned to Wielczypole very depressed, but I still believe we will win the war. I would love to pass this on to others. I think about my family and hospital in Szczebrzeszyn. I would love to give them the courage that is needed so badly in situations like this.

Probably tomorrow or the next day we will be going to Wlodzimierz by rail.

September 9, Railroad station   Yesterday at 7 A.M. we left Wielczypole. The orders came the night before. Today at 10 A.M. we were to start loading at the railroad station freight terminal in Lublin and depart at noon. Even though we arrived in Lublin at 8 A.M. the loading did not start until 7 P.M. We waited for eleven hours in the quarters of Hospital No. 2 next to the terminal. During this time there were eight major air strikes by German bombers. The first was around 10 A.M. I had just gone to the mess hall to have some lemonade when I heard three explosions very close by. The first bomb landed next to the hospital building (the hospital had a big red cross painted on the roof) about 100 m from me. Later I saw one demolished building, a few tall trees down, and a big hole in the ground. The second bomb landed by the elevator. Here there were casualties, killed and wounded.

Again, a few hours later, more bombers came. Some people went into the trenches, but a few physicians were still sitting on a bench with Maj. Wszelaki. When the bombers were just above us we heard the characteristic sound of falling bombs. In a fraction of a second we were lying flat on our stomachs—where will they hit? A second later there was a loud explosion, then a second and third. I looked to see what damage had been done. So far no casualties; only horses still in their harnesses were panicking and racing without drivers through the gate. One wagon shattered and barricaded the gate.

After some time, when we noticed that the bombers had gone, we started to get up—dirty, shocked, and with a feeling of complete helplessness and defenselessness. After cleaning ourselves, we began looking over the damage. The bombs felt as if they were less than 100 m from us, but their fragments flew over our heads. Three bombs destroyed a portion of the railroad tracks. We observed one large and two smaller craters. Pieces of steel weighing more that 100 lbs. fell not far from where I was lying, but no one around me was wounded. Now that we knew that all the men were alive, we began looking for our wagons and horses. Near one wagon carrying our luggage and equipment for the field chapel, a small bomb had exploded. The driver was only shaken, he saved the horses, but the wagon was completely covered with dirt. The second wagon with our luggage, and a few others, had disappeared. Soldiers began searching for them. After some time the wagons began returning. The last was the one with our luggage, but many items were missing, so we began looking. After a few hundred meters we spotted a suitcase, a little farther on, three more. I was pleased to see my own. At this time the siren announced a new air attack. I ran to a ditch where a few others were already hiding. Practically everyone prayed. Some civilians were shaking with fright. During the day we survived a total of eight bombardments.

A few times I hid myself in the basement of the hospital building, where I was unable to see what was happening and could only hear the explosions and fire from the anti-aircraft machine guns and artillery. I was very upset.

For no apparent reason, we were kept on the hospital grounds the entire day, without any shelter. Finally we began loading. Looking around the railroad station, I noticed several bomb craters. Our casualties were light: only five people killed and a few wounded. One of the dead was a military mail carrier. I myself had never, in any previous wars, been under this kind of attack.

At 7 P.M. the loading was finished and now we waited for departure. We were waiting to start moving any time now and hoped to reach Wlodzimierz while it was still dark. Finally at 3 A.M. our train moved slowly to the passenger terminal, 4 km from the freight terminal, and there we stayed until 6 A.M.

We moved out of Lublin very slowly. Everywhere we were able to see destruction, such as in Trawniki, where a dead man's corpse in a railroad uniform lay near the railroad tracks. In Rejowiec I was told that we would pass through Zawada and Zamosc. I was pleased and hoped I could call my wife from Zawada and she would be able to come along with my son to see me.

September 10, Sunday in a Train Car in Wlodzimierz   Yesterday at 2 P.M. we finally arrived in Zawada. I went quickly to the post office and right away was given a telephone connection to Szczebrzeszyn (important military call). My call was answered by Mr. Edward Cichonski, hospital administrator, but my wife was in the office at that time, so he gave the receiver to her. Mainly we talked about how to get her to see me at Zawada or Zamosc, but because she didn't know how to drive and all the chauffeurs were in the service, this was impossible. She was so nervous that she stopped talking. I received from Mr. Cichonski information about work in the hospital. Our call was short because others were waiting in line.

The railroad tracks in Zamosc were damaged, so we stayed in Zawada for a few hours. I looked to the highway hoping to see my Opel, hoping that my wife had finally found a driver. When at last our train moved on I still looked toward the highway beside the tracks. The highway was full of cars, trucks, and horse-drawn wagons going in both directions, totally out of control.

At the rail station in Zamosc the wife of Dr. Modzelewski was waiting for the train. An hour later we started moving.

I felt very bad about not being able to see my wife, and I thought how she must have felt, not being able to see me at the railroad station. I was even mad at myself for having called her. It would have been better not telling her how close I was to the hospital. Mrs. Modzelewska promised to talk to my wife.

Mrs. Modzelewska told us about the bombardment of Zamosc. From her, I found out that the city was in complete chaos, mainly because of the thousands of evacuees from the western provinces of Poland. She told me that my hospital in Szczebrzeszyn is under the control of Dr. Halacz, an evacuee from Zaolzie who arrived with his family in his own very expensive car. No information about the latest war events, no newspapers, no radio. Our good spirit is starting to fade. I see in some people complete nervous collapse. I try to fight this with all my will, but I'm beginning to ask myself what will happen if our army is defeated.

It is now 5:30 A.M. In a few minutes we will start unloading.

September 10, 1 P.M., Hotel in Wlodzimierz   After thirty-six hours on the train, dirty, dusty, and very tired, finally we unloaded. Waiting for further instructions, we stopped at the Red Cross station where we were able to wash, shave, and get breakfast of black coffee and black bread. It was excellent. For almost two days we existed in field conditions, eating only cold rations, so even this very meager breakfast tasted very good to us.

After breakfast we went to see our quarters in the Hotel "Europa." I was again with Dr. Modzelewski. Next to the hotel I met a friend of mine from Zamosc, Dr. Maj. Wladyslaw Kozlowski, who was traveling with the headquarters of the Polish Red Cross from Warsaw to Luck. He told me that the evacuation of Zamosc had just begun. I cannot believe that this is possible and that the danger of Germans entering the Lublin region is true. People coming from Lublin tell me that the damage to the city caused by air raids was very heavy, especially on the Krakowskie Przedmiescie and the Hospital No. 2.

In Wlodzimierz it is much more peaceful. Still there is heavy traffic. All the restaurants and coffee shops are full. One must wait a long time to get something to eat. No one has any true stories about the war situation, only rumors. Mostly it is the refugees from the western regions of Poland who are relating the gossip. This is terrible for the morale of the local population. During air raids people are running like crazy, pushing each other to be the first in the shelters.

What will happen now? I think it will be impossible for me to go to Szczebrzeszyn because in two days our hospital should be functional.

September 10, 8 P.M.   Around 5 P.M., not far from our hotel, without any warning, several bombs exploded. A few minutes later I noticed horse-drawn wagons carrying wounded to the hospital. Later I learned that three bombs exploded, one after the other. A few people were killed, the number of wounded is unknown. For the population of Wlodzimierz these first casualties were a real shock.

At 6 P.M., on order of the hospital commanding officer, all personnel assembled for administration of the oath. For all Catholic officers and enlisted men a Catholic field chaplain read the text of the oath. Afterward, for all the Orthodox, the same text was read by an Orthodox priest. Lastly, Maj. Wszelaki administered the oath to two Lutheran doctors and several Jews. I stood with a group of Catholic officers.

After the ceremony I went back to my hotel. On the way I saw a lot of military men from young lieutenants to colonels. They were looking for their units. Most of them are physicians from Lodz who received orders to move east and find their own units. I met old Dr. Col. Stefan Rudzki, who also was looking for his unit.

I tried to call the hospital in Szczebrzeszyn, but all the out-of-town lines were dead.

September 11   Early in the morning I left the hotel and tried to call again, this time from the post office, without any result. After breakfast Maj. Wszelaki gave the dispositions and assignments for the day. I was assigned to train two enlisted men to operate the fumigation equipment. I sat until 1 P.M. and watched them practice fumigating old straw mattresses. I felt terrible about this, but the army is the army and one does not ask for logic.

I found out from the county doctor that yesterday's casualties were much higher than I had counted. Thirty-two people were killed and over eighty wounded had been admitted to the hospital. This morning I observed the funeral of a young Jew. Everyone in attendance was in complete silence, without the usual loud crying and lamenting so common at Jewish funerals. Only men walked along silently, in complete resignation. One Jewish woman walked on the side, crying quietly. This type of funeral conduct had something very strange about it.

The organization of the hospital is coming along quickly and very well. The new high school building was assigned to the surgery unit. Workers installed additional electrical outlets for the operation of X-ray and post-operation rooms and other special quarters. Everything seems to prove that the hospital will be here for a long while. More and more doctors, mostly refugees from Lodz, began arriving at our hospital. They are all begging for any kind of assignment, requesting sleeping quarters, or asking for food or money.

During the day all streets are deserted, but in the evening, after the possibility of German bombardment has subsided, people leave the buildings and come outside. By then all the stores are open, but not too much can be bought; they are all empty. More refugees are passing through the city. They travel by cars, trucks, or motorcycles. Many people are using bicycles that have luggage hanging from them. Most are young males going east. Not too many are older men. The view of this exodus is very depressing and nerve shattering.

After a few hours of walking I decided to stop at the public library and take out a few books. I wanted to read *With Fire and Sword*, by Sienkiewicz, but it was out, so I took *The Ashes*, by Zeromski.

No news from the Western Front. All the radio information is very skimpy—only gossip, gossip, and more gossip. One has to try with all their will not to give up hope.

September 12   I spoke with Dr. Col. Rudzki, a very tall, heavy man with gray hair and a small beard. He is commandant of the military hospital for TB in Otwock, near Warsaw. A few days ago he received orders to evacuate the hospital. Now he is here in Wlodzimierz waiting for new orders. Very nice man. We talked about his experiences during World War I.

I met another physician, Capt. Slupecki. He was an army physician during World War I. I note this because I am very sympathetic to all officers of World War I, especially physicians.

Today for the first time we had lunch in the officers' mess hall. Next to me sat Dr. Rudzki, so we were able to finish our conversation. He told me he had read all my work printed in the monthly *Military Surgeon*. He is currently working on some heraldic articles about some known physician's families. He has one manuscript about his experiences as a front-line surgeon in the First World War ready for printing. But most important, he has not stopped working. He is a very interesting man.

During the day we experienced three air alarms. Between 3 and 4 P.M., German aircraft placed nine heavy bombs very close to the county hospital (with a big red cross painted on the roof). I was sitting in my hotel room. The whole building moved like during an earthquake.

Going back to the hospital I noticed Capt. Jedrzej Wachowicz, whom I had met last July in Iwonicz. He is an artillery officer stationed in Lodz. His battery now is in Wlodzimierz. He left his wife and two sons in Iwonicz. He has no way of knowing what has become of them.

Today on the streets I noticed very few civilian vehicles, mostly military. On the highway from Hrubieszow most of the cars and trucks are police vehicles carrying police officers from areas occupied by the Germans.

At the hospital the CO is still awaiting a new assignment for me, so I'm still watching my two privates fumigate mattresses. My blisters are killing me. Every step is painful, so I am trying to walk slowly.

Back in the hotel I am reading *The Ashes*. I'm reading very slowly to enjoy the beautiful language of Zeromski.

September 13   In the morning I drove to the barracks where our internal unit is located to check on the progress of installing the fumigation equipment. While I was there I visited all the facilities. The unit was installed in a two-story building in the center of a barracks complex. During peacetime it housed a sickroom. Everything was very dirty and neglected. I found sick people hungry, without breakfast, and without any attention. I learned that the orderlies hadn't arrived yet from their quarters in the city. All the nurses and kitchen help had left because they were afraid of the bombing.

Shortly thereafter a nurse and later a cook showed up. The location of the hospital wing between the old barracks was a big mistake. Every few minutes we were under German air attack. From the barracks to the town was a distance of 3 km and the physicians quarters were in town. Because of this, control over hospital activities is very difficult.

During lunch we had more visitors, Col. Maszadro, chief of sanitary services, with his deputy, Col. Laski. From them I found out that during the bombardment of Warsaw I lost two of my best friends, Dr. Col. Tadeusz Sokolowski, internationally known surgeon and chief of the Traumatological Institute in Warsaw, and Dr. Col. Tadeusz Kornilowicz, with whom I attended university first in Moscow and later in Cracow.

Today in Wlodzimierz they are digging deeper trenches. In some you see antitank guns. News spread that one company of German tanks is heading our way. Some military people keep saying that generally the situation is not so bad, and the Polish army can still repel the German invasion. Most of the devastation and casualties are from the air bombardments. This is very painful to the civilian population.

I spend all my free time reading *The Ashes*. I'm angry that we are wasting so much time waiting for breakfast, lunch, or dinner.

I am very glad that I am working on these notes.

September 21, Szczebrzeszyn   I survived a terrible week and I had no time to continue my diary. I scribbled in a small notebook dates and names to give me something to work with at a later date. Based on these notes I am describing everything that has happened since September 13. Those experiences are so painful, tragic, and shocking but they are so fresh in my memory that I have in my mind even the smallest details.

Early in the evening on September 13 I returned to my room and fell asleep by 8 P.M. Around 11 P.M. I woke up to loud knocking on the door. I opened it and in the corridor were two soldiers. One handed me a sheet of paper. I noticed that it was addressed to our CO, Maj. Wszelaki. I pointed to his room and again went to bed but could not sleep because of the loud noises coming from the next room. A few minutes later someone again was knocking at our door. I opened it and found Maj. Wszelaki dressed completely in his field uniform. He told me to start dressing and be ready in ten minutes. I woke up Dr. Modzelewski. I thought that probably a large transport of wounded had arrived and we were needed at the hospital. But when we went into the corridor we saw that other officers were already packing, so we did the same. A few minutes later Maj. Wszelaki showed up and told us, "Gentleman, I received orders to immediately evacuate the hospital to Luck. We will be going through Dubno and Krzemieniec to the Rumanian border. If any of you gentleman, especially the older ones, would like to stay and try to reach your own towns, you are free to do so. I cannot say more. You must decide for yourselves."

I was completely shocked. After further discussion I realized that the German army was rapidly moving toward the Bug River and Wlodzimierz would be taken in a few days. Their offensive is very fast and overpowering, and our Polish troops are powerless in trying to hold their positions.

In spite of all the bad news we still believed that the Polish troops would finally organize a strong line of defense. But now despair was taking over. Never in my life had I felt so helpless.

Quickly, in complete silence, we loaded our belongings onto a horse-drawn wagon. The loading was done in complete darkness, with some physicians fighting for a better location for their suitcases. I went with Dr. Modzelewski to the hospital building where our three platoons were quartered.

The city street lamps were out. New trenches crossed the streets every so often as a defense against tanks, and only narrow paths were left for traffic. Walking in darkness, I tripped over something and fell down. I dislocated the fourth finger on my left hand, but I succeeded in putting it back in place. The pain was terrible and my finger was badly swollen.

On the grounds of the hospital, soldiers were already loading horse-drawn wagons with provisions, office and sanitary supplies. All of this was done only with the help of flashlights with blue paper wrapped over the lenses, practically in complete darkness. Our hospital received only seven wagons, so we had to leave almost everything.

We left most of the equipment of Field Hospital No. 204 in Wlodzimierz. This hospital began operating on September 12, with three units in operation: surgical, internal, and contagious. We already had sixty-eight patients.

The hospital had operated not quite two days. Originally it was to be organized on the level of a clinic. We even had guinea pigs for laboratory research. The hospital was supposed to have 600 beds, 300 of them in the surgical unit. For this purpose the state high school, Copernicus High School, was used. This almost new campus was adjusted to the needs of the hospital with the necessary alterations. We were to leave everything, all the equipment (including three new X-ray units), all the bedding, all the surgical supplies, the pharmacy, dental unit, and the fumigating equipment so well known to me.

Around 2 A.M. the wagons were loaded and the platoons were ready to move out. Just before departure Dr. Modzelewski and I went to Maj. Wszelaki asking for his advice. He repeated everything that he told us before, adding only, "I can assure you that in this situation, if you decided to go home, it would not be counted against you as desertion." Finally he advised us to move out with the hospital so maybe in the future we would receive some new orders. Naturally we agreed with him.

Walking through the dark streets crossed with trenches was very difficult. I fell for a second time. I caught my foot in a rope between two abandoned cars. When we finally reached the highway to Luck we encountered other difficulties. The entire highway was crowded with military convoys, all types of motorized vehicles, horse-drawn wagons, and thousands of people on foot. Everyone was moving in one direction only—east. When daylight came a mass of people on foot and on bicycles added to the confusion.

It was completely weird. This whole mass of people, seized with panic, were going ahead, without knowing where or why, and without any knowledge of where the exodus would end. Large numbers of passenger cars, several official limousines, all filthy and covered with mud, were trying to pass the truck and wagon convoys. Most of the vehicles had Warsaw registration. It was a sad thing to see so many high-ranking officers such as colonels and generals fleeing together with their families. Many people were hanging on to the roofs and fenders of the cars and trucks. Many of the vehicles had broken windshields and windows, damaged hoods or doors. Much slower moving were all kinds of buses, new city buses from Warsaw,

Cracow, and Lodz and all full of passengers. After that came horse-drawn wagons of every description loaded with women and children, all very tired, hungry, and dirty. Riding bicycles were mostly young men; only occasionally could a young woman be seen. Walking on foot were many kinds of people. Some had left their houses on foot; others were forced to leave their vehicles abandoned.

Along the highway you can see hundreds of abandoned vehicles (lack of gas). Gasoline was hard to get; some people charged up to 200 zloty per liter. (The price of one liter of gas in August 1939 was 75 groszy. At that time the exchange rate with the dollar was 3.5 zloty per dollar.) Because of this people left their cars full of their belongings and went on foot carrying maybe a small bag. Once in a while you were able to see a well-organized convoy, mostly hospitals. Without any exaggeration one can estimate the number of people on the road at between 20,000 and 30,000.

Very slowly we went 12 km. The first few I walked; later I sat for a while on the top of a big flour bag, then back again on foot. My blistered foot made every step painful. The heavy coat and gas mask hampered all my movements, but the worst thing was the feeling of defeat. I was fighting with myself inside. What to do? Go farther or return home?

From the first day of mobilization I was full of enthusiasm. I was happy to be called for active duty because I was afraid that maybe the military would excuse me because of age. I was glad to be going to Lublin, hoping that I would be assigned to hospital duty where I could serve as physician and surgeon. I remembered well that during World War I, when I was mobilized to the Russian army, my first assignment was in a field hospital in Prussia, where already the first day after arriving I had my hands full of work.

But this time, at the start of things, I received first an assignment as chief of an X-ray unit, work that was unfamiliar to me. Dr. Modzelewski, a noted gynecologist, was made chief surgeon. When we both complained we were told by Col. Tabidze that no one changes assignments. In reality all assignments were made by a sergeant in someone's office who had found some notes in hospital logs. Without checking any professional background, no one can assign, especially older physicians, to work that is unknown to them. After ten days of waiting I received a new assignment, to check fumigation equipment, work that is normally done by an orderly. Later I was happy to have the future opportunity of working in the X-ray unit because another physician, Dr. Capt. Glowacki from Lomza, a X-ray specialist, was assigned there also. But we were forced to leave the X-ray equipment (still in crates) in Wlodzimierz. In a few days we lost everything. Twenty-four physicians, 1 dentist, 2 pharmacists, 1 chaplain, 4 officers, 48 medics, and 3 platoons of orderlies were now walking down the highway with only 7 horse-drawn wagons of equipment and provisions. That's all that was left of a 600-bed hospital.

Now our destination is Luck. Why are we going there? Probably to receive another order to go farther east or south to the Rumanian border. Are there some possibilities of new assignments? None. Hundreds of physicians from other hospitals are also walking, begging for work. Why are we going? And what is happening in my hospital in Szczebrzeszyn? Probably the hospital is full of wounded from the bombings and without medical personnel. How are my wife and son? Surely I am needed there more than walking on the highway. But is it true that my return to Szczebrzeszyn is justified and not desertion?

Slowly walking along I fought with myself deep inside. I carefully began to evaluate all the arguments for and against, but I was unable to decide. I was in turmoil inside and completely exhausted.

We finally stopped for a half-hour rest. Since Wlodzimierz, we had walked only 12 km. Maj. Wszelaki again told us that our situation is really desperate and our only salvation would be to reach the Rumanian border. He asked us again to make our final decision. He told us that since he is only forty-one he would attempt to go to Rumania and maybe later to France, but he felt that we were a little too old for that, and besides we are needed here to help the civilian population.

Dr. Modzelewski decided first. He took his small bag from the wagon and told me that he was going home. He had a very good friend at a ranch nearby, Mr. Kaczkowski, so he decided to go there first. I was completely broken, without any will to make a decision as to what to do. Now our hospital, or really what was left of it, began moving. I saw through my eyes all of the problems, long marches without any destination, and the waste of time and energy while constantly moving.

Then in one moment, after I realized that my own hospital and my own family needed me, I decided to return. I went to Maj. Wszelaki and told him of my decision.

I said good-bye to the other physicians and officers who were standing around the CO. At the last moment I was able to exchange two 100-zloty bills into forty 5-zloty bills. As I learned later, this was a smart move. We saluted, and I returned to the wagon to get my bag. Dr. Modzelewski and I waited by the road and watched the few remaining horse-drawn wagons and soldiers moving slowly east.

At the moment of my decision to return home I felt completely relaxed. Now I had one goal: to reach my hospital in Szczebrzeszyn as fast as possible.

While we were waiting and discussing what to do, we noticed a wagon driven by a peasant moving against traffic, going west. We stopped him and found out that he was returning to his village around Hrubieszow. He and his horses had been mobilized to move some military units, but since those units had been disbanded, he was going home and would be glad to give us a lift, thinking that with our uniformed presence no one would requisition his wagon.

First we arrived at Mr. Kaczkowski's ranch. There we met Dr. Rolski, a surgeon from Zamosc, who was currently assigned to the military hospital in Hrubieszow. We were received very well. After a good lunch, Dr. Modzelewski was outfitted in civilian clothes. I received an old coat and hat. We left our bags and intended to pick them up later, and so traveled very light.

Because of the very heavy traffic on the highway, we decided to use only dirt roads, traveling through villages unknown to me. We finally reached a ferry on the Bug River around the village of Uscilug. We were on the road the entire day. Around 2 P.M. we spent a whole hour lying in a ditch because German aircraft were bombing a railroad station nearby. Other than this delay we had a relatively quiet day. It had a calming effect to see people working in the fields, as was usual this time of year. The traffic was very light—no troops, convoys, or even solitary soldiers. Only once we noticed, far from us, a platoon of Polish cavalry.

Late in the evening we reached the ferry. Everything was quiet, but we could hear artillery fire not too far from our position. The two ferrymen were very surprised to see us, especially me wearing a uniform under an old civilian overcoat. "Captain, what are you doing? You are going directly into German hands," they told me. I was going home, hoping that the Germans were far enough away that I could reach my hospital without meeting them and without changing my uniform.

We already had the horses and wagons on the ferry when Dr. Modzelewski decided to stay the night. Our driver was urging us to go since his village was only a few kilometers away and he was anxious to reach his home. I had not decided whether to stay with Dr. Modzelewski or go on with our driver. One of the ferrymen suggested we use another ferry 4 km to the north. Our driver agreed. I left my officer's hat in the bushes, removed my uniform tunic, and put on the overcoat given to me at the Kaczkowski ranch. It was completely dark by the time we reached the next ferry. The ferryman there told us that on the other side of the river the Germans occupied a small village. Very quietly we crossed the river and stayed at the ferryman's farm. We slept in the barn on fresh hay.

The next day, Friday, September 15, we awoke early and left the barn. The village was waking up also, but we hadn't noticed any Germans. The driver had the wagon and horses ready and we left to go to his village, Teptiukowa, the commune of Moniatycze, located on a dirt road between Hrubieszow and Wlodzimierz.

When we arrived at the driver's house, his wife told us that the Germans had already been in the village for two days. She and her two daughters were happy to see the driver alive. They had feared for his life. She showed us into a nice large room where we ate a very good breakfast. Soon several displaced persons came by and asked us several questions. From them we also found out that the German soldiers stayed on the highway and were not stopping anyone walking or on horse-drawn wagons. I was gladdened by this news; it would be much easier to keep going.

The house was located on the bank of a small stream about 200 m from the highway bridge. Between the house and the highway there was an empty field, so I could observe traffic from the window. Soon I noticed a German scout car and one motorcycle. I watched the highway for quite a while as the traffic became heavier. Besides tanks and trucks loaded with troops, there were ambulances, field kitchens, and many motorcycles. On the bridge the vehicles slowed down, so I could observe more carefully. Across from me a small but well-organized German motorized column was moving. I noticed only one passenger car carrying some high-ranking officers; all the others were in scout cars. This column was going forward in victorious march, the same direction that a few days earlier I had watched our disorganized troops, by the thousands, being led by their officers in an escape stampede.

Time was flying and we had yet to decide what to do. The villagers told us that the Germans were not stopping anyone entering Hrubieszow. To be on the safe side, I ripped off anything that could identify me as a Polish officer. For 15 zloty I purchased a pair of old pants that were so tight I could use only two buttons. All my notes and my military ID card I left with the request that they be delivered to my friend Henryk Warchalowski in Hrubieszow. I also left my uniform and officer's belt.

Around 2 P.M. we were able to hire a horse-drawn wagon with a woman of the village as driver, and, appearing 100 percent civilian, we started toward Hrubieszow. Because of the German military traffic on the main highway, we decided to go by fields and dirt roads, but at one point we had to cross the highway. At the crossing point a group of German soldiers were standing, talking and smoking. Our woman was afraid to cross, but with a movement of his hand one of the soldiers signaled for us to proceed. This was my first close encounter with Germans.

We entered Hrubieszow from the site of an old military barracks. All the streets were deserted; the people were hiding. Once in a while you could see German soldiers. It looks like normal life is extinct.

Dr. Modzelewski stopped off at the notary, Mr. Zawadzki. I myself went to see Mr. Warchalowski, brother of the chancellor of the Warsaw Institute of Technology and a very good friend of mine. I found both of the

Warchalowskis home and very nervous. From them I learned that the owner of an auto dealership from Bilgoraj was going home and planned to travel through Szczebrzeszyn. I located him and we decided to travel together. I learned that he was supposed to travel with another man, also from Bilgoraj. I spent the night at the Warchalowskis and for the first time in several days slept very well.

Saturday, September 16, I awoke around 6 A.M. and went to see my companions. Dr. Modzelewski decided to stay in Hrubieszow and travel alone to Zamosc after the situation stabilized. Because he received an almost new suit from Zawadzki, he gave me his old vest and jacket. Mr. Warchalowski gave me a new gabardine coat so I looked much better now, only I couldn't remove the coat because of my tight pants.

Now we faced another problem: we were unable, for any amount of money, to rent a wagon. My friends were afraid of walking, because of rumors that some fighting was still taking place. So finally we decided to walk not on the highway but on the field roads. I said good-bye to Warchalowski and we started our journey through Werbkowice, Zawalowo, and Zomasc to Szczebrzeszyn and Bilgoraj. After walking for a few minutes another man from Bilgoraj joined us.

Through the open fields we reached a narrow-gauge railroad track, and following the tracks we came to Werbkowice. Before we left I bandaged my foot, but the blisters began hurting more and more. Every step was painful.

We left town and started down the dirt road. In town the people were nervous, terrified, hiding. Yet in the fields everything was normal. People worked as usual. Along the way we had not seen any Germans.

At one point the railroad tracks crossed the highway. Here we had to wait. A large column of German tanks was passing through. After a few hours of walking we came to the Werbkowice railroad stations. It was completely deserted and made us feel very sad.

Resting every hour, we finally arrived at the village of Frankomionka, in the afternoon, still in the county of Hrubieszow. We had traveled only 22 km, but my feet hurt so bad that we decided to stay overnight. We stopped at the village administrator's, who was well known to me, and we were received very well. After a good meal some neighbors came by and we discussed the general situation for several hours. I was very depressed about the news from these people. They were concerned only with their own fate, forgetting about their own country and nation. They all would like the war stopped, and the village administrator mentioned how glad the Ukrainian minority were of the German invasion.

The next morning, Sunday, September 17, after resting on hay in the barn, we awoke early, but my companions were in no hurry to begin another walk. I was the only one feeling impatient to get home.

We began talking about the German presence: are they stopping people on the roads? Are they interrogating or maybe shooting people? All different gossip. My companions were so frightened they even refused to drink water from the well, thinking it might be poisoned. Now again I wasn't sure what to do, to go alone or wait. It was still about 30 km to Zamosc. My feet hurt bad and it began raining, so in those conditions I did not feel like walking alone. Finally I persuaded them to come along with me. I located a refugee from Zamosc with a horse-drawn wagon who agreed to take us to Zawalow (around 8 km) for 100 zloty apiece. We were not ready to pay 300 zloty for this short trip. Finally around noon, after a long talk, he agreed to take us for a total of 35 zloty.

Once on our way the people we met told us that the safest way was to go on the highway because then the Germans would not ask any questions. From Zawalow we started walking, hoping that maybe we could find some means of transportation to Zamosc, a distance of around 18 km. Much later we came to the village of Miaczyn, where we rented a horse-drawn wagon to Zamosc. We went very slowly on the wagon. I noticed abandoned Polish tanks and other military vehicles on both sides of the highway, and also some buses where the local children were playing "cops and robbers."

Traffic on the highway later in the day was light. We passed Polish soldiers, naturally without arms, trying to get to their homes, many bicycles, and once in a while German motorcycles or cars.

Close to Zamosc I noticed several pieces of German artillery and tanks hidden among the trees. We entered the city from the suburb of Nowa Osada. In the marketplace German propaganda radio was blasting with the latest news. "Hallo, Hallo, hear this. Today Soviet Russia, in agreement with the German government, crossed the eastern borders of Poland." This terrible news was the last thing we wanted to hear.

We went downtown. Suddenly we spotted people running toward us. Some women shouted that the Germans were stopping all men. In a few seconds my companions disappeared. My driver turned the wagon around so I paid him and left. I walked down the side streets and stopped at Mayor Wazowski's. The servant told me that the mayor was sleeping, and since no one else was in the house, he refused to wake him up.

I walked farther. I passed the Bank Polski building and I noticed the windows with no glass left in them. I passed the house of county administrator Sochanski. Walking along I remembered the publication *Teka Zamoyska* and the constant consulting or fighting with Sochanski's wife during the meeting of the publishing committee. I walked past the empty bus terminal, past the city movie theater with its broken windows, past the house of school inspector Szczepaniec. I stopped but the entry door was nailed shut. Again I walked through the marketplace, where many German vehicles were parked.

After a few hours of wandering through the empty streets I came to a friend's house, Dr. Bogucki. I was positive that he and his wife would never leave Zamosc. Mrs. Bogucki herself opened the door. She was shocked to see me as I appeared—dirty, poorly dressed, and dead tired. She greeted me warmly and in a few seconds Dr. Bogucki made his appearance. Shortly thereafter we were joined by Mayor Wazowski, who still held that position, and also attorney-at-law Tomasz Czernicki, nominated by the Germans as commandant of the civil militia. Through the windows we could see the marketplace just as the German soldiers were destroying the well-known grocery store of Matel. They were loading some goods on the trucks, breaking furniture, and setting small fires. I was terribly depressed watching the German hooligans in beautiful Zamosc marketplace.

We all feel the same way. We were not yet ready to discuss the causes of our defeat, how within two weeks we had lost almost half of Poland. This is a fact, but we just cannot believe it. Now we are the witnesses to our beloved, beautiful, independent Poland falling, and we feel partly guilty about it.

It was too late to go home now. Curfew was set for 6 P.M., so I stayed at the Boguckis. All lights had to be dimmed and all the windows covered with black paper. Only the windows in the city hall were lit up because inside were the Germans. Through the marketplace every few minutes there passed German cars with their high beams on so the room where I slept was lit up also. This was a terrible night. Half the time I was reliving the past; half, I was thinking of the future.

Monday, September 18, I awoke very early and after breakfast began slowly limping toward Szczebrzeszyn. I hoped to rent a wagon or maybe stop along the way at one of the many farms belonging to the Zamoyski estate and there find some transportation home.

I had just walked half a kilometer when I noticed a wagon with two horses. I stopped the driver and learned that he had been taken from his field to help move military equipment and now was trying to return home, which was somewhere around Sandomierz. I explained that the best way for him to go was through Szczebrzeszyn, Frampol, and Janow. For driving me to Szczebrzeszyn I offered him 10 zloty. He agreed. We traveled slowly because his horses were very tired. I traveled in this manner the whole way.

The traffic on the highway was light: some people on bicycles or on foot were returning to their houses; horse-drawn wagons were carrying households; and once in a while German cars would pass.

As we approached the town I met several people I knew, but I was not in the mood to stop and talk. I was anxious to get home as soon as possible. I was still trying to persuade myself that my family was fine and I would find my wife and son unharmed.

Around 10 A.M. we entered the city. On High School Place there was a lot of German military equipment. On the street there were a few people standing around, looking. They knew me well. Only two weeks ago I was there in military uniform, and now I returned as a beggar. They were very surprised. They greeted me warmly. Finally we reached my hospital. The waiting room was full of people. I saw two nurses, and to avoid a big welcoming I ran quickly to my quarters. I found the door closed but in a few minutes chief nurse Maria Makowska came and with tears greeted me. After that my son and finally my wife came, looking very pale with red eyes full of tears. Soon everybody came to say hello.

I inquired about the work in the hospital. My wife told me that the hospital administrator, Edward Cichonski, left his post in a panic, giving all the provisions to the hospital personnel. After him several other people left, including some nurses and orderlies.

Before the Germans came, most of the patients were moved to Krasnystaw. Only seven wounded were left in the hospital but without any medical attention. We were lucky that young Dr. Mieczyslaw Krzypiak was passing through and agreed to stay. I say young because he received his doctor's degree from the University of Poznan on August 31, 1939. Staying with him was only chief nurse Makowska, a volunteer schoolteacher, Leokadia Hascowna, and my wife. I was very upset about the behavior of the hospital administrator. He was the one man in the hospital who was supposed to take care of all the administration, financial, household, and maintenance. I counted on his help, and his leaving the hospital showed complete disregard for his duties. He was very active in the civic life of the community, a leader of several organizations. He had a military draft classification of "D" and was over fifty years old. He even volunteered to be a so-called living torpedo against German warships in case of war. He had worked in the hospital for several years and was a very good and loyal employee. I was not disappointed as much with some of the other hospital personnel when they left, especially one young nurse, Wiktoria Szparowna. They were all frightened and went to their villages with the blessings of the hospital administrator. Because of this, I was so grateful to those who stayed on the job.

Soon after my arrival I began working. When the news of my arrival spread, people, especially Jews, brought to the hospital several wounded and ill. Now I had a good feeling of being needed again. After two weeks of doing nothing I now had plenty to do and felt like I was in the right place. My wife assisted me even in the operating room.

From the moment of my arrival the whole atmosphere of the hospital changed. Everybody was in the right place, knowing what to do and not interfering with the work of others. Once again hospital life became normal.

Around 3 P.M. when I left the operating room several German soldiers entered the waiting room. I went to them asking if I could be of any help. One who looked like an officer asked if I was Dr. Zygmunt Klukowski. He told me that I was to accompany them to their headquarters in town. I was not allowed to change clothes even, only shoes. I wore slippers because of my blisters. I had no time to say good-bye, even to my wife. At the hospital entrance I saw two motorcycles with sidecars. I was put into one under heavy escort, with drawn pistols. The other was occupied by the man who brought the Germans here. He was the same man who a few days earlier had taken a record player from my wife. Under escort I was taken to gestapo headquarters located in the high school building. Here, an officer with a very unpleasant appearance, through a translator, began questioning me. Was I a Polish officer; what had I been doing in the last three weeks; and, after returning to the hospital, why hadn't I registered? I answered that during the general mobilization I was called to active duty as a physician but later I was demobilized and returned home only a few hours earlier. Also that I had been the hospital superintendent for the last twenty years. After a very brief interrogation I was taken to the apartment of the high school teacher Bohun, with whom I had been in the military hospital in Wlodzimierz.

The apartment was completely empty of furniture except for two beds and a small table. The beds were being used as sofas where already several people were sitting; others were lying on straw spread on the floor. On the table were a few books and a photo album with postcards and pictures. Everyone looked through it, including me. When I was brought into this room the occupants began asking me about the situation on the outside, but I didn't feel like talking. I positioned myself by the window and began observing the school yard crowded with German tanks and cars.

Mentally I returned to the old times, to high school and teacher seminars so close to me. I thought about how many changes those schools had witnessed and what their future would be. In the apartment approximately thirty men were walking around, sitting, or playing cards. After a short conversation I learned that ten were hostages, five Poles and five Jews, and the rest were mostly soldiers. A few of the soldiers and one hostage, blacksmith Makar, were playing cards. They were very much involved in the game, and with their urge to win they were leery of their unknown partners.

I sat there for about an hour and a half. I was very worried about the hospital, about my wife, and generally about the future. To avoid complete depression I decided not to think anymore about the future.

Finally a German soldier came in with Vice-Mayor Zlomaniec. I was taken to the same officer as before. He told me I was free to go home under these conditions:

1. I can walk on the streets only between 6 A.M. and 6 P.M.
2. I have no right to leave the city. I can leave only in cases of medical emergency and only with special permission.
3. If the Germans found any illegal activities on my site, I would be shot.

Naturally I readily agreed and in a few minutes I was walking toward the hospital.

My arrest caused a sensation in the city. As soon as I stepped out of the gestapo building I was surrounded by hundreds of people, mostly Jews, showing me how happy they were at my release. On the way home I met my wife and my son who were running to meet me. At the hospital I finished my daily duties and after dinner requested a bed in the room next to the hospital lobby so I could better see what was happening in the hospital. I took a shower and went to bed completely dressed, except for shoes.

On Tuesday, September 19, very early in the morning, I started my day. First I had to check on all the provisions and medical supplies, then the daily visits of the hospital rooms.

Around noon, the hospital administrator came by. After a very unpleasant conversation, during which I freely expressed my opinion about his behavior, he started working. A few hours later nurse Szpyrowna came back.

The whole day I worked hard. During the day we were visited many times by German officers. They were very interested in my own quarters, which would be ideal as an apartment for their commanding officer and his staff. I was sure that we would have to move and used my last argument: my quarters are on the hospital grounds and we have experienced several cases of typhoid fever and dysentery, and besides the plumbing wasn't working. So we stayed.

Before I return to describing daily events, I must go back to the day I left home for my military assignment. This is taken from talks with the nurses, Dr. Krysiak, and my wife, and here I will try to describe what went on at the hospital during my absence.

When I departed on September 3, Dr. Felicja Warchalowska was left in charge of the hospital. On the next day, September 4, the county sanitation officer, Dr. Julian Tyczkowski, arrived from Zamosc with Dr. Zbigniew Halacz, an evacuee from Zaolzie. Dr. Tycykowski informed Dr. Warchalowska that Dr. Halacz would take over, in my absence, the duties of hospital superintendent.

On Wednesday, September 6, there were several air strikes. Every few hours people would rush to the ditches and shelters. The same day the first bombs fell on the Alwa manufacturing plant near Szczebrzeszyn.

Friday, September 8, the air strikes increased. People tried to avoid the open trenches and began hiding in the hospital cellar; this included the entire personnel, the infirm, and passersby.

Saturday, September 9, from early morning, the Germans were bombing the city. One bomb destroyed an apartment owned by the Jewish family Warman, on Targowa Street, killing five people and wounding seven. Other bombs fell on the grounds of the high school, also on the pharmacy owned by Mr. Szczyglowski, apartments owned by Mr. Guzowski, across from the hospital, and in a few other places, but without casualties. Two bombs fell on the grounds of the hospital, one next to the wall of the mortuary and the other 10 m farther away. Besides some broken plumbing, there was no other damage. All together more than twenty bombs were released.

During the air strikes all hospital personnel, patients, and some people from the city crowded into the cellar. Because of the lack of plumbing in the cellar, people sick with dysentery were forced to use buckets. One pregnant woman delivered a baby. By afternoon dead and wounded were being brought to the hospital. Dr. Halacz disappeared. Dr. Warchalowska and Dr. Spoz worked hard in the operating room. The same evening Dr. Mieczyslaw Krysiak arrived from Zamosc with a note from the county sanitation officer assigning him to our hospital.

Sunday, September 10, the evacuation of Szczebrzeszyn began. At first all the police officers left the city. Panic is spreading.

On Monday, September 11, some police officers returned. Dr. Halacz left for good. Also the young medical student, Samborowski, practicing as a medic, was unable to withstand the pressure and fled to his village, Plonski, in Krasnystaw County. The hospital was again under the guidance of Dr. Warchalowska. The number of wounded soldiers and civilians is growing. The hospital administrator went to Zamosc for instructions. After returning he passed on the instructions from the county sanitary officer to begin evacuation of the hospital. Dr. Warchalowska placed a call to county administrator Sochanski. He countered the order; no one moves, under penalty of death.

Today, September 12, panic is growing. My wife took the most necessary items and left with my son to some friends in the village of Kawenczynek, only 4 km from the city. In the afternoon again more bombardments. Again the high school grounds were hit. From the village of Brody the hospital received more wounded.

September 13. The tension in the city is growing. The military took over the city administration. A young lieutenant who had no prior administrative experience became city commandant. He began preparing the city for evacuation. At the hospital all civilians were dismissed.

Late at night Dr. Krysiak received an alarming call from the military commandant: "The hospital as an international institution will stay in place. But the military wounded will be moved to another hospital." The administrator said that he received an order from the military commandant to evacuate the hospital. As a result, fourteen wounded were moved out in the direction of Krasnystaw-Chelm. The hospital administrator Cichonski, nurse Szpyrowna, and a few orderlies left. Nurse Makowska left around 3 A.M. with all her belongings but came back at 6 A.M. She had taken her possessions to a friend. At the hospital only three wounded and five dysentery cases were left. Dr. Warchalowska decided to stay with her family in town. So in this critical situation only Dr. Krysiak and nurse Makowska, with about three-quarters of the orderlies, decided to stay at the hospital. During the night a few more wounded arrived. The first arm amputation was performed by Dr. Spoz.

In the afternoon Szczebrzeszyn was under heavy artillery fire. By late evening the first German troops entered the city.

Friday morning, September 15, some German officers inspected the hospital. During the day there was a lot of work, especially in the operating room.

In the afternoon my wife returned.

On Saturday, September 16, the hospital took in a few wounded and because of personnel changes was reorganized.

On Sunday, September 17, some unknown aircraft bombarded German positions outside the city. A hospital administrator arrived there from one of the villages. He stopped in to see Dr. Warchalowska, who was not in the hospital.

On Monday, September 18, around 5 A.M., seven artillery shells exploded on the hospital grounds. Several windows were damaged. At 10 A.M. I arrived at the hospital. Electric power from the Zamosc electrical plant was cut off and the city was in complete darkness. Because of the very short supply of kerosene and candles I had to change the hospital work schedule. After dinner, between 8 and 9 P.M., everyone went to bed. We had to wake up at 5 A.M. and begin working at 6 A.M.

September 20. Since early morning we noticed more and more troops going in the direction of Zamosc. But instead of the motorized columns there are more infantry and cavalry. It looks like the motorized spearhead has finished its assignment here and is moving rapidly farther to the east. Now the conventional troops are coming and heading north to Warsaw.

Yesterday, a general destruction and looting of the stores took place, Polish and Jewish. But since there are more Jewish establishments than Polish, the common statement was, "They are plundering the Jews."

The usual routine went like this. A few German soldiers would enter the open stores and, after taking some items for themselves, start throwing everything else out into the street. There some people waited to grab whatever they could. These people are from the city and also neighboring villages. Then they would take their loot home, and the soldiers would move on to the next store. If the doors were locked, the German soldiers broke in and the destruction went even faster.

Some private apartments were robbed also. The Germans would especially look for good food, liquor, tobacco, cigarettes, and silverware. From the pharmacy they took morphine and other narcotics.

With Dr. Warchalowska I went to the German city command asking for permission to move about in the city after police curfew hours, but we were told that this was not necessary since the curfew had been changed. We can now freely move about between 4 A.M. and 7 P.M.

I stopped in at the pharmacy. Everyone there is very depressed. I selected a good amount of supplies. I was very pleased when the pharmacist told me that he would rather see them in my hands, even though I was unable to pay now, than be taken by the Germans.

Around 5 P.M. we had another German visit at the hospital. This time a young, very elegant officer came in asking if we had any wounded Polish soldiers. He spoke French with my wife. Before he left I asked him if by chance we could receive some medical supplies. He said he would help.

Half an hour later he came by again, this time with a German doctor. He brought me some sterilized dressings and bandages. The German doctor promised me more help. Both were very polite.

That night was very quiet. At 5 A.M. on September 21 I went on my hospital rounds, checking if everything was all right. Then I began the routine work, like changing dressings. All day I was in the hospital, sometimes in the operating room, sometimes in the sickroom or in the administrative office. I had not even visited my own quarters, afraid that maybe, while I was there, some Germans would show up. It is important to catch them at the entrance, otherwise they would be searching everywhere in the hospital for me, making all the sick and particularly the wounded very nervous. Generally the German army personnel were not too bad, but the gendarmes and members of the gestapo were arrogant and extremely unpleasant. Lately we have been having more of these visits. The standard question always was, "do you have any wounded Polish soldiers, particularly officers?"

As always we observed troop movements. In the morning hours, a large contingent of German infantry and cavalry and all their necessary supplies moved from Zamosc toward Zwierzyniec. But from Zwierzyniec to Zamosc only motorized units were traveling, long columns of trucks and cars with ammunition, equipment, and guns of different caliber. From this movement it is impossible to get a true picture of what is occurring.

We have no news, no radios or newspapers, as always just rumors. The German soldiers tell me that Warsaw is taken and the war is over. They will soon go home and half of Poland will be occupied by the Soviets and soon Russian troops will be in Szczebrzeszyn. In the afternoon the mood of the Germans changed. Now they are saying that Warsaw, Lodz, and Posen are still fighting hard and that soon they will have to fight on the Western Front against France and England. One soldier told us that on the Western Front the Germans lost a battle. We now hear rumors that the general situation is changing. There is no way to check all the rumors because without electrical power our radios are dead.

Throughout the city more and more refugees from all over Poland are moving about, no more cars, trucks, or buses, only horse-drawn wagons, bicycles, and people moving on foot.

In town robberies are still continuing. Because most of the goods have already been taken, the real vandalism has started, the breaking of doors, windows, and even fires being started. The worst part is that local people and people from nearby villages are participating in these crimes.

The whole day I spent at the hospital with no desire to go into town.

September 22   In the morning I began my daily work. The entire day went very smoothly without any German visits. At noon my wife went downtown to buy a few items, such as cosmetics. At the apartment of the drugstore owner, Geszychter, she was able to buy one toothbrush, a few cakes of soap, and toothpaste. All were in broken packages and very dirty, but we had to take them. On the highway there were still many motorized columns, especially in the evening. No news, only gossip, gossip, gossip.

September 23   The entire day was very quiet. I stayed in the hospital without even going to my quarters. I sat in the main lobby and worked on plans to get provisions. Today I received 300 kilos of sugar from the Klemensow refinery and three milking cows from the Michalow farm, both part of the Zamoyski estate.

In the city looting is taking place everywhere. But because the shops are completely bare, the time has come for private homes and apartments. The German military police, instead of trying to prevent these crimes, seem to be on the side of the robbers and looters.

September 24   Throughout the night, without interruption, motorized units were moving toward Zwierzyniec. The tremendous noise of vehicles applying their brakes on the highway's sharp curves next to the hospital made sleep impossible. Finally the night came to an end and we began our work dead tired. This morning we could hear artillery from both the southerly and easterly directions. In town there are more rumors: a heavy engagement near Zamosc and the killing of a German general.

German soldiers tried to steal one big pig from the hospital ranch, but because of the terrible outcry from the patients, hospital employees, nurses, and even complaints by the physicians, they finally let her loose. The soldiers are still coming and trying to steal apples from our orchard, and naturally breaking the branches. They took over the kitchen and started to roast some chickens but finally left after I pointed out that we had several typhoid fever cases.

From day to day tension is rising. I try with all my power not to show that I too am very nervous. But I realize very clearly that only I can keep the hospital working and that everyone looks to me for guidance.

I cannot stand the presence of Germans in my hospital, but I must try to be polite. Today we had a visit from a German medical officer; he addressed me as *Herr Kollege*.

September 25   Yesterday until 11 P.M., there was a lot of motorized vehicle traffic on the highway and on the dirt road by the hospital. The cavalry moved in the direction of Blonie. Then everything became quiet. But around 5 A.M. heavy artillery began; by 6 A.M. it was all over. On the city streets there are few Germans. Some still occupy the high school. On Sokol Place the Germans set on fire many drums containing rosin. In the afternoon there was sporadic car and motorcycle traffic on the highway. Around 9 P.M. the last Germans left Szczebrzeszyn. It may be the truth that the Soviet army is coming. I cannot believe this.

September 26   All night there was absolute silence. At 6 A.M., I left the hospital to find out what was going on in town. I noticed a large number of unarmed Polish soldiers, very dirty and hungry, moving west in groups. They said they were disarmed by Soviet troops between Chelm and Krasnystaw.

Around 10 A.M. the streets were full of marching soldiers. This time between the ranks of the unarmed Polish you can see German soldiers. This was a very terrible picture. I still remember that a few weeks before this mass of unarmed, dirty soldiers were members of the Polish armed forces, the pride of our nation. But we have not seen Russian troops yet.

At 11 A.M. I heard some motorcycles. I went out to see what was going on. From Zwierzyniec came two motorcycles with sidecars carrying three soldiers in each. One car carried officers and flew a white flag, and later one more car arrived with soldiers. What does this mean?

Around noon I received a young boy with a mutilated hand. He had tried to disarm a German bomb. I had to amputate his arm. Still, by evening, the Soviets had not shown up. During the night Mayor Franczak came back with several clerks. He began to organize a civil militia.

People are returning, not only those who had fled the city because of fear of bombings, but also those who had been discharged from the military.

I received two visitors at the hospital: Dr. Grot, a well-known internist from Warsaw, and Dr. Oczkowski, director of the hospital in Noworadomsk, both in officer's uniforms, trying to reach their cities. After a good supper they both received civilian clothing and left.

I am sure that tomorrow we will have Soviet troops in Szczebrzeszyn. I still cannot comprehend the situation and cannot become accustomed to the new routine.

September 27 The whole night I slept, without undressing, in the hospital lobby to be ready for any emergency. It was generally quiet, but I noticed the dreadful effect that the coming of Soviet troops was having on the hospital personnel. I remember very well the same feeling I had in 1918 when I worked at the hospital in Symforopol in the Crimea.

Last night four Polish soldiers showed up and gave us five crates of surgical instruments, dressings, and pharmacy equipment. They came on an army horse-drawn wagon. Naturally I received these supplies with gratitude. This morning we started to unpack and sort out all the items so essential to me. For two old civilian suits and two coats they "donated" two good horses and a wagon.

Around 5 A.M. the first Soviet soldiers entered Szczebrzeszyn. After a short stay at city hall they left again. A few hours later I noticed several civilian Communists wearing red bands on their left arms. Around 4 P.M. I left the hospital to find out any news. I saw Polish soldiers from whom the Communists were taking belts, haversacks, and map cases. The Communists took the administration into their own hands.

The county Communist committee from Zamosc sent a factory worker, Kardyga, to organize a local committee; he came with a few other Communists. The local Communists greeted them with red flowers (salvia). In the new Communist militia I noticed a few faces that were known to me (Talanda, Goleniak, Sudak, Kowalik, Kowalikowna). I was surprised to see in the Red militia some members of patriotic organizations and two letter carriers from the post office.

Just before dark I noticed a large group of Polish soldiers coming into the city. The Communists tried to take their possessions, but the local people standing on either side of the soldiers took so strong a position that they retreated. But in a few minutes the Communists declared a new curfew. Anyone out walking between 6 P.M. and 6 A.M. would be shot.

Very tired and depressed I came home. I was thinking about how long we would be able to hold out like this.

September 28 During the night I had to help in a complicated birth when the midwife called for my assistance. In the morning I noticed some commotion across from the hospital. At the local bakery, for the first time in ten days, you could buy white bread. People went crazy about it.

At 6 A.M. I received a wounded woman. Someone had thrown a hand grenade into her house and wounded a few sleeping people.

At noon I went to city hall, which was the temporary headquarters of the Red Militia. I talked with Commandant Talanda to establish rules of survival for the hospital. He and his assistant, Sudak (my former patient), addressed me as "Comrade Doctor." From them I learned that a band of local hooligans had started destroying the Zamoyski castle in Klemensow. The militia was unable to prevent this and had requested help from Soviet troops in Zamosc.

From Zwierzyniec I received a patient ill with meningitis. He came here from the hospital in Zwierzyniec and was escorted by Mr. Seroka, the former postmaster and now hospital administrator. He mentioned that his small hospital was overflowing with more than 120 wounded soldiers. Dr. Wroblewski finally received some temporary assistance from a displaced physician.

We now have only 26 sick and wounded, but a few are very grave cases requiring special care. We are being helped by two volunteers. Miss Leokadja Hascowna and Mrs. Maria Wadowska both agreed to work at night, which was a great relief.

September 29 Yesterday evening several trucks carrying Soviet troops passed by the hospital. One car stopped at the hospital entrance. I saw an officer, typically dressed in a long Russian military coat, start walking around and giving orders in Russian. After some time they left. I can't believe that I'm witnessing the truth and not dreaming.

I had a hard night. Some of my patients are really worrying me, such as the wife of a Polish officer. After a normal birth she started an extremely high fever and very rare eclampsia. One of the nurses stayed with her the whole night. At 6 A.M. we once again received a young man with a mutilated hand, and to save him I had to perform an amputation once again.

Around 8 A.M. several Russian armored cars entered the city. Staying in the hospital entrance, I observed officers and soldiers and listened to their conversations. I have to admit, I like them better than Germans.

Up until noon our work routine was normal, but just after noon we received a visit from a Russian officer and three soldiers. They came to take my car. After a long conversation in Russian the officer asked me if maybe I could give him some sheet metal. So after receiving five large sheets of metal roofing, he decided that "Comrade Doctor" really was in need of a car. During our conversation I noticed that I had some difficulty with Russian, but overall I spoke it fluently. One of the soldiers was from Moscow. He assured me that I would be unable to recognize Moscow and Petersburg. Both cities are growing rapidly.

In the evening Dr. Michal Kowalik, originally from Frampol but now working in Bilgoraj, stopped by, asking for dressing material. His small hospital was caring for 240 wounded. He was the only doctor, because Dr. Pojasek still had not returned. He was forced to send several badly wounded to the hospital in Zamosc, located in a high school that is used as a surgical unit.

Every day it is more difficult to keep personnel matters in order. In the last five weeks we have changed from Polish city administration, gone through German, and now Russian administration. One big relief is that we finally have electrical power back. So we are not in darkness anymore with only kerosene lamps and candles; we have our electric lights back.

September 30   This morning around 6 A.M. we received several wounded brought directly from a battlefield by horse-drawn wagon. They were to be sent to Zamosc, but since our hospital was closer, we had to minister to them. One officer, Wierzbicki, died during transport and was taken directly to the mortuary.

A few minutes after the arrival of the transports a large crowd assembled outside the hospital. Men started moving the wounded from the wagons to the receiving room. First we moved the most serious cases. Hard work all day. Around noon we had used up all the linens and hospital garments. Soon, news spread about this and people started bringing in shirts, underwear, sheets, and pillowcases. The town women delivered coffee and tea in big buckets and later brought in plenty of good chicken soup. Girl Scouts, under the guidance of Miss Zofia Jaworska, began a general clean-up of the rooms and corridors. Young women from the Polish Red Cross began nursing duties both day and night. Even the Communist town committee represented by Sudak and Wit Naszynski delivered a few hundred kilograms of flour and grits.

It gave me such a good feeling to see everyone helping. Our three big hospital wards were full of wounded. I was proud that we managed to supply every one of the wounded with his own bed. In the other hospitals half of the wounded were on the floor. The hospitals in Zamosc and in Bilgoraj are so full that the wounded, because of the lack of mattresses, are lying on hay or straw spread on the floor. The medical services there are very primitive. Officers who had been treated by me and later moved to other hospitals tried to be moved back to Szczebrzeszyn.

As I mentioned before, all of the wounded were brought directly from the battlefield. This was the last battalion of a group commanded by Col. Koc. This battle was fought against German troops at the village of Zwola, county of Bilgoraj.

October

October 1   Today our hospital admitted more wounded: first, seven Russian soldiers; later, Polish officers and soldiers, a total of over seventy patients. All were wounded during the same night battle in Bilgoraj County. I was kept very busy from 6 A.M. to 11 P.M. All the beds were full so we started laying some of the wounded on mattresses on the floor. Throughout the day local women brought in all kinds of soup, compotes, coffee, and tea. The hospital personnel worked around the clock, giving the same attention to the Russian and German soldiers as to the Polish. Then someone told the town committee that some Soviet soldiers were hungry and not being cared for. So we had an investigation conducted by a special committee headed by the Communist Naszynski. After the investigation he publicly announced that the accusations were false.

Today the director of the museum in Luck, Lt. Julian Niec, a doctor of philosophy, died of head and brain injuries. He was brought to the hospital in very critical condition. I know his name from some journals, but I cannot remember the subjects. Between other cases I received two very serious ones: Maj. Konrad Zelazny from Posen and a man known to me, Capt. Stanislaw Lis-Blonski from Lublin, a known civic leader. Both have mutilated legs and will probably face amputation.

I am so tired that I cannot think straight.

October 2   From 5 A.M. until 10 P.M. I worked without interruption. I am terribly tired. This morning we had to amputate the leg of Capt. Lis-Blonski just below the knee. I have a lot of help now. Yesterday Dr. Wladyslaw Borkowski, a surgeon from the hospital in Starachowice, arrived. He was called to active duty but was not given an assignment, so after waiting around for several days he decided to go home. Near Frampol he was stopped by Russian soldiers. At the same time many wounded Polish and Russian soldiers were brought in. After administering first aid, he decided to move the wounded to Szczebrzeszyn. Naturally he is staying in my quarters.

I have received much help from other local physicians also. Dr. War-chalowska, back in the city, is on duty again. I put her in charge of the women's and infectious isolation wards. Dr. Spoz and Dr. Borkowski each have one surgical ward. I myself took charge of critical cases, but admin-istration and general organization took up too much of my time.

Around noon a Russian military physician came by to visit wounded Soviet soldiers. He was an assistant surgeon of the university clinic in the Ukraine. He told me some interesting stories about medicine in the USSR.

More rumors spread in the evening. The Russian troops were supposed to withdraw, and the Germans come again. This created a real panic in the Jewish population.

October 3 During the early morning Russian troops brought in a few more wounded to the hospital. The whole day we worked very hard without any chance to rest. The smell of decomposed human flesh surrounds me.

October 4 Polish officers and soldiers were put into a Russian internment camp in Szczebrzeszyn. The camp had some very poor guards and many soldiers escaped. At night my very good friend Lt. Col. Dr. Kazimierz Rytter, from Zamosc, escaped and came to me for help. He stayed over-night, and after changing into civilian clothing he helped me with the wounded. He performed surgery on Maj. Zelazny.

He recited to me the events of the last day of fighting by the group com-manded by Col Koc. He read the last order of the day signed by Col. Koc, beginning, "We are the very last detachment of the Polish army fighting on Polish soil." Lt. Col. Rytter was so moved that, with tears in his eyes, say-ing only, "I cannot read this anymore," he left the room. Dr. Borkowski, who was also present, completed reading the order. Wounded Maj. Zelazny started crying together wih the nurses. I had a hard time holding back my tears.

Lt. Col. Rytter left for home this evening. Before leaving for Zamosc he wrote a few lines in my diary: "I saw in these hard times for us something that will brighten my days—in very primitive conditions, the best in med-ical help, particularly by the staff and the hospital in Szczebrzeszyn. I salute all the staff members, doctors, nurses, orderlies, and volunteers of this hospital."

October 5 This morning the Russians came for their wounded and sick and left the city. All the local Communist committee members and Red Militia disappeared. The red flags that we were forced to display after the arrival of the Red Amy were taken down.

Rev. Kapalski, the Catholic priest, organized a relief committee to help the wounded. Maj. Zelazny donated 600 zloty to the committee and Capt. Lis-Blonski, 500. The committee decided to donate all the money to the hospital. This is really a big help.

I do not feel too good.

October 6   I have the flu. I know from last year that my heart is too weak for me to work through this illness, so I decided to stay in bed. I am lying down still dressed, so in case of an emergency I will be ready. I would like to be in good health by tomorrow because we have so much to do, and I am sure that without me the work would slow down. I was unable to force myself to stay in bed, so I visited some wounded amputees.

My head is very heavy from lack of sleep, fatigue, and fever. I cannot think straight and I'm lying here only half sleeping. Our ordeals of the last four weeks have been so terrible that it would be easy to experience a complete breakdown of the nervous system. Only hard work prevented this, particularly when we began to receive wounded soldiers. We worked sixteen hours a day and a few times even eighteen. Thankfully, with so much intensive work, one has no time to think about anything but the wounded.

Completely unexpected to me, I was able to put the whole population to work, not only city people but those from the nearby villages also. Some of the same people who only a few days earlier were robbing the stores now came with help. They are caring for the wounded Polish soldiers. Local women prepared food; village women brought bread, milk, chickens, eggs, apples, homemade wine, juices, and even candies. They are even happier when they can distribute things by themselves. They brought dressings, sheets, and one elderly woman even brought a large first-aid kit belonging to a disbanded volunteer fire brigade. Young girls came to help attend to the wounded but seemed particularly interested in young officers. Girl Scouts worked hard cleaning the operating rooms and corridors. Some women even took laundry home to wash. The relief committee members, along with Fr. Kapalski, were trying to buy eggs, butter, wheat, sugar, pigs, and calves, so I received much help from them. Without this all-around effort the hospital would not be able to function. I am glad to see the good mood and appreciate the help being given to the wounded soldiers by these people. I was so pleased that this effort put my hospital in such good standing. According to people who had been through others, my hospital gave the best care. I was told this by Russian physicians. They pointed out that only in my hospital and in Sokol the wounded are not lying on straw-covered floors.

Today was a very pleasant day. Because of a Jewish holiday traffic was almost at a standstill. No German or Soviet soldiers. The Germans are supposed to come tomorrow. This afternoon, according to the old customs, the city caretaker walked through the streets singing the old song for citizens to keep watch over their houses against fire and robbers.

October 7 Yesterday evening I had a very high fever. This morning my temperature was still very high, and I felt terrible. I spent the whole day in bed. Dr. Spoz is now in charge of the hospital. I am still very much involved in hospital life, so I must have an information briefing about the wounded a few times a day.

I am particularly worried about Maj. Zelazny. It appears that he is facing another amputation.

The city is quiet; the Germans are not here yet. Many Jews left Szczebrzeszyn with the Soviet army, especially those who were part of the Red Militia.

October 8 I feel much better today. My temperature is normal but I am still very weak. It appears I have to stay in bed another few days. My heart is very weak. Both Dr. Warchalowska and Dr. Spoz even advise me not to talk. Dr. Brokowski had to make another amputation of Maj. Zelazny's leg. I feel so sorry. He is such a good man. I am glad that because of my illness I was unable to make the amputation myself and was even unable to assist.

Yesterday Dr. Wroblewski from Zwierzyniec visited us. He talked about his hospital. For 104 wounded he had five physicians but not one surgeon. Probably he will send some wounded here to Szczebrzeszyn.

Today a small German column passed through the city in the direction of Zamosc. One car stopped by city hall and an officer, in very good Polish, requested that a big sign in Polish be removed. The sign read, "Germans will never take our city."

Late in the afternoon a Polish officer came to me and in the name of all the wounded handed me 300 zloty for the hospital.

October 9 I have no more fever and tried to get up, but my heart is still very weak so I must stay in bed. The Germans are already in town. A few German soldiers came to the hospital inquiring if we have any Germans or Russians, and also how many total wounded we have.

Prices on everything are going up so it is difficult to provide the hospital with all its needs. Today a pound of butter was 10 zloty, a pound of bacon 5, milk 35 groszy per liter, eggs 35 groszy each, and poor-quality meat, 1.5 zloty per pound.

October 10 It appears that the Germans will be here for a long time. They are seeking quarters for 150 men. We have a new city commandant. From the first moment they put the Jews to work cleaning the city. Today, for the first time in weeks, we had a normal open market as we usually do on Tuesdays. Many villagers came to sell their goods. Around 3 P.M. some people began destroying Jewish shops. Mayor Franczak requested the help of German soldiers to stop this. After firing a few shots into the air, the German soldiers began searching for stolen goods. In a few minutes the people disappeared, but the military police began searching all passersby.

October 11 Today, for the first time in a while, I walked around for a few hours. I even went to see what was happening in the hospital. My wounded soldiers are better and some can be released. We discharged around twenty. Everyone will receive one kilo of sugar, a donation of the Zamoyski estate refinery in Klemensow.

The town is crowded with Germans. They are quartered in all the larger houses. Most of them are from Austria and some from Vienna. In general the Germans are trying to clean up the city. For this work they are using only Jews. Jews must sweep the streets, clean all the public latrines, and fill all the street trenches. Plastered everywhere are German notices giving an idea of what we can expect in the future.

We must return all arms. We must record all contagious diseases. The police curfew is from 10 P.M. until 5:30 A.M. The restrictions applying to Jewish shops change from day to day. Sometimes the Jews are allowed to open their shops, and sometimes they are not. It seems that most of the orders are aimed at the Jews.

One German soldier told me that in a few weeks we would have a permanent Soviet occupation. I cannot believe this, but in this war anything is possible and we have already had a few surprises.

Many German troops are moving toward Zamosc. It appears that they are to concentrate on the Bug River, the new demarcation line between Germany and Soviet Russia.

Today Dr. Josef Zelazny, the superintendent of the hospital in Jaslo, stopped by to inquire about his family. His wife went east with other refugees and was supposed to leave messages for him at the hospitals along the way. He came from Lublin, but so far we have not received any messages from his family.

October 12 Today was very quiet without any important happenings. I have many administrative problems, some orderlies are sick with the flu, and some have gone to help with the potato harvest, so the nurses have to take over the cleaning work. Among the volunteers the early enthusiasm has disappeared. At first the young girls and women came in such numbers that we were forced to send some home. It is difficult to get even a few Girl

Scouts to help. The hospital is dirty and it smells, but it cannot be helped. The people are helping with the potato harvest.

In the city the Germans are cleaning the streets with the help of the Jews. All the Jewish shops are still closed and in the others there is nothing to buy. The well-known Kollataj department store is so empty that you can only buy floor wax and toilet paper.

October 13   The German military commandant told the mayor that a concentration camp will probably be established in Szczebrzeszyn. This is very sad news.

The Germans decided to regulate the free market. They published a price scale, but for items not listed the maximum that may be charged is 50 percent over the prewar price. They established a rate exchange with the mark: 1 German mark equals 2 zloty. This makes everything even more difficult to buy, and no one wants to sell for the legal price; for example, no more meat for sale.

The Germans posted several new regulations. I am noting only a few:

> "All men of Jewish religion between the ages of fifteen and sixty must report at 8 A.M. on the morning of October 14, at city hall with brooms, shovels, and buckets. They will be cleaning city streets."
>
> "All people of Jewish religion can move freely on the city streets only between 6 A.M. and 6 P.M. Their houses and apartments shall be open for police inspection at all times."
>
> "All radio receivers shall be deposited at city hall in two days, with the names of the owners attached. Jews shall add under their names 'Jude.' "

Jews are staying home, not going out.

October 14   I was in bed the whole day because of my weak heart. Every few minutes someone came to me with news from town. Yesterday the Germans established a new city administration. As acting mayor, Jan Franczak was installed, as vice-mayor, Borucki, a former street cleaner with a good knowledge of German who requested us to address him as "Herr Doctor." All the other clerks were the same as before.

Today is Saturday but the Germans required that all Jews work at cleaning the streets, even though it is a Jewish holy day. The Germans are treating the Jews very brutally. They cut their beards; sometimes they pull the hair out.

Yesterday, on orders of the German military government, a young German doctor came to the hospital asking for a signed requisition for all medical supplies needed by the hospital. I had this requisition form ready in advance. Today I received many of the items that I requested and even some that I had not requested. I was told that more are coming.

October 15   Somehow I made it from my bed, but my heart is in very bad shape. At noon, with my wife, I took a horse carriage to Zwierzyniec. This was the first time I'd been there in two months. Everywhere you can see the traces of war. Around the railroad station and the Alwa plant there are many bomb craters. The highway is partially demolished and half of the village of Brody is burned down. Along the highway you can still see carcasses of dead horses and shattered vehicles.

In Zwierzyniec everything is quiet. At the marketplace you can see a few destroyed buildings. At the hospital and the Pozerski apartments there are sixty-nine wounded, most of them lying on hay spread over the floor. Dr. Wroblewski also assigned four rooms from his own house to be used for the wounded. Everywhere there are many displaced people from all areas of Poland, waiting for the possibility of returning home. I spoke briefly with young Jan Zamoyski, chief administrator of Zamoyski estate. He is worried about the future of the material that has been compiled for the 350th anniversary of the Zamoyski estate and that is to be published in *Teka Zamojska*. One of the estate officials, Gustaw Swida, told me that approximately 1,000 Germans will arrive shortly, and it will be a problem to quarter so many. I was also told about the destruction caused by German soldiers in the estate offices. The estate archives, though, are still supposed to be intact.

In Szczebrzeszyn the Germans are organizing a militia. Approximately sixty people were called for these duties. They are organized as an auxiliary police unit. They wear on their left arms white bands with a number and insignia, *Hilfspolizei* in German, and below that *Milicja* in Polish. On the first day a German major, now town commandant, told the new "police" that all brutalities against Jews have to be tolerated since it is in line with German anti-Semitism policies and that this brutality has been ordered from above.

The Germans are always trying to find new work for the Jews. They order the Jews to take at least a half hour of exhaustive gymnastics before any work, which can be fatal, particularly for older people. When the Jews are marched to any assignment, they must loudly sing Polish national-al songs.

In town there is more and more talk about the Russians returning and about battles between German and Soviet troops somewhere along the Bug River and other locations.

You can feel the nervousness of some of the people who fear the Jews. Sorry to say, but some citizens are as equally brutal as the Germans are toward the Jews.

The town commandant, who is staying in Dr. Warchalowska's apartment, insists that the Germans will never pull back from this region. Who is behind all these rumors? I do not know.

October 16   In the early morning I went to city hall. At this time the military commandant was meeting with the new civilian administration. The entire city is crowded with Germans. The stores are again open, but the waiting lines are a few blocks long. Persecution of Jews is increasing. The Germans are beating the Jews without any reason, just for fun. Several Jews were brought to the hospital with their buttocks beaten into raw flesh. I was able to administer only first aid, because the hospital has been instructed not to admit Jews. They asked me for affidavits stating that they are unable to work. Knowing that this will make the situation worse, I advised them to go to the German military physicians who are, so far, giving aid to civilians.

Just after lunch Dr. Borkowski left the hospital. He helped me for more than two weeks. Now he is going home. I feel sorry for him because of his 160-km walk.

Around 4 P.M. a German military doctor, Oberstabsarzt Kreutzer, M.D., together with other Polish-speaking German officers, came to inspect my hospital. He asked many questions about the wounded and about my general needs. He told me that all the wounded would be transported to the military hospital in Zamosc, and we had to prepare ourselves for receiving more contagious cases, particularly typhoid fever. He was very polite and promised to help.

October 17   Today we once again had an open market. Many horse-drawn wagons came from nearby villages with produce. The stores are full of buyers. I stopped by city hall and learned that the German administration is planning to organize a new county, Szczebrzeszyn. This new county will combine the following communes: Sulow, Rodecznia, Zwierzyniec, Nielisz, Wysokie, Mokre, and even Old Zamosc.

More and more Jews come to the hospital asking for release notes from work. Only when it is really necessary are we giving those releases, with doctors' signatures, mostly mine and that of Dr. Spoz.

Tonight I was called to treat a Jew who had been terribly beaten by a German gendarme. But after giving first aid and a prescription, I was unable to do anything more. The hospital again received a transport of about fifteen wounded.

As required by the new regulations, I turned my old, broken radio receiver in to city hall, but the new one was hidden outside the hospital, in one of the villages, to be used in case of need.

October 18 We worked the whole day without any unusual interruptions. I stayed at the hospital without going into town. This morning the Germans started moving some male Jews to work outside the city. Some more wealthy Jews were able, through bribes, to avoid any work or gymnastics. The Jewish women whose relatives were taken to work almost started a riot against the rich Jews. The German police decided to take all those Jews to the city jail.

October 19 Since the morning hours I was kept very busy. Besides, I am not feeling well. Around noon a German military doctor sent in a few dozen Jews, bakers and butchers (only five Poles), for physical evaluation. They were scared to death. After I gave them a thorough examination a German doctor gave a talk about hygiene at work, particularly in bakeries and meat-cutting places. His speech was in German and was translated into Polish.

I went to bed very early because my high fever had returned.

October 20 Today is my twentieth anniversary as hospital superintendent. Exactly on October 20, 1919, I was put in charge of this hospital. All the personnel came to wish me another twenty years. From the nurses I received nice flowers, roses and carnations, and from our kitchen, a cake that I shared with the nurses and especially with the wounded soldiers. I went to the ward where Capt. Lis-Blonski was being treated. He gave a nice speech in my honor.

From city hall I received new regulations signed by the military commandant. Some are very interesting reading:

"Since the war is over, by request of Adolph Hitler, the German army does not see the Polish people as enemies but as friends and will help in restoring order and prosperity."

"The German army will tolerate the existence of Jews, and they will receive help, depending on their behavior."

"All Jewish taxpayers in the city of Szczebrzeszyn are requested to provide by October 25, 1939, information about their assets. All cash, jewels, gold, list of realty holdings, all goods in stores, antiques, and others. Anyone who disobeys this ordinance faces seizure of all possessions and jail."

"All members of the Polish armed forces and all males of draft age shall, by October 20, register with city hall."

Today a German doctor brought me medical supplies including injections. He seemed glad to be able to help.

October 21 This morning I received a visit from Dr. Wladyslaw Kwit, originally from Dubno. He just rented an apartment in Szczebrzeszyn and will try to open his own medical practice. I am curious how he will make out. So far private practice is practically nonexistent, and we do not have any Jewish patients at all.

From military commandant Von Bassevitz I received an invitation for *Abendessen*, dinner, for tonight. This invitation was written in accordance with the requirements of social etiquette, with all the titles so popular in German life. Because of my fever I was glad to send a nice letter, with an apology, that I was in no way able to attend. I copied a letter that had been prepared for me by a translator. I am glad not to be able to attend this event, but on the other hand I am also sorry, because there would be much to write about.

Today the Germans ordered that the patients who were not too severely wounded would be moved to the military hospital in Zamosc.

It appears that the Germans would like to have all Polish military wounded in one place and have all the civilian hospitals ready for who knows what uses.

October 22 People who attended last night's German dinner told me that nothing major happened. After a short speech by the city commandant and a short address by Mayor Franczak, there was a very unpleasant speech by Vice-Mayor Borucki who started with "Heil Hitler." Not even all the Germans answered "Heil." Even during daily conversations with the Polish, Germans were not using "Heil." Young Jan Zamoyski came late and left after a few minutes.

The whole day was very tiring and nervous. Around 10 A.M. the Germans announced a special alert. All Jews were taken from their houses and apartments and moved to the marketplace, just across from city hall. The Jewish women had to stay inside their homes. No one was allowed to enter the marketplace except Germans and members of the militia. Anyone coming to town was turned back.

People who were attending Mass in the Catholic churches were kept there for a few hours. I was told that at St. Catherine's Church, next to the hospital, the old priest started singing songs prohibited by the Germans, such as "God who has defended Poland for so many centuries, give us freedom again."

Around noon the Jews were moved in a military fashion from the marketplace to the city hall. No one knew what would happen. Later in the day

Mayor Franczak's son, a young militia man and a student at Lwow Technical Institute, came by and told us what was happening.

The Germans were taking Jews for field work. At one house an old Jew tried to hide in the loft of a barn. The ladder gave out and he fell on one of the German soldiers. The Germans considered this a violent act against the administration. Altogether, eleven Jews were arrested and put on trial by a German military court. The Jews decided to ask the Catholic priest, Fr. Cieslicki, to intervene. A delegation composed of yesterday's dinner guests tried to explain the situation to the Germans.

After the Jews were assembled on the grounds of city hall, the Germans began robbing their houses. Merchandise from the Jewish stores was brought into the streets, to be transported away by truck. This evening during the court session the Jews were acquitted. All Jews being held at city hall were free to go home. The consensus is that the story about the ladder was just an excuse to confiscate the goods from the stores.

New rumors that we soon will have a new administration. These rumors are not taken seriously anymore. People have lost their self-criticism. This is because they have lost all contact with the world. No newspapers, no radio, only rumors. Once in a while someone who has a hidden radio receiver will break some news, but the same news repeated a hundred times will lose its reliability.

October 23   Today, just before noon, Maj. Konrad Zelazny passed away. We had done everything possible to save him. From talking with officers and soldiers who served with him I learned that he was a very brave man. For him an order could not be changed and had to be obeyed.

I am very worried about Capt. Lis-Blonski. He is not doing very well at all.

In town things are fairly normal; only the Jews are under constant pressure. I was told that yesterday at the marketplace the Germans whipped a great number of male Jews, even a rabbi. Today his wife came to me crying. She heard that tonight the Germans would start killing Jews. She asked me for help.

During the afternoon we had a visit from notary Rosinski, from Zamosc. He told us about his own experiences since the first day of the war. From him I learned that a good friend of mine, Klebanowski, superintendent of schools in Lublin Province, shot his wife and later himself the moment the Germans entered the city.

The whole afternoon we heard artillery fire.

October 24   About the artillery explosions from yesterday. They were caused by the Germans detonating bombs and shells still lying by the sides of the highway. We had imagined some other actions.

Last night the German administration left the city. Only fifty soldiers commanded by one sergeant stayed in Szczebrzeszyn, but around 10 A.M. a new detachment of German soldiers, under the command of a new city commandant, arrived.

Today for the first time I received a copy of the newspaper *Lublin Voice*, dated October 22. It is printed in Polish, but instead of a prewar size of twenty-four pages it has been reduced to two. No news, just some official German announcements. The rest is all inquiries about missing persons, a list of official prices, and a digest of a few books. Because we had not received any newspapers since the early days of September, we read it.

October 25   Today the new school year for grammar school children officially began without any interruption by the Germans. At the hospital everything is normal.

October 26   Yesterday afternoon there was once again a change in German command. It is impossible to even guess what this means. Today the German administration decided to arm the militia. Nine militiamen received arms.

Around 4 P.M. more news: the Germans will be taking hostages soon. Personally I am worried about Capt. Lis-Blonski. It looks as if we will be unable to save him.

October 27   A normal workday. I am finishing the last pages of *The Ashes*. It is relaxing to read this masterpiece of Polish literature.

October 28   Today the wife and daughter of Capt. Lis-Blonski came to the hospital. They had been searching for him, and yesterday someone in Lublin mentioned that he was in Szczebrzeszyn. I am so glad that he is still alive.

October 29   I now have much more work because Dr. Spoz stopped coming to the hospital. We are receiving more and more patients, and some are critical cases. I am very tired. It seems that you cannot trust people, especially if you are unable to pay for their services.

I have to check on everything, even the smallest details. All the rumors make me sick. You hear so many stories, knowing they are all gossip, but you still react to them. If the news is positive, everyone is happy, but the negative news makes people completely apathetic, without any will to control themselves.

Today I finished *The Ashes*. It took a long time for me to read it. I began reading in Wlodzimierz, but I was forced to stop several times. Today I will begin reading *With Fire and Sword*, by Sienkiewicz. These types of Polish literary masterpieces, which I have known for years, are helping to keep me calm.

October 30 Today even the German officers began searching Jewish homes, taking all cash and jewelry.

A new gestapo detachment arrived in the city. From Zamosc bad news: the power station has only sufficient fuel for two weeks of operation, so we started preparing ourselves for darkness.

Today the new school year for high school students began with services in the Catholic church. This will be a difficult year for students and teachers. No school books, no school supplies, and because the high school building was taken over for gestapo headquarters, classes are to be held in the afternoon at the grammar school.

October 31 Today at 5 P.M. Capt. Lis-Blonski passed away. He was in the hospital for four weeks, and even though he was on the critical list the entire time, his personality was very warm, having an almost healing effect.

November

November 1 Through Szczebrzeszyn, everyday, more and more Jews are traveling. Some are riding on horse-drawn wagons, but mostly they go on foot. Men, women, and children, with all their possessions, are going east. They have been expatriated from western Polish regions; they are maybe going past the Bug to Soviet Russian occupation areas, or maybe they will stay in the Lublin region, which is supposed to be reserved as a temporary settlement for Jews.

November 2 Today the German police searched practically all private homes looking for arms, ammunition, gas masks, and military equipment. We are expecting this at the hospital also.

Yesterday and today I released nine patients, one captain (Rylko), two lieutenants, and six enlisted men. I still have twenty wounded soldiers but no officers.

November 3 Today we all attended the funeral of Capt. Lis-Blonski. After the flu, I've been spending all my time at the hospital. From the hospital gossip I get the feeling that maybe the Soviets will come again.

In all my spare time I'm reading *With Fire and Sword*.

November 4 Today Capt. Lis-Blonski's widow left Szczebrzeszyn. She left the hospital without even saying good-bye. She just left without saying a word to the doctors, nurses, or any hospital personnel. We tried hard to save this brave man during his more than four-week stay in the hospital. His case was critical. Keeping him alive during this period depended on the know-how of the physicians and nurses, but understanding his death takes into consideration his own resistance, his age, and heart condition. No one knows how many sleepless nights I spent worrying about his life.

November 5 German patrols are cruising the city. Once in a while they stop at the hospital. They walk through the corridors and enter some of the wards. We have new police curfew hours. Instead of 10 P.M., you can now walk on the city streets only until 7 P.M.

November 7 Yesterday and today nothing really important occurred, only typical hospital life. Last night we received two Jewish women who had been shot during a house robbery. These types of cases are now almost daily events. We have several patients at the hospital who have been wounded during robbery attempts.

November 8 Today I went to see the German military commandant. I went myself, because yesterday when my nurse stopped at city hall with the standard release forms for the wounded, he asked about me. During our short conversation he inquired about the needs of the hospital, particularly dressings and other surgical supplies. He was rather polite.

I stopped to see Bohun, the schoolteacher who was with me at Military Hospital No. 204. He told me what happened to the other hospital personnel since the time that Dr. Modzelewski and I both decided to return home.

They went first to Luck, then to Rowno, Sarny, and farther through Maniewicze to Kowel; from Kowel to Chelm, and from there through Krasnystaw and Fajslawice to Lublin. From there everyone went on their own. This was on October 8; we left Wlodzimierz on the night of September 13. This long journey would have been exhaustive. I wonder if with my bad heart I would have survived it, going in a circle and trying to avoid both the Germans and Russians.

November 9 In the morning a few Germans with Red Cross arm bands wandered through the hospital for several hours. They looked everywhere, all the rooms, the kitchen. They checked the inventory of surgical instruments, opened all cabinets, went back to the kitchen pantry and even to the private quarters of the staff. It appears that the Germans might have special plans for using our hospital. During the afternoon a German military doctor came from Zamosc with new regulations regarding wounded Polish soldiers. He told me that in a few days all the wounded would be transported to Zamosc and then from Zamosc to Cracow. There might be some delay because before Szczebrzeszyn the hospital in Tomaszow has to be evacuated. From now on I must report every Thursday the total count of patients in the hospital, particularly the wounded. I cannot release anyone from the hospital without first notifying German authorities.

From Zamosc we have bad news. The Germans are beginning new repressive measures. Today around 2 P.M. they arrested the county administrator Sochanski, Mayor Wazowski, Fr. Zawisza, and three Jews. They are kept as hostages. People are deeply distressed. No one is sure what will happen to them during the next few hours.

In the city there are new regulations. The German administration formed a new tax office. This office will work out new laws. By tomorrow, November 10, all Polish military uniforms, belts, blankets, and other goods shall be turned in to the German military administration. The penalty for not obeying varies from arrest to death. Naturally, under these conditions it is hard to survive.

Because all government and county employees, families of Polish military personnel, and all those receiving government pensions have not been paid in two months, they are starting up a black market, buying and selling tobacco products, sugar, food, salt, coffee, tea, and anything else you can think of. Some people are making a good profit.

Everybody is very tense and nervous. Myself, I feel that my nervous system is starting to give up.

November 10   Last night the German military authorities posted new requirements that all former Polish reserve officers have to report to city hall by 10 A.M. Not everyone was aware of this. I myself found out about this order around noon. The German military commandant explained that all former reserve officers would be transported to Germany but would receive all courtesies. Everyone involved has to appear again Monday, November 13, for further instructions. Some reserve officers such as teachers and city clerks must obtain a deferment from the German civil authority and report their whereabouts in the city twice a week.

At 2 P.M. I reported to the deputy commandant. He told me that because I am a hospital superintendent I would automatically be excused, but that I still had to report on Monday.

Another regulation required that all cars, trucks, and parts be turned into the German authorities. After reporting that I own a small passenger car, I was told that because I am a physician I can keep it, especially since it is private and not a government car.

All these regulations, particularly those pertaining to prospective transportees, were received with much anxiety. The prospect of being deported to Germany is not very exciting.

Tomorrow is November 11, Polish Independence Day. You can feel that people are waiting for something to happen, but at the same time it seems that the Germans are more alert also.

November 11   Independence Day. Girl Scouts with their leader, Zofia Jaworska, came to the hospital with flowers and cookies for all the wounded soldiers. From two grammar schools children marched to church, where services performed by Mgsr. Szydlowski. After Mass, children from School No. 2 were dismissed by the principal, Misiolka; but children from School No. 1 returned and were dismissed by principal Wegierski after one period.

Students from the high school were absent from the service. In speaking with the principal, he told me that in today's situation he felt that an Independence Day celebration was inappropriate, and because of that he decided to keep school open.

The absence of the high school students from the church service was noticed by the people. Up until today the principal had been popular, but he has now lost many friends.

A few people went to Zamosc to obtain from the *Landrat* papers allowing them to stay on their jobs. He officially informed them that the whole thing is a mistake and there are no plans to move former Polish officers to Germany.

Who is right, the military or civilian authorities? We will find out on Monday.

Last night there was a small celebration of Polish Independence Day at the home of the mayor. The German military commandant and his deputy were present and behaved politely.

For some time we have been hearing that desertions by German soldiers are increasing. All stores received instructions not to sell any civilian clothing or even fabric to the German military. I was told about some instances of desertion, but without proof I will not repeat them.

From some unknown sources the news is spreading that a few English aircraft were seen over Zamosc. The Germans are very nervous about this. Yesterday an aircraft was seen flying between Labun and Zamosc.

November 13   At 10 A.M. I, along with a small group of Polish reserve officers, went to German military headquarters. The city commandant, a lieutenant, asked who among us had taken an active role in the war. Only five of us had been mobilized. We were taken to another room where we waited for half an hour. After a brief interrogation three reserve officers were arrested—Malkowski, Majdan, and Pomaranski—and one hour later were sent to Zamosc. One officer, Siciarz, who had been wounded in the leg, was released but had to report for a physical examination by a German doctor. I myself was released because of my position as hospital superintendent, but I was selected as a hostage and told I must report twice a week, Tuesdays and Saturdays. A number of other persons were selected as hostages: Mayor Jan Franczak; Principal Wiktor Jozwiakowski; owner of the flour mill, Drozdzyk; owner of the tobacco shop, Jan Malinowski; and a few others. The number of hostages will be increased, we were told.

I had lost two hours of time and left very mad, grinding my teeth.

On returning to the hospital I learned that on November 10 the Germans conducted a very detailed search of the Bernardin monastery in Radecznica and arrested two monks, Father Superior Duklan Michnar and old Fr. Stefan Puklicki, who was very ill with tuberculosis.

November 14   Today I learned more details about the search at Radecznica from some very well informed people. All the monks were ordered to leave and go to their families in nearby villages. A monk of German origin, Fr. Maksymilian, was left in charge of the monastery buildings and estate. Two eighty-year-old brothers also received permission to stay. The theological seminary was closed and students sent home. The search was very detailed; in some rooms the Germans even ripped up the wooden floors. All the gold and jewel votives were "confiscated." No one was to mention the theft under penalty of death.

Today the Germans began searching for homes of railroad workers in Zawada and Szczebrzeszyn. Now they are leaving the Jews in peace and beginning to persecute the Christians.

I had a visit from Judge Mazurkiewicz. He, as well as other government officials without any income, had begun selling his possessions. I purchased from him a pair of galoshes and two pairs of socks.

November 15   Last night I went to bed early. Around 10 P.M. I was awakened by loud noises on the street. When I reached the window to see what was going on, I saw a huge fire burning across from the hospital. I sounded the alarm to alert the hospital personnel and have them ready in case evacuation was necessary, and then I went out onto the street. Jewish houses next to the synagogue were on fire. I wondered why the sound of Jewish women crying and lamenting was absent. The Germans were fighting the fire and trying to contain it so the buildings on either side would be safe. The German police barricaded the street and evacuated all tenants. The other streets in the city were deserted because of the curfew. This prevented the assembly of spectators so typical in times of public disasters. I could hear pistol and rifle shots. Jews were not allowed to take anything from the burning houses. The city commandant himself was coordinating the goings-on. He insisted that the Jews themselves had started fires at four places in the city. In three spots the fires had been extinguished before spreading; this one across from the hospital was the only dangerous one. I was worried because of its position close to and directly across from the hospital. The sick and wounded were ready for evacuation, as were all personnel. The important hospital equipment was ready to be moved to the hospital orchard and garden. The Germans finally assured me that the fire was under control and the hospital was safe. The city commandant posted guards to see that I didn't give any more than first aid to any Jews. Several Jews had been beaten by German soldiers, and some had been shot. I received one man with a gunshot wound in the arm, and after first aid the Germans took him away.

After three hours the fire was extinguished. All Jews in the city received instructions to assemble in the marketplace. German soldiers pulled Jews from their homes by their hair, beating them and constantly shouting. The Germans were shooting continuously. Jews were crying and lamenting. I saw Jews being pushed by the Germans with their bayonets. I saw an old man unable to walk being carried by two old women. Finally around 5 A.M. it became quiet.

This morning several Jews were held as hostages and taken to jail; all others were released. The Jewish population was ordered to pay 10,000 zloty as penalty for starting fires and another 10,000 as a bond against future occurrences of this kind.

The whole affair with the fires being started by Jews appeared very fishy. Why would the Jews start fires at four places in the city, and particularly next to the synagogue and house owned by the rabbi? What reason would the Jews have for trying to destroy their own heritage?

Today I admitted to the hospital a Jew with a gunshot wound to the head. Normally, many people would be shouting and crying and accompanying the patient, but today only his wife came to me, terrified, asking in a low voice if I would look at him. I admitted him without even thinking about repercussions. I also received a Jewish woman with a bayonet wound to her buttocks.

I decided to see for myself the area destroyed by fire. You can still see hot spots. The people in the city are very depressed. It looks like this might be the beginning of a new era of the German administration.

November 16 Everyone is talking about the fire. The German statement that Jews themselves started the fires appears more and more reasonable. During the interrogations it came out that several Jewish occupants left these homes a few hours before the fires started, taking with them their belongings. In the area destroyed by the fire, several houses had been empty since September, when their owners had left. These homes were now being occupied by Jews from other regions. The Germans had been preparing new regulations. Any persons living in houses abandoned by their legal owners had to move out and the properties would be taken by the city. The evicted Jews swore that if they left no one would be able to move in.

It seems the Jews expected the start of the fire, but it took the Germans completely by surprise. Within a few minutes the trucks were ready to evacuate. The German detachment stationed in the high school building prepared for evacuation by breaking down the fence in a few places, to have some additional exits besides the main gate. The Germans set up machine gun stations. But about the origins of the fire there are only assumptions; no one knows anything for sure.

Yesterday the Germans searched the grounds of the Alwa manufacturing plant and the homes of all employees. They were searching for arms. At the same time a detailed search was made at the home of the attorney Paprocki, in Szczebrzeszyn.

November 17 This morning Mrs. Aleksandra Mianowska, the Polish Red Cross delegate from Cracow, visited my hospital. She is checking all the hospitals in the Lublin region to collect information on wounded and sick soldiers of the Polish army, particularly those from the Slask and Cracow regions. At the same time she is looking for her husband who is missing somewhere in Bilgoraj County. He was wounded during a bombardment and disappeared. She left Cracow a week ago and, after traveling through Lublin, arrived in Szczebrzeszyn. She informed me that on November 6 the Germans arrested almost all the professors and senior instructors at the University of Cracow, and on November 11 all the professors of the Catholic University in Lublin. I am shocked by this news and feel very depressed and nervous. I know now that the Germans are not only trying to destroy us economically but are also trying to destroy our cultural life.

Today another search was carried out, this time at the Malkowski farm, in Rozlopy, not far from Szczebrzeszyn. They found an old BB gun and a radio receiver. Mr. Malkowski was arrested. His son, a reserve officer, was taken a few days earlier along with other officers, to a camp in Zamosc. Nobody knows what will happen to old Malkowski.

I am counting on another "visit" very soon at the hospital. To be sure that I am "clean," I burned most of my correspondence. I'm worried about the future of my library. After moving some of my most valuable items, I still have more than 5,000 volumes and several hundred folders with drawings, newspaper clippings, and other collectibles.

November 18 Today, for the first time, I went to report myself as a POW to city hall. On the alphabetical list of officers they put a small star by my name and that's all. Old Malkowski was released due to the intervention of the mayor. Young Malkowski somehow was able to escape from the camp in Zamosc.

We constantly hear about new searches and arrests. We live under continuous pressure, waiting for something to happen here. Some of the Jews tell me that no one undresses at night to sleep. Even small children sleep with their clothes on. They are all afraid of the possibility of fire, robbery, searches, or arrest.

November 19 Yesterday evening Mr. Rosinski arrived from Zamosc. He told me about the new life-style in his city and also that the county administrator, Sochanski, was released from jail.

November 20 Today the Germans received the 10,000 zloty penalty from the Jews. This afternoon a German officer came to Szczebrzeszyn and in the name of the German military high command closed our high school. He was unable to give any reason for this action, mentioning only that the high school in Zamosc was closed also.

The whole day I heard rumors that the future life of my hospital is in jeopardy. I don't know anything for certain, so I haven't even begun evacuation procedures.

November 21 I had a visit from Lt. Col. Stanislaw Sosabowski, commanding officer of the ninth Infantry Regiment. He is trying to reach the eastern regions of Poland and had come from Warsaw. From him I learned many details about life in our capital city. I listened with regret to tales of the destruction of buildings and the removal and shipment to Germany of major museum inventories, libraries, and archives.

November 22 A normal workday. I received information from Zamosc that the county offices will begin a normal work routine any day now. Hopefully I can count on some financial help. So far I have been forced to provide hospital support by myself through donation and, sorry to say, the black market.

November 23 I spent the whole day inside the hospital. During the afternoon I began reading once again *The Deluge*, another classic by Sienkiewicz. I was always fascinated by the episode about the siege of Czestochowa. Reading this I was able to forget our slavery.

November 25   Nothing happened, and it is not necessary to repeat rumors.

November 26   You can feel the lack of basics more and more. Most money is gone and people are trying absolutely everything to get cash. People find many ways to get money for the most important items to support their families and themselves. People are selling and buying without any organized plan. Even children are involved in selling matches, cigarette papers, shoelaces, and even home-baked cookies and cakes. Some people have opened coffee shops and restaurants. In one of his houses in the marketplace Maj. Malinowski started a new restaurant, the Citizen's Club. Most of the clientele are German soldiers. Yesterday Paprocki started a new establishment, Cafe-Club-Bridge. The owners are Paprocki, Mrs. Mazurkiewiczwa, the judge's wife, and Mrs. Swiderska. Yesterday my wife and I stopped by with some friends to see how the café was doing. There were many Germans, but we were seated in a separate, small room and were able to speak freely.

Returning home I learned that in Zwierzyniec Mr. Engelhardt and in Nielisz Mr. Stankiewicz were arrested. During the search the Germans severely injured young Stankiewicz, only sixteen years old.

November 28   Today I reported again to city hall. In the future I have to report once a week, on Tuesday. It is harder and harder to buy food; prices are rising, particularly for butter, for which we pay 6 zloty, and eggs also. Soldiers are buying food to send to Germany.

I was surprised that besides the general hike of all prices and the devaluation of the zloty against the mark the legal exchange with the dollar is the same as before the war: 1 dollar equals 5.4 zloty. I found this out by paying my quarterly insurance premium, *Assicuratione Generali Trieste*. According to my agreement, all premiums are to be paid in zloty based on the dollar exchange rate.

November 30   This afternoon I received a visit from two German physicians from Zamosc. Both doctors asked several questions. They wanted to know the maximum number of beds I could provide. They inspected the operating room and were surprised at the lack of X-ray equipment. They asked why we didn't have electric stoves in the kitchen. They seem to be looking for a hospital with modern equipment to be used by the Germans. Now I am really worried about our future.

December

December 1   Everywhere you can feel unusual excitement and commotion. Prices are still going up, particularly on food, and its supply is ever more limited. The Germans are buying more and more for shipment to Germany. Yesterday, last night, and today we noticed an increase in motor vehicle traffic. Particularly at night, many military ambulances went in the direction of Zwierzyniec, but armored cars, motorcycles, and trucks towing heavy guns moved toward Zamosc. People feel that some important event is shaping up in the future. We know that all furloughs were canceled by the German army, and we can see how nervous they are now. The city streets are crowded with people. Jews don't hide anymore. Some have already returned from territories occupied by the Russians. They are more sure of themselves. They are not being taken for any labor.

One of the Bernardin brothers from Radecznica, in civilian clothes, went to Lublin to inquire about Fr. Duklan. On his return he stopped in to visit. From him, finally, I learned some news about what had happened. Fr. Duklan is in prison along with seventy-four other priests. Four bishops, Fulman and Goral from Lublin, and bishops from Kielce and Wloclawek are also imprisoned. Only bishops receive restaurant food. The priests have to eat German food from the prison kitchen. They can receive packages from the Polish Red Cross only once a week.

December 2   The entire day passed without any interruption, but we are all uneasy. What will happen to the hospital, and what will we do, where will we go, where will we live, and what should we take with us? We are not living from day to day but rather from hour to hour, because the Germans only give a twenty-minute notice to people they decide to evacuate. You can take only a part of your personal belongings, leaving all furniture, books, and other articles behind. Naturally this feeling doesn't help our normal activities, but I cannot be surprised at anything.

I sent the hospital administrator to Zamosc to try to find out what is really happening from county officials. He was told that the same two German doctors were visiting hospitals in Zamosc and were checking them closely. We are powerless against any decision. Yesterday during a show at the city cinema theater a German officer declared it off-limits to Poles. The theater has been taken over for the use of Germans only. It can happen at the hospital also. We are ready for the worst.

In Zamosc the people are depressed. The living conditions are very difficult. Prices are rising again. Tea is sold for 150 zloty, and coffee is 50 zloty per pound. Here in Szczebrzeszyn things are the same. Today it was impossible, at any price, to buy butter, meat or eggs.

Today some business took me past the high school. The Germans are building a new garage and repair shops on the grounds. Now it appears that they will stay here for a long time.

December 4 What will happen to the hospital? Maybe the Germans will take it from us. We don't know yet. But everything is possible, so I rented a small apartment in Budzynski's apartment house, on Zamojska Street. We can move there at any time, but so far things haven't changed. News of the world never comes to us. As always we hear only rumors, which can be more or less plausible, but we are in no way able to check them.

December 5 Today we had a big open market. The marketplace was full of horse-drawn wagons between which German soldiers were snooping around. They were looking for butter. On the streets leading into town guards with machine guns were located. The Germans checked all the baskets carried by peasant women. With the help of city civilian employees they weighed the butter and then paid 5 zloty per pound. The women who had any butter left took it to the marketplace and sold it for 6 to 7 zloty per pound. This type of action was typical of the Germans.

I registered again at city hall and I was told that very soon the German administration would change again and we would have German police instead.

December 6 This morning I was called for medical consultation to Zwierzyniec. There I learned something of German conduct. On Sunday, December 3, the Germans executed Jan Lys, the son of a forest ranger from Wygoda. He was charged with hiding arms. He was a young boy discharged from the army a few months ago. Under the impression that in the future he might need guns and ammunition, he hid them. The German soldiers buried the body where the boy had been shot. After a few days the parents received permission to bury him in the Catholic cemetery but without any public assistance. A few hours after the funeral a large wreath with the sign "We Salute Fighters of Free Poland" was placed on his grave by an unknown person.

The saddest thing is that the boy was a victim of denunciation by his own neighbors. Even the Germans admit that on several occasions their investigations of hidden arms are based on denunciations.

Yesterday during a search in the village of Obrocza the Germans discovered arms and other military equipment. Now searches every night are common in different villages.

Going back to butter purchased by the Germans at a low price: all this butter was taken to the creamery and wrapped in 1 lb. packages; 144 lbs. were shipped to Germany but 160 lbs. were sold to the public at 6 zloty per pound.

December 7   Today Zdzislaw Cielecki, a young medical student from the University in Wilno, reported to me. He came on recommendation of my friend Dr. Bogucki, from Zamosc, asking for work as a medic in my hospital. He had been in the army, wounded and since released from the hospital. In no way will he be able to go to Wilno. I agreed, but I am sure there will be some legal difficulties with city hall.

Today there was the funeral of a German soldier killed during the reconstruction of an area of the high school—an unsupported wall collapsed, killing the man. There will be an investigation. He was buried in the military cemetery on the grounds of the high school.

Not far from Zamosc the German gestapo arrested Boleslaw Wnuk, a well-known civic leader and member of the Polish *Sejm*.

From the radio we received bad news. Part of the Zamosc region, including Szczebrzeszyn, will be established as a concentration camp for all Jews from Poland, German, and Austria, and we are supposed to be relocated to Germany. Nice future!

December 8   I went to the Klemensow sugar refinery. Production is at full speed, but the mood of the workers has changed. It is difficult to work under constant surveillance, knowing that all production will be going to Germany. Today the official price is 1 zloty, 20 groszy per kilo. To buy sugar it is necessary to obtain a special permit from the *Landrat* in Zamosc.

December 9   As I mentioned before, the Germans were conducting searches in the village of Obrocza. I finally received some "true" information. The Germans began a search for a military motorcycle supposedly hidden by Michal Gmys. Naturally, he denied having any knowledge of it. He was arrested. A few hours after his arrest his wife delivered a motorcycle to the Germans.

Around Szczbrzeszyn more and more robberies are occurring. Last week a band of robbers entered the Bramski farm in Gruszka Zaporska, then the parish hall, in Tworyczowo, and last night the Matrasiowa farm in Tworyczowo and the Huskowski farm in Sulowiec. During the robbery of Mrs. Matrasiowa's farm, her son, a high school student, was wounded in the leg. The mother brought him to the hospital in the morning. She told how the robbery took place. Around twenty robbers were involved. Five entered the house, two went to the stable, and the rest stood guard around the farm. All were well armed, some even had machine guns. They arrived around 9 P.M. and stayed until 2 A.M. The house is well lit by electrical power from a nearby flour mill. Upon entering the house the leader of the gang fired one shot, wounding young Matras in the leg. After terrorizing everyone else, the leader started to help the wounded boy. He applied first aid and apparently had a good understanding of it. After feeling around he finally removed the bullet from the left leg, then sterilized the wound and suggested that the boy be brought to me for further medical treatment. Then the robbers collected cash, jewelry, and silverware and started eating and drinking. Two began playing the piano, and according to witnesses played very well. In the end they raped two women. Finally they left, saying that if anyone told the authorities about the robbery the farm would be burned down.

All the people on the neighboring farms are living in constant fear, particularly since they are without arms and completely helpless against the well-armed bandits. The German military administration is not taking any action. It appears that they are trying to avoid any contact with the organized bandit groups for fear of losing soldiers. The Germans patrol the villages only during daylight hours. Once evening comes, and throughout the night, they stay in their quarters, not moving from them at all. This type of inaction by the Germans is helping to increase banditry.

December 10 Strange things are occurring with foreign currency. The official exchange is 5 zloty, 40 groszy for 1 dollar, but the black market is paying 60 zloty or more. I found this out myself when I sold 20 dollars to a Jew for 62 zloty per dollar. Single dollar bills are less attractive than 10- or 20-dollar bills. Simple explanation: most of the dollars are purchased by Jews who are afraid the Germans will eventually take all of their currency, so they are hiding the bills by sewing them into their suits and coats.

December 11 As I expected a robbery took place at the Siemiatowski farm in Widniowka. I do not have any details yet.

During the last few days we can see German repression against the Jews growing. Every day fifty Jews have to work on the public streets. Before, the rich would pay the poor to work; now everybody has to work. They are marched to and from work with uncovered heads, without hats or caps.

I spoke with the Fr. Maksymilian, who was left in charge of the Radecznica monastery buildings and household items. During the search the Germans were looking for the treasure of Wawel castle, which was evacuated in September from Cracow. He is sure that the arrest of the seventy-four priests and four bishops is linked to this treasure.

The robbery at Widniowka took place at 6 P.M. There were eight men involved.

Late yesterday evening I received two patients, evacuees from Posen. They talked about their ordeal. It is hard to believe but it is true. One hundred sixty people were brought by train to the railroad station in Szczebrze-szyn. They had been staying in the village of Brody. But one morning they were split into small groups and taken to other villages, namely, Ro-zlop, Sulowa, Deszkowice, Michalowa, and Radecznica. Many small children and some pregnant women, in the last weeks of pregnancy, were among them. They come from all classes of life, but originally they all were taken from Wagrowiec. They are workers, farmers, teachers, clerks, bankers, and merchants. Even Dr. Wladyslaw Likowski, the county physician, is among them. They had twenty minutes to pack all necessities and could bring 200 zloty. The people were held in an old military barracks and then loaded into unheated railroad cars. First their destination was Zamosc, but then, as I've mentioned, they were dispersed to the cities and villages. What will they do here? Nobody knows. From Wagrowiec the Germans evacuated everyone, not only those who came there after World War I, but even those whose families had lived there for centuries. The German soldiers were extremely brutal. One of the sick that I received at the hospital, a bookkeeper, had been so severely beaten that he will require long hospitalization.

Today I admitted a young woman. She had been beaten by German soldiers and was brought to the hospital unconscious. Later she told me that she had just purchased a few pounds of butter. Germans tried to take it from her and she started fighting. One German kicked her in the stomach and the others beat in her face.

December 14   Yesterday some Germans came by the hospital twice, asking if I had a German named Kuhn. The first time only three soldiers came, but the second time there were six, all carrying rifles. It looks like this Kuhn just deserted.

A few days ago I finished the last volume of Sienkiewicz's trilogy. Now I am beginning to read *World History*, by Trzaska, Evert, and Michalski. I started with the Middle Ages but the reading is very difficult. It looks like during the few months of war I've lost the ability to think clearly, so that in no way am I ready for any scientific work. But in today's situation it feels completely normal.

We live in constant fear, knowing that at any moment we could be thrown out and wondering how to provide for the hospital. There are more problems than you can imagine. We are now living in two small rooms. Because of the heating problems I cannot use my library or study.

The atmosphere in which we are living—always thinking about the future, about the lost nation, about the destruction of Polish cultural heritage—is so heavy a burden that no strength is left to even start any mental task, especially writing.

December 15 Today I met Dr. Likowski, the county physician from Wagrowiec, who was deported with his whole family. He told me in detail about his family having to be ready in forty-five minutes. Also during this time he was severely beaten. After being held in a military barracks for several days, he was finally taken by train to Zamosc and now Szczebrzeszyn. He wants to open his own medical practice. After talking with other evacuees I am amazed at their good spirits. They are positive that they will all be back in their own homes after the complete defeat of the Germans.

From Zamosc I received news about the arrest of Gregor, director of the Bank of Poland.

The Germans came to the hospital twice today and looked everywhere, but they stayed completely clear of the infectious ward.

December 17 In anticipation of some new and important events, people seem to be extremely tense and nervous. Fantastic rumors. They are all supposed to be from British radio (BBC). Optimists try to believe any good news. Pessimists see everything in black, but their number is very small. Most people believe that the war will be over soon and we will in the end be victorious. Some people commented about the prophecy of St. Andrew Bobola (over 300 years old) that our slavery will be over after 101 days, which would mean December 8. Others said that in Czestochowa, on the miraculous picture of Our Lady, the so-called Black Madonna, the date December 12 appeared. Still others mention the well-known mind reader, Ossowiecki, who once said, "In 1940 I would not like to be a German."

I pray that we will have the strength to hold out against the physical and mental pressure and not sink into apathy and resignation.

Personally, I strongly believe that very soon the days of our slavery will be over, that we will again survive, and I am burning inside thinking about the magnitude of the work facing us in rebuilding our nation. Many times I have contemplated how this rebuilding of our culture, so badly destroyed by the enemy, will be performed, and how quickly. As I think about this, I try to forget that I am already fifty-five years old.

December 18 Today there is new excitement. The news spread that all Germans stationed in Szczebrzeszyn will leave soon. Yesterday evening no one mentioned this, but today a young German soldier who was friendly with a few of my wounded arrived to say good-bye. He was shaking as he told us that surely he and others would go to the Western Front. Conversations began between the German soldiers and the civilian population because of the news received by a German medic. His family was killed during a British bombing of his town; only one child survived. Today a Russian car with two officers was seen on the city streets. This afternoon, news came from the military commandant that around 200 Jews would be moved to Szczebrzeszyn from Posen, and the *Landrat* in Zamosc ordered that all Polish evacuees be located in villages around the city but not in the city itself.

What does all this mean? We don't know. Motorized traffic is increasing. The whole day trucks and cars traveled in all directions. During the afternoon a few trucks stopped at the bakery just across from the hospital to load bread and flour.

I worked on moving my library from the hospital to the rented apartment in town. Some particularly valuable books I stored in the homes of several friends. We are all asking ourselves what the next few days will bring.

December 19 Last night 180 Jews, evacuees from Wloclawek, arrived in Szczebrzeszyn. Almost all are women and children; there are only a few men, mostly older, because the young ones were kept in Zamosc. Local Jews are taking care of them. I heard that another 300 will be here soon.

Yesterday one German company left. Two others are supposed to follow soon. The Germans do not like this at all and they are very depressed. A German medic again mentioned that they would be moved to the Western Front and soon we would have German police and SS.

Today, during all my free time, I moved my books.

December 20 Today, stopping in to see me was Stanislaw Nowinski, my former student from the teacher's seminary in Szczebrzeszyn, where for several years I taught hygiene and was also the school physician. Now he teaches in Pulawy County. He showed me a form that all teachers are to sign. One side of the text is in German, the other is in very poor Polish. The text is as follows: "Under oath I am stating that I was a member of the following military or political organizations _____ . Further I am stating that it is not known to me that either me or my wife is not of Aryan origin. I am aware that Aryan origin means a person who in the last three generations had not one drop of Jewish blood, and that racial origin has nothing to do with religion."

This afternoon the Germans posted new regulations. From Friday, December 22, all Jews ten years old or older, when walking outside, had to display a white band with the Star of David on the right sleeve. All stores must display signs stating that they are either Aryan or Jewish. The bands and signs can be purchased at city hall.

Yesterday from London British radio broadcast the news that only 20 km from Zamosc a small group of Polish soldiers was trying to reach the Hungarian border. Being so near to Zamosc we should know about this.

Last evening I moved more books.

December 21   New regulations were posted. Without written permission from the *Landrat* no one had the right to remove any articles from the county. We see more and more restrictions, each making our lives more unbearable.

December 22   Despite the request that all Jews wear bands showing a yellow Star of David, so far not one Jew has obeyed.

Today I learned that in Zamosc the Germans executed Dr. Polakow, a university professor, and in Lublin Fr. Bocian from Suchowola, and also nine men from the same village, including a nineteen-year-old boy. The reasons for the executions are not clear. The priest and the nine men were executed possibly for removing and burying in a different place the body of a German soldier in Suchowola. This was done without the permission of German authorities.

December 23   All owners of cars and trucks were ordered to deliver their vehicles to city hall. I was advised to take my car to Zamosc and obtain a permit from the *Landrat* to keep it. So, because I had no gasoline, I chained my car behind a horse-drawn carriage and slowly made my way to Zamosc. I could not accomplish much; because of the coming holidays the *Landrat* had already left, so I was to come back after Christmas.

Zamosc is not as I remember it. At city hall, the county buildings, and even the university red flags with black swastikas flew. Germans are everywhere. They are in all the stores, restaurants, and coffee shops. I stopped at a print shop and a German soldier was buying 1,000 postcards showing city hall and printed with German New Year's greetings. The proprietor told me that he had received an order for 6,000 more postcards to be delivered the next day. In Kapicki's bookstore I saw the same: Germans buying postcards.

Walking along I saw several German announcements posted at street corners. I verified from them that the executed physician was Dr. Maj. Michal Polakow. While walking through the streets I did not meet one person I knew, even though I have many friends in Zamosc. Most people stay inside. They don't like to see the Germans walking around in large groups or see their swastikas or cars.

Not too many Jews were on the streets either, but of the ones I saw, several wore the Star of David on their sleeves. In Szczebrzeszyn, not one Jew has obeyed that order.

December 25   Last night, around 10 P.M., two German soldiers inspected all hospital wards. They even checked the infectious rooms. Many times they asked if all the patients and wounded were Poles. It seems to me they were searching for someone.

I received for my collection several printed and typewritten German instructions. A few are interesting. On December 1, 1939, the chief German forest ranger signed a note to all German officials in Zamosc County that read, "All wood used for heating or construction that was illegally taken from any forest after September 1, 1939, must be delivered to the local forestry station or paid for."

From the military commandant, Field Order No. 8, dated December 19, 1939, puts into detail what I stated on December 22:

1. All owners of shops and stores shall hang in the store window a sign saying, "Aryan Business" or "Jewish Business." The signs can be purchased at city hall.
2. All Jews, men and women of age ten or older, must wear white arm bands displaying the Star of David. Arm bands can be purchased at city hall.
3. This takes effect on December 22, 1939.
4. Anyone who disobeys may be arrested and fined.

On December 18, 1939, a new regulation was posted at city hall: "Because of the upcoming holiday season, all houses must be cleaned and painted white."

In spite of the strict orders, I have not yet seen one Jew wearing a star. Maybe this is in connection with the change of the city commandant, which is to be very soon.

December 26 The new German company, which arrived last night, began its stay by once again destroying Jewish establishments, but everyone expected this, so it surprised no one.

Yesterday an announcement was posted by the new military commandant: "All Polish women who are walking with German soldiers are asked to register at the 'Public House' for better acquaintance. Their names will be kept in strict files and never published."

Many people stopped to read the announcement. The Germans noticed this and removed it quickly. But it is true that some young girls went with German soldiers, particularly officers, and the announcement helped to stop this.

December 27 I went again to Zamosc regarding my car. The *Landrat* is still on vacation and his deputy, a very ugly type, wouldn't even listen to me. But at the police office a German *Feldwebel*, speaking good Polish, told me to keep my car and come back when the *Landrat* returns. This *Feldwebel*, a Czech, spoke good Polish with me and his friendliness was in complete contrast to the other Germans in the *Landrat* office.

For the first time since the outbreak of the war I stopped by to see the county administrator, Sochanski, and his wife. We greeted each other warmly and spent a few hours talking.

I came home really disturbed. During the last few hours I learned more details of the executions of people I knew. It is really hard to live in slavery.

December 28 Yesterday when I was in Zamosc I stopped at the county office. The clerks were sitting there doing nothing, only talking among themselves. No one worked. I spoke with the secretary, Mr. Burzminski, and asked what kind of help the county could give to keep the hospitals in Zamosc and Szczebrzeszyn running. After this conversation I lost all hope. I have to run the hospital by myself, but how? The situation is so bad that 70 percent of my patients cannot pay and the others pay only a portion of the normal fees. So now I have a dilemma. What to do?

Today I called a meeting of all the staff members and personnel to explain the situation. Beginning January 1, 1940, I will be unable to pay normal salaries, maybe just a small amount, enough to survive. I have to start drastic savings. We are closing the special staff cafeteria. Everyone will be fed from the hospital kitchen. The kitchen will serve more meatless meals and the amount of butter, eggs, and dessert will be reduced. Naturally my popularity dropped by several points. Also I was forced to talk about other disciplinary matters.

December 30 A few days ago a single bandit armed with a rifle and hand grenades attempted to rob the Marian Doroszewski farm at Szperowka, near Szczebrzeszyn. The people inside were ordered to stand with their hands above their heads. Somehow the people tried to disarm the man, but he threw a grenade, killing Marian Doroszewski and wounding himself. While lying on the floor he threw another grenade, this time killing himself and wounding another person.

Yesterday a German *Feldwebel* who is deputy city commandant visited the hospital wearing street clothes. In civilian life he was a chemist and instructor at some school. He promised to help. He seemed like a nice person.

Today the *Ortskommando* began the registration of all Jews who left the city with the Soviets and later returned. Those Jews are to be deported to the Russian occupation zone.

Life Is Nerve Shattering

January

January 1 Probably never in the history of Poland has a New Year's Eve been so sad. The only New Year's greetings were hopes that our slavery will soon end. Every day this slavery is harder to accept. Everyone waits for the end of this situation, and no one thinks that it will remain like this for too much longer. I personally believe that our defeat is temporary and that we will survive. I am sure that the strength of the Polish nation will finally win this struggle. I am always glad when the day comes to an end because I feel that we are closer, by one step, to final victory.

We see very few Germans walking on the streets. I am happy because I still cannot get used to their presence.

January 2 We are completely broken by the news that reached us about executions in Warsaw, Lublin, and other cities. I was particularly shaken by the execution of some people who were very close to me from scientific or civic life: Professor Bialobrzeski of the University of Warsaw, a noted physicist; Judge Bryla, from the Lublin appeals court; Presiding Judge Sekutowicz of Lublin; Professor Czuma of Lublin University; Fr. Niechaj; and others. I received information about the execution of more than one hundred men in the village of Wawer, near Warsaw. This news makes all of us more and more nervous and worried about our own destinies.

Today Dr. Wroblewski, from Zwierzyniec, stopped by to see me. He told me about the tailor-made hunting trip designed for German dignitaries at the Zamoyski estates, but all estate officials, including young Zamoyski, refused to participate. During the hunt some German officers shot a few pheasants and had them delivered to Zamoyski, but he would not accept them and sent them back.

January 4 Just yesterday Jews began wearing the Star of David arm bands, some on the right arm, others on the left.

Today the *Ortskommandant*, Capt. Jensen, visited the hospital. Appearing very elegant and well behaved, he seemed extremely interested in hospital activities and asked if he could be of any help. When I showed him the still unrepaired damages received by the hospital in September (mostly from air bombardment), he promised that soon everything would be put in good repair. As he was leaving he told me that he is very satisfied with the way the hospital is being run. Maybe some naive person would believe that he is really interested in the hospital, but not me.

On the streets we see fewer Germans now than during the last few weeks. No military patrols; guards are posted around the high school and city hall only. At night only militia patrols move through the city.

January 8 Some people get used to a new way of life sooner than others, even if it is slavery. In a small city like Szczebrzeszyn nothing can be hidden. Yesterday the family of our mayor was celebrating the birth of his first grandson. At the end of the festivities a late guest showed up, a German officer, and he sat at the family table. It is interesting to note that the father of the newborn is an officer in the Polish army, now in Rumania.

Today I went to Zamosc. From the German authorities *(Standartsamt)* I received a permit to keep my car, but I can use it only traveling to and from a sick person. So I brought the car back to the hospital.

Among my friends in Zamosc I could sense very low spirits. They seem to believe in rumors because nobody knows what the truth is anymore.

A few days ago seventeen people, including one woman, were shot in a small high school garden. The executions could be seen from the county offices.

At the headquarters of the Red Cross I observed very heavy traffic. The new volunteers, including a few judges, lawyers, and women, were kept busy. It seemed that many people went there for help. For the hospital I obtained a large bag filled with bandages and a big carton containing medicines.

After visiting the Red Cross I went to the public library. It was crowded as never before. The number of subscribers is over 1,000. No Jews are allowed to borrow books. Each day around 400 people exchange books. This can be due to the fact that people are staying home more than before, par-

ticularly during evening hours, because no one is allowed to walk the
streets after 8 P.M.

January 9   Very cold. This morning we had temperatures of −10°F. The
Germans are feeling the cold and have begun confiscating all fur coats. Yesterday the German police took all sheepskin coats from passing villagers
and left them only in jackets.

Today at our weekly reporting session we met a new German captain
who told us that our region is now part of the so-called general government,
a new German administration with headquarters in Cracow. He asked us to
obey all German laws and to be loyal to German authorities. From now on
we have to report only every other week.

During this visit I met with the high school principal, Jozwiakowski.
He told me that he and the mayor were called in and advised by the mil-
litary commandant about the speeded-up reconstruction of the high school
because a new company of soldiers (120 men) will soon be moved to
Szczebrzeszyn. Principal Jozwiakowski saw the damage caused by the
Germans to the almost new buildings. The gymnasium was converted to
an auto repair shop. To accomplish this it was necessary to remove portions
of the walls. In the auditorium, window openings were converted to antitank stations.

January 11   We are freezing. The temperature dropped to −20°F. No one
goes outside. All the stores are closed. Only bakeries are open but only for
a few hours a day. It is especially difficult to find bacon, sausage, or butter.

Today I was called to treat a sick Jew with frostbitten feet. He brought
some merchandise here from Warsaw by rail. Crying, he told me about being beaten at the Warsaw railroad station by some passengers and being
thrown from the car. Part of his merchandise was stolen. Finally the train
conductor hid him in a cargo car where he remained for twelve hours until
he reached Rejowiec. For another twelve hours he traveled from Rejowiec
to Szczebrzeszyn, all in unheated cars.

It is cruel, but some Poles are imitating German methods.

January 12   I received a personal invitation from the city commandant
to attend a double-feature program at the movie theater. Two films were
supposed to be shown, a political review and a comedy. Naturally I decided not to attend, but I was really interested in how this would be presented and who would be there. So I asked a young medic to represent the
hospital and go to the presentation of the political revue. The Germans
asked him about me, why I had not attended and how many ill were at
the hospital.

January 15 Notary Rosinski from Zamosc and Mr. Kazimierz Zieleniewski, a librarian from Warsaw, paid a visit. Mr. Zieleniewski, who is here as an evacuee, began working at the sugar refinery as a bookkeeper. He promised to write about his experiences during the last few months.

January 18 It is cold, down to −10°F. All the stores are closed. Prices are high whenever the stores open. For the hospital, wholesale prices are: bread, 1 zloty per pound; rye 70 zloty per 100 weight; wheat, 90 zloty; flour, 160 zloty; eggs, 40 groszy apiece. With these prices I will no longer be able to support the hospital without outside help, but at the same time I cannot count on any outside help.

Today the German military theater began performing in town. The city must provide quarters for a few hundred soldiers arriving soon.

Today the gestapo from Zamosc questioned Fr. Cieslicki, asking for a list of all Catholic organizations active in the deanery, with membership and financial statements. They seem to be keenly interested in the assets of all Catholic organizations.

In Zamosc Prof. Stefan Miller, director of the Zoological Institute, was arrested.

According to new regulations you can walk around until 8 P.M. To enforce this, the Germans are stopping people and charging them 1 zloty per minute after 8 P.M.

January 20 Freezing temperatures are still holding. The very thick hospital brick walls are so cold that the inside temperature of 40°F in the evening drops to 32°F in the morning. With this temperature it is impossible to sit in one place. I began a new working assignment, a new cross-reference system about Polish physicians. I included all the information obtained from reading biographies and articles. I am noting physicians by name, the publication where their name is found, the date of printing, and page number. This takes a lot of time but I am relaxing mentally, forgetting about the worries of the day, and particularly about the future of my hospital.

Every day it is more difficult to supply the hospital with food and other goods. Many items are sold out completely; for others you must pay extremely high prices. Grits are 1.5 zloty; sausage, 7 zloty. It looks like the prices will go up even higher because the Germans began registering all livestock. Even at the hospital we must give a complete list of all pigs and chickens. In some areas the Germans are branding not only cows but also pigs. The branded pigs have to be specially fed and can be butchered only for the use of the German army. The peasants have plenty of money so they are not anxious to sell. But because they are not able to buy, they drink every day, and during the evening many drunks start singing on the streets. It is interesting to note that patriotic sentiment has been increasing lately. You can hear every patriotic song including the Polish national anthem. The same happens in the restaurants and bars. In one of the local bars there was a confrontation begun between some peasants and a group of German soldiers. The soldiers left the bar, afraid of what might happen.

January 22   Last night I was called twice to attend to Dr. Likowski, who suffered a heart attack. At night the city looks very strange, as if it were dead. No one walks. No patrols, no guards, all windows are covered with black blinds. Only at the market place I noticed a few dimmed lights.

From friends I found out about the arrest of the journalist Zbigniew Klaudel, publisher of the weekly *Truth*. The reason: some prewar articles in his paper. At the same time the very popular Wladyslaw Klokocki was arrested, but in his case for black marketeering.

The gestapo are still questioning the presidents and secretaries of all civic and professional organizations. The president of the Young Farmers, Skiba, was arrested.

At the Zamoyski estate in Zwierzyniec the German military command appointed a new administrator to manage everything owned by the estate: farms, mills, refineries, and forests. Of course, it is a uniformed German.

January 23   Today the free market was larger than normal and full of surprises. Every horse-drawn wagon coming into town was stopped. The Germans were searching for cash. All 100-zloty bills were confiscated. This is in line with the new regulation that all 500- and 100-zloty bills are to be given to German financial institutions and will be exchanged sometime in the spring for a new type of money to be printed by a new exchange bank. It will open soon. The second surprise was the search of all wagons leaving town. In this case the Germans were searching for rye and wheat. These commodities were purchased by them at 32 zloty per hundred weight, which is the maximum price called for in the official price list. At the free market the price for a hundred weight is 80 zloty. Anyone involved is in a panic. As a result of this the next free market will be completely empty.

Today a detachment of German gendarmes arrived in Szczebrzeszyn and started organizing their offices at city hall. So again we will have new authorities. As of now the same military commandant is in charge. The Germans again began organizing a Polish police force. So far members of the prewar police are involved. They carry no arms, wear civilian clothes, and on the left arm they wear a green band with *Policja* spelled out in black letters.

January 24 Following yesterday's search for rye and wheat the Germans stopped all deliveries of firewood. The search for 100-zloty bills continues.

January 25 Stankiewicz, the secretary of commune Nielisz, who was arrested a week ago, was executed in Zamosc for hiding weapons. The Germans notified the commune but not the family.

Today the Germans ordered all school principals to take from the students handbooks of the Polish language as well as history and geography texts. In every Szczebrzeszyn school, in every classroom, children returned books. But still some students are refusing to give them up.

This is making me feel worse. I am in shock and deeply depressed.

January 26 Each day is the same, it seems routine. Civic life is nonexistent, it has completely stopped. People try only to make ends meet. They are involved only in supplying the necessary means of survival. Besides this, only gossip.

We really do not know what is going on, not only in our own surroundings, but, more important, in the world. We look to see in which direction the Germans are moving, counting guns, tanks, and other military vehicles, hoping that from this information we can guess what is really happening. We try to hear conversations of German soldiers. This is our only clue to news of the Western Front. Once in a while I receive a copy of a Polish-printed but German-published newspaper, such as *Nowy Kurier Warszawski*, from Warsaw, or *Goniec Krakowski*, from Cracow, but this news is all made up, so you can trust only the advertising and missing persons columns.

We do not have radios, and anyway, information that is supposed to be from the BBC is so contradictory that it can't be trusted. So we are completely cut off from the world, from intellectual life, and have only one goal, survival. But no one even knows what awaits us in the near future, or who will survive. Thank God I have my goal: to save my hospital. I know that soon it will be in demand.

This morning some unusual excitement. It was announced that no one is allowed on the streets between 10 A.M. and noon. We don't know what this means. People stayed home and looked through the windows, but before noon some went outside and soon traffic became normal.

We learned later that a German general arrived for a full inspection of the military barracks and the authorities were ordered to keep the public away from him.

At noon I admitted a pair of Jews, evacuees from Lodz, both with typhoid fever. As requested, I notified city hall and as a caution a guard was posted at the apartment where they had lived. Fifty-three people were already living in that apartment building and now will have a fourteen-day quarantine.

From the villages of Brody and Kawenczyn I received information that the German gendarmes confiscated all money from villages, not only 100-zloty bills. They took money from passersby also.

January 27 Today the Germans again confiscated money. They stopped people on the streets and searched every traveler. They even searched some houses. Our cook, Miss Osipowiczowna, was stopped and searched. To avoid any loss she had money hidden in her boot.

This afternoon I admitted another case of typhoid fever and again reported it to city hall. This sickness really has the Germans worried.

January 30 The most important event of the last few days is the spread of typhoid fever, particularly among the Jews living on Zamojska Street, near the high school buildings which are now barracks for German soldiers. The German military command announced new regulations. No one has access to the barracks. All Jews who worked there were dismissed, and Germans are cleaning their quarters themselves. Soldiers are not allowed to walk on the city streets; they are confined to their barracks. No one can walk on the sidewalks next to the barracks. All restaurants and bars are closed, including Maj. Malinowski's Citizen's Club and Mr. Paprocki's Cafe-Club-Bridge. The Germans moved out of some of the houses on Zamojska Street.

Every new case of typhoid must be reported to the military command. Today for the first time I admitted typhoid cases from Krasnobrod. The lice crawling on the Jews from Krasnobrod cannot even be described.

February

February 1 I visited Zwierzyniec, the headquarters of the Zamoyski estate, to beg for firewood and flour and to talk about employment for former county administrator Sochanski. I met with Debczynski, the estate administrator, and young Zamoyski, but finding a job for Sochanski will be difficult. Zwierzyniec has changed. It's full of Germans, especially at the estate offices and clubhouse. The first floor of the estate headquarters has been taken by the Germans for use as a supply room and sickroom, *Krankenstube*. Everywhere you see German signs.

I spoke with several friends. They are sure that by spring we can count on heavy fighting. The Germans are building heavy fortifications around Zwierzyniec. The soccer field has been completely destroyed. Other fortifications are being built around the villages of Obrocz, Frampol, Tarnogrod, Labun, Tomaszow, and Belzec.

From today on bread can be sold with food stamps only. The daily ration is 1 lb. of bread per person, with the legal price being 35 groszy per pound for dark and 45 groszy for white.

February 3   Freezing temperatures are still holding, down to −10°F. I have problems with hospital supplies; in particular we are lacking fuel. Our supply of coal is almost exhausted and firewood prices are extremely high. For one cord of oak you pay 50 zloty.

I went to the sugar refinery in Klemensow. From the manager, Mr. Wyszynski, I received a hundredweight of sugar and from Attorney Muszak one wagonload of hay and straw for the horses. So I've come to begging to support the hospital.

February 5   Today the gendarmes searched the Jewish stores looking for any kind of fabric, soap, and food.

From early morning people are waiting in line in front of bakeries and markets to buy sugar and bread. Lately butter is being rationed also. People wait for hours just to get a few ounces. Some are selling it on the spot to Jews. (Jews are not allowed to buy butter in the stores.)

February 6   Today we have new administrative changes. The city commandant is still Hauptmann Jensen, but he is in charge only of military affairs. All POWS must report to him. Public administration, including regulating food supplies, is left up to the mayor and the city council. Public safety is in the hands of the military gendarmes and German police. The Polish police, now in uniforms, and the militia are to help the Germans maintain public safety.

February 7   This morning, I watched a long line of people waiting for the bakery across from the hospital to open. Until 8 A.M. only Poles were allowed to buy, then Jews could start. But not all were able to because by a few minutes after 8 A.M. all the bread was sold out.

As I watched this spectacle I remembered standing in line in 1918, in Symferopol in the Crimea, to get food for my wife, my son, and me. I stood the whole night to finally be able to buy a little bread, meat, and sugar. I clearly remember standing among people who spoke in every language of the former Russian empire as I read *Physician Aphorisms* by Hippocrates.

I visited city hall and learned that in Szczebrzeszyn there are eight active bakeries, three Polish and five Jewish. The Jews have been instructed to buy bread only in Jewish ones. But they are buying as much as possible in the Polish stores even though they never patronized them before. Now Polish bakeries have been ordered not to sell to the Jews, and the police are to enforce this order.

Today colorful posters were plastered all over the town "requesting" that all men and women ages sixteen to fifty sign up for volunteer work in Germany. All unemployed and welfare recipients must register for this program. Of course, this announcement makes people very uneasy.

February 8   I went to the forestry inspectorate in Kosobudy to ask for firewood, and from there to Zwierzyniec. I spent a few hours in a very peaceful world. First I traveled the beautiful road through the forest, then I relaxed in Mr. Otto's living room. There, in the forest, you can forget all about war and the Germans. Out there my nerves relaxed. But then on the road to Zwierzyniec I saw hundreds of abandoned military and private vehicles covered with snow. This was a very unpleasant picture.

February 9   Every commune received quotas for grain delivery by February 18. Zwierzyniec must deliver 12,700 hundredweights, Sulow, 16,000. Even the city of Szczebrzeszyn must give 3,600. Those numbers are so high that neither commune will be able to deliver. And what will be left for our own people?

Thinking about the rising prices and the ever more limited supply, people are grabbing whatever they can, without even paying attention to the prices. Today I purchased a few hundredweight of flour at 140 zloty and cereal for 2 zloty per pound.

The regulation on selling bread to the Jewish population changed again. Jews can buy bread at Polish bakeries after all the Christians have left.

February 10   The freezing weather is still with us. All stores are closed. Once in a while you can see a group of people, usually Jews, standing by a house. There the German police are making a search, looking for any hidden items. Lately Polish stores and homes have not been involved.

Today Dr. Tyczkowski, the county sanitation officer from Zamosc, stopped at the hospital. He came to say good-bye because, as of now, Szczebrzeszyn has been moved from Zamosc County to Bilgoraj County. The following communes have also been added to Bilgoraj County: Radecznica, Sulow, Zwierzyniec, and Tereszpol. I am deeply disturbed by this news because I don't know too many people in Bilgoraj and it is also much farther than Zamosc. I am worried that there will be no one who can help me with the needs of the hospital. I hope that this will not occur for quite a while.

Around me people are taking this attitude: wait until spring. In spring we are expecting big events, hopefully a large British offensive on the Western Front. Everyone is sure that the new Polish army, formed in France by Gen. Sikorski, will take part in it. The Germans are waiting for something to happen also. When young people asked permission to hold a dance, the Germans refused, saying, "In a few weeks the living and the dead will be dancing here without music."

February 14   Still cold. It is so cold that our normal life has practically stopped. People are waiting for warmer days. The only place that people seem to go is the German movie theater. At the entrance is a big sign, "Jews Are Not Allowed." But people are still going, and the small Krzeszowski theater is always full. People don't realize that by going to see German movies they are supporting the German war effort, because the profit is helping to equip the German army.

Some people, in particular unemployed women, are very friendly with the Germans and have changed their apartments into public houses where the soldiers spend the whole night.

And how is it with going to work in Germany? I was sure that there would be no volunteers, but the recruiting is going rather well. A few transports from Szczebrzeszyn and Zamosc have left already.

February 15   The notary Rosinski visited. For several hours we talked and planned for the future.

February 17   I was visited by the teacher Bohun. He is kept busy trying to start underground organizations in cooperation with Zamosc. He asked me to join. Naturally I agreed without even thinking twice.

February 18   I met a woman, wife of an official of the Zamoyski estate. She had just arrived from Chelmo. For some time I've been receiving alarming information about the execution of the mentally ill patients of the psychiatric ward at Chelmo Hospital. I asked her if this really happened. She verified that it was true.

All the mentally ill were shot with machine guns, but under penalty of death the hospital personnel are forbidden to talk about this crime.

It is so hard to believe anything as terrible as this.

February 19   I feel very bad both physically and mentally. My wife and son are both down with the flu. I am fighting this by taking every precautionary measure. I know what will happen to the hospital if I become bedridden. A normal flu with my heart condition will put me in bed for about two weeks.

I am very depressed by everything I see and hear. I never expected the morale of the Polish population to sink so low, with such a complete lack of national and personal pride. More and more people are volunteering for work in Germany, sometimes whole families, and not only from our town but also from surrounding villages. From my hospital a few people volunteered also, including a cook who has worked here for the last four years.

I've heard about a growing number of denunciations usually about hidden weapons. Most denunciators are women.

As I pointed out before, the German movie theater is always crowded with people, and what now seems interesting is that evacuees from the Posen region attend it also.

Some of the girls are having very intimate relations with the Germans. As I think of this, I can visualize as a contrast the sight of a handcuffed Prof. Miller being escorted through the streets of Zamosc.

February 20 Yesterday there was another change in the German police force. The new policeman began their work by beating Jews.

Today I went and reported myself as a POW to the German military commandant. His office is the principal's office of the high school administration building, well known to me for over twenty years.

February 22 I left the hospital very early in the morning to see a group of people leaving for work in Germany. From surrounding villages a total of 135 persons and from Szczebrzeszyn a total of 45 more left. One thing is good: most of these people are known troublemakers, and their departure is rather good news for the general public.

Events seem to prove we are part of Bilgoraj County. Yesterday the county administrator in Bilgoraj requested from city hall quarters for 1,000 Jews to be moved here soon from other cities.

February 25 The mood has switched to growing excitement once again. People are expecting something important to happen. Different rumors are circulating throughout the city. Some people say that the Germans themselves are unsure of their future and are beginning to criticize the Hitler administration and are fearful of a general uprising in Germany.

February 26 The excitement is still growing. Radio news, though illegal, sometimes reaches us. Some local events have built suspense, such as the Germans ordering a new alarm siren from the machine shop in Szczebrzeszyn. People saw British aircraft shining reflectors over the city of Zamosc. This supposedly started a panic in German circles, so much so that some German officers are moving from the city to the suburbs.

In Szczebrzeszyn police searched the homes of retired teacher Billecki, and school gardener Koprowiak for hidden radios. In both cases nothing was found. People say that this was a denunciation.

German police, speaking good Polish, searched Jewish homes looking for hidden goods and beating Jews for no reason.

February 28 Now everything is calm. As I suspected, there were no British aircraft over Zamosc. People were just saying what they wanted to hear.

Our situation is the same as before. Talk has stopped about us being moved to Bilgoraj County. More and more people are being called for labor duty in Germany. Today eighty-two men were called. Volunteers are not registering anymore. People are worried about our youth. People say that the Germans are forming youth labor camps for children from fourteen to eighteen years of age. A special notice concerning this matter was printed in an official German journal, but so far no specific instructions have been given as to how to carry it out.

February 29 Today I received a few typewritten leaflets concerning actual events taking place in Szczebrzeszyn: one about Jews, one about a girl the Germans called "Charlotte," and a third about an affair concerning leather.

First about "Charlotte." She is Leokadia Hascowna, the grammar school teacher who worked as a volunteer in my hospital during September 1939. She is now dating German soldiers and her behavior is questionable.

About leather. During a search the Germans discovered a large supply of shoe leather. It was found in a Jewish store. Two-thirds was shipped to Germany and one-third was left at city hall for distribution to the Christian population. But before any distribution was organized, city employees had divided everything among themselves.

The leather affair was described by retired teacher Bielecki in a poem he had written. He was very well informed about the leather situation from the local offices. But his poem is the worst I have ever read. I am noting this poem in its entirety because it tells about the feelings and actions of some of Szczebrzeszyn's people.

Christ and Leather

In front of the Church stands a monument to
Christ encircled by flowers.
This monument—a symbol of God's kindness,
Shows how to love your neighbors, and fight your enemies.
So those who are humble bow their heads.
Those who walk past with bowed heads are
shoemakers, tailors, bricklayers, officials,
and dignitaries, and they remove their hats.
One evening during autumn,

A fat man stands there, humbly praying, and he is saying,
"Christ, at your feet, O Lord, I beg for help, as soon as night comes.
Save the leather, from this costly
Possession I will make shoes, so my
Feet will not freeze, and I will make
A belt. It is good to help a neighbor.
Everything will be done diligently and well as it should be
In your care even a thief believes,
And I will give you as an offering the
First Brigade's old playing cards.
O Lord, you know it is winter and we will play cards.
Heaven will help us with these ideas,
Those who sleep at work, and when
It occurs, to clear away timid thoughts.
One of my comrades, a hero, O Lord, returned
From Kowel. He fought there.
He hid leather in a grave in the cemetery.
A thief stole it, now he is in mourning.
Everything is in the Polish way, established from above.
One perishes from hunger, the second steals leather,
The third steals fabric for underwear,
The fourth, a deserter, fights for our country.
The fifth makes good money in the parish.
All, O Lord, are 'Ready and United,'
So I would like to serve my country well, as long
As my foot does not slip."
He looked around, with a sigh of relief, at
The feet. Among the flowers he carefully placed his treasure.
Now he breathed freely, and took his hat,
Happy that he had hidden his leather well,
He left. But from the distance you can hear
People searching for new prey—to extract people's tears.
And in a minute silhouettes are seen, grabbing leather from the feet.
He calls from a distance, "Lord, forgive me, I pay my tithe on time.
I will give as an offering one penny, or another new coin,
If only to be sure that my head will not fall because of leather."
This is nothing strange. O Poland, quite a few
Are robbing for themselves.
Around the theft there is no shame.
They laugh at the name of Poland.

March

March 2   You can sense depression in our town. People talk constantly about the men being taken for labor in Germany. At city hall you see more and more Germans from the labor bureau. Yesterday the Germans requested another 200 men for the next transport. No one is volunteering. Now people are receiving individual summonses to report to the labor bureau in Zamosc. Many people have asked doctors to sign excuses because of illness or hardship. I sign them, but I am not sure if they will help—probably not. A lot of men are hiding. Many who so far have not received any summons stay home and avoid walking the streets. I am deeply worried about the deportation of our youth to labor camps.

It has already been a half year of war and occupation. It's hard to believe. We are living, waiting for a change.

March 4   Since early morning people have been active on the streets, in particular around city hall. The German police, with the help of the Polish militia, are going from house to house registering all Christians between the ages of fifteen and fifty who are suitable for labor. The populace is upset, especially the women. A large group of women assembled before city hall and began shouting and demonstrating against the mayor and other officials. They demanded to know if the two daughters and the son of the mayor are also registered for labor in Germany.

We do not have any news from the outside world. We are not aware of what is occurring or how the fighting nations stand or if spring will bring us any changes.

March 5   The worst time of the day is morning when I awake with the knowledge that I am facing another day filled with troubles and worries, a day that I must spend in an atmosphere of slavery, dimming the joy of living.

Today, again, one transport with about twenty or so people left for work in Germany. New registration procedures have begun. People are very much disturbed, particularly parents of young girls.

The weather is terrible. Snow is falling, so all roads are practically nonaccessible. Snow flurries have stopped motorized traffic. To clear the roads the Germans are using hundreds of Jews. As they work they must sing Polish national songs.

Today at the hospital I admitted a few new cases of typhoid fever. This time they are Jews evacuated from Kalisz.

March 6   Today new regulations concerning the registration of Jews between the ages of twelve and sixty were posted. Naturally, a panic is spreading among the Jewish population because of their fear of labor camps.

The Germans conducted more elaborate searches, looking for radio receivers. At teacher Bielecki's place, during a second search they discovered a radio. He was arrested. A second receiver was found at the home of the grammar school principal, Wegierski.

March 7   I am very disheartened to see people dressed in clothing made
from old Polish uniforms, such as caps, coats with civilian buttons, every
type of tunic, trousers, and belts. Many times these articles of clothing are
worn by people who never served in the military. Some have even altered
the military overcoats into jackets. In the physician's office, during consultations, I can still see military underwear, with many of the stamps visible.
Even women are wearing underwear made from old Polish shirts that still
show a military stamp. There is even a new fashion. One style of boot is
made from leather and military blankets. Women find them popular. People
who never served in the military wear this clothing. It is sad to see our
public property ruined like this.

March 10   Yesterday I went to Zamosc. The roads are covered with snow,
so no cars can get through. Around Szczebrzeszyn the Jews are clearing
the streets; in Wielacza the peasants do it, but around Plonsk even the Germans work. In Zamosc there is a complete collapse of morale. The streets
are almost deserted, including the area around the Czerski apartments, not
far from the university, where the Germans established a new gestapo
headquarters. Here, as in our own Szczebrzeszyn, no one gets any news of
the world.

March 16   One week has passed. Nothing much has happened, but the
temperature rose and the snow began melting. The Germans mobilized
more Jews to clean the city.

On March 13 a new transport of young people was sent for labor work
to Germany, but it was limited to a handful. People are hiding to avoid
deportation.

The registration of Jews continues. Dr. Likowski and Dr. Spoz are
checking people with real or fake illnesses. I have examined many people
myself, but I am not sure if my recommendations will be honored by
the Germans.

A recently posted new regulation forbids Jews from walking on the
city's main streets on Saturdays. As of yesterday we are officially part of
Bilgoraj County.

I do not feel good at all. My heart is really troubling me. I am afraid of
the future. I am not able to do any mental work. For the first time in my
life I am spending time reading the most absurd novels, anything to stop
thinking about reality.

March 19   Today 130 people were supposed to report for work in Germany. Twenty horse-drawn wagons were ready to transport them to

Zamosc. Only 2 people showed up, and one was extremely ill. With a physician's statement as proof, this person is sure that he will be sent home from Zamosc.

The German administration is not functioning at all. As of today no one knows if our town is in Zamosc or Bilgoraj county. New regulations, mailed by the *Landrat* in Zamosc, are in German. Other new regulations from Bilgoraj are in Polish. The military commandant is not sure whom to listen to. Yesterday we signed a petition to the governor in Lublin that would allow us to stay in Zamosc County.

March 20 Today I received some official papers. One was from the *Ärztekammer* in Lublin. It orders all doctors to correspond officially only in German. County physician Dr. Tyczkowski sent this to us in Polish, but the next day another announcement was signed by him in German as *Kreisarzt*. In this one he said that Jews can be treated only by Jewish physicians, nurses, dentists, medics, or midwives. The reason: "Typhoid fever and other infectious diseases are mainly in the Jewish population, so it is necessary to isolate Jews from others." I don't know what will happen in Szczebrzeszyn where there is not even one Jewish physician.

Today Dr. Stefan Jozwiakowski returned from prison. He looks very pale and is not talking about his ordeal.

March 27 On Easter we had notary Rosinski from Zamosc as a guest. Yesterday seven people left for Germany, but almost one-hundred were called. From Zamosc we admitted more and more typhoid cases, mostly Jews, evacuees from Lodz and Wloclawek.

March 28 Today new regulations were posted. On order of the *Landrat* from Zamosc's city hall, meat consumption on Fridays is prohibited.

March 29 Yesterday Dr. Spoz went to Zamosc to clear up once and for all the question of whether we have a right to care for Jewish people. He spoke with health department officials. I just received an answer: "It is illegal to give any medical attention to the Jews, just as it is illegal to admit Jews to hospitals. Jews can be treated only by Jewish physicians." But what do we do if there are no Jewish physicians? I had a difficult situation. I was called to see a sick Jewish man. I went to him wondering whether anyone was spying on me. I feel terrible. On my prescription I even omitted the name of the sick man. So now we come to this: the main goal of every physician is to give medical help, but now it becomes a crime, punishable by imprisonment.

The Germans are still attempting to cut us off from the world. Yesterday they confiscated radio receivers from Mayor Franczak and Vice-Mayor Borucki. Until today they had special permits to own radio receivers and listen only to German stations.

March 30 In Zwierzyniec a German military company started rioting because of bad food. After a short while things calmed down, but special punishment duties were ordered.

In Zamosc, Mr. Sochanski was arrested again. Along with him the Germans arrested Dr. Col. Gorniewicz, a veterinarian; Maj. Mucha; Capt. Sliwinski; and in Kosobudy, forest ranger Byczkowski.

April

April 1 Today our clocks were advanced one hour.

I went to Zamosc. People there are talking about the recent arrests and searches in the city and neighboring counties.

In Krasnystaw County Mr. and Mrs. Suchodolski, from Moscisko, and in Tomaszow young Grzegorz Lipczynski were arrested.

In Zamosc new propaganda action has been started by Ukrainian patriots. Mudry, former vice-speaker of the Polish parliament, has been here for weeks.

Along with Dr. Tyczkowski and Dr. Bogucki I went to see the *Standartarzt*. We tried hard to explain the necessity of receiving permission to admit Jews into the hospitals. But he insisted that it was of the utmost importance to separate Jews from others. He will promote a new regulation to start a Jewish clinic in Zamosc for all neighboring counties. Only until the start of this clinic will we be able to admit Jews.

April 3 Today the Germans took from my hospital the last wounded Polish soldier. He was Jan Lugowski, who had one leg amputated. He was taken to Zamosc where the Polish soldiers are kept. So with his departure one chapter of our hospital life has closed.

April 6 Upon the request of the county administrator in Bilgoraj, the mayor invited several people to attend a meeting regarding labor work in Germany. Fifty invitations were mailed. But besides a couple of city officials, everybody excused themselves. Only the son of the mayor and teacher Bohun showed up, but Bohun had a special interest in seeing what was happening. So practically every intellectual boycotted the meeting. Naturally the Germans noticed this.

Today again new regulations were posted. The most important ones concerned the exchange of old zloty for new ones printed by the German bank, Bank Emisyjny. This started a panic. Some people began hiding old zloty, others are trying to buy whatever they can; on the other hand merchants are either hiding their goods or selling them for extremely high prices. So far no one trusts the new German zloty. Otherwise, nothing is new.

April 9 Today German gendarmes ordered that I give up my car. They were very upset about a few parts being missing. The whole day they stayed after me, and finally in the afternoon they had several Jews move my car to city hall. I was told that if by 7 A.M. the next morning I did not present the missing parts I would be fined 2,000 zloty.

April 10 With the help of a mechanic I knew we started the engine around noon, but I was fined 50 zloty for not keeping my car in running condition. I kept the receipt for the 50-zloty fine as a souvenir.

During the last few days the Germans have been looking for cars and trucks. Young Zamoyski lost his car in Zamosc and was forced to return home in a rented horse-drawn wagon.

New regulations. We can walk until 9 P.M. Milk, butter, and cheese are prohibited at the free market but can be purchased in special stores. But the worst one is that from now on we are not permitted to fire or hire anyone without written permission from the German labor bureau. In Zamosc the labor bureau will fill all vacancies with its own people.

And so the conditions of living and working are getting harder every day.

April 11 The military police took over my garage and then stored the Zamoyski car in it. They are constantly here on the hospital grounds.

April 12 On order of the county administrator a special meeting of all teachers was held. It was called by the school inspector, Szczepaniec. German officials were present also. The main item on the agenda was the labor problem in Germany and the recruitment of volunteers. The Germans would like to have a larger number of volunteers and keep deportations to a minimum. After this meeting Mr. Szczepaniec stopped by to visit. From him I learned that, according to a new reorganization chart, the public library in Zamosc is now a part of the Lublin District Department of Propaganda. The librarian is still Mrs. Gorczynska and the personnel are the same but certain books have been removed from the shelves. Jews are not allowed to have library cards. As of now, 1,500 people are using library services.

April 13   The main topic of conversation in town regards information received by hidden radios about the fighting in Norway. People hope that
maybe now more military action that can bring about some changes in our
lives will begin.

April 16   Today there was an inspection of livestock. My hospital lost one
good horse. Produce prices are rising. A liter of milk is now 80 groszy; butter, 12 zloty; bread on the free market, 1.5 zloty.

During the last few days I noticed heavy German military vehicle traffic. Most military convoys are moving toward Zwierzyniec. In Zamosc
there is an increasing number of German soldiers. Every day several troop
trains are leaving Hrubieszow.

Finally we have nice, warm weather, but tension is increasing also. We
are awaiting some important events.

April 19   German troops in Szczebrzeszyn are on alert. We were witnesses
to night exercises. On the hospital grounds the Germans installed machine
guns. The whole night we listened to the shooting. It was hard to fall asleep.

At city merchant Zlomaniec's place the Germans discovered an old car
with several parts missing. He was fined 1,000 zloty.

April 25   The days are passing slowly. We are trying to get any news from
the outside world, hoping that we will finally hear something good. We are
living under daily increasing pressure against us by the German authorities. Sorry to say but the mutual relations among the Polish populace are
not the best. We are lacking a uniform stand against the Germans; all the
rumors, intrigues, and denunciations are growing. Life is difficult because
of new restrictions issued practically everyday. Lately, the amount of butter per person per week was reduced by half. The only commodities you
can buy freely are potatoes, barley, and sauerkraut.

Yesterday we received a new order. This time all items made from copper, nickel, and lead, such as candle holders, flatware, candelabras, and
kitchen pots, must be taken to a German collection place. The same with
all iron gates and fences; they must be dismantled and given to the German
war effort.

We now have the new money, but people don't trust it so the exchange
is going very slowly. The stamped 100-zloty bills are difficult to use. No
one wants to take them. They can be exchanged only at the bank. The
reason is simple: there are too many bills circulating with counterfeit
stamps.

During the night more patrols check the city. They are made up of one
soldier, one gendarme, and one policeman. They stop everyone walking
about after curfew. They enter homes where light can be seen through

blackout curtains, even though there are no rules about any air raid preparations. But the most upsetting thing is the way some women are behaving, staying with and driving with German soldiers. I've seen this myself.

Because of denunciations the gendarmes are finding items that have been hidden at different locations. They do not have to search at all after entering the houses; they know exactly were the contraband has been hidden. At Biziorek's in Szczebrzeszyn they located a minibike. Today at the Alwa factory they ordered the surrender of a truck, but they knew all along where it was hidden.

We are still caught between Zamosc and Bilgoraj. Both counties send us instructions. Of course, this creates chaos.

May

May 19   For three weeks I have been unable to write. I am afraid that my notes may fall into German hands. There are some people in the city who say that I am writing a daily diary and that I am collecting information from the people known to me in the Zamosc region. I was forced to destroy some of the materials and to hide the loose pages of writing in different places, so I can later rewrite them in a special notebook. I received confidential information from city hall that the gestapo and police have a special interest in the activities of all local physicians.

Life is more difficult now than even a few weeks ago. We live from day to day, glad when the day has ended without any extraordinary events. We are not sure what will happen tomorrow. No news. The few people who still have radios have dismantled the receivers and hidden the separate parts. The use of radios by German officers who live in private quarters has stopped also.

The fighting on the Belgian-Dutch front is being followed with interest. Everyone hopes the war will enter a new phase that will decide our future.

New German orders, mostly those referring to labor work, are having a very depressing effect on the population.

The volunteering for labor in Germany has completely stopped. The Germans are stepping up the registration of all young people, so all young men and women born between 1915 and 1924 (from fifteen to twenty-four years of age) must register with the *Arbeitsamt*. This announcement caused a panic among parents and their youth. Fewer and fewer young people can be seen walking on the streets. Some are hiding in small villages or in the forest. We are particularly worried about the future of the young girls. Because of information obtained from Warsaw, we have learned that some young women have been placed in Germany's public houses.

More and more news about the raids in Warsaw and Lublin is reaching us. We are awaiting raids here in Szczebrzeszyn. Most young boys are not sleeping in their own homes anymore. They stay in barns, in fields, or in the forest. Recruitment for forced labor in Germany is a terrible blow to our national future. The Germans are trying to destroy our most valuable asset, our youth.

It is difficult to hide anyone because of growing denunciations. The meanness of some people has no limits. A few days ago I watched as the Germans transported a young boy, Kowalik from Bodaczow, in handcuffs. During a search of his house the police found a machine gun. He had been betrayed by a woman. The commandant of the local police was saying, after a few drinks, that he had been ordered to find a few confidants. He had several volunteers. Who they are we do not know for sure, so in this case I am not giving any names.

The new money printed by the German Bank Emisyjny is here. Different people have different attitudes toward the new money, but suspicion is widespread. People try to spend the new money first, because of the possibility of devaluation. Many people, including peasants, who have enough money are trying to keep the old bills.

Food prices are rising. Butter sold on the black market is going for 18 zloty. It is hard to get eggs because the Germans are exchanging 4 kg of eggs for 3 kg of sugar. Peasant women would rather have sugar than money.

A very good friend from Warsaw, Ludwig Gocel, a noted book collector, came by several times. He is involved in the black market. Together with notary Rosinski we spent several evenings talking about our future and our hobbies, so we were able to forget the present.

With Rosinski we talked about our underground work. He is very much involved, along with Zygmunt Pomaranski and Col. Mackowski. My own activities are limited to collecting money, colportage of an illegal press, and collecting historical material about the occupation. There are many emotions connected to the action on the Western Front in France.

The German company that has been here for almost half a year is moving out. The German police are already gone. Only a small unit of the Polish police is still here.

We are still somewhere between the county of Zamosc and the county of Bilgoraj. We receive orders and announcements from both.

May 25 Yesterday and today the Germans began arresting the Communists who were active in committees and other activities during the short period of Soviet occupation. Yesterday Kardyga, former chairman of the county committee, was arrested; this morning he was dead. His remains were delivered to the Zamosc mortuary. Whether he was hung or died from a beating is not known, but it appears that his death was probably caused by a beating.

In Szczebrzeszyn they arrested Sawic from Szperowka; Radzik from Przedmiescie; Kowalik, as hostage for his son; and a married Jewish couple named Bleiwas. They are searching for more. It looks like the good relations between the Germans and Russians are breaking up.

The young people are still living under the pressure of deportation to Germany. Even during the Feast of Corpus Christi, on Thursday, May 23, not many young people took part in the annual procession.

May 27   More and more talk about Soviet troops. The Jews are sure that we will have them as our allies. This makes us very nervous.

May 29   Yesterday, just before midnight, a transport of 1,070 evacuees from Kutno, Wloclawek, and Lodz arrived in Szczebrzeszyn, mostly women, children, and older men. They had been removed from their homes with only fifteen minutes given to pack their necessities. They were allowed to take only 20 zloty per person. At the transit camp in Lodz, all young people between the ages of fifteen and twenty-four were removed and shipped to labor camps in Germany. After a few days the rest were loaded into freight wagons and moved east under military escort. They arrived in terrible condition, resigned to their fate, completely broken, in particular those whose children had been taken to the labor camps. Every evacuee curses the Germans and they all want revenge. Local people are taking care of the evacuees. In a few days they are supposed to be relocated to several villages around Szczebrzeszyn.

The political news is not too good, so instead of the excitement of a few days ago, we now have complete resignation.

May 31   Again today we saw how brutal and inhuman the Germans are. For the last few days their horse-drawn wagons have been moving evacuees in the direction of Bilgoraj, mostly young children and many of them are ill. Today I admitted four of them with symptoms of mental disorder.

The news from the Western Front is not good at all. Generally, a depressed feeling is becoming evident and some people are showing signs of giving up. The uneasiness concerns deportations to Germany. Increasing rumors tell us that tonight the Germans will begin arresting our youth.

June

June 1   Those rumors materialized. Last night the gendarmes and police searched homes looking for people who had already received a summons but never reported to the *Arbeitsamt*. They arrested fifteen people and sent them to Zamosc. This is not the end because another thirty-five received summonses. It is possible that the Germans will begin street raids in other cities to fulfill their quota, because the people who had received summonses disappeared. Young people are hiding wherever they can. The young daughter of Dr. Likowski stays at my hospital the whole time. She is a medical student and works as a practical nurse. Mr. and Mrs. Sekutowicz arrived from Zamosc with their seventeen-year-old daughter, and I admitted her to the hospital as a TB case. Now the Germans have begun a new method, taking parents in lieu of young people.

June 3 The whole night we waited for more arrests. Even though this is Sunday there are very few people in the churches. In our town yesterday was quiet. So far no one has been arrested. But this morning there came alarming news. In the village of Sulow unknown people killed former teacher Chytros, who began working with the Germans as a denunciator. At 6 A.M. an entire company of German infantry with gestapo and gendarmes, moved into the small village only 7 km from Szczebrzeszyn, and we really worried about the future of the people there.

June 4 I received some information about the investigation into the Sulow killing. The police were trying to establish the motive for the crime, robbery or political. All the peasants were tortured. Usually the interrogation would start by putting the men into a wooden barrel, head down, and then beating them on the legs until they were barely able to walk. Several people were taken hostage. The search of the victim's house disclosed several guns and pistols and pieces of German uniforms. After several hours the hostages were released. Deportations have stopped. Some people returned to their homes from hiding. The feeling is that we will have a break until June 10, but then more energetic deportations of our youth will take place.

June 5 Last night an alarm sounded. A fire raged at the Alwa manufacturing plant. I went to see. A boiler room was on fire. An investigation proved that the cause was a hand grenade.

Today the police killed a known bandit during a wild fight in Brody forest. He fought and threw hand grenades but was finally shot.

June 7 Yesterday two companies of German infantry left Szczebrzeszyn. Now we have only a few German soldiers, but a new quartermaster has arrived.

New arrests in Zamosc County: in Czerniecin, Stanislaw Huskowski and noted writer Pawel Krzowski; in Zamosc, Mrs. Sliwowska, president of the local Red Cross chapter; Nowacki, vice-mayor; and a few others.

June 9   This morning we were shocked at the news of Mayor Jan Franczak's arrest and also the high school principal, Wiktor Jozwiakowski. Both were transported to the prison in Zamosc. These arrests are puzzling. The mayor was very loyal to the German authorities and always tried to cooperate. Principal Jozwiakowski dedicated himself to family life ever since the Germans entered the city. Police are looking for teacher Piotr Bohun, but he has disappeared. We are waiting for more arrests.

I received confidential information that I am on the list of people to be arrested.

June 10   Since early morning the gestapo has been in town, but so far no arrests. I have made several preparations in case I am arrested. Detailed instructions were given to the hospital staff, my financial situation settled with my wife, and finally a small suitcase was made ready.

New curfew was posted: Christians can walk until 10 P.M., but Jews, only until 7 P.M.

June 11   I reported for the first time to a new city commandant. He seems very disagreeable.

A group of Germans came form Zamosc and began a roundup of Jewish men on the streets. They chased after the Jews throughout the city. Later they transported them to Zamosc for work detail and returned them to Szczebrzeszyn late in the evening.

We received the bad news that Italy has joined Germany in the war against France and England. Now the people are really apprehensive.

June 13   I went to Zwierzyniec, where I was informed about a strike in the lumber mill owned by the Zamoyski estate. The Germans who worked there notified the gestapo. After a short investigation and the beating of several strike organizers, the workers returned to the job. The next day several came asking for medical excuses.

June 14   This afternoon more bad news. Paris has fallen into German hands. Everywhere the Germans are flying swastika flags. The city is even more depressed.

June 16   The news from France is terrible. People are emotionally broken. Some have lost all hope. What will happen now? What will happen to Poland?

June 21   I barely survived the last few days. I am putting on paper everything that happened to me and everything my eyes witnessed. I am writing this quickly, still under the sensation of the last few days' events.

As I mentioned earlier, after the arrest of the mayor and high school principal we expected more arrests, but after a few days of waiting we became so used to it that we began thinking that this was merely a nerve-wracking situation and we started breathing normally. But on the afternoon of Tuesday, June 18, I received confidential information from a very reliable source that the next morning at 5 A.M. I could expect the gestapo at the hospital and that a few people in town would be arrested. Even though I was completely prepared for the eventuality of arrest, I carefully went through all the instructions to the hospital staff and my wife and then went to bed to await the arrival of the undesired guests.

On Wednesday, June 19, I awoke at 5 A.M. I went to the hospital garden where I could observe the street from the old brick walls. From there no one could notice my movements. Around 7 A.M. I returned to my quarters and after breakfast began reading a book, hoping that the information about the arrests was wrong. But around 8 A.M. I received a call from the hospital lobby that the Germans were there. As soon as I came through the door, at the threshold, I was surrounded by four German gendarmes. A Polish policeman stood in the corridor. One of the gendarmes, a sergeant, held a pack of individual warrants with the one in my name on top. He asked me if I was Zygmunt Klukowski and then told my wife to prepare supplies for five days because I was under arrest and would leave with them. He ordered me to take him to my private quarters. There I was submitted to a personal search; the Germans looked through my pockets and wallet. At the same time others searched all closets, cabinets, my desk and my wife's, throwing everything on the floor for no reason. They looked through my photo album and took three pictures of young men, two in Polish uniforms, one in civilian clothes. They asked me who they were and answering them was easy because I knew they were outside German borders. In my study only my desk was searched; most of the library shelves were left alone. From my collection of art prints a German gendarme took an album of Kamil Mackiewicy's drawings entitled *German Purgatory—My Experiences in Prison Camp*. This is really a wonderful collection of drawings from World War I. The gendarme was amused and asked me why there are so many soldiers in different uniforms in this book. I was afraid that he would take it, but after looking through it he dropped the album to the floor. The entire search took a maximum of forty minutes. As a result only the three pictures and the military ID of Dr. Borkowski were taken. During this time my wife was preparing a rucksack full of food, which was very heavy.

The Germans gave me very little time to change. I left the hospital with the staff, personnel, and even patients standing around, crying, to see me off. My wife walked me out and a young medic carried my rucksack. I took only a raincoat and light luggage.

First we stopped at the gendarmerie post in city hall. There were three others there, teacher Kiciak, from Zwierzyniec, someone I didn't know, and Franciszek Sierkowski. In a few minutes more people arrived. First was Rev. Josef Cieslicki, dressed in civilian clothes, then old pharmacist Jan Szczyglowski. He was arrested in lieu of his son Czeslaw, who was not home during the search. Later Kafarski, who had a long white beard, teacher Kilarski, Councilman Andrzej Przysada, a well-known farmer and civic leader, and a few more I didn't know were arrested. In total, eleven men.

At 1 P.M. we were taken to a red bus waiting for us outside. Many people stood by to see us leave. Some women were crying. In charge of the escort was a gestapo man with three stars on his collar. Generally he was calm; only a few times did he shout at Borucki and translator Krol. The other gendarmes behaved rather properly. I noticed that all were small men. My wife cried constantly, but one of the soldiers told her to stop because in a few days I would be home. The front part of the bus was taken up by the gestapo and gendarmes. We were seated in the rear. I was between Rev. Cieslicki and Szczyglowski. The bus was long and rather comfortable. Shortly thereafter we left.

We came to Wielacza and stopped at the parish hall. Here we waited for some time. Finally more prisoners were brought to the bus, Rev. Czekanski and teacher Gunia.

Around 2:30 P.M. we came to Zamosc gestapo headquarters at the Czerski apartments (near the cathedral). Here the gendarme who searched me at the hospital returned the three pictures and Dr. Borkowski's ID. We stayed there for quite a while and finally moved off through the city. First Kosciuszko Street, then the bus terminal, Staszyc Street, and the marketplace, all in the direction of the railroad station. I noticed the streets were deserted, no one was walking, a very unusual sight in Zamosc.

So far it was difficult to figure out where we were going. But finally I noticed the bus turning on the street leading to the military warehouse known as the Rotunda. Finally the bus stopped and we were taken through the gate. Above the gate a sign read, "Temporary Internment Camp for Political Prisoners."

Inside the Rotunda we were stood in a row against the wall. We were called for another search and interrogation.

Waiting for my call, I looked around. I saw a large, round, athletic field divided by a barbed-wire fence. On the right was a gate. Behind this gate was an area reserved strictly for prisoners. There was a well-kept lawn with a nine-yard-wide running track around it. From the track eighteen numbered doors led to eighteen cells. On the athletic field the exercise had just started. Among the prisoners I noticed civil engineer Andrzej Bielawski.

I looked around the waiting room to see what was going on. As their names were called the prisoners went to the long table where gestapo officials searched their pockets, registering the amount of money and asking questions. First teacher Gunia was called. After a short time he was escorted to the field and ordered to run three laps. Second was Rev. Cieslicki. The third name called was mine. The first question was about *Geld* (money). I removed the bills from my wallet. The translator, a young man in civilian clothing, told me I had brought too much, but he put 180 zloty after my name. Checking my luggage, they confiscated a pocketknife, fork, and spoon. They were looking for cigarettes and tobacco. I was really sorry to lose my pocketknife, which I had kept for twenty-five years.

I was assigned to cell no. 8. I entered the enclosure. The gestapo were busy registering new arrivals, and because the guards were occupied in exercising prisoners on the track, I moved slowly toward cell no. 8 and reached it without being noticed. In this way I avoided any physical exercise. I looked around. The cell looked like a normal cellar with a high ceiling, brick walls, and no floor. The floor area was compressed dirt. There was one small window, and a door opened out to the exercise track. In the door there was an opening a little above head height. Through the small opening I was able to observe what was going on outside. All cells were alike, connected with a two-yard-wide corridor without any doors. The prisoners were able to move from cell to cell, even though prison regulations forbid such contact. Inside the cell I noticed a lack of furniture. Along the walls some straw was laid down to be used as beds. The first impression was very doleful.

I took for myself a space by the door. Next to me was old Mr. Szczyglowski and after that Rev. Cieslicki, Rev. Czekanski, Kafarski, Kilarski, Kiciak, Przygoda, and two men unknown to me. Altogether there were fifteen people in the cell.

Outside on the field gestapo exercises were taking place. People were standing in two rows. The German guards gave the commands in German—"Attention, left turn, right turn"—and then had the prisoners run three laps around the field. All of this was conducted brutally with the beating of the prisoners.

After a short while our cell's turn came. A young gestapo officer along with a prisoner, Prof. Werner, now the camp commandant, entered the cell. Prof. Werner was able to explain that we had just come in and a few of the older men had heart problems, so the German agreed to take only nine of the younger men for training. The Germans assigned Rev. Cieslicki, who showed a very good physique in civilian clothes, as commandant of our cell.

After all the cells were put through the physical fitness exercises the doors were locked. Whenever German guards came by and looked through the window, those in the cells had to come to attention. Usually Rev. Cieslicki gave the command. After a few hours of staying in our own cell we started visiting others. I went also and met a few friends, such as school superintendent Szczepaniec, notary Rosinski, lawyers Bajkowski, Czernicki, Sikorski, and Legiec, engineers Bielawski and Klimer, county physician Dr. Tyczkowski, presiding judge of the appeals court Cybulski, Judge Laparewicz, Prof. Fenc, school principal Przybolowicz, a few teachers, former students of mine, and many others I knew by sight only.

They all told me of their arrests this morning and being brought to the rotunda prison in small groups. Practically every one of them had to run three laps around the track. Those that moved slowly were beaten with wooden sticks. I was told by witnesses that Count Aleksander Szeptycki from Labun, who was seventy years old, was forced to run; after three laps he was ordered to keep going, and a few yards later he fell dead of a heart attack. Then the gestapo called a horse-drawn wagon and took the old man to the city morgue. It was a terrible sight, but the gestapo acted as if nothing had happened.

I came back to my cell. Standing by the door and looking through the small windows I noticed more buses with prisoners. A large group had arrived from Tomaszow. They were ordered to stand in a row facing the wall, and after registration they had to run three laps carrying all their belongings.

Among the prisoners I noticed Dr. Cybulski, a very heavy man of my age who was running in an overcoat, carrying a large suitcase and blanket. I was sure that he would not make it and would die as Count Szeptycki had.

The people from Tomaszow were put into cell no. 8. It appears their leader is the high-spirited Dr. Cybulski. Cell no. 8 was definitely the most joyful one.

The next group was from Krasnobrod. Here the oldest was Msgr. Wojcikowski, almost eighty years of age, then Sen. Fudakowski, Dr. Lastawiecki, and a few others. Very late came a small group including Zamoyski estate administrator Debczynski and director of estate forestry Kostecki. The Germans were extra brutal in the handling of Mr. Debczynski. I saw a German with a whip hit him twice over the head. Then he was forced to run three laps around the track, which for an overweight man was difficult. After him Kostecki was forced to run six laps.

I watched and watched. A very tall, older priest dressed in a long cassock had a hard time running. A gestapo man ran next to him and hit him so hard with a stick that the priest fell down, losing all of his luggage. One young man who refused to answer questions during the interrogation was forced to run while singing the Polish national anthem. After three laps he was given a block of ice. With ice held against his chest he ran eight times around the training ground. I found out later his name was Sozanski and he

was a member of the Polish Olympic team. Many of the runners were
beaten with wooden sticks.

Just before dark we were called for an evening roll call. We had to stand
at attention in front of our cells. Gestapo men counted us and at the same
time beat us with sticks, whips, or fists. Old pharmacist Szczyglowski was
hit twice.

After roll call the time came for the delivery of parcels received by the
camp. All the parcels were on the grass and had paper notes attached.
When Prof. Werner called a name, the prisoner had to answer loudly,
"Present," and after receiving the order to step forward had to run quickly
to his package, pick it up, then run back. The gestapo stood and watched,
making sure that everything was being done quickly, but only a few times
searched the parcels. After this we were told that all cigarettes, tobacco,
cigars, and matches had to be turned in. In a few minutes a large amount
was confiscated. After being reminded that in the event of an escape we
would all be shot, we returned to our cells.

Now a new game began. At the sound of a whistle we had to run
quickly from our cells and form a double line. If it was not fast enough we
had to repeat it. This was difficult, especially for the older men who never
had any military training. In our group old Mr. Szczyglowski was practically carried out. I held him under one arm and Przygoda held the other
side; only in this way was he able to move fast enough.

It was long after 9 P.M. before we finally were allowed to rest in our cells,
and we each received a cup of ersatz coffee. The coffee was delivered to us
by the Polish Red Cross. We had enough food with us but no one ate much.
We were given nothing to drink for an entire day. The coffee tasted excellent and we blessed the Red Cross for it.

The padlocks on our cells were closed and the Germans finally left us
alone. It was already very dark. We noticed another group of prisoners arrive, but they were taken directly to their cells without any exercise.

We made ready to sleep. No one undressed; some men just took off their
jackets. I took my shoes off, spread my blanket over the straw, and used
my suitcase as a pillow, but I could not sleep. It was necessary to go
through all the events of the day, to go over all the insults and abuses, to
work out a psychological approach to withstand new harassments that we
can count on in the future. Besides this, I thought of my family and my
hospital, my personal future, what the Germans would do to us, and where
we would be deported. Of course, I also thought of our nation. Our political situation, after the defeat of France, is very grave.

This first night in prison was very difficult. Around midnight I fell
asleep for a couple of hours but later tossed and turned from one side to
the other. Though the small opening in the door enough light came in to

outline the silhouettes of the prisoners, who were sitting or lying. This scene reminded me of a drawing by Jacek Malczewski from a Siberian camp in 1870.

By 4 A.M. no one was sleeping. We started walking between the cells, talking about the past and the future. Prof. Werner as camp commandant was everywhere. He showed us how to keep the cell clean, so the straw would be stacked neatly along the wall, and he showed us how to make a broom from the loose straw and sweep the floor with it. He told us that if the gestapo guards would find some floors dirty, the beatings would start with the so-called cell commandant. So we began cleaning very early. In these conditions we attained maximum efficiency.

But the worst thing was a lack of buckets. We were taken to the restrooms late in the evening. When we asked the guards to let us go later the answer was, "Hold it until 6:30."

Exactly at 6:30 A.M. the Germans opened the first three cells and let us go in pairs to the toilets, outside the Rotunda. The toilet, or so-called latrine, was a pit with a narrow board supported by two vertical boards. The board was the seat. I must confess that even though the general atmosphere was not too pleasant, the view of the seat occupied by older and overweight gentleman made me laugh.

After all the prisoners had used the latrine, we began cleaning the training ground.

Lack of water to wash with or even drink was difficult to withstand. There was a water cistern and guards allowed prisoners to go to it with bottles, but it was almost dry. Only once I filled half a cup. I took a few sips and cleaned my eyes with a wet handkerchief. I was lucky.

The guards were not paying much attention to what we were doing, so we walked on the field and talked with prisoners from other cells. Early in the morning a new prisoner arrived, Mr. Ossowiecki, from Zamosc. Prof. Werner was expecting the arrival of the gestapo around 8 A.M. After talking with the guards they agreed to give us a warning. At the sound of whistle we were to reenter our cells.

A few familiar gestapo agents arrived on the field and the normal prison routine began again. We were ordered to stand at attention while Prof. Werner gave the report. Then a roll call was taken. After we were locked in our cells again, the Polish Red Cross began distributing black coffee. During this time new prisoners arrived. We looked on and noticed that some gestapo were in uniform and some were in civilian clothes.

A little later a gestapo man called for Sen. Fudakowski. After a brief conversation the senator went to his cell and in a few minutes was outside again, but this time with his overcoat and luggage. He was taken to the gate and given a pack of cigarettes; he was free. We envied him.

Later a fat German in a civilian Tyrol outfit came by. He was the German administrator of the Zamoyski estate. He came to talk with Mr. Debczynski. He was allowed to talk to him only through a barbed-wire fence. The small package he carried was searched very carefully by the gestapo.

Around 11 A.M. we were assembled on the field. We were marched in military formation. The gestapo gave marching commands to Rev. Zawisza. He marched along giving instructions such as, "Left, right, left." The Germans were very brutal, beating those who could not keep up. This took about an hour. For some of the older men it is very difficult. A few men who were unable to walk fast enough were forced to run three laps.

We then stood at attention and Prof. Werner called out those men's names who were to receive parcels. Gestapo agents checked to see if we were standing correctly. One prisoner smiled. He was ordered to run three times around the field. Without expecting it I heard my name. I ran quickly to the center of the lawn where Prof. Werner handed me a small parcel. I was completely surprised. I took the parcel, but the gestapo cut it open with a knife. Several bread rolls with butter fell out. As fast as I could I picked them up and ran back.

Around 12:30 P.M. we were finally allowed to go to our cells. We were tired so we sat on the straw. I opened my parcel of bread rolls and butter. The short note with my name on it that was attached to the parcel bore the characteristic writing of Mrs. Bogucka.

While sitting and eating rolls and drinking black coffee from a beer bottle I heard someone call Rev. Cieslicki and my name too. We both stood up quickly to see a tall German in civilian clothing holding a piece of paper in his hand. He asked if we were from Szczebrzeszyn and told us to gather our belongings and follow him. As fast as I could I packed my suitcase and left my food for the others. I was not sure what this meant, to be called along with a priest. It could mean transportation to a concentration camp or to another prison. We stood for a while by the cell door. Finally the same German ordered us to follow him to a registration table. A gestapo agent in uniform, who spoke very good Polish, came over to us.

I noticed several people from Szczebrzeszyn standing, facing the wall. I recognized young Czeslaw Szczyglowski and Rev. Wladyslaw Klos. The man at the table began questioning me: was I a physician at the Szczebrzeszyn hospital, and how many other doctors did I have to help me? He also asked if we had any cases of typhoid fever. Hearing this type of questioning I was hopeful that I would be released. In my head I was saying "Glory to the louse." I answered all the questions to the satisfaction of the gestapo official. Finally he asked me the name of the German division physician. This I was not able to answer. He went wild, pounding the table with his fist, and finally yelled, "Out." So I asked him, "Where? Maybe home?" He shouted again, "Out, out, out." A guard escorted me from the room and out through the gate to freedom. I didn't even have time to say good-bye to my companions. I know for sure that some of them saw me go to the gate.

Finally I stood outside the Rotunda walls. I could not believe that I was free. Slowly I began walking toward the city. The day was very hot. I was dressed warmly so I had to stop every so often to rest. I met several women who were standing, looking at the Rotunda. Their husbands, sons, or fathers were prisoners. A few of them asked questions that I was not able to answer.

Through almost empty streets I finally reached Bogucki's house. There I really felt free. After a shave and a shower I waited for my wife who was in Zamosc trying to find out about me. When she returned she was very surprised to see me.

I was very tired and terrorized and afraid that maybe I would see the gestapo men from the camp, so I stayed at Bogucki's house. I sent the maid to ask Mrs. Werner to come to see me as I had a message for her from Prof. Werner. After seeing her we went to the railroad station to catch a train to Szczebrzeszyn. We traveled as far as Zawada with former high school principal Adam Szczerbowski, who had just returned from Lwow. He had changed; under Russian occupation he became very pale and appeared malnourished.

As soon as we reached the Szczebrzeszyn station I called the hospital to send a carriage for us. My call was not only received by the hospital but it also spread the news of my release so quickly that at our 6 P.M. arrival in town we were greeted by a large crowd of people, mostly Jews, who had assembled to greet me. The same thing happened at the hospital. Not only the personnel but most of the patients were waiting in the lobby. Even the old town ladies were kissing me with affection. This spontaneous greeting was completely unexpected. For several hours people came to our quarters. Many of them had relatives in the prison and wanted to learn of their future.

After a long bath I finally went to bed. All of the small things that make up a daily routine now gave me complete satisfaction. But I was still very tense, so after a few hours of sleep I awoke and started going through the details of the last few days. I knew that this time I was very lucky: first, I'd spent only one day in prison; second, it so happened that I didn't run around the training field; third, no one beat me. I am not even counting the fact that some of the Germans shouted at me.

Many times I had heard about the beatings during interrogation, but what I had witnessed surpassed all the rumors. I was unable before to comprehend the methodic disregard of personal dignity, how human beings could be treated much worse than any animals, while the physical abuses that were performed with sadistic pleasure clearly showed on the faces of the German gestapo. But I have to stress that the behavior of the prisoners was magnificent. No one begged for mercy; no one showed even a trace of cowardice. Everything was received with clenched teeth. In times like this people would rather die than endure this kind of treatment, and here everyone realized that any reaction by one would bring terrible consequences, including death, to many. So all the insults, mistreatment, and abuses were received calmly with the knowledge that they bring shame and disgrace to the German people.

During the time I was at the camp I saw around 200 people. Most of the prisoners I knew personally. [Translator's note: A complete list of names is in the Appendix. It is interesting to note that many of the prisoners were highly educated: Catholic priests, 18; lawyers and judges, 13; teachers, 19; physicians, 6; engineers, 7.]

June 23   I am still not back to normal. Now I can feel how much the events of the last few days have exhausted my nervous system. I found out that my quick release from prison was due to the request of the local *Ortskommandant*. He is afraid of a typhoid fever epidemic, and after personally checking the contagious ward he began calling the county officials in Zamosc and later the German governor in Lublin requesting my immediate release.

June 26   I went back to Zamosc, past the Rotunda. I felt very nervous. I noticed guards at the gate and also some cars. I felt shivers as I started to think about last Wednesday.

Yesterday most of the prisoners were moved to Lublin. Only a few were released: Dr. Tyczkowski, Prof. Werner, old Szczyglowski, Rev. Wojcikowski, Rev. Koziolkiewicz, and a few others. Just after my release some new prisoners were moved into the Rotunda: Mayor Franczak, high school principal Jozwiakowski, and teacher Wysocki.

In Zamosc people live in constant fear. They talk in low voices, moving quickly without looking around. It is feared that more arrests will follow. I spoke with some and they asked how it was in the Rotunda. Naturally I was unable to tell the truth to the wives and daughters of the prisoners. You have to be very careful when you talk. Before release every prisoner must sign an affidavit that he will not reveal the details of prison life. Only Rev. Cieslicki and I were released before the gestapo started the new rules.

I stopped by to see the Sochanskis. Mr. Sochanski had just come back from the prison in Lublin. The few months of imprisonment were evident on his face. After speaking with him I found out that life in Lublin prison is much worse than in the Rotunda in Zamosc. We talked about the latest happenings. I was really shocked about the news of the famous wall-size painting by Jan Matejko, *Prussian Tribute* (the ceremony of the Grand Master of the Teutonic Order swearing allegiance to King Sigismund of Poland), which was removed from the Cracow Museum in 1939 and stored in Zamosc. Now it is back some place around Cracow. The move was made by an underground organization.

June 30   Today I spoke with administrator Debczynski in Zwierzyniec. He had been moved from Zamosc to Lublin prison and was finally released yesterday. The employees of Zamoyski estate are awaiting new arrests.

July

July 1   Today the Germans ordered that all horses be assembled at the marketplace to have their tails and manes cut. The Germans are trying to steal everything.

July 3   Today is the first day of registration for the new school year. The new classes are supposed to begin on September 2. All teachers received notices that they must stay home during summer vacation, without any exceptions.

July 5   Since early morning the gestapo have been patrolling the streets. They ordered from city hall two large, well-furnished rooms. People are again nervous. Some are even leaving home. People are again talking about new arrests.

July 10   The gestapo are in Szczebrzeszyn every day. We do not know what they are doing. People seem used to their presence and, for the moment, life is normal.

July 12   Tension is growing again. People fear that we are facing new restrictions and mass arrests.

From Zamosc I received terrible news about the executions in Lublin of more than forty people. All of them were from Zamosc. The list of people included: member of the Polish *Sejm* Boleslaw Wnuk, Vice Mayor Nowacki, Maj. Mucha, Capt. Sliwinski, and journalist Klaudel. I have a difficult time believing this is true.

In all the city and county offices there is complete disorganization. Many high-ranking officials have been arrested; some took leaves of absence. The clerks that have stayed on the job are so nervous that it is impossible for them to do their normal work. All offices are open but not functioning.

Again we hear more and more news about the possibility of military action between Germany and the Soviets. It seems likely because the number of German troops assembled along the Bug River is growing constantly. Around Szczebrzeszyn we have three divisions. In town only the officers have quarters. I met Dr. Leszczynski from Lubaczow. He recently fled illegally with his family from Russian occupation.

Yesterday, in the event of another arrest, I had my small suitcase ready. This time as before I instructed my hospital as to procedures in case I was forced to move out.

It is so difficult to live in this kind of situation, when at any moment you can be arrested, taken from your family, taken from your line of work, beaten and ill treated by the German gestapo.

July 16   I went again to visit Zwierzyniec. Everyone is very excited about the movement of German troops. People now strongly believe in a military conflict between Germany and Russia, maybe not tomorrow but in the near future.

All of Zwierzyniec was shocked by the inhuman behavior of German forest inspector Klitzing. Before the war he was a forest ranger at the Zamoyski estate. He knew everything that went on in the estate forests, and he even took part in civic activities. But now he is more German than the highest gestapo official. A few days ago, while on patrol, he noticed two young boys grazing a few cows in one of the estate forests. He was very much upset by this and without any explanation shot one boy. The fourteen-year-old boy, son of a shoemaker from Obrocza, was there legally working as a herdsman with the forest ranger. After being brought to the hospital the teenager died. His remains are already five days in the mortuary pending investigation, but the German was set free. It is legal for Germans to shoot Poles and Jews.

July 17   This day was very hard for the Jews. For the last few months they had relative peace. The exception: every day forty people would be taken for work to Zamosc, Bodaczow, or the local barracks. Otherwise everything was quiet. I am not counting sporadic beatings or shooting by the Germans or the police. But last night we received a notice that Jews from Szczebrzeszyn must provide five hundred men for labor camps in Germany. This notice almost started a riot. My hospital was stampeded by people requesting medical excuses from labor. Later the Jews appealed to both Zamosc and Bilgoraj counties and to the labor bureau. Lublin eventually reduced the number of "requests" from 500 to 130. Just this morning the recruitment of Jews began. The so-called *Judenrat* assigned 130 young men to be recruited but only 98 showed up. The rest went into hiding. The gestapo came from Zamosc and started a search. Horse-mounted gendarmes went everywhere. Young Jews just standing in the marketplace were separated from their mothers, fathers, and other relatives. Some were beaten. Even members of the *Judenrat* were whipped. German soldiers using beautiful Polish horses taken from our own cavalry searched the nearby villages and trapped a few young Jews. For others they took fathers as hostages. The *Judenrat* president was severely beaten and later was ordered to lie for one hour on his stomach in the center of the marketplace.

After a few hours the Germans marched the Jewish column to the railroad station to be loaded onto a freight train bound for Germany. The column was guarded by Germans on horses. Lamenting and weeping Jewish women followed behind the marching Jews. Many Poles stood by and watched. Some of their faces showed no sympathy at all; some of the people even laughed and joked. After the first group left the Germans notified us that other groups will follow. During this time all Jewish businesses were closed and street traffic was minimal.

During the afternoon new regulations were posted. The mayor, Borucki, is asking people to obey the new police hours. In the event of Polish people still walking after 10 P.M., the curfew would be shortened to 8 P.M.

July 18   All the Jews are nervous now. They expect more recruitment for the labor camps. By a new order of the mayor all Jews between the ages of sixteen and fifty must report every morning at the *Judenrat*. No Jews can leave the city without a special permit. Anyone outside the city without a permit will be subject to severe punishment and deportation.

July 23   During the last few days a large number of troops have passed through Szczebrzeszyn, and, what is even more interesting, they seemed to be moving in all directions. Now even French cars can be seen. More and more officers and soldiers are seen wearing similar red ribbons with white and black stripes. This must be a new military decoration.

Everywhere you can see many troops. Zamosc and Zwierzyniec and even the small villages are full. It's difficult to comprehend what this means. Maybe it is true that war against the Soviets will start soon. Who knows?

The general mood of the thinking population is sadness. On one side we see the victorious German army, victorious so far on all fronts. On the other side, after the defeat of France, there is only England, who must withstand all the pressures of German might. What will happen if England gives up fighting on behalf of others? What will happen to us? I still believe that things will change and that finally we will be victorious.

Yesterday I received a short letter from a girl in Kassel, Germany. She was an orderly who volunteered for work in Germany and now is begging me to do anything to bring her back. She cries that the Germans are treating the laborers as slaves and their treatment of Poles is worse.

Today our hospital was officially transferred from the Zamosc County Health Department to the Bilgoraj County Health Department. For two hours we held a reorganization meeting. Today the military command in town changed again and we began reporting to a new *Ortskommandant.*

The county surgeon from Bilgoraj, Dr. Snacki, visiting Szczebrzeszyn, called all the physicians together and gave us the new German regulations concerning the treatment of Jews. We are not allowed to sign any notes, such as labor releases, for the Jews. We are not allowed to attend to any Jews. After I questioned this by saying that in Szczebrzeszyn there is not even one Jewish doctor, the Germans agreed that the hospital can give medical attention to Jews only one hour a day and only when no other patients were present. But we still have no right to admit Jews into the hospital except in case of infectious diseases such as typhoid fever. So I was forced to release from the hospital a few Jews I was treating for other reasons. Many of them I kept in the hospital to protect them from being deported to labor camps and not because of any illness.

The conditions at the labor camps are terrifying. There are two camps around Zamosc, one in Bortatycze and another in Bialobrzeg. The work there is digging deep trenches. The trenches are part of a system to dry out existing swamps and prepare the land for future cultivation. The workers are standing in water the whole day. They are very poorly fed and live in filthy barracks. The barracks are located several kilometers from the job sites, so besides the long hours of work the camp inmates must walk another two hours a day to and from the camp. During the walk the Germans beat the prisoners with their fists and with sticks.

Typhoid fever is spreading, particularly in Bialobrzeg, and all cases are sent to me because the Zamosc hospital is not yet ready for this type of problem. Sanitary conditions in the camps are terrible. Never in my life have I seen so many lice, even in the Russian revolutionary camps during World War I. All inmates are young men ages seventeen to twenty.

July 26 Late last evening the mayor was notified that a new transport of 1,000 evacuees is coming to Szczebrzeszyn. At 6 A.M. I left my hospital to find out more details. It was true; a transport arrived around midnight. Some of the evacuees stayed at the village of Brody, but more were brought to Szczebrzeszyn. They have been temporarily settled in the market hall and in the unfinished apartments of Antoni Jozwiakowski, on Zamojska Street. The mayor was able to obtain some straw to be laid out on the floor as bedding. No other buildings were ready since all schools and the movie theater had been taken by the German army. I went through both accommodations; they were horrible. Completely exhausted people were lying on the straw. Women, older men, and children, mostly small children, were all sleeping completely clothed even with their shoes on. I noticed that no young people were present. I found out that all teenagers had been transported to labor camps in Germany.

I spoke with some of the people who were already awake. A week ago, in all the villages around Gostyn, the German police showed up at night. People were given less than an hour to pack and be ready for deportation. These people are all small farmers having ten to fifty acres of very fertile soil apiece, the best in all of Europe. Some others are from Wielun and Kutno counties. The only exception is the family of the principal of the teacher's seminary in Gostyn. The Germans allowed the deportees to bring along only a few personal items. The deportees were assembled at the old factory in Lodz. They stayed there several days and were subjected to personal searches during which all their money was confiscated. All the teenagers were deported to Germany. During this time the Germans beat the prisoners with sticks.

It was necessary to organize a supply of food for the evacuees. First we organized the delivery of milk for the small children and coffee for the adults, then we prepared for lunch and dinner. I visited the evacuees several times. They were very pale, tired, and dirty, and yet they talked in detail about their ordeal. It seemed that particularly the women were full of hatred toward Germany and Germans. Some people cannot hide their urge for revenge.

They had been forced to leave their homes where their families had lived for hundreds of years. They were herded like cattle, pushed and beaten on the road from their villages to the railroad station. People who were too slow were shot. They were kept for one week in Lodz at a factory and then later on a train. Almost all the small children are ill with diarrhea. We treated over one hundred cases. I admitted several people to the hospital, including an eighty-year-old women. Some are so exhausted that others have to feed them while they lie down.

These people are all to be relocated in different villages in the Zamosc region. What will they do, how will they live? Hundreds of them who were farmers became beggars in one hour. They were thrown off their own property and sent away homeless on a long trip. The worst of it is that our own farmers do not have enough even to feed themselves and many times have refused to help.

July 28   For the first time I met a good German. A few days ago a German car hit a ten-year-old boy from Brody. The German officer riding in the car ordered the driver to take the injured boy to the hospital. He later came by himself to ask about the boy. I was surprised to see how worried this officer was about the child. He asked if he would recover, if there were any broken bones or internal injuries. He mentioned that he had children of his own. He comes to the hospital every day with toys and candies. He even went to see the child's parents a few times.

Today he and I had a long conversation. He is a reserve officer. He fought in France and has been decorated twice. He has a doctorate in philosophy, was an assistant professor at a university, and recently held a high position in a bank. He is sure the war will end soon, in any case before winter.

Yesterday afternoon a new announcement: Jews are prohibited from walking on the city streets after 7 A.M., and Christians after 8 A.M., until further notice. This was because the German governor general Frank was passing through the town. All the streets were swept and even the street gutters received a new coat of white lime.

At 7 A.M. the Jews were hiding. Christians were trying not to be seen either. Around 8 A.M., from Zamosc, instructions came that changed the original order. Christians can walk on the city streets anytime. Police patrols can be seen everywhere. It is official: Gov. Frank will be coming.

Around 11 A.M. a group of cars passed through the city escorted by scout cars armed with machine guns. On his way Gov. Frank visited the Alwa manufacturing plant. Chief engineer Waligora was forced to stand by the gate and greet Frank. When his car came to a stop the German guards quickly took up position around the factory. Mr. Waligora says that they executed the deployment perfectly.

At the entrance to Zwierzyniec a special gate was erected. The road from the gate to the estate offices was decorated with flags. In Bilgoraj, Frank was greeted by enthusiastic Ukrainians. This afternoon he returned to Zamosc.

August

August 1   Yesterday I visited the Red Cross in Lublin. I have not ridden the train for quite a while. Looking at the passengers I saw a new type of traveler, one you would not see before the war. Dealers of small goods, so called sack merchants—or *Temporis Belli*, as the Russians called them during World War I—carried sacks. In my car there was no luggage, only sacks, large and small. In Rejowiec during a change of trains I noticed people fighting for better seats. Women were the most expert in fist fighting and cursing. When it came to cursing they used Polish, Russian, even German words. I had a great time listening to the best repertoire of cursing I had ever heard in my entire life. Coming back at night without any lights was not very pleasant.

Lublin is very different. The streets are crowded with Germans, particularly gestapo and SS. There are many German stores with German signs. The Rutkowski coffee shop and the Radzyminski restaurant, the two best establishments in Lublin, have been taken over by the Germans, with signs now reading, "No Polish allowed." On the street corner of Krakowskie Przedmiescie a new German street sign reads, in Gothic, "Krakauer Strasse." On one side of the street all the houses are destroyed. I looked at the cathedral in the old marketplace. The entire front was in ruins, only two columns were left, but the interior was mostly intact.

The Polish Red Cross headquarters has a lot of work. I met with the president of the chapter, Dr. Czerwinski, and his deputy, Dr. Danielski. Both men had been released from prison just a few days ago. From them I learned about the arrest of several physicians: Voit, Kossowski, Lerkam, Freitag, Fijalkowski, Dziemski, and others. Drozdz and Dobrzynski were sent to the Oranienburg concentration camp. Young Dr. Waclaw Niechaj was executed. He was born in Szczebrzeszyn and graduated from high school in Zamosc. During summer breaks in his medical studies at the University of Wilno he worked at my hospital. So I knew him well. He left a wife and small child.

Germans and Ukrainians are taking over all administration. At the Sisters of Charity Hospital the superintendent, Dr. Modzelewski, was removed and a German appointed. Naturally he began his duties with a complete reorganization. In these conditions the Polish doctors find it much more difficult to work.

Yesterday young Czeslaw Szczyglowski was released from the concentration camp at Oranienburg, along with Szczepaniec and a few others, but notary Rosinski is still there.

Late in the evening German police searched the hospital grounds looking for copper and iron.

August 2   A friend of mine, Dr. Edward Stocki, from Cracow, stopped by to visit. From him I learned about the shipments of extremely valuable books from the university library and collections from the national museum to Germany. Many monuments were destroyed. Most of the university professors have been deported to Oranienburg concentration camp where seventy-seven-year-old Prof. Kostanecki died of blood poisoning.

August 5   Mayor Borucki decided to convert the partially destroyed synagogue into a city movie theater. He commissioned an architect, Klimek, from Zamosc, to begin design work. As soon as the Jewish community found out about this they sent a delegation to me asking for advice and wanting to know what I could do to stop the project. But what can I do? I advised them to appeal directly to the mayor.

Since early morning gendarmes have been arriving and with the help of German police began removing merchandise from Jewish stores, to be given to a Christian cooperative.

August 8   Today around noon the gestapo conducted a search of the home of our close neighbor Michal Brylowski. Brylowski, a sergeant in the Polish army, lived there with his wife, father, and son. The gestapo did not find Brylowski so they arrested his wife and younger brother Zygmunt, a teenager in high school, and sent them to prison in Zamosc.

The Jews are lamenting and crying. Three hundred men must go to the labor camps. They received personal summonses. They must be ready to report on Monday, August 12.

The other cause of anxiety is the news that the German authorities have decided to relocate the Jews from Zamojska Street and also the market-place. Where they are supposed to go, and if they will find a place to live, nobody cares.

August 11   The Jews are very nervous about the deportations to the labor camp. I was told that many people who received personal "invitations" had left town. So the remaining Jews were fearful that the Germans would arrest any available person just to fill the quota. They are expecting some action by the Germans soon.

Yesterday an eleven-year-old Jewish boy, Israel Grojser, was killed by a stone thrown at him. Today I treated a young Jewish woman with a head wound. Many Jews are coming to the hospital and asking for admission, but under direct orders from the Germans I was unable to admit them without a permit from the *Ortskommandant*. So far I have received only one such permit.

Today my wife and I went to Zwierzyniec. On the road I saw many Jewish males fleeing the town. I have never seen the Jews so nervous.

August 12   The whole night Jews were leaving the city. Standing at my window and looking through binoculars I observed the street. Fleeing and hiding were not only Jews who had received their notices but many others also. Out of 300 men called for deportation, only 50 showed up, so the Germans began a general search. Besides the gestapo, the German and Polish police, a few city clerks, and Mayor Borucki took part but without any real success. A few Jewish men were arrested, but all the old ones were released. So only a handful of deportees were moved to the railroad station, and only women and young children waved farewell to them.

Around noon the German police announced through loudspeakers that all Jews who refused to be deported would be shot, without any hearing or trial. I do not know what the end result will be. I know only that the Germans are not ready to give up on this issue.

Around noon I had a surprise visit from Rev. Cieslicki. I was positive that something important had occurred if the priest came to me like this; it's never happened before. He came to me to discuss the case of the former Orthodox church in Szczebrzeszyn. It is an interesting story, but to understand it we must back up in history.

There stands in Szczebrzeszyn a former Greco-Catholic church built in the sixteenth century. After the abolition of the so-called union by Russia in the late 1860s, the church was reopened as Orthodox. But just after World War I it was closed due to a lack of parishioners. The unoccupied building was falling apart. In 1938, when the conversion of the Orthodox to Catholicism began, (in the Zamosc region this was promoted by Gen. Olbrycht) a group of people led by Rev. Cieslicki and engineer Waligora decided to remove the old metal roofing material.

When I found out about this destruction of a historical building I requested the intervention of the county administration in Zamosc, without any result. Finally, with the help of notary Rosinski, I received an order from the historical society in Warsaw halting the removal of the roofing and ordering the restoration of the church. The outbreak of the war stopped the work.

Rev. Cieslicki informed me of a visit from a man who was supposedly a representative of an Orthodox group demanding the removal of metal roofing from the parish hall and the small church in Tworyczow, to restore the abandoned church. Now Rev. Cieslicki wanted to know all the historical details about it.

August 13   Today was another free market day; many people but no Jews. The villagers refused to sell anything to the few Jewish women who were there. Because of this, prices fell on all products. For butter one must pay between 8 and 9 zloty, instead of the previous 12–14 zloty. Germans paid even less. People are willing to sell with little profit instead of giving items to the Germans for next to nothing.

Last night the military police searched for Jews but without any result.

August 14   At midnight another search for Jews began. At first a few city clerks went around. The mayor established a bounty of 5 zloty payable

by the Jews to their captors. I observed the search from my window.
Around 5 A.M. a new group of gendarmes arrived from Zamosc and a new
search began.

As I mentioned before, I used binoculars for observation, and this time
it was a mistake. In the morning a group of soldiers was searching a house
across from my observation point. I was so involved in watching the behavior of the soldiers that I did not see a German officer walking on the
streets. But when he started shouting I realized that I was in real trouble.
Within a few minutes this officer and a few soldiers were inside the hospital. My wife had enough time to throw the binoculars through the window, into the garden. The German officer began the investigation by
saying that the possession of binoculars by a Pole is illegal. I explained to
him that I had no binoculars and that I was only covering my glasses with
my hands because of the rising sun. He asked more questions but left after
a few minutes. After he left I understood why my wife had been gesturing
and whispering "pants, pants." I wore a sleeping gown without pants. She
talked about this the whole day.

As a result of the raid, two trucks loaded with Jews went to Zamosc.
The raid had been very brutal. The Jews were beaten and kicked without mercy.

The Jewish people left in town are in a quiet desperation. Most of them
do not have money for food, and because of the restrictions merchants are
refusing to sell to Jews. I have reliable information about this from our hospital butcher, Lejzor Zero. He is hiding out in one of the small villages, but
his wife and four children are still in town. To help them we buy food ourselves and then give it to them.

Around noon I went to Zamosc. I came back terribly depressed. Upon
entering the city I noticed that all the iron fencing around the cathedral and
other buildings had been removed. On the lawn across from the cathedral
stands a statue of Our Lady. The monument lost its head during the bombardments. Church authorities erected a wooden cross in front of the
statue. The news that I had received a few days earlier about the execution
of forty-three prisoners was verified. City hall had received formal verification along with a complete list of the executed.

Mr. Szczepaniec told me about conditions in the Oranienburg concentration camp and about notary Rosinsk. It sounds terrifying.

I said good-bye to the Sochanskis. They are moving from Zamosc to
Cracow. We talked about starting up the publication *Teka Zamojska* again, as
soon as the war is finished. I am sure that we will be working together
again in the near future. It is difficult to get used to the food card system.
Because the stores in Zamosc are better supplied than those in Szczebrzeszyn, my wife wanted to buy a few household items. For everything you

need cards. Through a connection my wife was able to buy a few small items. She hid them in her handbag because the Germans search all packages taken from the stores. I am noting this to show our living conditions.

August 16   Germans are taking more and more Jews from the surrounding villages. This is taking place in all the villages, not only those in our county, but in other counties also. Trains filled with Jews are moving them to Belzec.

We just received new information about mass arrests in Warsaw. New announcements were posted about the registration of all officers—active duty, reserve, or retired. For not registering the penalty is death. Another registration will begin soon which will include all men between the age of sixteen and twenty-five.

There is more talk about the possibility of a German-Russian war. For some time now no one discussed it, but the increase in military transports had changed all this. Large transport trains are moving in the direction of Hrubieszow and Belzec. On the highways there are many military convoys, including a large number of ambulances marked with red crosses.

Everyone lives in a very tense atmosphere, waiting for something to happen. It is a very tiring situation, nerve shattering to the point that one does not want to live any longer. But it is necessary to show a good face and hold on.

August 18   Yesterday the gestapo searched the village of Radecznica and several people were arrested in the monastery. At this time I have no details.

A very unpleasant event occurred in Twaryczow. A farmer, Jan Wasilik, reported to the gestapo that his brother, an army sergeant, had arrived from Warsaw with a gun and some illegal pamphlets and began to distribute them to the people. He turned his brother in after a quarrel. The gestapo began reprisals. His brother disappeared, but his father and two other farmers were arrested. I learned this from Wasilik himself, and he even said that his actions had been correct. He told me this while picking up his wife from the hospital. In Sulowiec, mechanic Wladyslaw Papuga was arrested. He has been charged with belonging to an underground organization.

August 20   Today I visited Bilgoraj. All physicians from Szczebrzeszyn and Zwierzyniec were notified by chief county physician Dr. Snacki to report at 9 A.M. for a meeting with the new *Landrat*. The physicians from Szczebrzeszyn went on an old truck. We drove rather fast. I hadn't been on this road since the start of the war. I looked around and saw many abandoned and destroyed cars and trucks alongside the highway. Otherwise, everything looked normal until we arrived in Bilgoraj.

As soon as we entered the city I realized the magnitude of its destruction. The city practically is nonexistent. Buildings are destroyed and burned. Nothing has been rebuilt, so you go through dead streets to the main marketplace where only one building stands. Today the city begins on the street leading in the direction of Tarnogrod and Solski forest. The county administration offices, police, courts, and other offices are located there. Only a few other streets are still intact. Never before have I seen destruction like this.

On the main street one can see signs in German, the same at the county offices. We reported ourselves as Polish reserve officers to a German civil clerk named Predolak, who speaks Polish very well. Because of our appointment with the *Landrat* we were processed very quickly, ahead of a long line of other people. Many are here only because the penalty for not registering is death, and this is the last day of registration. Many people are afraid that this registration will cause us trouble.

After 9 A.M. we physicians were presented to the new *Landrat* who had the rank of *Kreishauptmann*, a man thirty years of age. As other Germans had informed us, he was a big shot, married to the sister of Rudolph Hess, deputy to Hitler. He sat in a big chair behind a large desk. On the wall behind him there hung three big portraits, one each of Hitler, Goering, and Hess. Dr. Snacki made the introductions. He started with me as superintendent of the hospital. The conversation was limited to only answering questions asked by the *Kreishauptmann*. Dr. Likowski was the translator. I did somehow manage to ask him to intervene with the county supply department about the assignment of coal for the hospital. Without asking any more questions he made a short phone call and then told me that the first coal truck was on the way. He pointed out that the heating problem next winter looked very bad but he would try to supply the hospital. He asked me about the number of patients we have in the hospital and stated that he will visit my hospital in Szczebrzeszyn very soon. Then he talked about the hospital in Zwierzyniec. At the end of the meeting he stated that in case we receive special night travel permits we must not use them for private situations.

After the short meeting he dismissed all the physicians but asked Dr. Likowski and me to stay. During a quick conversation he asked how many horses the hospital has and if the superintendent has a personal carriage. I explained that yes, I did have a personal carriage, because my car had been stolen from me. He stated that he would like to have a nice carriage also. So I gave him the name of a manufacturing company in Zamosc, Korba and Kabas, known as builders of the best carriages in the area. He wrote the name in his notebook and asked if the same people built sleighs. I answered yes, the best sleighs.

As I was leaving the county offices I met old Rev. Koziolkiewicz, pastor of Bilgoraj Church. He told me about the destruction of his church and how three days ago the gestapo evicted him from his house, allowing him to take only clothing and books. Now he is staying with a parishioner.

As we left Bilgoraj I noticed a long line of horse-drawn wagons entering the city with a group of around 100 evacuees from the western region of Poland. I was very much depressed about Bilgoraj, one of hundreds of towns destroyed by the war and today ruled by the Germans.

Late in the evening the well-known writer Jerzy Plomienski from Warsaw paid a visit. He now lives in a small village near Hrubieszow and is looking for any type of work.

August 21   During the last few days there has not been any action against the Jews, so they started coming back to town. Now more and more Jews can be seen on the streets. But today again a new detachment of gendarmes came and began searching for Jews. Now it is posted that all Jewish men must report by 3 P.M. tomorrow in Zamosc for final selection to labor camps. So far only the sick and specialists have been excused—specialists such as shoemakers or tailors who cannot be easily replaced by Christians.

August 22   This morning all Jews living on Zamojska Street were evacuated. The only exception is dentist Bronsztein.

August 23   Today a German military physician from Lublin inspected my hospital. The inspection was very detailed. His search was very thorough, and he behaved politely, not like the one I observed in Zamosc.

August 26   New regulations were posted in town. Because of their importance they were announced through the use of posters and loudspeakers. I kept a copy as a document characteristic of the actions of the New Regime:

On August 24, 1940, the city administration is beginning these new regulations regarding the Jewish community.

All Jews are prohibited from walking on Zamojska Street.

All Jews are prohibited from entering city hall.

All affairs of the Jewish community will be handled by the mayor in the quarters of the *Judenrat*.

Anyone not obeying these regulations will be prosecuted.

These regulations are not binding for members of the *Judenrat* or workers in German barracks.

Signed, Borucki, Mayor

August 27 Today I learned more details regarding arrests in Radecznica. The gestapo were there looking for the Benedictine brother Apolinary. He was not home but the Germans took his notes, correspondence, and books and then arrested people close to him. Also Polish sergeant Josef Marek and the family of building contractor Szumanski were arrested. During the search the gestapo discovered an old gun. They arrested fourteen additional people, including Rev. Emil Seroka and the wife of teacher Zdunkiewicz. They were transported to prison in Zamosc.

August 29 All Jewish stores, including coffee shops, beer bars, and even small soda places, were closed and put up for auction. During the auction some local citizens began bidding as partners with the Jews, the original owners.

The order prohibiting Jews from walking on Zamojska Street is not being obeyed. They are there as always.

September

September 1 Today is the first anniversary of the war, so I am going back over the year's events to evaluate the situation. I am reading my diary to see if events have taken on a different meaning or significance. Looking at all the facts I am more and more convinced that short notes written under fresh impressions have more meaning as historical documents than elaborate writing done after a long time has passed. Time will change not only the details of the events but, most important, the feelings of the writer.

In my half century of adult life this year has been the hardest one. So far I am alive and happy that, despite everything, I have survived. I am still in good psychological shape and hopefully my heart will allow me to withstand more blows.

From the intellectual point of view this year has been a complete disaster. I was unable to study, to perform any kind of scientific research about the history of medicine. My collection of books increased by only a few volumes. I was able to collect some documents regarding the German occupation and our fight against it. This is not satisfactory. Besides, I am still living with the fear that my collection can fall into German hands and be destroyed.

As of now we are stifled in our intellectual life. We know nothing about what is happening in the world concerning art, literature, or music. In Poland it looks like we are dead. During the past year not one new book was printed, with the exception of Polish-German dictionaries. No more Polish newspapers, weeklies, or magazines. Newspapers printed by the Germans in Polish in Warsaw, Cracow, or Lublin are even worse than the original German ones. No one buys them. Once in a while we find some illegal underground papers such as *Walka, Pobudka,* or *Szaniec,* printed in a very primitive style, and the news they give is always old and not too reliable.

The same with radio information. People use their imagination. We are not being informed of any events around the world or how the war is progressing. But we are trying to learn anything that will keep our spirits higher and force us to believe in a good future and final victory. People live completely occupied by their own personal problems and the struggle for daily food. Some who are involved in the black market are doing well, but everyone is trying to survive until the end of the war, hoping that we will win. We must protect ourselves against the invasion of influence of not only the Germans but also the Ukrainians. The Ukrainians are beginning to invade our area with the blessing of the German administration. Here in Szczebrzeszyn we now have a Ukrainian judge, Stocki, and two lawyers, Hrecyna and Zaborski. An organization of Ukrainians unknown to us is beginning a campaign against Mayor Borucki.

We are exhausted. Life is nerve shattering. We are living in uncertainty about what will happen to us, not in a month or a week, but in one hour.

We live under the constant threat of search, arrest, beating, evacuation, and death, with the last one maybe not being the worst because of the treatment of prisoners in German prisons and camps. Slowly we become used to it. We are prepared for everything. We know that casualties are common in this type of fight and that we face even more terrible times. But we wait to be witnesses to the war's end and our final victory over this evil enemy.

From all sources of news, many times not reliable, we try to learn the real situation of the fighting nations. We are glad that in view of the fast fall of Holland, Belgium, Norway, and the final capitulation of France, our own fight in September 1939, particularly around Warsaw, showed Poland in a completely different light in the eyes of the world. Our involvement in the fight in Norway and France gives living proof of the worth of Polish soldiers.

Our position against German occupation is firm. The entire population, with minor exceptions, is showing pride in our national heritage. The efforts of the Germans to form a Polish government are completely fruitless.

Last September we suffered a terrible blow, but today it is clear that against German military might this was unavoidable, since we were the first to fight. The Germans have occupied Poland for a year. They have tried to destroy our Polish culture and everything that is Polish. Everywhere the Germans try to enforce the rules of German national-socialistic life, but we treat them as a temporary evil, hoping that soon they will be defeated and our revenge will come. We are glad that this gives us more strength to fight against the German occupation and that, in spite of our defeat, we believe in our final victory and our bright future.

Today, even though it is a sad anniversary, it is a normal day in our fight for survival. On the streets, because of the nice weather, many people are walking.

September 4   The headquarters of a German division arrived in Szczebrze- szyn. On the streets you can see many officers and soldiers. One wagon full of straw for the hospital was confiscated by the Germans. We purchased it with hospital money. Our driver tried to explain this. Intervention by the mayor had no result. He only assured me that he will try to supply the hospital with double the amount of straw.

September 7   A Jewish physician, Dr. Henryk Pomeranz, from Cracow, ar- rived in our city. By order of the German authorities the Cracow medical association gave him only twenty-four hours to close his practice and leave the city where he had practiced for many years as a gynecologist. He vis- ited me today. Of course, he is not pleased with his evacuation to Szcze- brzeszyn and hopes to return to Cracow.

September 9   This afternoon I was standing by the window in my room when I witnessed an ugly event. Across from the hospital are a few burned-out Jewish homes. An old Jew and a few Jewish women were standing next to one when a group of three German soldiers came by. Sud- denly one of the soldiers grabbed the old man and threw him head first into the cellar. The women began lamenting. In a few minutes more Jews ar- rived, but the soldiers calmly walked away. I was puzzled by this incident, but a few minutes later the man was brought to me for treatment. I was told that he forgot to take his hat off when the Germans passed by. German regulations require that Jews must stand at attention and the men have to take their hats off whenever German soldiers pass. The old man, named Bryka, was talking with the women and had overlooked the Germans. As a punishment for this he was thrown head first into a deep cellar. After attending to his head wound I had to send him away. I was not allowed to keep him in the hospital.

During the last few days the Germans have again begun beating Jews on the streets.

September 14   I finished reading a book by Poraj, *Caserns and Nightmares*. This book, published only a few months before the war, deals with life in today's Germany. The book is full of quotations taken from Nazi leaders, including Hitler's *Mein Kampf.* Reading this book I was in shock trying to imagine what would happen if Germany wins the war.

I think that the best way to show the Germans as they really are, their aggression and their threat to the freedom of all nations, would be to translate and print Hitler's *Mein Kampf* and other books such as the Polish *On the Trails of Smetek,* by Wankowicz, and *The Earth Gathers Ashes,* by Kisielewski. This should open people's eyes.

We feel excitement now in connection with the air battles between England and Germany. We are trying to follow news of air attacks on London and Berlin. The information we have is from German newspapers, talking with German soldiers, and from letters from deportees to German labor camps. By observing German behavior we are trying to learn about the morale of the German army.

We have heard lately that suicides have occurred, particularly in German officers' circles. A few cases in Zamosc and Szczebrzeszyn are known to us. Desertion and general insubordination are supposed to be increasing. We do not know how much of it is true.

Our lives are filled with growing suspense as to what the future will bring to us. We await some big events that will decide our fate. Even though some people are afraid of the unknown future, we are confident of the final English victory.

September 16   On Saturday, September 14, the new school year began. Teaching will be very difficult. The school buildings are now German barracks, so the city council assigned as a temporary school an unfinished apartment house belonging to Mr. Antoni Jozwiakowski, on Zamojska Street. The rooms there are so small that the children are crowded like herrings in a barrel. Maybe later one portion of the city hall will be assigned to accommodate the school. We are lacking school books and school supplies. They were stolen by the Germans.

September 17   I am very much disturbed by the news I received today. It is a formal notification of the execution of a few people I know. From the village of Czerniecin, Stanislaw Huskowski and Pawel Krzowski. I knew them both very well. Stanislaw Huskowski was a well-known farmer. After finishing agricultural studies at the University of Cracow, he had a prize-winning farm in Czerniecin. Following his execution the Germans evacuated his wife and two children.

Pawel Krzowski was a very interesting person. He was the son of a small farmer from Czerniecin. After finishing high school he attended Warsaw University and studied Polish literature. He was very much involved in Polish culture and folklore studies and printed several articles about them. He had a few large works ready to be published by the Academy of Science in Cracow. Just before the war, publisher Lucjan Kapicki in Zamosc purchased from him the rights to a book about life in a small village.

He always had new ideas; he read many different books. His scale of interest was very large, but he was completely lost in his own ideas. He tried to keep in close contact with the most noted historians, but due to his way of life he hadn't made many friends. Always dirty, unshaven, and sloppy, he tried to borrow money from everyone. As a rule he never returned books borrowed from the libraries; for example, the university library in Wilno was looking for him, charging him with the theft of several books. Certainly he was a very talented man, but he lacked the basics when it came to relations with others.

September 19 Yesterday I received information about the death of civil engineer Andrzej Bielawski, from Zamosc. He died in the concentration camp at Dachau. He had been arrested on June 19. I had been with him in the Zamosc Rotunda. As a long-time employee of the county of Zamosc, he was a very popular person. A very good musician, he performed at all the charity concerts, playing cello. This sad news caused many people who knew him to cry.

September 20 Yesterday I went to Bilgoraj regarding hospital business. I received only good words but no real help. The most urgent questions about money to run the hospital were not answered. Crucial problems, such as the cost of the maintenance of the hospital buildings and grounds, were left unsolved. So again I realized that I could not count on anyone's help and I would have to fight alone to keep the hospital operating. I would have to find a way to pay for everything, even through black marketeering, which I have been engaged in for a year already.

In Bilgoraj there is more and more Germanization. Everywhere there are new signs in German. Buildings have been taken over for German offices, stores, and clubs. New buildings have been built for German use. The streets are crowded with Germans and you hear only the German language. Their behavior is typically German: they are sure of themselves and are trying to show that they are in power over our land. This was so disgusting that I came home with a severe headache.

During the last few days we have observed some airplanes over Szczebrzeszyn. Today, around 3 P.M., very high in the sky a small white plane circled a few times over the city. The sound of the plane made people very nervous. Is it German or maybe British? Some people swear that the plane dropped leaflets.

September 22   Today a celebration and services were held in the Orthodox church, or rather the walls without a roof. A young Orthodox priest performed the services. Many people came, particularly Catholics who attended the services out of curiosity, to see the service performed in a half-destroyed church in ruins and full of rubbish.

September 25   Yesterday in three villages, Kawenczyn, Kawenczynek, and Topolicza, farmers were arrested for not delivering the assigned grain quota. Michal Brylowski was released from the prison in Lublin. He had been arrested a few weeks ago. Even though he is not talking, we know that during interrogation he was severely beaten. His wife and younger brother are still in prison.

Today a few gestapo officers came from Zamosc and ordered certain Jewish women to be brought to city hall. When the women came, one gestapo officer began reading a list of Jewish names and explained that those men had been shot for illegal black market activities. When the Jewish women began crying the Germans only laughed.

September 27   Throughout the city there are more and more military patrols. At 7 P.M. they watch for any Jews who are still on the streets. Then at 10 P.M. they stop everyone and cite them with a 10-zloty fine. Besides the military patrols, new special patrols are cruising. They are composed of one gendarme, one *Volksdeutsch*, and one Polish policeman, the so-called, blue police. These patrols are supposed to eliminate all black market activities. They stop passersby and search for food and other black market items.

Today around 4:30 A.M. I awoke to the news that a German patrol was entering the hospital. I quickly went to the window and saw three German soldiers. I was sure they were coming to arrest me or hospital administrator Cichonski or medic Cielecki, but after a few minutes of suspense I learned that they were here to take a car from the garage. This small incident is proof of the nervous state in which we live.

September 28   Very early this morning Mayor Borucki came to see me. He told me that late yesterday the United States of America declared war against Germany and Italy. He said that he heard this personally while listening to German radio news in some German officer's quarters. This was blessed news, but during the day no confirmation came of it.

September 29   No news about the United States. I do not know what the mayor had in mind spreading this kind of news and assuring us that it is true.

There are more patrols on the city streets. They are stopping passersby and checking identification papers. Yesterday they stopped and searched German military vehicles looking for some Communist leaflets printed in German.

I am not buying so-called Polish newspapers, but lately I began reading the Russian paper *Novoje Slovo*, published in Berlin. Sure, it is a newspaper fully supporting German policy, but it contains news from Poland never printed in other publications and also news about Russian life.

A few days ago I had a real surprise. Through Ludwik Gocel, a well-known bibliophile from Warsaw, I was able to buy a small book published in Lublin in 1724. This book, by Dr. Jerzy Fonklefen, has a long title, *Treasures about People's Health, including Short Descriptions of Internal and External Sickness of Women and Children and How to Cure Them.* It is interesting that the best-known scholars of the history of medicine, such as Estreicher, Gasiorowski, and Zieleniewski, never mentioned this book.

In general this little book is a popular course in gynecology and obstetrics, with several interesting observations. It shows the high standards of medicine in eighteenth-century Poland. Because this book is unknown to historians of medicine, I already have a plan to write an interesting article about it.

October

October 1 The villagers are very much disturbed that the Germans are taking everything that they raise, so today at the free market there was nothing to buy, no butter, no eggs.

Today was a good day for the Jews because almost all of the men taken a few weeks ago to the Belzec camp were returned. For this the Jewish community paid 20,000 zloty. But around Polish circles tension is mounting again. Someone spread news about new arrests that are to take place in a few days.

This morning several people were arrested. This has to do with not fulfilling the grain quota. So in Deszkowicze teacher Padzinski and in Sasiadka, farmer Gryba were arrested. For the same reason two farmers from Deszkowice, two from Sulow, and one from Zrebiec were evicted. Their farms were given to evacuees from the western regions of Poland.

October 3 All attention is on the grain quotas to be delivered today. Even my hospital must deliver 12 bu. of grain as a first installment. I was threatened with arrest, but after a long conversation I finally received a postponement until November.

For a few weeks we have been hearing about leaflets distributed to German soldiers. These leaflets were the reason for the search of even German military vehicles. Today I received a copy of such a leaflet. It was addressed to the German soldiers, in German, and signed by the Communistic Committee of German Soldiers. With good logic the leaflet shows that Germany has no chance of winning the war and begs the soldiers to request an end to it and save what can be saved. It is written very well and makes a good impression.

October 4   The Germans started to build a new military airport right next to the sugar refinery. All bricklayers, carpenters, and other construction workers from Szczebrzeszyn are being forced to work on this project.

Several people who say that they are well informed are sure that war between Germany and Soviet Russia will start any day. I have been observing some very unusual behavior by the Jews. They are buying guns and ammunition, particularly pistols, and paying very high prices. This gives us much to think about. What will the next day bring to us?

October 7   Around midnight I admitted a young pregnant woman already in labor. A German patrol had stopped her wagon for a search. They looked everywhere, even checking the poor woman's clothing. Lately Germans have been stopping wagons and searching them for hidden goods.

Most of the farmers who had been arrested and evicted for not fulfilling grain quotas were sent to the labor camp in Belzec. Their families were allowed to stay in their villages only if the new farm owners agreed.

October 8   Today during the weekly free market the German air force, using guns and bayonets, arrested all Jewish men and sent them for labor at the new airfield. The *Judenrat* agreed to fulfill a labor quota and also sent workers to the airfield.

Besides the one airfield near the Klemensow sugar refinery, the Germans have begun building a few others. One is near Zamosc and one at Teodorowka, near Bilgoraj, where the agriculture junior college will be rebuilt as a German flight school.

October 10   The work around the airfield is going strong. Motorized construction equipment is running day and night. The new barracks are starting to grow almost like mushrooms. It will be interesting to see why the speed of construction is so important. For sure it is a good reason.

October 14   Tonight a new group of evacuees from Zywiec and Sucha arrived in Szczebrzeszyn. This was a large group of over 1,000 people, mostly the elderly, children, and the sick. Around sixty people requested medical attention. Eight were admitted to the hospital, including two women in labor. The evacuees were temporarily housed in warehouses filled with straw. In the hospital kitchen, from 2 A.M., we prepared food for the evacuees. Around noon the mayor requested the help of all citizens. The city administration was not prepared for an emergency like this and help was not sufficient. Seeing this fills you with the urge for revenge.

October 17   No news, only rumors. We know only what we can read in the German newspapers. By my own observations more and more Germans, in particular officers, are drunk at night.

The German administration "requested" that city hall establish a public house to be used by German soldiers only. Mayor Borucki began organizing the first legal bordello in Szczebrzeszyn. He rented a large house and even engaged a matron to run the operation. The day of the grand opening was set, but then the German commandant gave a twenty-four-hour notice closing the bordello and dismissing all personnel. So this was the end of Szczebrzeszyn's bordello.

Work on the airfield is progressing quickly, but the workers are complaining about their treatment. The Germans are beating the workers for no reason, Poles as well as Jews.

Yesterday the Germans searched the house of meat cutter Ryzner. They discovered a lot of bacon, sausages, and smoked meat. He was beaten very badly. Along with him, another butcher, Wiatrowski, was arrested. Both were sent to prison in Zamosc. All other butchers live in constant fear, so it is impossible to buy any meat.

Today, by order of the German administration, city hall made the following announcement:

> The German administration notified the city council that during the last few days unknown persons destroyed military telephone lines. This is an act of sabotage. Because of this the city council is warning all citizens of the city of Szczebrzeszyn that in the event of another act of sabotage on telephone lines, twenty men will be shot.
>
> *Szczebrzeszyn, October 17, 1940*
> *Signed, Mayor Jan Borucki*

October 19   We now have new police curfew hours. All Aryans are allowed to walk on the city streets until 11 P.M. instead of 10 P.M., but Jews can walk only until 7 P.M.

October 20   At 4:30 P.M. two German officers entered the hospital. Hearing a loud conversation, I went to see what was going on. A young officer stood on the stairway leading to the attic; the other, a captain, held a package. After a brief conversation I learned that both officers came with the order that immediately a large Red Cross flag was to be hung on the roof. They handed me the flag and left. Both officers were completely drunk. Later I was told by our custodian that four other officers with a Red Cross flag were seen on the streets; eventually they moved off in the direction of Blonie.

What does this mean? Why must we fly the Red Cross flag at night? At first we thought that war with Russia had begun and that soon Russian airplanes would be overhead. I noticed very heavy traffic on the highway.

October 24   Constant worry about the future; always waiting for gestapo visits keeps us nervous. We know that every day a few gestapo officers come from Zamosc, always looking for something. On Monday, October 21, they searched two bookstores, one owned by Olczyk, the other by Kimaczynski. They were looking for historical books, maps, portraits, and postcards with historical scenes. They took some and ordered the owners to destroy the rest.

A few people from Szczebrzeszyn were summoned by the gestapo in Bilgoraj. After returning they refused to talk about their interrogation, but the general feeling is that the Germans are beginning an investigation of Mayor Borucki. Many people have signed requests for his removal.

Yesterday I witnessed two German officers arrest the nineteen-year-old son of Dr. Likowski. He was escorted to jail. Later, from Mayor Borucki, I learned that young Likowski and a few more boys were too aggressive toward the Germans. They stared them straight in the eye and never stepped aside to allow them to pass. They were all released but warned that the next offense would be enough to have them deported to a labor camp.

Today two German soldiers came to the hospital and requested the return of the Red Cross flag left here by the drunken German captain.

It is interesting to note that when not on duty the Germans walk the city streets unarmed, no pistols or bayonets.

We have heard that discipline in the German army is very poor. Cases of desertion are increasing and soldiers are complaining about the prolonged war.

October 31   For the last few days I have not written in my diary. Nothing much has happened. But yesterday we learned about the outbreak of war between Italy and Greece. Lack of news is difficult to withstand, but lately any news showing German problems is a blessing. The garrison in Szcze-brzeszyn is beginning to organize for departure.

Because of the upcoming Independence Day holiday on November 11, we are sure that more arrests will take place. Last night the Germans showed up at teacher Lopuszynski's apartment. To avoid arrest he jumped through a window dressed only in his underwear.

Right now I am sitting in my quarters after a day of work. I feel that I am almost free of psychological apathy and am ready to once again begin my historical studies. I am reading the work of Lelewel. I've begun making notes about medicine in old Poland, particularly in and around Lublin and Zamosc.

November

November 4 Members of the German air force began surveying parts of the city. It is hard to figure out for what; maybe for anti-aircraft artillery, or maybe for signal installations, but surely not for pleasure.

A few days ago a new transport of evacuees, about 1,000 people from around Zywiec, arrived in Zwierzyniec. But this time the organization of help was well coordinated. At the head of the welfare committee is Jan Zamoyski and his family, so everyone is trying to help.

Today is the last day for the delivery of the grain quota. Throughout the whole day horse-drawn wagons full of grain have been coming to town. Farmers are fearful of arrest, so they are bringing their quotas on time.

The few farmers that were arrested previously have been released from the camp in Belzec, but their farms are still confiscated.

November 7 A few days ago Jacek Jakimowicz was released from Oranien-burg concentration camp. He looks terrible, pale, undernourished. He looks so bad that he is almost unrecognizable. Along with him Stanko, director of the lumber mill in Krasnobrod, and one teacher from Zamosc were released.

Radio news is not reaching us. From the newspapers we awaited the results of the election for president of the United States on November 5. Everyone is glad that Roosevelt was reelected. We hope that he will bring the United States closer to active action against Germany.

A few days ago I received some unexpected excitement. A farmer from Szperowka who was hiding two large radio receivers, one of mine and the other belonging to the hospital administrator, probably acting under stress and fear that the Germans could discover both, arrived at the hospital by horse-drawn wagon. He overlooked the possibility of a German search; he just arrived around noon and unloaded both receivers by the entrance.

Both receivers were completely useless: one was full of water from being stored in an old cellar; the other one was destroyed also. We had to throw them into the river behind the hospital.

November 9   A midwife from Krasnobrod told me about the celebration of All Saints Day. In their local cemetery approximately 300 soldiers and officers of the 1939 campaign are buried. On their graves 180 wreaths were laid, with uncounted numbers of candles. Two large red and white Polish flags were installed, one with the Polish white eagle. By the large grave of the unknown soldiers, which were covered with battle helmets, one sparkling clean rifle with a belt and cartridge pouch was placed. Many white and red lamps were lit. A second rifle was placed on the grave of Maj. Gluchowski.

The cemetery was crowded. Never before had so many people attended services. Most of the people were assembled around the military graves. All of this was in front of the German terrorists and made a colossal impression. That evening the local priest removed the flags and the Polish police took one of the carbines. The other one is still on the grave of Maj. Gluchowski.

November 11   For the second time we are spending Independence Day in captivity. Last year we had some observances, such as the school children attending church services. This year November 11 was a day like all other days. Even at the churches attendance was no different from any normal day. But in my own mind I still remember the old days of freedom.

I have a few events from the Zamosc region to record. Ten nights ago the gestapo and some German gendarmes searched the home of the German administrator of the Zamoyski estate, *Treuhander* Streich. The search was very thorough, so that even floor planks were removed. As a result, Herr Streich, dressed in a nightgown, was arrested. The gestapo had not even allowed him to dress. His home was sealed and a guard posted. Three days ago the gestapo came again for an even more detailed search. What happened to Streich is anybody's guess. As we found out, he was involved in activities with some Bavarians. This is even more interesting because Streich was a member of the Nazi party and a personal friend of Goering and Gov. Frank.

Engineer Klimek, from Zamosc, stopped by to see me. From him I learned a few details of life there. From Hamburg came bad news. Young city engineer Stanislaw Molicki was killed.

In Zamosc the Germans are everywhere. The city hall is restored and the offices of the German administration are already moved in. Civilian city hall is in the old county building. The beautiful Citizen's Club building is now the German officers' casino; the city movie theater is now a *Soldaten-heim*; the brand-new building on the marketplace is the new *Deutscheshaus*; the big Czerski building next to the cathedral is gestapo headquarters. New buildings are in the planning stages as new streets cut through the city. On both sides of Lwowska Street the Jews are digging trenches and installing air-raid shelters.

The Germans are taking good furniture, carpets, and paintings from private houses, not only Jewish but Polish also.

November 15   In Zwierzyniec there is great excitement. The Germans found out that for some time spare wheels, tires, and other parts from military vehicles were disappearing. One day they arrested a small boy who was caught taking parts from a car. During an investigation and beating he gave out a few names. The Germans first went to see Lalik, son of a poor widow, where they discovered car parts. He was taken to jail. Then a second boy, Burdzynski, son of a midwife, was visited and more items were found. He was arrested also. That was yesterday, but today gendarmes arrived at the house of brewery executive Zienkiewicz, where in his thirteen-year-old son's room they found a German carbine, a few bayonets, a field telephone, and many other small items. During the search the boy escaped, but his father, teenage sister, and a young maid were arrested. I do not have any more details, but we are all deeply disturbed by the situation. What will happen depends on one thing—if the army gives this investigation to the gestapo or handles the case itself.

November 18   When young Zienkiewicz found out that his father and sister had been arrested he gave himself up. His sister and maid were released as well as the other boys. Only old Zienkiewicz was taken to prison in Bilgoraj.

November 23   Yesterday I went to Bilgoraj to straighten out a few hospital problems. Along the entire highway the Germans were putting up new telephone lines to be used by the new airfields. The new communications line will connect all the new airfields, three in Bilgoraj County and four in Zamosc. It will finally end at the Russian border. In Szczebrzeszyn a new telephone line runs across the hospital grounds.

As I traveled I noticed much heavy construction activity. Wood barracks are everywhere. Those ugly buildings are changing the character of many villages, especially the many barracks that were erected around the hospital.

The normal calamities of war, like hunger, poverty, and venereal disease, are spreading. German authorities ordered that all women involved in prostitution must be registered and periodically checked at the hospital. In the event of venereal disease German soldiers are to give the name of the woman by whom they were infected. The sick women from both counties, Bilgoraj and Zamosc, are to be sent to the hospital in Szczebrzeszyn. As of now I have thirty-two cases, but I was told to be prepared for many more. Most of the women with venereal disease are professional prostitutes. They are very hard to handle, being familiar with prison life. They constantly fight among themselves. There are cases of escapes from the hospital, so now we must lock them in for the night. But some are young girls also, even as young as sixteen, who were first raped and later started prostitution as the only way to support themselves. Many are evacuees from the west, without parents and families.

November 24 Today former Szczebrzeszyn mayor Jan Franczak returned from the concentration camp at Dachau. More than half a year he spent at prisons in Zamosc and Lublin and later in concentration camps in Oranienburg and Dachau. I was told by people who had visited him that he is completely sick, looks terrible, and his feet are so badly swollen that he cannot wear shoes. He is a complete wreck, both physically and mentally. People talk about him; some say that he was too soft with the Germans. I am not able to give any opinion, but if there was any softness in his relations with the Germans he paid for it through torture in prison and later his time served in the concentration camps.

   More news: in Dachau a well-known civic leader, Stanislaw Kowerski, from Zamosc, died.

November 28 Yesterday I was visited a second time by Jerzy Plomienski. For several hours we talked, mostly about the losses of Polish cultural life and what is happening to our scientists and writers. Many have been killed; many are still dying in German camps. In Lwow, Professors Bartel, Bujak, and Romer have died. Zelenski is teaching French in the Ukrainian university. Those who are still alive are fighting for their very existence. Some are involved in black marketeering, but without any experience in selling or buying they cannot make a living. Some are staying at friends' farms. Some, like well-known graphic artist Tadeusz Cieslewski, who is now a waiter in a Warsaw restaurant, are trying to start new lives. Others are trying to make a living by selling their collections, so from Prof. Henryk Moscicki I purchased a few books. Not all of them give up. Many, after a short time of apathy, again begin the intellectual life. Of course, our defeat and the collapse of France were hard blows, the same as the hardships of no food or other necessities are difficult to take, but most accept it. One is Prof. Plomienski, who has one room in a small village in Hrubieszow

County and works diligently at his studies. He is preparing a new work to be printed at the end of the war.

I stopped by today to see Franczak. He looks better but his time in prison and concentration camps will leave the stresses of his ordeal with him until the end of his life.

We talked in general terms, nothing personal, nothing about his prison experiences. But without words people can say and understand much.

December

December 1 Today I went to the Klemensow sugar refinery hoping to receive some sugar for the hospital and some mill cake for the horses. The last time I was there was three months ago, so I was curious to see the many new barracks built to house the German flyers.

I came back with an unpleasant feeling. Some weeks ago a new man was assigned by the German governor as deputy engineer. His name is Molinski. Very shortly after his arrival chief engineer Wyszynski resigned. The new man is a good engineer who knows sugar production, but the way he handles himself with the old employees, including Mr. Wyszynski, is not correct. His actions united the employees against him. He forced Wyszynski, a seventy-year-old gentleman, to resign. Wyszynski is the best specialist in his field. And he and his family helped the refugees. Around forty people were housed and fed on his small farm in Pniowek. He was very popular with the factory workers and had held his position for more than thirty years.

Now about Molinski: it is clear that he will go at the same time the Germans do.

December 5 The events of the last couple of days have started some commotion in town. Hooligans entered St. Leonard's Chapel in the cemetery; they destroyed a small altar, removed all the votives, and cut the painting of St. Leonard with knives. No one was arrested. Some people say the Germans did this; others say the Ukrainians.

What happened to Rev. Cieslicki is proof that you are not even safe in your own house. He was evicted. The parish hall was converted into an officers' club. Even the intervention of the *Landrat* did not help.

In Klemensow there is new excitement. This time the gestapo and the SS began the registration of all workers. Everyone was forced to sign forms. It appears that after completing refinery work the workers will be shipped to labor camps in Germany.

Banditry is beginning again. In Widniowka the bandits robbed the farm of Mr. Siemiatkowski for the second time. At the time of the robbery a dance was being held in the village, so the bandits showed up and danced for a few hours.

I'm sorry to say that I have nothing positive to write about, only that here and now no one is giving up the fight and we all live with the strong belief that our slavery will end and that we will finally regain our independence.

December 7   A few days ago the administrator of the Zamoyski estate, Mr. Debczynski, was arrested again, this time supposedly in connection with the arrest of Streich, the German *Treuhander*. He was taken to Lublin prison.

December 10   The German authorities have decided to organize the medical profession into so-called medical guilds. And so in Szczebrzeszyn, the city with only a few physicians, we now have the Great Medical Guild of Szczebrzeszyn, with Dr. Likowski as the head of the new organization. Today was the first meeting of the guild. Besides physicians, pharmacists, dentists, midwives, medics, and hygenists, including Jews, were also present. The meeting was very short. Not one of the physicians spoke. We were very upset that we had been ordered to appear; we do not like being ordered around by the Germans. The entire structural organization of the guild is ridiculous. Through our actions at the meeting we showed how we felt about it.

December 12   The Germans are confiscating furniture for their new officers' club. They removed furniture from some homes in Szczebrzeszyn, including dentist Bronsztejn's. Mostly they stole the beautiful furniture from the Mogilnicki estate in Krasnystaw, with some antiques dating back hundreds of years.

December 14   Another flu. During the last few days everyone around me has been sick. I was fighting it, taking pills and injections, but finally my body gave in. I am lying here in fever with a very heavy head and I feel that my heart is slowing, as is normal for me during a flu. I think very calmly about the possibility of death. I worry about the possibility of death. I worry about my family and my hospital. Still I would like to see the end of the war.

December 18   Today, finally, I feel better, no injections. For the last two days my life has been in jeopardy.

December 29 I am still very weak and I am not able to leave my room. Most of the time I am lying in bed, waiting for my heart to improve. During the last few weeks I have been thinking about my youth in Moscow. I wrote down some short recollections of that interesting time. Maybe this will be of some worth to someone.

Writing these memoirs and at the same time breaking away from the daily routine of our slavery conditions has hardened my nerves. I am still physically weak but my mental capacity is back fully once again. I am full of energy and have the urge to work and plan publishing. Only because of such a close call with death, I realize that I do not have much time left. I must do everything possible not to waste even a minute, because I still have so much to do.

From the people who visited me I was able to gather only a little information about the events around us, about new regulations pertaining to buying milk products and about arrests for selling meat and bacon. Another one is an order prohibiting Poles from using the railroad from December 23, 1940, until January 2, 1941 (during the holidays).

Yesterday in Szczebrzeszyn a Polish policeman, Wieliczko, committed suicide. He shot himself in the heart. He was pronounced dead on arrival at the hospital in Zamosc.

The List of Casualties Is Growing

January

January 4   For the last few days we have had snowstorms like never before. All highways, roads, and railroad tracks are snowed in. Thousands of people are working in the massive cleanup. For snow removal the Germans are taking not only Jews but farmers from all of the villages. It is a constant job. As soon as the roads are cleared another snowstorm comes and the people have to start again. All communication is dead, buses and trains are out of commission, and there has been no mail delivery. In the city most stores are closed. The city seems to have shut down. Yesterday the citizens had some real "amusement" as they watched Mayor Borucki, who was personally involved in beating Jews who showed up late for roadwork.

A few days ago a young girl, personal secretary to one of the German officials in Zwierzyniec, came in for compulsory treatment. She was escorted to the hospital by a gendarme. She appeared very elegant, maybe eighteen years old. She is Polish; her name is Alfreda Soltysiak. She said that after finishing Kunicki High School in Lublin she worked in Katowice, where she learned German. She likes the Germans so much that now she works with the gestapo. She even showed a gestapo ID card. At one point she was even ready to call the gestapo in Lublin to report a young boy named Osuch who was talking very negatively in obscene language about the Germans. Medic Cielecki finally persuaded her not to do it. I am noting her name here to record one of many strange cases of shameful behavior.

January 10 For some time things have been quiet. We heard about some arrests but they were for black marketeering and not political. Now a change is occurring and again we are worried. There is talk once more of upcoming German arrests aimed at intellectuals and also of new deportations to labor camps. Most arrests are expected in Warsaw, where the Pawiak prison is preparing to take more prisoners. The Lublin prison, an old castle, is doing the same. Because of this people feel depressed, but we still believe in final victory over the German devil.

We have new cases of spotted typhus, not typhoid fever. A German physician, a gynecologist who has never seen this disease, has stopped by several times for observation. He asked me to show him how cupping glasses work since they are not used in Germany.

Drunkenness is growing. More and more people are drinking, and naturally there are more drunken fights, but it appears that the Germans are rather pleased about it. Today Mayor Borucki, who likes to use alcohol himself, was forced to suspend two clerks and one driver because of drunkenness.

January 14 Three days ago gendarmes, with the help of soldiers, began stopping people, apparently looking for anyone coming from Warsaw. In Marszycki's boardinghouse they conducted a very thorough search, as they did in all other places known as temporary quarters for people from Warsaw. At the same time everyone stopped on the streets had to present their ID. Personal searches were conducted only of people from Warsaw. It seems that they are looking for some items smuggled out of Warsaw that are unknown to us.

Yesterday they were looking for a woman dressed in a gray overcoat.

January 15 All night there was very heavy military traffic going in the direction of Zwierzyniec. I haven't seen such heavy traffic for a long time. In town there are rumors that furloughs of German soldiers have been called off. At the same time we hear that in the Zamosc garrison several officers, even some gestapo, have been arrested for taking bribes. People involved in studying political events are sure that something big will happen soon.

January 18 In Bilgoraj County there were new arrests. Three persons, including one priest from Tarnogrod, were executed; others were transported to prison in Zamosc. More arrests occurred in Lublin and Warsaw. In Zamosc a new group of 1,000 evacuees from Posen arrived. Over 100 people were sent to Deszkowice. This month we again expect a new transport of evacuees in Bilgoraj County, this time 4,800 from Posen. I have this information from a county doctor who is asking for help to organize medical services for such a large group.

Winter is here in full force, with freezing temperatures and blizzards. In these conditions the poor evacuees are dying by the hundreds, especially the young children. The last transport was held up for seven weeks in Lodz in unheated barracks with little food. Many children were sick with the measles. They were later transported in unheated cars.

This is very depressing news. On the bright side, we received information about British victories in Africa. We are delighted, but we still would like to know when our suffering will end.

January 20   Just on the edge of town on Frampolska Street the Germans built a new rifle range. Small amounts of ammunition have turned up missing. The city council posted an announcement signed by the mayor stating that the Germans see this as sabotage and if it does not stop they will shoot several hostages.

Today a hearing was held at city hall regarding the drunkenness of three city employees, Krzyzanski, Kitowski, and Krukowski. They were warned that they would all be fired from their jobs if this was repeated.

I am very much disturbed that we have not had any news, for more than a month, from notary Rosinski in Dachau. Previously he had sent short notes twice a month.

January 22   Today the hospital administrator went to Zamosc. People there are awaiting new mass arrests, similar to those of June of last year. Many people are leaving Zamosc to stay in places where they are not known. In all offices work is at a standstill. Employees are unable to work because of nervous stress. So far there have been only a few arrests, all related to black market activities. Only a Jewish contractor, Braunsztein, was arrested for sabotage, even though he was doing contract work for the Germans.

A few days ago a German officer notified us that in one camp near Vienna forest ranger Byczkowski was killed, as was postmaster Radzik in Oranienburg camp.

I am very pleased that we received a letter from notary Rosinski, in Dachau, and that he is well.

Robberies on public streets have begun taking place. Yesterday around 6 P.M. Fedorowicz, an employee of the Alwa factory, came from Zamosc with 15,000 zloty cash, withdrawn from a bank. Near Zawada a young man asked for a lift. A few minutes later he pointed a gun at Fedorowicz, took the briefcase, and left. The driver and another passenger, Kleban, were so completely surprised that the robber left without any protest. (Later I learned that this was an act of sabotage by an underground organization.)

January 28   The German authorities seem to be preparing for some new initiatives. Again yesterday there was registration of Jews, probably having something to do with labor camps. Another order was issued by the mayor calling on people to volunteer for labor work in Germany by January 31. The announcement was written such that everyone knows new deportations will begin if volunteer registration is low.

From different areas comes news about the arrests of professional people. Life now is very nerve wracking.

January 31   Only one young woman signed up for volunteer work in Germany. Since yesterday the Jews have been allowed to walk the streets without formally greeting the Germans. We do not know how to explain this. Jews must still take their hats off when passing German soldiers, because a Jew was beaten by the Germans for not taking his off.

February

February 3   Today I received news that Dr. Marian Sulewski was arrested in Izbica. He has been in hiding since last June and thus has avoided arrest. Many people are being held in Krasnystaw. In our city and in Zamosc only a few people have been arrested lately, all for black marketeering, but people are still waiting for something big to happen. Today in Szczebrzeszyn the gestapo spent the whole day going over a list of people registered as legal residents of the city.

February 5   Today I attended a *Sondergericht*, special court, in Zamosc as an expert witness against two women, formerly my patients. Both were charged with infecting German soldiers with venereal disease. I went to the trial with mixed feelings. When I tried to enter the court building through the main entrance I had to turn away and find a back entrance because of a sign reading, "Jews and Poles Not Allowed." I of course turned around and entered through the side entrance. There the German signs were mixed in with old Polish ones. All court clerks spoke German, while janitors and custodians spoke Polish.

In the courtroom three judges in black uniforms sat behind a long table. The prosecutor was dressed in a light-green uniform, and the defense attorney wore a long black robe.

The two women had been brought from prison and they freely admitted having sexual intercourse with soldiers while knowing that they were sick. Several times I had advised them about this, but they did it only to support themselves. One was a seventeen-year-old girl, an evacuee from Posen. She mentioned that her father was a captain in the Polish army, but she didn't look like a captain's daughter. Because of their admittance of guilt, I was not asked to testify. I was happy that it turned out that way. Because of their action my testimony did not influence a guilty verdict.

The prosecutor asked for five years hard labor for the older women and four for the younger. The court sentenced the girl to one year and seven months in prison. How much the older one received I do not remember.

After the hearing I was asked to sign some papers in the court office. Observing the way this German court operated, I came to the conclusion that luckily this is only a temporary state of justice.

I left Zamosc glad to be going home.

February 7   A forestry ranger, Kulinski, from Kosobudy, died in the Dachau concentration camp. He was only twenty-five years old, one more victim from the Zamosc region. Still not much news about Rosinski. I ask myself if he will be able to survive.

February 10   Today I went to Zwierzyniec. Around the hospital the Germans constructed ugly wooden barracks, painted gray for anti-aircraft camouflage. I heard much gossip: Szmidt beat up Adam Karpinski in a fistfight, the Germans confiscated some goods at Kostecki's place, supposedly belonging to Ajzen in Szczebrzeszyn, and so on.

The estate administrator is no longer in prison but in a cell in the Lublin gestapo building.

February 12   I have not been as depressed as today for quite some time. Dr. Waclaw Drozdz, from Lublin, died in Dacha. We attended the university together in Cracow. He was a very popular physician and was president of the Polish Medical Association. Yesterday in Lublin Dr. Poradowski was held as hostage. Every tenth hostage was shot, including Dr. Poradowski.

In Szczebrzeszyn the gestapo are still checking registrations in city hall. Today they stopped Kitkowski's wagon bringing people from Zamosc. After a search they confiscated some of their belongings. The relief committee posted a new announcement asking people for donations of food and clothing because a new transport of evacuees will arrive soon.

February 13   Since early morning more Germans are engaged in searching passersby. This afternoon four truckloads of gendarmes with full armament arrived. We feel that something is about to happen.

February 14   The Polish population spent an extremely nervous and trying night. Many young people left town; many others, including elders, did not stay in their own homes; many more slept fully clothed. The reason: more than 100 gendarmes stayed the night in Szczebrzeszyn.

All day today the gendarmes patrolled the city streets, stopping and searching everyone. All roads leading into the city were blocked and all wagons searched. On one of the streets a ten-year-old grammar school pupil, son of Stocki, the physician from Cracow, was stopped and searched. Gendarmes searched his briefcase, all his school books, and even his clothing.

It is possible that this is connected to an event in Kawenczyn. A woman, Biziorowa, got into a fight with her son-in-law Gnypel and went to the Germans saying that he had a hidden gun. The search of the house was without any result, but gendarmes arrested Gnypel and the woman's son, who by the way has a very bad reputation. After all this Biziorowa somehow got a rifle and took it to the gendarmes. During an investigation she said that the peasants are preparing a revolution against the Germans and that they have many hidden arms and illegal publications. So the gendarmes again went to Kawenczyn and searched all the houses, again without any results. Finally they arrested the stupid woman.

The nervousness in town is not over yet. During the dark hours the streets are deserted.

A few days ago, in Zamosc, Zygmunt Pomaranski, former owner of a bookstore, was arrested. He was very active in the underground.

February 15   More and more gendarmes are coming to town. Everyone on the streets must show an ID. Again a young school pupil was searched. The gendarmes even took his pencil and fountain pen. The youngster's crying did not help. The same occurred in all villages around the city. All routes are patrolled, and a truck armed with machine guns is posted at the crossing of Rozlopska highway and Michalowski Route. Definitely there is a reason for all of this. But what?

In town there is no more salt—all sold out. People again are talking about important events, but no one really knows anything.

Rev. Chroscicki from Old Zamosc died in Dachau.

February 19   The story of Kawenczyn is not over yet. Yesterday I saw gendarmes escorting a few horse-drawn wagons filled with villagers from there. Among them I recognized Jan Lazorczyk, a well-known farmer and a very intelligent man. I learned later that during their interrogation the Germans were very brutal and many of those taken were severely beaten. A few were released, but the rest are still in jail.

From Zamosc comes bad news. First, the public library will be closed and moved from the old building. Second, the apartment house where Rosinski lived will be evacuated and all apartments used as quarters for

German officers. Rosinski's sister is still trying to save his collections and furniture.

Any day now we are counting on mass arrests in connection with forced labor in Germany. A few physicians received statements that they have been selected to perform medical examinations of people assigned for labor camps in Germany. I am glad I was not selected.

Yesterday afternoon Germans arrived at mason Michalski's house. Without asking any questions they went directly to the cellar, removed portions of the brick wall, and found several items, including fabric taken from Ajzen's store in Szczebrzeszyn. It would be interesting to know how they obtained this information.

February 20   Last evening around 7 P.M. three bandits entered the home of Pereta, the owner of the flour mill. Holding guns, they demanded 20,000 zloty and jewelry. Pereta gave them 2,400 zloty, so they left without taking any jewelry.

February 21   From Zamosc came news that yesterday Kazimierz Rutkowski and his wife, Janina, were arrested. He is an executive of an insurance company and was active in the organization Friends of Books. She is an instructor at the teacher's seminary. Along with them a university student and son of a judge, Pacewicz, and a clerk of an insurance company, Maria Bleszynska, were arrested. The reason for the arrests is unknown.

In Zamosc new obituaries about the deaths of many people were printed in two languages, first German, then Polish.

February 22   Today a telegram came from the Dachau concentration camp about the death of Michal Kafarski, a merchant from Szczebrzeszyn. He was arrested on the same day as I was, June 19, 1940, and we were in the same cell in the Rotunda in Zamosc. He was a very quiet man. He suffered much during the revolution in Russia. He was always calm and controlled.

February 23   Today Mrs. Kamila Kopcinska called me from Zamosc with the news that notary Rosinski died in Dachau. I have never in my life been in such a state of grief over the death of a friend. I cannot control myself; I cannot cover up my tears.

With his death I lost my best friend and co-worker in my seventeen-year-old study of the history of the Zamosc region. We did everything together. I always consulted him when I planned for the future. No one gave me more support. Now who will take his place? I cannot foresee any work about the Zamosc region without Rosinski. People like him are hard to find. They come along only once in a while.

From our close group of friends, only I am still here, alone and very sad.

A few days ago, when writing my memoirs of 1918, I described Henryk Rosinski. I was sure that he would survive and would come home to us. But it is different now.

I do not know how long I will be able to work, but I know that my duty is to finish, as soon as possible, all my memoirs about life in the Zamosc region and the tremendous influence on it by Henryk Rosinski.

When I began writing my memoirs I was sure that the first one to read the manuscript would be Rosinski, and I was sure that he would be the first one to criticize, only his criticism was always productive, demanding still more work. I am sure that he would be glad about my reconstructing in writing this important period in the history of the Zamosc region.

Now I must speed up my work to conclude it as soon as possible. I must type everything because no one can read my handwritten notes.

This will be my tribute to my best friend.

February 24   I cannot come to myself. The more I think about the death of Rosinski, the more I can feel the loss of the most distinguished member of the citizenry of Zamosc.

February 25   Today I was supposed to go to Zamosc, but my driver never showed up, so I stayed home. I felt too tired to ride a horse to Zamosc.

From Dachau came news about the death of the Zamosc deputy postmaster, Marek Wojciechowski, arrested in June of last year.

The list of casualties is growing.

February 26   I went to Zamosc to meet with Rosinski's sister and find out about his death. He died on Friday, February 21, the same day that I wrote about him in my memoirs.

The obituaries concerning his death were posted, but regulations have it that German is on top, Polish below. This is in effect the persecution of a dead person's memory. It is not enough to persecute people while they still live. Rosinski's death had a tremendous impact in Zamosc. People feel a great sorrow in the loss of a great citizen.

I spoke with many people. Even now everyone still believes in our final victory.

Yesterday in Zamosc there were new arrests: surveyor Stefanek, and Judge Wladyslaw Pajewski. From Dachau came news about the death of attorney Kulik from Hrubieszow.

I stopped at the public library. People stand in line for books. So far the library is in the same place. Mayor Wazowski assured me that he had a place to move this library and museum in case of evacuation.

February 28 A few young people, so called Golden Youth, with my former student Piotr Jozwiak as leader, were totally drunk and were arrested. The list included Piotr Jozwiak from Brody, Chwiejczak from Zurawnica, and Bortkiewicz and Wybacz from Szczebrzeszyn. They were thrown into the city jail.

March

March 2 Since early morning there has been heavy traffic. More gendarmes are in the streets. They removed all horse-drawn wagons from the marketplace. People are nervous again.

On Thursday, February 27, services were held in Zamosc Cathedral for notary Rosinski. A woman told me that very few people had attended the Mass. People were afraid that a massive attendance would be seen by the Germans as a political demonstration. A few gestapo came in civilian clothes. Through the suggestion of one Polish policeman, solo singing and cello music was dropped. Yesterday a service was held in Szczebrzeszyn.

By order of the governor in Lublin new announcements were posted. Jews are prohibited from living within the city limits, and all people are reminded about police hours. Anyone stopped after curfew will face three months in jail or a 1,000-zloty fine. All permits allowing movement after curfew are revoked. New permits will be given only by the office of the governor general in Cracow, and only in special cases such as physicians and nurses. So far not one of the local physicians has applied.

March 3 Today there is a big sensation. Last night four youths who had been arrested on February 28 escaped from the city jail. More gendarmes are now stopping people and searching homes. All country roads are patrolled constantly. People are afraid of repressions. More people are leaving the city, now even women. Tension is mounting as we await new reprisals.

March 5 So far no new arrests. People seem to be breathing more freely. We do not know how long this will last or even if the Germans will forget about this escape.

March 8 A few days have passed without any major events. So far there have been no reprisals in conjunction with the escape of the four young men. But the Germans are searching in all the villages and forestry stations.

We are again very much involved in trying to find out what is going on in the world. The news that German armies have entered Bulgaria was a big surprise. Now talk about war between Germany and the Soviets has begun to be a big topic once more.

In Zamosc someone noticed a German truck loaded with road signs, *Nach Lemberg* (to Lwow). In Hrubieszow, Tomaszow, and other villages close to the Russian border the curfew has been changed. No one is allowed on the streets after 7 P.M. This curfew is strictly enforced.

At the airfield near Klemensow construction is going full speed. In the forest the Germans are installing ammunitions depots.

This evening we received news about the assassination of the director of the theater in Warsaw, the German actor Igo Sym. Because of this act, several people were arrested as hostages. The Germans announced that if the assassins were not found within three days, all hostages would be executed. Many people are upset that we will again lose the important ones. The list of hostages includes a few university professors, a well-known physicist, lawyers, and artists.

A few days ago another transport of evacuees arrived in Szczebrzeszyn, this time 200 persons. So far no group has had as many sick. I admitted more than twenty, mostly small children and very old people; three have already died.

March 10   I am very tired. This life—under constant fear of arrest, constant struggle to supply my hospital, and constant uncertainty of the future for already 1½ years—is shattering my nerves.

I believe in British victory but I am not sure that I will see it because of my physical condition. My heart is slowing visibly and nothing is pointing to a quick end to the war; everything seems so complicated that the struggle may go on for years.

In Poland we see complete devastation in all facets of life. Our best people are dying by the thousands. People can be replaced, but the worst is the destruction of our national culture. How will Poland look after a few more years of devastation? I have an urge to work like never before. I feel that now every person must strive for maximum effort to survive and give others a goal for survival.

As for myself, I live with the constant fear that maybe I will not be able to finish what I have started. So I have to rush, because we do not know what the next day will bring. I have to organize my manuscripts. I have to type so that in the future they will be easy to read. I type in duplicate, hoping that at least one copy will survive. I try not to waste any time.

But under what circumstances is this work proceeding? It is so difficult to force one's self to do normal mental work. Almost every day brings some events so terrifying that you cannot concentrate. Constant news about arrests, executions, death in concentration camps, and torture in prison keep the mind away from productive work. *Nulla dies sine Linea!*

Every few hours someone comes to tell me that the gestapo are looking through some lists at city hall, that gendarmes are stopping everyone on this or that street, that so and so was arrested. And so it goes on.

People try to predict what will happen tomorrow. Some hide in town, others move to the villages so they will be unknown. We have many new-comers here who hope that in these new surroundings they will not be recognized. Everyone does await arrest though.

I have my small suitcase packed and ready near my bed, in the event of arrest. At night my shoes and suit are ready, so I can dress quickly.

I am still here only because of my hospital; otherwise I would move to Warsaw, where I am practically unknown, and wait there for the end of the war. In this nerve-shattering situation productive work slows down.

But now, realizing my responsibilities, I am glad that I have my hospital and can still be a help to others, and that my mind is constantly occupied, so I have no time to think about what might happen the next day.

March 17 It has been quiet during the last few days. In fact, there has been an unusual relaxation of nerves. We are carefully watching for any military activities in our area.

More and more troops are quartered around us. More barracks have been built. Between Szczebrzeszyn and the Klemensow sugar refinery they stretch in long rows facing each other. Around Klemensow and Zwierzyniec, mostly around the hospital, are garrison areas. People are disturbed because of the gasoline depots around Rudka. There are a few large areas near the refinery where the gasoline drums are stacked three rows high, even in the castle gardens of Klemensow. Besides gasoline, other materials are also stored.

At the airfield construction work continues from early morning until late at night. Air force personnel arrive constantly. Motorized traffic is increasing. This seems to be proof that something big is coming. In every building the windows are prepared for blackout. Even at the railroad station blackout blinds have been installed.

The last two days have been full of worry. On Saturday, March 15, my son Tadeusz disappeared. After returning from school around 3 P.M. he just left the house. By 5 P.M. he had not returned, so we began a search, which had to be called off at the curfew hour.

We spent a terrifying night. Finally in the morning we resumed our search. We learned from someone who saw him that he had traveled through Blonie, in the direction of Kawenczyn. My wife went there and asked for information. A few hours later I learned that he had spent the night in Topolcza. I went there and found out that he had already left by morning. We looked everywhere. Finally today we found him in Zwierzyniec, where he had spent the night at the pharmacy. By 10 A.M. he was home. When I saw him I could not help but cry. He wouldn't tell me the reason for running away from home, but he said that he was happy to be back.

March 18 After a few days of relatively quiet time, once the people grew used to sleeping quietly at night, new arrests occurred.

Early this morning in Szczebrzeszyn the following arrests were made: Mayor Jan Borucki, translator Krol, sanitary worker Adamczyk, bank director Michal Pawlik, drugstore owner Buchaczkowski, and hardware store owners Staniszewski and Stelmaszczuk. No one knows the reason for these arrests. With the exception of Pawlik, all are originally from western Poland. Borucki has lived in Szczebrzeszyn for several years.

This evening I received news from Zamosc about more arrests. So far these names are included: Tadeusz Burzminski, along with his wife and fourteen-year-old daughter; Sobolewska, the wife of a school inspector, and her two teenage daughters; Zygmunt Syrek, a teacher; Cieslinski, also a teacher, attorney, and member of the Polish *Sejm* (congress); Tomasz Czernicki; Antoni Wisniewski; Karpowicz, a district attorney; Zolcinski, a sanitary inspector; Mackowski, a retired colonel, along with his wife and two sons; Stasiak, a bank employee and his wife; Kowalczyk, a retired sergeant; Burlewicz, a court employee; and Maria Grzechnikowna, an insurance employee. More names are sure to follow.

March 20 In Zwierzyniec more arrests; people are disturbed. Pastuszynski, an employee of the Zamoyski estate, Kaminski, a retired officer, and his wife, and Newlaczyl, a retired railroad worker, were arrested. The prison in Zamosc is full.

March 21 More arrests are expected; since yesterday people have been talking. We can expect arrests at night. Even some names are being mentioned. Again people are not staying in their own houses; some are leaving town. We fear arrests of teenagers because lately young people from Wieloncza, Zawada, and Niedzieliski were deported to labor camps in Germany.

Influenced by these events I prepared myself for arrest; even my heavy winter coat was ready. My wife stood at the window an entire night looking for gendarmes.

We are mentally exhausted.

All railroad freight shipments are canceled. German troops are conducting exercises around Szczebrzeszyn.

March 25 No more new arrests have occurred in Szczebrzeszyn. In Zamosc there have been a few, but people are ready for more.

Yesterday, in one of our local churches, services were held for Kafarski, murdered in Dachau.

There is heavy military traffic on all highways and secondary roadways. Gendarmes are stopping and searching every horse-drawn wagon. No one knows what they are looking for this time.

Lately we have not obtained any newspapers—no German ones or even Polish papers published by the German administration.

Here in Szczebrzeszyn a small bookstore recently opened. You can buy mostly German books and magazines there, but once in a while it is possible to buy some Polish books, mostly about nature and travel, published by the Polish library in Warsaw. The prices are very low. For Lepecki's *Sowiecki Kaukaz* and Ficinski's *Twenty Years in Parana* I paid only 2 zloty, 20 groszy each; for Pawlowicz's *In the Sun of the Far South* I paid 3 zloty, 50 groszy.

March 28 Still we do not have any world news. It looks like even the distribution of illegal press has stopped. We do not believe in German propaganda news, but we worry when they tell us of their political victories in the Balkans. It appears that England has its hands full in the future and the war will maybe last a few more years. Here our lives are more and more difficult; we are in constant fear of the next day.

We await the beginning, any day now, of new deportations to labor camps because the number of volunteers has been very low.

All around the Szczebrzeszyn railroad station there are new anti-aircraft shelters being built. We observe the constant movement of German troops. The repair and construction of new roads in the direction of the Russian border are progressing rapidly. We hope that war between Germany and the Soviets will break out any day now.

March 29 Tension is growing again. The German behavior is strange and everyone notices it. Young people hide or leave town at night and return at daylight. It is a tiring life.

I began reading travel books and continue writing memoirs.

March 31 In Zamosc, Sobolewska and one of her daughters and Rutkowska were released from prison; in Zwierzyniec, Pastuszynski was released.

Here in Szczebrzeszyn there is nothing new. German soldiers walk everywhere, drinking and singing.

April

April 1   Today is the 400-year anniversary of Jan Zamoyski, one of Poland's most famous political figures. Even from before the beginning of the war a huge celebration had been planned, including a special meeting of the Polish Academy of Science, to be held in Zamosc. We were planning several publications dedicated to the memory of this great Pole. I am sure that now only a handful of people will remember this anniversary. A few weeks ago I talked with young Jan Zamoyski about this. To my surprise he told me that even he had completely forgotten the event. I feel sad as I think about the present, compared to what we had hoped to have.

April 3   I went to Bilgoraj. The highway, which had been repaired a few months ago, was again in terrible shape. From Zwierzyniec to Bilgoraj roadwork is continuing at full speed. The wooden bridges are to be replaced by concrete ones. There is very heavy traffic, mostly hauling construction materials. Around Zwierzyniec, besides the wooden barracks, there are many tents. Next to the hospital in Bilgoraj the Germans put up a large building to house a 1,000-bed army hospital. Last week a building containing a brand-new X-ray unit burned down. What we see points to a fast and thorough preparation for the new war.

During the last few weeks several people have been arrested in Bilgoraj and also in the village of Goraj. Rev. Wielgosz and the director of the cooperative, Huzar, were arrested in Bilgoraj. Also in Tarnogrod sixteen people, including Rev. Kimaczynski were arrested. (During the first war Rev. Kimaczynski was an assistant pastor in Szczebrzeszyn.) In Zamosc I have heard of only a few arrests.

More German troops arrived in Szczebrzeszyn. The German air force took over all the school buildings, so again our children are without the possibility of an education.

April 5   Today all prisoners were taken from Zamosc to the railroad station and transported somewhere. Where, we do not know, but probably to some concentration camp.

Traffic is increasing. Many military trucks loaded with supplies and equipment are using the highways. More and more troops keep arriving. People are afraid of losing their houses. The same in Zamosc.

During the last few days some white planes have been flying high above the city. People say that they are Russian.

A few days ago the wife of a Ukrainian physician from Cieszanow, a village located on the Russian border, stopped by to visit. They live under constant fear of Russian attack. All stores are closed. All Ukrainians were ordered to turn in their radios. Until now they had permission to use radios.

April 7 This morning a German soldier on guard duty committed suicide. Before this case was cleared and finally accepted as suicide, people were convinced that the Germans would execute several hostages on charges of murder.

Today Yugoslavia and Germany are at war. People are happy and hopeful that maybe Turkey will fight against the Germans. Because of this news spirits are high.

April 10 My nephew, architect Jan Klukowski, from Warsaw, has been visiting for a couple of days. We talked and talked for hours.

This afternoon we learned about the Germans' progress in the Balkans. This is depressing news. What will happen if England collapses? I don't even want to think about it.

Today in Sulow a commission for the registration and physical examination of people being sent to Germany for labor was to begin working. Approximately 580 people were called in, but only a few showed up and they were invalids completely unfit for any physical work. As I found out, the post office was able to deliver only about thirty notices; the rest were returned, marked "Refuse to Accept."

April 14 Second day of Easter. The traffic on the highway never has been as heavy. From 4 P.M. until 10 P.M. German troops have been on the move from Zwierzyniec toward Zamosc, infantry and supplies. The vehicles all have special blue lights. Yesterday many motorized units went in the same direction. It was very strange to see mounted artillery units pulled by six horses.

Everywhere there is unusual readiness. German civilian employees were ordered to stay put. The sugar from the Klemensow refinery was loaded into rail cars and shipped west, mostly to warehouses around Cracow. There has been some news about British success in the Balkans.

Work on the airfields has not stopped. Even though yesterday was Easter Sunday, work progressed as if it were any normal day. At this time, from what we can see, war between Russia and Germany will start any day now. Many people are standing on the sidewalks to see the German troops. We all hope that this war will start now and help England on all other fronts.

April 15 The movement of troops goes on. Delivery of German newspapers has been interrupted. The news we receive is complete fantasy and cannot be trusted.

Yesterday in Zamosc two women employees of an insurance company were arrested.

Attorney Bajkowski, from Zamosc, died yesterday in a concentration camp.

April 16   Yesterday all lights at the Szczebrzeszyn rail station were blacked out, even the signal lights. All vehicles travel with blue covers over the lights.

The highway to Hrubieszow is in such bad shape that troop movements have slowed down. The road workers are unable to keep up with the repair work. Vehicles move constantly, without interruption.

April 18   The troop movements are still heavy. From early morning until late at night units have been moving toward Zamosc. The Germans placed anti-aircraft machine guns around Klemensow and on the high school roof. Three locations have also been selected on the hospital grounds.

Yesterday the Germans removed from the attic of the grammar school buildings all books and teaching supplies. They were piled up on the playground and burned.

Many people are looking for rooms in the small villages so they can leave the city. They are afraid that in case of war between Germany and Russia Szczebrzeszyn will be hit hard.

April 21   The troop movements continue. Today city hall received new announcements concerning the blacking out of all windows. The war comes closer.

April 22   Troop movements continue. All sugar from the refinery has been shipped out. Germans are bringing aviation bombs and storing them in the refinery warehouses.

I am preparing myself for the eventuality of evacuation from Szczebrzeszyn. I put some of my manuscripts into two packages, hoping to ship them to Warsaw. But what to do with my books? I do not know, but in the meantime I am typing my notes.

April 26   Never in my life have I seen so many motorized troops. The movement is now in the tenth day and still very strong. Yesterday heavy guns were moved. The houses shook and the roadway is completely destroyed. There are parked military vehicles everywhere, so that even crossing the street is difficult. One interesting item: every vehicle has wooden blocks tied on the sides. People say that the blocks are for use when the vehicle gets stuck in the mud. Others say that the blocks will be used while erecting tents.

At the hospital we have been ordered to dig more trenches and to cover all windows.

In town all stores are closed or empty. There is no place where bread can be purchased.

Many people are packing and preparing to leave the city. Some are panic-stricken, thinking about the possibility of air bombardment. We await the start of the war any day now.

April 28 This morning a group of German medical corps officers visited my hospital. They informed me that a portion of the building will be taken for a German military hospital. It will be hard to survive with Germans that close around us. But nothing has been decided.

It has been raining without interruption for days. I never remember it raining as hard as this year. Most of the hospital grounds are underwater. The fields are flooded and water is up to the highway. Regardless of the rain, the highway traffic is still very heavy.

Provisions are hard to find and prices are going up. Supplies are short. The city bakeries have enough flour for one day only. What will happen later no one knows. For grits and flour one must pay 4.5 zloty per pound.

Now, after the arrest of the mayor, we feel the lack of coordination in city planning. At city hall there is complete disorganization.

Everyone is sure that war will start any time now, but besides the troop movements we do not see any sign to indicate that this is true.

People are nervous, packed and ready to move out.

April 30 Rain is still falling. Flooding is spreading. It has never before been like this. This is the worst flooding of this century. Any fields with new crops are destroyed. We are facing hunger next fall and winter. It will be impossible to seed the fields again. Tomorrow is the first of May.

May

May 3 Yesterday I went on hospital business to Bilgoraj. By horse-drawn carriage this was a very long journey. There were many military vehicles, but civilian traffic was practically nonexistent. Everywhere you could see roadwork. Most concrete bridges are completed already; in some places the highway has been widened. The people in Bilgoraj are sure about war with Russia, yet the population is calm and no one is preparing for evacuation. Here people are not as nervous—not many are packing or even talking about moving out. They stay in their own houses, not like in Szczebrze-szyn, where men hide at night.

After returning home I learned about the excitement in town. By order of the military, city hall notified all citizens that men between the ages of fifteen and sixty years must report to work on the airfield by 7 A.M. to-morrow. Only physicians, veterinarians, and public employees are excused. This announcement affects the city of Szczebrzeszyn and the communes of Sulow and Radecznica. The penalties for not going are heavy, including death. Altogether 4,000 people will be working without pay. The speedup of the building program at the airfield must be connected with the upcoming war. People coming from the Russian border are telling us about the preparations for war on the Russian side. They say that Russian radio is becoming more and more aggressive toward the Germans.

May 6 In the city since early morning there has been a general panic. Germans are stopping all men, Aryans and Jews, and are sending them for labor at the airfields. During all of this beatings are a normal part of German conduct. From the window I observed them. With special satisfaction the Germans beat people who were well dressed and looked like white-collar workers.

All workers are under constant surveillance. One soldier with a rifle looks after ten workers. The work now starts at 6 A.M. and ends at dusk. The hardest work is in the flooded areas where the workers stand knee-deep in water. Some people who signed in as sick were examined by a young German physician. Only a few were dismissed.

Now the Germans have organized a civil defense. Dr. Likowski was put in charge. Today the commandant of gendarmerie stopped by to inspect the hospital cellars. He told me that he is requesting the installation of electrical power and telephones in the cellars, for use in case of air raids.

Everyone talks openly about the upcoming war.

May 8 In the Jewish population of Jozefow an epidemic of spotted typhus erupted. Yesterday I admitted nine cases. Soon after that I went to see the German military commandant to report that I have new cases of an infectious disease and to ask that the hospital be off-limits to all German soldiers as a precaution against spreading this sickness among the German troops. Within an hour signs were posted proclaiming the hospital off-limits to all Germans. This way my hospital will be safe and not taken over by the Germans.

Thousands of people are working at the airfields. This is very hard work, particularly for people not used to physical labor. More and more people have been sent to the hospital for treatment and observation. I had to assign one ward only for Jews. The hospital is full and I have so much to do that I have no time for writing.

A new mayor has been selected: Josef Hejno, a blacksmith from Szcze-brzeszyn. I feel that this is not the best choice.

Today we had an inspection of our blackout preparations. The Germans checked all the windows. One officer told me to be prepared for the admission of a large number of wounded, but he never said from which of the enemies we can expect air bombardments. On the highway there is still very heavy traffic. The villages around Szczebrzeszyn are full of soldiers.

May 11 I admitted another group of spotted typhus cases from Jozefow. We finally received information about people arrested from Szczebrzeszyn. All are in the concentration camp at Auschwitz, except Borucki and Buchaczkowski, who are still being held in Zamosc.

May 12 Today I received confidential information that two large barns have been assigned by the Germans to be used as morgues.

May 14 The preparation for war is at full speed. On the marketplace there are new anti-aircraft trenches. Also new trenches have been dug by the city pharmacy and in the parish garden. The city commandant today ordered that one room in the hospital be converted into a civil defense ward in readiness for occupation by twelve men. In the health center a ward is to be prepared for a women's squad. The Germans are building concrete shelters for themselves in the cellars of city hall. Many people from Klemensow have been forced to move out and many more are ready to move. But moving is another problem. All the villages are full of soldiers, in many cases owners of the houses were thrown out to make room for the Germans. Naturally the Germans are stealing many valuable small items that can be carried in their pockets.

Traffic is even heavier, daytime as well as night. From Bilgoraj came new instructions regarding civil defense. Current events are typical of a prewar atmosphere. In the hospital there is plenty of work. I have been on my feet the whole day.

May 18 A few days went by without any special events. Yesterday we received a new announcement signed jointly by *Kreishauptmänner* in Bilgoraj and Zamosc that the work at the airfields can be done by unemployed people only and that arresting and placing people into forced labor situations was an administrative mistake.

Since yesterday the atmosphere in town has been changing. We received information about new arrests in Janow. People here feel we will have the same again. Many do not sleep at home.

May 21 Today I learned about new German barbarity. In Sulow the Germans tried to arrest and send some people to work at the airfields. A few men tried to escape, so the Germans started shooting. I admitted two people very seriously wounded, twenty-one-year-old Stefan Bartnik and twenty-two-year-old Adam Wylupek. Both are on the critical list. Naturally the villagers are upset.

Traffic is still heavy. We feel that war is close but nothing is happening. This is very tiring.

May 23   Again tension increases. Work at the airfields is progressing very rapidly. We have to prepare our civil defenses and carefully cover all windows. We have a very heavy workload. The hospital administrator went to Bilgoraj. People at the county offices await big, new events. The *Kreishauptmann* received orders not to leave the county offices even for a few hours.

A few more arrests have occurred in Zamosc: Wisniewski, for the third time, and a Hungarian; and in Nielisz, teacher Mazur. People are saying that the gestapo have a list of twenty-two people to be arrested in Szczebrzeszyn.

Yesterday was the Feast of the Ascension. By order of the German military commandant the holy day was moved to Sunday. The same will happen with Corpus Christi. People are very upset. With the exception of city hall and German offices, everything was closed anyway. People celebrated the holy day feast as always.

May 24   Yesterday we again had news that America had declared war against Germany, but no confirmation.

Today several German officers and soldiers from the Air Force Sanitary Unit visited the hospital and requested to see the spotted typhus cases. I took them in groups of three through the infectious wards.

May 25   Today the Germans brought to the morgue the body of a soldier who had drowned in the river.

May 26   Today the city commandant, as chief of civil defense, called a meeting of several people involved in the preparation of defense of the city. Present were Dr. Likowski, Dr. Spoz, fire chief Ostrowski, and me. He informed us that on May 29 a special alert will be called to check the readiness of groups involved in civil defense of the city. The fire brigade, sanitary squads, and hospital will be involved. He read to us the instructions received from the district civil defense office. Now I can readily see that the Germans are preparing civil defenses very well and in detail, and they expect air attacks. But still there is no news about war activities. The rumor about America going to war was just that, a rumor. Today not even

Germans commented about it. No newspapers were delivered today, so we do not know what is occurring around the world.

May 27 Since early morning you can sense excitement. Last night the gestapo ordered wagons with good horses. Last night in Radecznica the secretary of the commune, Wasniewski, and in Podlesie, young Pruffer, were arrested. Around 10 A.M. I received a warning that I would be arrested along with postmaster Pazdziora and Mayor Hejno. Some people asked me to leave town and hide for a few days. I was thankful for their good intentions but said no. In today's hospital situation with the typhus epidemic my duty is to stay here. But I prepared myself for the possibility of arrest. I waited for it the entire day. Against my daily routine I did not type any notes.

I received bad news. In the Zamosc prison Dr. Marian Sulewski, from Jzbica, died of spotted typhus. In Tomaszow Dr. Cybulski was arrested again, and in Janow Dr. Kuczewski was put into prison.

May 30 Yesterday an air-raid alert was called to check the readiness of our civil defense, including the blackout of all windows. Sorry to say that this was much better organized and performed than the one in August 1939. At that time people ignored the possibility of war. But now, after the experiences of September 1939, and because of German pressure, everyone responded and the alert went very smoothly.

Today at 8 A.M. there was a fire alert. The fire was supposed to be in an apartment next to the hospital and a bomb was supposed to have wounded several people at the marketplace. The fire brigade responded to the fire call and the civil defense squad helped the wounded. The drill was accomplished but still there was some minor disorganization.

New arrests occurred in Zamosc. In Szczebrzeszyn gestapo activities are increasing. What will happen in the future is anybody's guess. Now not only men but also some women hide at night.

Food prices are rising. A hundredweight of flour is 800 zloty, a pound of tobacco leaves, 120 zloty.

Today again more troops moved through Szczebrzeszyn.

May 31 Today's news: at 8 A.M. diplomatic relations between Germany and Soviet Russia were broken. The military traffic that has been so heavy on the highways increased even more. On the highway next to the hospital, military vehicles passed—heavy guns, tanks, squad cars, pontoons, trucks loaded with soldiers and supplies. Today, just before noon, the border guards from around Belzec were seen moving west, in the opposite direction.

More traffic signs have been posted. There was one of special interest to everyone. It was posted on a highway curve near the hospital. It read in German, "*Gefährliche Kurve*"; in English, "Dangerous Turn"; but in direct translation to Polish, "Dangerous Whore."

June

June 1   We spent another day filled with excitement. I was awakened by my wife around 4 A.M. She told me that Germans were in the lobby and asking to see me. I dressed quickly, took my physician's white coat, said good-bye to my wife and son, and went to see what was going on. As I left my quarters I was confronted by a gestapo officer, a sergeant of the gendarmes, and two gendarmes armed with rifles. The gestapo officer asked me about an old retired hospital helper, Jozef Waszczak, who still lived on the grounds of the hospital, and also about Michal Krukowski. I explained that I did not know Michal Krukowski and that he was not a patient in the hospital. I was asked to show my ID and ordered to go with one of the Germans to look for Krukowski. I still wore my physician's white coat as we left. The gendarmes locked my wife inside our quarters so that she was unable to see where they were taking me.

On the street the gestapo man was very nervous. He wanted Krukowski. He was so mad that a few times he pulled my beard, but being prepared for the worst, that was not so bad.

No one was out walking at that time of the morning. I saw only a few groups like ours walking slowly from one house to the next. I was sure this was a special search on Zamojska Street, but there wouldn't be too many arrests because many people were hiding.

The gestapo man ordered me to start knocking on doors asking for Krukowski, so I went from door to door. People were not willing to open doors or windows.

At the Kimaczynski apartment we woke up some German officers who were staying there. Then one of the gendarmes told me to try the house of a small restaurant owner. Finally at the house of Mrs. Marszycka I learned that Krukowski was not Michal but Feliks and that he was a driver with the fire brigade who was living at the fire station. We found him sleeping, and after a short interrogation the Germans ordered him to dress. All of us went to the marketplace where several more groups such as ours were already assembled. In one I saw Dr. Likowski with a small suitcase. In a short while we were escorted to the gestapo headquarters.

There was very heavy traffic on the way there. At the office of the local gestapo commandant several high-ranking officers were talking with a few individuals in civilian clothes who spoke good Polish. A few guards with rifles and one with a machine gun stood watching us. I noticed several people I knew, and more were coming in.

Everyone was called in for a short interrogation and their personal information was noted on separate pieces of paper. Through the movement of an officer's finger I was called to the table a few times. But my name was not on a certain piece of paper he was holding so I was told to wait. I noticed two men standing facing the wall. One was engineer Stanislaw Kobielski from Brody; the other was my medic, Zdzislaw Cielecki.

Too many people were assembled in the office so we were told to move to the marketplace where we were loaded onto a large truck with long benches. We sat there waiting. I was still wearing my white coat when somebody handed me an overcoat. The truck was filling up fast.

I noticed the following people around me: Dr. Wladyslaw Likowski; accountant Ksawery Leszczynski, who never lost his good humor; Galka, an employee of the Alwa plant; Pozdzik, Galka's eighteen-year-old cousin; a court clerk, Lucjan Drozd; Piasecki, director of a bank in Bilgoraj; owner and engineer at the Alwa plant Aleksander Waligora; university student and medic in my hospital Zdzislaw Cielecki; a retired hospital helper, Jozef Waszczuk; a policeman and German informer, Brzescinski, who had been involved in many searches and arrests and who was hated by Jews and Poles alike; a merchant, Feliks Wiatrowski; Chief of Police Antczak; diner owner Mr. Zeidicowa; Lucjan Michalski, released only a few days ago from a Warsaw prison; Jan Kubielski; glazier Mrozowski; and merchant Kriukow. Also there were a few more unknown to me.

When finally everyone was inside a gestapo man began reading names from forms prepared during the interrogation. My form was not there because I was never interrogated. When he finished I told him that I was not on the list. He looked at me, spoke with a gendarme standing next to him, then told me to get off the truck. I did this as quickly as possible and took with me my small suitcase. I gave my one loaf of bread to my medic. A gendarme took me to the gestapo officer who had conducted the interrogations. He was ready to leave but stayed to ask me questions. He finally told me to go home. He did not have to tell me twice. As fast as I could I started toward home, but after maybe 100 yards I was stopped by a German soldier. He ordered me to go with him. We went to the gate of one of the apartment houses where another solider stood guard over a young Jew lying on the pavement. The soldier asked me if I was now free and told me to take care of this wounded man. I ran as fast as I could to the hospital. In a few minutes I was back with a stretcher. The German soldiers were still there waiting. The young Jew was taken to the hospital. He had a wound in his thigh that had completely shattered his bones. In the presence of the Germans he had not uttered a sound, even when he was laid on the stretcher. I know that his pain was not easy to withstand. During surgery two gendarmes entered the operating room to take his name and address.

So in one moment I changed from a prisoner into a physician. I was still on the street when my wife and son joined me. They stayed close to the truck and waited. My wife had been hurt by a blow to her back. We were together again. This was the third time I had escaped from the claws of the Germans.

At home I was told what had occurred during my absence. First about my medic. The Germans had not even asked about him. When he learned that the Germans were in the hospital, he dressed himself and left through the window. But instead of hiding somewhere in the garden, he jumped over the wall and began running in the direction of Blonie. After a few minutes he was stopped by a military guard. The guard took him to the gestapo, where he was held as an escapee.

With administrator Cichonski it was a completely different story. A nurse notified him when the Germans took me from the hospital. He dressed and waited. A short while later a gestapo official came, this time asking for him. Again a nurse notified him and escorted him to the infectious ward. From there he escaped through the window and hid in the garden. During this time the Germans searched his room. They returned three times, searching other rooms, including my study and the kitchen area. In his room the search was very elaborate, even to the point of removing the floorboards. When they left they locked the room and took the key with them. The only item taken was a briefcase containing 4,000 zloty. Now we must wait for a special commission to enter the room.

It was difficult for me to begin normal work, but at the same time it was necessary to put myself in control, especially after losing the help of my medic and administrator. It is difficult to express my feelings. This can be done only by someone with literary experience and time, but not through short notes such as mine.

During the day I received information about arrests in Zwierzyniec. The following people were arrested: forest inspector Tomasz Kietlinski, forest ranger Michalic; and two brothers, Bohun and Marian Gulinski. Stanislaw Dubicki, an employee of the Zamoyski estate, was killed during an escape. When he saw the gendarmes he began to run. The Germans began shooting and hit him, but he kept running. Finally, while crossing the river, he collapsed. He died on the other side. With his death the underground lost a good man. He was a squad leader.

More people were arrested in other villages, but I do not know their names. In our town there will be many more people arrested, even though many men do not sleep at home.

June 2   After yesterday's experience I still feel very disturbed. Even now I cannot control myself. It is so hard to concentrate, but I have so much work that I am sitting in my office and writing even though it is midnight.

June 3   Today at 6 A.M. I was already at work in the hospital. I am still not used to the absence of my medic and my administrator. I have to do everything myself.

This afternoon the *Kreishauptmann* from Bilgoraj County came by, along with Dr. Snacki. I had to give a report about yesterday's happenings. They are trying to secure the release of Dr. Likowski and my medic. I hope they will succeed.

I went with Dr. Snacki to the village of Big Brody, 1.5 km from Szczebrzeszyn, where the German teacher Otto Wojan came down with spotted typhus. We visited his quarters and also talked with one of the two female German teachers. We visited the school area. This is only a ten-year-old school. All buildings have been taken over by the German military, but one large room is reserved as a classroom for German settlers. I saw a large picture of Hitler and a huge swastika on the wall.

In all the surrounding villages the Germans are confiscating grain, potatoes, and mostly livestock. Dr. Snacki told me what had happened in Goraj, where the Germans were taking food from the Polish people. When the Germans searched one of the houses an old woman would not give up her loaf of bread. She refused to give it to the Germans, holding it close to her chest. One soldier started to shoot. She fell, still holding the bread. So the soldier shot through the bread and killed her. She was buried holding the loaf of bread to her chest.

On the Feast of the Pentecost the SS in Rudka, near Zwierzyniec, began a real pogrom against the Jews. Several were beaten and their possessions were taken or destroyed. A few Polish people were also hurt, but three Jews were killed.

June 4   In relation to the escape of administrator Cichonski, I received a visit from Captain "Piotr" (later called "Adam"), who is commandant of our region of the underground's so-called Home Army. He came to find out what was still in Chichonski's room. He was particularly interested in some photographs. He was a good looking, very well built, a very self-confident, tall man—a typical professional soldier. I spoke with him in the hospital office behind closed doors. I asked him to undress and even signed a prescription so that in the event of German intrusion it would appear to be a normal physical examination.

We are living like hunted animals. Because of so many arrests in so many different places, you can see complete disorganization and chaos, and people are losing any energy to fight back. Everyone is sure that if not today then maybe tomorrow they will be arrested. Most men go to work only part-time, trying to stay home as much as possible. At night they leave town. I stay at the hospital without going out. But I am not thinking about hiding or escape. I am prepared for the worst. At night I have my small suitcase next to my bed. We are all very nervous and very tired. Only hospital work keeps me going.

The gestapo search the town constantly. Today again a new group arrived.

June 5 This morning a gestapo official visited the hospital—the same one who had searched Cichonski's room—to give me the room key. I refused to accept it, saying that by order of the *Kreishauptmann* everything in the room had to be cataloged. He was angry, even cursing obscenities when he left. Not too long after his departure a three-person commission arrived from Bilgoraj, including the German deputy *Kreishauptmann*, inspector Hulak, and the accountant Podolinska. Soon two gestapo men joined them. I recognized one. He was an investigator at the Rotunda in Zamosc. Both gestapo men stayed outside the hospital, probably afraid to enter because of typhus. The county people took the key to Cichonski's room and we all entered. The deputy *Kreishauptmann* excused himself and disappeared.

In Cichonski's room all the accounting books, receipts, and other items belonging to the hospital were separated from his belongings. Then the rooms were again closed and sealed. All items removed were carefully counted and described.

Yesterday gestapo officials searched houses occupied by known Communists and their sympathizers. The Jew Goldman was arrested because his son is now in Soviet Russia. Along with him Sawic from Szperowka was arrested.

This evening more gestapo arrived. I received news that a large truck usually used to transport prisoners is now in town, to be prepared in case of arrests. I repacked all my personal items into a rucksack because luggage is not allowed anymore.

On the highway and side roads there is heavy military traffic.

June 6 I have much work. From early morning until late at night I was at the hospital. Finally I retired to my quarters.

Night approaches and the time for night searches and arrests is getting closer. People again are leaving the city for their nightly wandering. They are exhausted, both physically and mentally.

June 7   Because of unusually heavy military traffic, all civilian movement was halted for several hours. You can see many different types of troops. They seem to be traveling in the direction of Zamosc. Only empty vehicles travel in the direction of Zwierzyniec; occasionally a motorcycle or passenger car does also. The situation is the same as during a war when large fighting units begin to move.

We received news from people arrested a week ago that an epidemic of spotted typhus is growing in Zamosc prison. I have lost any hope that Dr. Likowski and my medic will be released.

June 8   Today is Sunday, a very quiet day.

June 10   Two days passed without any excitement. From Zamosc came some rumors that in prison my medic was beaten so severely that he lost consciousness. The whole town is feeling sad because of that. Now I can see how much people really appreciated his work at the hospital.

In Zwierzyniec Mrs. Ribenbauerowa, an evacuee from Pozman, was arrested. She had been very close to the German administrator of the Zamoyski estate, Streich. She owns a small diner in Zwierzyniec.

June 11   Highway traffic is still very heavy day and night. I have never seen anything such as this in my entire life.

In Szczebrzeszyn the free market was called off for the fourth week.

June 12   Last night more troops were being moved, all in the direction of Zamosc. Around 2 A.M. the military orchestra began playing German military songs. Singing, shouting, and tremendous noise continued all night long. On all public roads civilian traffic is prohibited. Only people walking or riding on bicycles are allowed; no horse-drawn wagons.

Today I had a surprise visit. Around noon a tall, well-dressed man in his thirties arrived at the hospital and asked for a private conversation with me. I remember seeing him a few times, and I was aware that he is involved in underground activities.

When we were alone in my office he told that the 4,000 zloty taken from Cichonski by the gestapo belonged to his organization and that I had to give him that amount of money. I was completely shocked and told him that I was unable to give him that money. Then he gave me ten minutes to change my mind. If I didn't give him the money he would send some of his people and take it by force. I was outraged and said that I would not give in to any kind of threats. The conversation we were involved in was long. He spoke loudly and with arrogance. I was calm and self-controlled. I told him that I should really throw him out of my office, but knowing that he too was under pressure, I did not. Finally he calmed down. He told me how he had been treated in a German prison. He now had to find the means to support several people of the underground, giving monetary support to families of prisoners. After a long conversation I agreed to give him 500 zloty as my donation and another 700 zloty as a personal loan to be paid back in three weeks. After a few more minutes of conversation he left.

An hour later a man named Antoni Koczan came to pick up the money. He brought with him receipts written on pieces of thin cigarette paper, signed by county commandant Wisman.

This whole incident and particularly the way the money was requested seemed really fishy to me; and this person, the "county commandant," left a very unpleasant feeling.

June 13   Today the gestapo arrested Feliks Krukowski. He was taken to Zamosc prison. From the prison we received news that the release of Dr. Likowski and my medic was temporarily impossible. From information I received it appears the rumors about medic Cielecki's beating were not quite true.

From Auschwitz we received information about the death of farmer Michal Adamiec, from Kawenczyn, and store owner Huzar, from Bilgoraj.

Traffic on the highways is still very heavy. The number of tanks and motorized equipment is unbelievable. More troops are arriving in Szczebrzeszyn every day. Several apartments were evacuated to house them. Even city offices were forced to move out to the small school building.

In the hospital cellar, by request of the city commandant, a new stairway was built and a telephone installed. Another telephone was installed on the church tower, close to the hospital. It is possible that the hospital cellar will be used as a shelter for German staff officers.

During the last twelve days I was so busy in the hospital and so nervously tired that I was unable to do any mental work. My writing has stopped. Finally, yesterday I once again began working on my memoirs. But the work is going very slowly. I was hardly able to put even a few sentences on paper.

June 14   Today I stood on top of the hospital wall and observed the military traffic. In one hour, around noon, between 500 and 600 vehicles passed by, but in the afternoon the infantry began marching. As I observed I asked myself, Where are these troops coming from and where are they going? When will this war finally start? And what will the future bring us?

Yesterday the gestapo searched a small factory and house owned by engineer Kobielski. No one of the Kobielski family was home, so they arrested an old man and a sick teacher, Stafania Lewandowska, who was staying there as a guest. During the search the gestapo behavior was brutal. The teacher was hit in the face several times.

June 18   The last few days passed quietly. Traffic has been slowing down. Last night was very nice and peaceful. There were no trucks or cars on the road and no patrols on the streets. But today we have noticed an increase in air traffic. More airplanes are coming to Klemensow and the other nearby airfields.

Food prices are rising. More stores stay closed every day because the merchants do not like to sell at the legal price.

Some people are still trying to leave the city. There is a general feeling that Szczebrzeszyn will be a dangerous place to be because of the surrounding airfields. But people who have left the city are facing a new danger. Robberies are increasing. So either way is no good, if you stay or if you flee.

June 19   Today is the first anniversary of last year's mass arrests. I am trying to remember everything, even the smallest details of my stay in the Rotunda prison in Zamosc and particularly the other people who were there. I feel very sad when I think about all the killing and death of last year. I am still remembering my friend Rosinski.

The highway traffic is increasing and so is the air traffic. Everyone, even the Germans, are talking about the upcoming war with the Soviets.

Today a new mayor, selected by the Germans, arrived in Szczebrzeszyn. He is Andreas Kraus, a Ukrainian, now a so-called *Volksdeutsch*. He stopped in a few times. He speaks Polish very well.

June 21   Since 10 P.M. last night very heavy tanks and other armed vehicles rumbled without interruption, almost throughout the entire night.

At 7 A.M. I received instructions from Bilgoraj County to have the hospital ready for any event. I must be prepared to admit large numbers of wounded. Because of this all Jews who are ill with spotted typhus must be moved to two Jewish buildings across from the hospital. German police and "blue police" began evacuating the tenants of those buildings, giving them thirty minutes to pack and move out. Policeman Tatulinski was very active in this evacuation.

Around noon I went to city hall to talk about food supplies for the hospital. Everyone there is working on improvements and organization of the civil defense system. On the highways traffic is increasing. All vehicles are traveling in the direction of Zamosc. Once in a while abnormal congestion stops the traffic completely.

Gendarmes arrived at the hospital to check on our readiness and also to check the cellar.

All civil defense units, fire brigades, and sanitary units are on full alert. All street vendor stands have been removed. New anti-aircraft trenches are being dug. At night members of the civil defense units are allowed to go home.

Late at night traffic began slowing down. German soldiers began checking the window blackouts. Around 10 P.M. they arrived to investigate why one of our windows was lit up. Across from the hospital the German officer quarters were blacked out also.

June 22, 8 A.M.   At 1 A.M. heavy bombers from the surrounding airfields took off toward the east. Until 4 A.M. the constant roar of the bombers and the planes was hard to endure. We are sure that war between Germany and Russia has begun.

At 6 A.M. I went to see what was going on in town. Everything now is completely quiet. Even the highway traffic is down to a minimum. No one knows anything for sure, but some people are anticipating Russian air strikes.

June 22, 9 P.M.   People are talking. Some are saying that this is only a general alert. Others say that the war has already started.

There is heavy traffic again; above us there are many planes. Finally, from a few railroad workers I learned that the war has indeed begun. A railroad engineer, Borowicz, told me that he had to report tomorrow at Rawa Ruska railroad station, and Rawa Ruska is on the other side of the Bug River, in the area now occupied by the Soviets.

We have new police hours, from 7 P.M. until 5 A.M. All windows must be blacked out and all civil defense units are on full alert. People fear a Soviet air attack taking place tonight. Highway traffic is extremely heavy. Planes are flying very low and are noisy. We await whatever will come.

June 23   Last night again we heard the tremendous roar of the flying bombers. We would like to find out any news about the fighting but we hear only rumors. To note them all would be impossible and would take several pages.

The fact is that Soviet troops are fighting. The railroad workers who were supposed to go to Rawa Ruska are staying in Zawada. The situation has changed and trains are only going as far as Krasnobrod, not even as far as Belzec.

June 24   Last night again large tanks came by, one by one in a long row. The weight of each one is so much that the roadway is being completely destroyed. Until now the roadway was holding up, but it is clear that in a few days even light cars will have trouble using it. Outside the city you can hear the artillery and other detonations. We have no news yet about the fighting. All high-ranking officers, including a few generals, left the city in the direction of Blonie.

Because of the damaged roadway, traffic on the highway is slowing down and German road patrols are having a hard time regulating it.

Tonight there are very few Germans left in town. The soldiers began removing telephone lines.

June 25   Today passed quietly. Traffic is slow. Most German troops have left; others are preparing to leave. Some houses taken over by German officers were returned to the owners. The gendarmes began packing, using Jews for help. It is a difficult situation to understand, since we do not have any news about the front, only rumors. Today there were more airplane flights.

Today one Soviet aircraft was spotted above the airfield. Now by order of the German air force no one has the right to approach the perimeter of any airfield. Soldiers on guard duty have orders to shoot anyone approaching, without any warning.

By order of the military commandant homeowners must dig an anti-aircraft trench near their houses.

Some people say that Russian troops will advance and we will again be in Russian hands.

June 26   Last night was quiet. Since early morning heavy motorized traffic continues. German papers are not printing anything from the German-Russian front.

June 28   Yesterday passed quietly. There was heavy traffic on the highway but only in the direction of Zamosc. Air traffic was very limited.

Today I received from Bilgoraj an order to prepare the hospital for the admission of around fifty wounded Russian soldiers.

Yesterday around 3 P.M. the military command left the city. All buildings occupied by the troops were vacated. The high school building was wide open. People ran there to take anything left by the Germans, especially straw mattresses. I requested fifty mattresses from the police, but I was told that because they are military property the police have nothing to do with it. Later, the new mayor, Kraus, sent to the hospital twenty-eight mattresses and some straw. Now I can prepare for the Russian wounded.

Again around 10 P.M. more tanks passed by the hospital. Under the weight of these monsters the whole road shook. Our old hospital withstood the vibrations. Only some dishes fell from the shelves, otherwise no damage. The roadway is completely destroyed. The concrete sidewalk is broken into small pieces. The tanks stopped at Blonie and Kawenczyn, where small houses were severely damaged.

This morning came new orders from Bilgoraj. I must prepare the hospital for 100 wounded Russian soldiers, not 50. We started to lay mattresses on the floor because all the beds are occupied.

On the main highway and near the hospital the traffic is terrible. We feel something in this continuous movement that was unknown until now: tension. It is all very tiring. We do not know anything for certain about what is really occurring. From the Germans you cannot get any information at all. They are not talking.

June 29 Nothing new today. The constant traffic is so tiring that some people are beginning to show signs of nervous breakdown. No news from the front, and the fighting already is in the eighth day.

Ambulances passing through town are transporting German wounded. From Zamosc I received notice that because Dr. Bogucki's hospital now has 160 Russians I can expect a transport at any time.

Last night came a new announcement. All men, Aryan and Jews alike, between the ages of fifteen and sixty must report for work at the airfield.

Today the commandant of gendarmes inspected our cellars. In one of them he wants to establish a new operating room. At the same time he ordered me to assign a room for thirty patients who might be injured by gas.

July

July 1 Today for the first time newspapers printed an official military communiqué. German troops are advancing and took the following cities: Kowno, Wilno, Brzesc, Dynaburg, Kowel, and others. People are sad because everyone wished the Russian troops well, hoping the Germans would take heavy losses.

Around town everything is normal, but more and more bombers are flying east.

July 3 No news. Some people say that a Russian counteroffensive recaptured Kowno, Wilno, Brzesc, and Lwow.

Today from Zamosc prison the following people were released; Kriukow, Michalski, Galka, and Pozdzik.

Our town seems totally deserted. The military is gone. The mayor moved back to city hall. Most people have returned to their homes. Traffic is very light.

July 4 Tonight bandits robbed the Wroblewski farm in Gorajec, wounding one person. A second robbery took place in Sulow where the commune office was attacked. During the shooting with police one bandit was killed.

At the hospital a gestapo official tried to find out where the wife of hospital administrator Cichonski is now living.

There is no more talk about a Russian counteroffensive. It appears the Germans are advancing.

Everything is quiet in town. There are not many military vehicles; it seems that the military reserves have already passed through Szczebrzeszyn. What we see now are big trucks hauling destroyed aircraft.

July 5 Today I went to the forestry station in Kosbudy for firewood for the hospital. In the forest everything is so quiet that I really enjoyed my journey. It is hard to imagine that such quiet places still exist in Poland.

July 6 Today is Sunday, but at the hospital routine work makes it like any other normal workday. I do not like Sundays anymore. I am irritated by people who dress up and walk the city streets without any purpose.

We read all the German newspapers to learn what is occurring on the German-Russian front. This war is the main topic of all conversation; no one talks about anything else.

I personally am very tired. I try to separate myself from all the daily tasks and concentrate on my work of writing memoirs of the Zamosc region. I sometimes have to force myself to work; at the same time I realize I don't have much time left. I type all manuscripts in duplicate hoping that maybe one copy will survive.

July 8 A few days ago schoolteacher Tuckendorf found an artillery shell. He tried to disarm it, but it exploded and a piece of it hit him in the vicinity of the heart. He was killed instantly. Yesterday was his funeral and many people attended.

Late yesterday evening a German flyer shot a young twenty-two-year-old Jewish woman to death. Naturally, not only Jews but the whole population is very much disturbed by this crime. During the funeral probably every Jewish woman from Szczebrzeszyn took part.

On the highway there is practically no traffic. It appears the troops have advanced to their new positions. So far we have not received any wounded Soviet soldiers. I personally feel that we will not receive any.

July 11   During the last few days nothing much has happened, so I didn't work on my diary. Because of the very light traffic it seems to me that the front has moved far to the east. Now we can concentrate on our domestic situation.

I received news about some of the prisoners in Zamosc prison. My medic works with the prison gardener, so he is outside his cell all day. More and more prisoners are ill with spotted typhus. Pilat, the owner of a small store in Brody, died of it. Rev. Gomolka from Zamosc and accountant Podwinski are very sick. They have not been moved to the hospital but are now in an isolation cell, without any medical attention. Engineer Aleksander Waligora was moved to the prison in Lublin. Last week an accountant from Bilgoraj, Kucharski, was arrested. He is very popular.

This morning we received news that in the future there will be an amnesty. So many letters were sent to the governor general and to the Polish Relief Committee in Cracow begging for the release of prisoners. I sent a formal request for the release of my medic, but I have no hope that it will help.

I admitted more Jews with symptoms of spotted typhus. One of them is named Wulf Badzzdrow ("Badzzdrow" means "Be in good health").

July 14   Because of successes on the Eastern Front, we again are allowed to use railroad trains. Police hours are changed. We can walk freely from 4 A.M. to 10 P.M. During the last few days no one obeyed the curfew hours. People walked about until late at night.

July 17   I have only bad news to note: new arrests. In Zamosc I was told arrests were limited to former Polish military personnel, mostly retired officers and sergeants. Surveyor Stanislaw Czerski and high school custodian Tracz were arrested. Accountant Podwinski died in prison from spotted typhus. The gestapo are constantly snooping around Szczebrzeszyn. They searched the home of school principal Kopyciak in Brody. He was not home at the time of the search, so he is still free. Tension is mounting; no one knows what will happen tomorrow.

July 18   In Szczebrzeszyn a visiting farmer, Wroblewski, from Gorajec, was arrested. The gestapo are looking for four young teachers, all members of the underground: Turowski, Pozdzik, Koczon, and Kryk. They were able to slip away.

July 19 Today the gestapo again searched the homes of the four teachers, but they have disappeared.

July 25 The gestapo are searching for another teacher, Turowska, who was married only a few days ago. She and her husband, Rajewski, and court clerk Postulski, have disappeared.

Yesterday a new medic, Tadeusz Blachuta, a former cadet from the Polish Military Medical Academy, began working in my hospital. Since the outbreak of the war he has been working as a deputy forest ranger in Bilgoraj.

July 28 The days are very monotonous so I don't have much to write about.

Yesterday I went to Zwierzyniec. The Germans are gone. On the highway there was very light traffic. Speaking with some of the people I learned some local news about the behavior of a few executives of the Zamoyski estate and their wives. The name that was mentioned most often was Maria Kostecka, wife of the director of forestry. She is seen constantly in the presence of German officers and even invites them to special parties in their honor.

We are receiving unconfirmed reports about German defeats on the Eastern Front.

August

August 4 For the last few days I have been busy writing my memoirs of the past twenty years. It is difficult to compare life today with life as it was before. Just after World War I we began rebuilding our nation. We worked hard, knowing that we were building a strong Poland. Today we work hard also but only to survive and help others survive.

Today's life is very repetitive, filled with anxiety and restlessness, and only faith in our victory keeps us fighting for survival. I am the lucky one. I can work in my profession to help people and still have time for writing my memoirs and history of the Zamosc region during the years between the two wars.

No concrete news. I cannot trust the German newspapers. The military situation has changed so no one is expecting a Soviet attack. We feel that the front has moved farther east.

All civil defenses were demobilized as of August 1. But the Germans are counting on the possibility of gas being used in the future. At the hospital we received brand-new gas masks for all hospital personnel with instructions (in German) on how to use them.

There is practically no military in Szczebrzeszyn. Only once in a while the airmen from the nearby fields come into town. Especially at night they begin drinking, making lots of noise, and beating Jews.

August 6   After a few quiet days there is new excitement. At 8 A.M. all those who had received a summons to report for departure for labor in Germany were supposed to report. No one showed up. This was a free market day and the streets were filled with villagers. The Germans began arresting people and taking them to a large, empty warehouse. Several people were beaten. The so-called Polish "blue police" helped the Germans with this. About 200 people were arrested, but only 100, mostly young women and girls, were taken by truck to the railroad station in Zwierzyniec. Throughout the entire city people were hiding and trying to escape. Many people came to the hospital hoping that here they would be safe. We watched this with clenched fists and grinding of teeth.

August 9   Yesterday from Zamosc I received information that around twenty people were moved from the prison to an unknown place. Among them were Dr. Likowski, medic Cielecki, Kobielski, and Zamosc mayor Wazowski. I have lost all hope of their release.

Twenty specialists from the sugar refinery in Klemensow received summonses to report to the labor bureau. The chief engineer sent a request asking that they be exempt from any labor in German camps. We are expecting new arrests.

August 10   A nightmare has hit us. Word has it that all twenty people removed from the Zamosc prison were shot. I cannot believe this. I am sure, at least I hope, that this is gossip, but you can expect anything from the Germans. I am very much disturbed.

About the twenty specialists from Klemensow: when they arrived at the labor bureau they received special cards. The cards stated that the specialists are vital to German victory and cannot be removed or shipped elsewhere.

August 21   A few days have gone by without anything too much out of the ordinary, so I decided not to write. The rumor about the execution of twenty prisoners still has not been confirmed.

I received new orders. Now all women are to be released from the hospital after their venereal disease has been reported to the labor bureau. Today for the first time a clerk from that organization came to the hospital for three women. They will be sent to labor camps in Germany.

Yesterday Dr. Witold Gadzikowicz, a professor of hygiene from Warsaw, going on vacation to one of the nearby villages, stopped by to visit. He is a very pleasant, older gentleman. We talked for several hours. He has not given up under the pressure of very difficult living conditions. He is working on several new books to be printed after the war. One is a new handbook of hygiene.

September

September 3   After a very nerve-wracking and demanding two years of work without any interruption I decided to take a vacation. I had to sign a special request form for the *Kreishauptmann* in Bilgoraj, who, after asking me some questions, finally gave me twelve days of vacation. I decided to go to Warsaw. The last time I was in our capital was July 1939. I was a little afraid of this journey, knowing that in today's situation travel by train is not very pleasant.

On Sunday, August 24, I went to the train station to get reservations for the 4 A.M. train to Warsaw. There were many people waiting even though the cashier's window was closed. When the departure time passed I went through the private door into the cashier's room. The cashier was sleeping on one bench and another railroad employee was sleeping on the other. I woke up the cashier and he told me that because of a locomotive breakdown we can expect a minimum three-hour delay. So I went home, intending to be back at the station around 8 A.M. When I came back I learned that the train had been canceled. So I went home again. Finally around noon I was able to buy a ticket for the second-class seats (first class was reserved only for the Germans). With difficulty I was able to get into the car, but I was forced to stand in the corridor. At every station more and more people tried to get in.

In Rejowiec we were supposed to change trains, but because of the mass of people ready to switch I decided to take the same train to Chelm and from there take another to Warsaw. I was lucky because I finally got a seat.

On the train I observed behavior I was not used to. Passengers shouted at each other, and the types of obscene words exchanged between them were far beyond my vocabulary. Women were the main artists when it came to this way of talking. Almost all the passengers were petty smugglers who knew all the tricks of the trade.

I stayed in my seat until we arrived in Warsaw. The cars were without any lights; all stations had very dim lamps. In Warsaw there were no lights either. Finally I was able to rent a so-called ricksha. The ricksha is a World War II invention. It is a three-wheeled bicycle with a seat for two passengers in front and a driver who pedals in the rear. All streets were completely dark so I had a hard time orienting myself as to where we were going. After a one-hour ride I finally reached my nephew Jan Klukowski's house.

Early the next day I started on my walks through Warsaw. Leaving my nephew's house on the Sixth of August Boulevard I noticed a burned-out building, the Ministry of Defense, but the sight of one destroyed building cannot be compared to whole streets in ruins, like Nowy Swiat, Krakowskie Przedmiescie, Pilsudski Place, and others. The ruins have been cleaned up; debris from the streets and sidewalks has been covered with plywood. But the worst for me to see were the ruins of the royal castle.

I passed through the Jewish ghetto a few times. It is almost impossible to figure out how something like this can happen. All points of entry are guarded by Germans. High brick walls around the perimeter divide the Jewish ghetto from the rest of the city. Traffic on the streets is rather heavy; many stores are open. That's how it looks from a streetcar. A few streetcars go through the ghetto but without stopping. From a friend of mine I learned that the mortality rate in the ghetto is very high, especially among the poor Jews, who are living in terrible conditions.

Before coming to Warsaw I was told that the cost of living here is very high. The prices are high on many items and out of reach for the average person, but with enough money you can buy anything. In the restaurants prices are not so high, so even by paying the legal price you can have a good meal, but the quantity is very small. In general I have to say that while staying in Warsaw for a total of seven days I was never hungry, and I didn't have to spend too much money on food. It is difficult to get bread or fat, but vegetables are cheaper than in Szczebrzeszyn.

The worst financial situation is among the so-called intellectuals and the people with fixed incomes. Pensions are very small and many retirees are very hungry. Some people exist solely on soup given through charity organizations and churches. People dress worse than before the war. Most wear old clothes because to buy new ones would be too expensive. But you can still see some very elegantly dressed people, because many speculators are making good money on the black market.

I was really surprised to see how the streetcars were operating. As a rule most people don't buy tickets. The conductors are not in a rush to sell tickets. Those who do buy them return them to the conductor who sells them a second time. The reason for this is simple: all profits from streetcar operations go to the Germans. Many people don't pay, saying that they will never support the German economy.

Making a living is most difficult for university professors, artists, and others who have little practical knowledge of surviving. As an example, Prof. Wladzimierz Antoniewicz, chancellor of Warsaw University, is working as a stocker in the boiler room of a building. Prof. Henryk Moscicki is selling his collection of books. Graphic artist Tadeusz Cieslewski is working as a waiter in a small restaurant owned by Puchalski, located on the corner of Chmielna and Zgoda streets. One day we went there to speak with him. Of course, he has had enough of that kind of work, but he is glad that he has at least that as a means of survival. He has begun writing novels and has a nice collection of manuscripts. He is still full of energy and hopes to publish as soon as the war ends. I can give several similar examples.

I was lucky to be able to meet with some of my old friends. Former county administrator Pryzinski is now in real-estate sales. In September 1939, as a colonel in the army reserve, he was called to active duty and was badly wounded in the head. Zubowicz, a very popular attorney from Zamosc and a former senator, is now a notary public.

What I was looking for was to meet people engaged in selling books. I was able to admire collections of books and prints dedicated to the 1831 uprising, owned by Ludwik Gocel, and ex libris collections of Prof. Tadeusz Wolski. I met with Dr. Konopka, noted collector of books about the history of medicine. He is now working on a physician bibliography with almost a half-million entries. Adam Englert showed me his collections, which are very well known and contain memoirs and biographies, but he has only half what I have in Szczebrzeszyn.

Every Wednesday at the home of Stefan Rygiel fifteen collectors meet. I was invited into this select group and attended their forty-ninth meeting. Present were Marian Gumowski, numismatist; Stanislaw Dabrowski, historian; Krolikowski, graphic artist; Adam Englert; Slonecki, painter; Adam Solecki, numismatist; Ludwik Gocel; Wdowiszewski; Gieysztor; Kram; Cielek; Gerquin; Dr. Konopka; and me.

In a big album everyone has a page dedicated to his own collections. Because this meeting was dedicated to me, Stanislaw Dabrowski entered a new page with my initials, Z.K. I spent a few hours in a warm atmosphere with friends, something I do not have in Szczebrzeszyn.

I visited Maj. Wszelaki, the commandant of the field hospital where for a short time in 1939 I was a physician. He told me some details I was unaware of about the last few weeks at the hospital. Some of it contradicted what Bohun told me after his return to Szczebrzeszyn.

Maj. Wszelaki is very upset about Bohun. He told me that after the war he will press charges against him for stealing horses and a wagon, and for desertion. At home Bohun told me about his promotion and heroic actions.

We talked also about the last visit to Wlodzimierz on September 13, 1939, of Col. Maszadra, chief of sanitary services, and his staff. Now I can see how misinformed Maszadra was. From him I learned that the following doctors were killed. In reality Col. Dr. Tadeusz Sokolowski, surgeon, is now in England, Col. Dr. Tadeusz Kornilowicz, is now in a POW camp in Germany. Maj. Wszelaki informed me also about what happened to two other doctors that I knew from the field hospital: Dr. Witkowski was killed and Dr. Wronski, from Radom, died in a German camp. All the papers of the field hospital were destroyed, so it will be difficult to reconstruct the events.

After talking with Maj. Wszelaki I have the impression that he has already forgotten several things. Now he says that at the time the hospital was moved from Wlodzimierz he gave Dr. Modzelewski and me the order to demobilize. In reality it was not an order but rather a suggestion, leaving the final decision up to us. This decision has caused me many nervous emotions.

I met two of my close friends from the University of Moscow, attorney Jan Gadomski and his brother Jerzy, superintendent of schools in Lwow. We talked about our lives in Moscow (before World War I) and I left with them a copy of my "Memoirs from Moscow," for review and critique. I hope that with their help we can jointly publish a book about Poles in Moscow.

I stayed in Warsaw for a total of seven days and rested as never before during the last two years. Warsaw is still the capital of Poland. The amount of illegal press is very impressive. All the news from the BBC is printed twice a day. People speak Polish. You can hear German only in German offices. Some professors are writing new books and authors are writing new novels, all to be ready for printing as soon as the war is over. My nephew is working on "How to Solve the Housing Problem."

In general people in Warsaw are very positive that the end of the war will come soon. They are more informed and can take a more logical stand against any German action.

You can see propaganda slogans in many places. They are proof that the Polish population is very much opposed to German rule.

Everywhere you go, you can see a big letter *V*, put up by the Germans as a symbol for victory. Next to the letter *V* some unknown person added "*erloren*," which means "is lost."

I saw a German propaganda poster showing a destroyed Russian cross. Someone added, "So looks that cross of Christ the King destroyed by Germans in Posen."

Speaking about the Germans: the officers and soldiers are drinking heavily. Around the barracks black marketeering is growing. Soldiers sell not only items stolen from Jews, like jewelry, suits, or silverware, but also parts of their own equipment. You can even buy pistols and ammunition.

Overall I was very happy about my visit to Warsaw, but then I was afraid of the journey back home.

First I went to the west station where I obtained a third-class ticket to the central station. There I was able to buy a second-class ticket and forced myself into a seat. Our train to Rejowiec experienced a two-hour delay, but the train to Zamosc was still waiting. From there I had to stand the whole way. Finally around noon I arrived home. It is interesting that during the entire trip I was not asked once to show my ID papers. I returned home without any problem.

September 6 After returning from Warsaw I went for three days to the Siemiatkowski farm in Witniowka. While there I completely forgot about the war. When I finally returned home I became tense once again.

After coming back to my routine work at the hospital I was once again in the middle of events. First I learned that Tomasz Kietlinski, director of forestry at the Zamoyski estate, had died in Auschwitz. In Bilgoraj, inspector Hulak was arrested. The reason for his arrest was that he began collecting clothing for the families of men killed in the concentration camps.

About the people arrested in Szczebrzeszyn and then held in prison— Dr. Likowski, medic Cielicki, Kobielski, and others—there is no new information, but some people say they were all executed. This is frightening.

Yesterday all civil defense units were called for a five-week-long exercise. It looks as if the Germans are expecting some counteraction by the Russians.

Overall the feeling is optimistic. People are sure that the Germans cannot survive a winter in Russia. I am not sure, but I would like to think that we will be able to withstand German pressure.

September 13 In Auschwitz chief forest ranger Michalik died. Sawic from Szperowka and Ribenbauerowa from Zwierzyniec were released from Lublin prison. This morning Grzeszkowiak came back to Szczebrzeszyn after his release from the Dachau concentration camp. He was there for more than a year.

September 15 All the rumors about the execution of the twenty men are true.

Today the gestapo called the families of the executed to tell them sabotage was the reason for their execution.

Executed were: Dr. Wladyslaw Likowski, age fifty-four; Zdzislaw Cielecki, medic, age twenty-four; Jan Kobielski, age thirty; Ksawery Leszczynski, accountant; Lucjan Drozd, court clerk; Piasecki, accountant; Brzescinski, policeman; Mrozowski, glazier; Jan Borucki, mayor; Jozef Waszczuk, retired hospital helper, age seventy-five; and Buchaczewski, pharmacist.

From Zamosc the executed were Michal Wazowski, mayor, along with his fifteen-year-old son, and Rev. Gomolka. The other names I do not remember.

When I think about this I personally feel very lucky because I was detained with all those people on June 1. But I was able to survive. No one knows what will happen next time.

September 24   Almost ten days have passed and I have not noted anything. The same story as always: who was arrested or who died in the camps.

Naturally, I do not know the names of everyone arrested in the area. Arrested in Zamosc were: an employee of the sugar refinery, Przegalinski; in Sulowek the owner of the flour mill, Hajer; and in Tarnogrod attorney Olenski and two physicians. Last night the gendarmes requested from city hall a registration list of all inhabitants and for 1½ hours went over the list and made notes. Now everyone is asking who will be next.

Yesterday 600 Russian POWs were moved through Szczebrzeszyn. I watched them carefully; they appeared very tired and showed symptoms of malnutrition. For the night they were housed in a military barracks. Many people, Aryan and Jew alike, brought them food. One prisoner escaped.

From Auschwitz come news that policeman Sierpinski has died.

September 30   The last few hours were filled with excitement and suspense. At 6 P.M. yesterday I was notified that the gestapo came to town with several trucks, surely for searches and arrests. Many people left town to hide in the nearby villages and forest. At night I heard the Germans moving about on the sidewalk next to the hospital. They read the signs about spotted typhus and typhoid fever, so they left. But they took with them from Szczebrzeszyn barber Romanowski and from Mokre Lipy the pastor, Masztelarz. The gestapo searched for his assistant, but he escaped. From Zaklodzie they took Galezowski, owner of the flour mill; from Radecznica, Dr. Gawlik, a teacher, and Planeta, a clerk; and from Zwierzyniec, Nowosinski, director of a lumber mill, and Latomski, director of a furniture factory. Also they took the Wysocki brothers: Rog Wysocki, the owner of a diner, and Wandzio Wysocki, a butler at the Zamoyski estate.

From nearby villages there were more arrests, but the names at this time are unknown to me.

Everywhere arrests are daily routine. More people were transported to Germany for labor camps.

From the news it appears that the Germans received some setbacks and that retaliation against the Polish population is in direct connection with the gathering of Polish troops in Russia. But this is not a substantiated statement, only suspicion.

October

October 4 Yesterday another transport of Soviet POWs, around 15,000, passed through. This time it was different. They all looked like skeletons, just shadows of human beings, barely moving. I have never in my life seen anything like this. Men were falling to the street; the stronger ones were carrying others, holding them up by their arms. They looked like starved animals, not like people. They were fighting for scraps of apples in the gutter, not paying any attention to the Germans who would beat them with rubber sticks. Some crossed themselves and knelt, begging for food. Soldiers from the convoy beat them without mercy. They not only beat prisoners but also people who stood by and tried to pass along some food. After the macabre unit passed by, several horse-drawn wagons carried prisoners who were unable to walk. This unbelievable handling of human beings is only possible under German ethics. Some people said that among the prisoners there were many Polish people taken by the Russians to Siberia in 1939. Today they were forced to move farther in the direction of Zamosc.

October 5 This afternoon another group of Soviet POWs was moved through town. Because today is Sunday, many watched. Bread, apples, and other goods were placed on the sidewalks on both sides of the street. Even though the soldiers from the convoy started shooting at them while they fought for food, the prisoners did not pay any attention to the Germans. The Germans stopped the convoy and forced people to remove the food before they moved out. Finally they agreed that the food could be put on a wagon and later be divided among the prisoners.

The entire Polish population, not only the Jews, were very sympathetic to the Russian prisoners.

I can still see, even though I close my eyes, those poor Russian soldiers, looking more like the skeletons of animals than humans.

October 12 Last week another group of POWs passed through our town. After spending the night outside the barracks they were forced to march on. They took along three dying comrades. All three were dead after only a few kilometers of walking and were buried along the highway. The mayor told me that the prisoners received one pound of bread each day and no other food. Almost every day some prisoners escape. There was more shooting this time.

Nowosinski and Latomski were released from the Lublin prison.

Everyone is watching military events in Russia. The Germans say they will destroy all Russian military power before the beginning of winter; that means in a few weeks.

October 15 Today new police hours were posted. You can walk the streets only from 5 A.M. until 9 P.M. This is most likely due to the changing of clock time by one hour. The black-out of windows will now be strictly enforced.

October 16 Today a delegation from the *Judenrat* came to see me. These Jews asked me to intervene with the county officers in Bilgoraj to try to stop a Jewish physician from coming to Szczebrzeszyn. They do not want a Jewish doctor in town. The reason is this: if the city has a Jewish physician, all other doctors have no right at all to help the Jewish population. The *Judenrat* feels that the few Polish doctors in Szczebrzeszyn are doing a very good job.

October 17 Today in Zamosc Dr. Boleslaw Modzelewski died of a heart attack. He was very popular. Even though I knew him for almost twenty years we never became close until we were in the same military hospital and staying in the same room.

In the concentration camp three people died: Zygmunt Syrek, a teacher, Zolcinski, and Stasiak, all from Zamosc. The list of casualties does not end.

October 20 Today is my twenty-second anniversary as superintendent of Szczebrzeszyn hospital, a long time. It is also the second war I have survived here.

October 23 Throughout the county the epidemic of spotted typhus is spreading, mainly among the Jews. More and more sick people have been admitted to the hospital. Today the German authorities met to deal with this epidemic. Present were the county administrator, the mayor, the commandant of police, a delegate of the *Judenrat*, and all physicians, along with county Dr. Snacki. Everyone at the meeting met the new Jewish physician, Dr. Bolotny.

By direct order of the *Kreishauptmann*, the *Judenrat* must open a public bathhouse for Jews only. All Jews must shave their heads and cut off their beards. Regulations on taking baths will be organized along with a procedure for disinfecting clothing. For not complying the penalty is arrest. I just do not know how this will be accomplished. I have my doubts.

For some time there has been talk about the evacuation of several villages and the quick transport of Poles past the Bug River. How much truth is involved only the future will show. We are upset by these rumors, but from the Germans you can expect anything. Not knowing the future is nerve shattering and causes people to just quit whatever they are doing. I feel this myself.

Most of those arrested in Tarnogrod were released, including two physicians, Dr. Woyciechowski and one other. Only the teacher is still in jail. Tadeusz Burzminski, from Zamosc, died in Auschwitz.

November

November 2 The last ten days were typical working days without any unusual happenings. The epidemic of spotted typhus is spreading despite all precautions. More people were admitted to the hospital. We have no more beds or mattresses, so I was forced to put two patients into each bed. Several physicians in the area are victims of this sickness: Dr. Kuczynski, in Komorow; Dr. Rozenbush-Szpiegenglass, in Zamosc; Dr. Atlas, in Tyszowice; and a Jewish physician in Goraj.

The production of sugar in Klemensow is going full speed now. Every day the Germans take two wagons of beet by-product to feed the Russian prisoners.

November 6 Two days ago a German gendarme stopped by and asked for the address of medic Cielecki. Later he visited the widow of Dr. Likowski and gave her a few small items taken from him during his arrest. Now it is true; they were executed. It is hard to believe.

Today we experienced the first snow. It is cold and muddy. The best way to spend time is to stay home. People are afraid of winter because we lack coal and firewood. We have news from Warsaw that full transports of German soldiers are arriving there for treatment of frostbite. There is more and more talk about a German war with America.

November 8 Yesterday I received information about the evacuation of the village of Skierbieszow and a few others in Zamosc County. Today I received more information. All Poles in Sitaniec and Bialobrzegi were evacuated. This afternoon the inhabitants of Niedzielisko, a village 7 km from Szczebrzeszyn, received a German order to be ready for evacuation but to stay in their homes until then.

This news makes people very nervous. No one wants to do anything. They ask why it is necessary to work if the future is so insecure. My wife and I have gathered all necessary clothing into one place, to be ready in any event. I can see this attitude even in the hospital, where I am having a difficult time pointing out that we are here to help others. The work atmosphere is bad, and the cold is not helping; it can be felt even inside the buildings.

As for myself, I have an urge to work. During my free time I write my memoirs, hoping that somehow they will survive.

A few days ago all the German police left town with full equipment. We do not know why and where.

Rev. Masztelarz, Galezowski, Gawlik, and Planeta were released from prison.

November 9   Again there is more and more talk about evacuation. People are naming the new villages already evacuated. There are many rumors. Even though we all live so close to each other there is no way to have true information. More villagers are bringing furniture and household items to town and leaving them with relatives or friends, but here the inhabitants are not sure of the future either, especially when we have information that Zamosc is also on the list.

We hope that the Germans will be forced to give up all evacuation plans because of the situation on the Russian front.

Now I have a new worry. The new hospital administrator, Ludwik Adamski, is sick with spotted typhus. He is only thirty years old and has been working only a few months, since the escape of Cichonski. His condition is grave and I am really worried.

November 10   I admitted to the hospital a young man, Jan Radziszewski, from Przedmiesce. He was captured by the Germans around Kiev with his wagon and two horses. He was wounded and has had his right hand and part of his foot amputated.

There are more rumors about the evacuation of Szczebrzeszyn, so people have begun packing.

November 11   Early this morning we were notified that the evacuation of villages has been temporarily stopped. People find it hard to believe.

Here is more information about evacuees. The Germans treat them very badly. They are housed in military barracks in Zamosc. The mortality rate is high, particularly among the small children. We do not know for sure if this is true.

November 12   I have a slight case of the flu, so I am staying in bed. I hear rumors that in some of the villages farmers are destroying their own crops by spraying potatoes with naptha and starting fires. They are also killing their livestock. They are trying to destroy everything so the Germans will find nothing when they arrive. After the destruction the farmers move out. Some people feel this has something to do with stalling the evacuation.

November 14   My administrator is now listed as critical. We are doing everything possible, but I do not have much hope.

The German police have returned to Szczebrzeszyn. They had taken part in the evacuation of a few villages. Assistance was given to the police and soldiers by German colonists and people signed on as German nationals, the so-called *Volksdeutsch.*

In Zawada the Germans are storing more bombs in the new warehouse.

People again are talking about upcoming evacuations. They are puzzled as to why no Jews have been evacuated lately, only Poles.

November 21 Day after day passes slowly without anything substantial to report. If I were to note all the rumors, my diary would be several volumes thick.

There are more rumors about evacuations but nothing for sure. So it is unwise to write anymore about it.

Now the Jews are not sure what to think. After a relatively peaceful length of time some Jewish men were arrested yesterday and are to be transported to Germany.

The city administrator in Szczebrzeszyn received an order to remove from the registration list the names of all people executed during the last few weeks: Dr. Likowski, medic Cielecki, Brozd, Leszczynski, Piasecki, Waszczak, Borucki, Buchaczkowski, Brzescinski, Mrozowski, and Jan Kobielski.

November 25 On Saturday, November 22, the hospital celebrated something unusual. On that day I admitted the 1000th patient this year. Never before in the history of Szczebrzeszyn hospital have so many patients been admitted in a year.

On Sunday, November 23, I began feeling ill. To my own and other physicians' astonishment I had come down with diptheria, which at my age is very unusual. For two days I was very ill, but today I feel much better.

Today from Auschwitz came news about the death of butcher Feliks Wiatrowski.

This morning the German school inspector stopped by to review all the books in the city library. He was definitely looking for something. But Mayor Kraus, shortly after taking office, went through the books and hid some. I am a little worried about my own collection.

December

December 1 Because of my weak heart I am still in bed. I am practically separated from the rest of the world. News comes to me rarely and it is very skimpy.

Administrator Debczynski was released from Lublin prison. Tomasz Czernicki came back from Auschwitz, and Andrzej Przysada, from Dachau. A young physician, Dr. Stefan Matuszewski, came to us from Warsaw. He will help me in the hospital. He took his final exams during the war.

December 9   Yesterday a wedding took place between Miss Rajewska and Mr. Kozlowski. During the reception dinner the gestapo burst in. They were searching for the brother of the bride who had recently married the sister of Jan Turowski. The young groom and Turowski both escaped. A few people were arrested after a lengthy interrogation. The bride, Rajewska-Kozlowska, was the only one held as late as 9 A.M. the next morning. She was severely beaten. But at 10 A.M. the gestapo arrested her again. During the second arrests the gestapo searched the house next door, belonging to Mr. and Mrs. Gramez. During the search Mrs. Gramzowa was badly beaten.

Today we received the big news about a Japanese-American war. Everyone is thrilled, but there are no details.

December 10   Mrs. Gulinska, in Zwierzyniec, received a telegram that her twenty-seven-year-old son, Bohun, died in Auschwitz. He was a very well built man in excellent physical condition. He had been arrested along with his younger brother Marian. After a few weeks of imprisonment in Lublin, he was transferred to the Auschwitz concentration camp. Even a young man in good physical condition cannot withstand the terrible treatment of the so-called German death camp. Bohun was very popular here. The news of his death saddened everyone.

December 13   Now, finally, there is a German-American war. Everyone is happy today. Now we are completely sure that Germany will be defeated, maybe even by next year.

December 16   Today Dr. Snacki, along with the director of sanitary services for the county, the German Pradelok, visited my hospital. Pradelok, who speaks Polish very well, worked before the war in German intelligence and spent a few years as director of the German travel agency. He was a frequent visitor in the most expensive Warsaw cabarets, like Adria and Gastronomia. He told us his budget for running the travel agency was 2.5 million marks per year.

Inspector Hulak, from Bilgoraj, died in Auschwitz.

December 21   We try to trace the events of the war. Even in the German newspapers it appears to be true that in Russia and North Africa the situation of the German army looks very bad. German newspapers are talking about the necessity of strengthening and aligning all along the Eastern Front. This will be achieved by pulling the troops back. This is a very nice explanation of a typical retreat.

The epidemic of spotted typhus is still taking many victims. Somehow my administrator, Adamski, recuperated, but our cook, Helena Osipowiczowna, is now very ill. Because of those two people being out of commission for some time the administration of the hospital is suffering.

A couple of days ago I went to Zamosc to have some X-rays taken. In the Zamosc hospital there are many spotted typhus patients but no Jews. All ill Jews are housed in two barracks in the Jewish sector of the city. I was pleased to learn that the city museum, evacuated from its own building, is now located in an old apartment house on Ormianska Street and is still under the direction of Mr. Kabat.

I was pleasantly surprised to learn that Prof. Otto Werner is now the mayor of Zamosc. I have no time to meet with too many people, but I feel that everyone is exhausted. The constant question is when will it all end.

December 31 Tomorrow we will start a new year. We all believe that this will be the last year of the war. From all fronts we receive news of German retreats. The winter this year is very fierce. There is much snow and freezing conditions are making motorized units practically immobile.

We watch as military ambulances and trains go west, loaded with wounded and frostbitten soldiers. Most frostbite occurs on hands, feet, ears, noses, and genitals. You can judge the desperation of the German military situation by the fact that Hitler has taken direct responsibility for all military action in Russia.

We have noticed disorganization in the German administration. For example, in the county offices you cannot solve any problem at all because the employees think only about their own future and make decisions based on the future.

Here in Szczebrzeszyn there is new action against the Jews. On December 26 it was announced that under penalty of death all Jews must surrender all fur coats, fur hats, fur collars, fur gloves, fur muffs, and any other clothing made of fur. Now most Jews are trying to hide all fur articles, but some are giving them away. Dr. Bolotny took to the *Judenrat* about 12,000 zloty worth of his own and also his wife's furs. At anytime we expect the same for the Polish population. Some people are boiling mad, but some are happy because this fur business shows that the Germans are suffering. The temperature is very low. We lack fuel and people are freezing, but everyone hopes for an even colder winter, because it will help defeat the Germans.

The only large supplies of coal and firewood are at the gendarmes station. Today a few gendarmes, who come daily for the dressing of their abscesses, complained that it is too cold inside the hospital. I pointed out that we do not have enough coal to heat properly. Within a few hours we received from them some coal.

The black market is booming now that the dollar is so high, 100 zloty for 1 dollar. A 5-ruble gold piece goes for 600 zloty or more.

Evacuations have stopped. Some evacuees from Skierbieszowo were relocated in Bilgoraj County. The German military authorities oppose the deportation of evacuees past the Bug River. They are afraid of having them too close to the front. But the population is ready for anything.

Two days ago in Lipowiec several people were arrested for nondelivery of the grain quota. They are now in prison in Bilgoraj and are taken every day for hard labor in the Hedwiczyn Quarry.

From Zwierzyniec I learned that Komora was killed.

Many people are dying, but everyone still alive feels sure that our time of revenge and victory will come.

Will We Be Evacuated or Maybe Shot

January

January 5 Today, by order of the German authorities, all skis over 170 cm in length and boots beginning with size 41 must be brought in to city hall. Nothing about fur items, but we expect that very soon. In the villages, police have begun confiscating sheepskin coats from the farmers. On the city streets no one wears fur, because there have been cases where the Germans took the fur, leaving men only in suits and women in dresses.

January 7 Yesterday in Sulowiec the commandant of Polish police, Jozef Siuda, was killed. One policeman, Franciszek Oleszewski, was wounded in the leg. The murderer, the known bandit Matfiej, escaped. German gendarmes began searching for him and a few others, without any result. The bandits left Sulowiec with their families, so the Germans burned down their houses.

This morning a young physician, Dr. Bronislaw Nizewski, only twenty-eight years old, visited my hospital. He is assigned to Sulow commune to help fight the epidemic of spotted typhus. He is very nervous and close to a complete breakdown. He informed me about his experiences in the Auschwitz concentration camp. Terrifying.

January 12   In Zamosc, Roman Niedzwiecki, city hall usher, known to everyone as "Romcio," died of a heart attack. He was one of the most popular people in Szczebrzeszyn. For years he delivered legal papers to the populace. Today was his funeral and many people attended.

January 14   Among the Jewish population there is increasing nervousness. Two Jews were arrested and executed for hiding furs. Today six Jews were taken as hostages because of low fur collections. For the same reason all members of the *Judenrat* in Bilgoraj and Tarnogrod were arrested.

January 15   Very cold. This morning the temperature dropped to −15°F. We received information about the growing number of frostbite cases on the Russian front and the beginning of a spotted typhus epidemic in the German army.

In nearby villages the number of typhus cases is increasing; but on the other hand, the epidemic among the Jewish population is decreasing.

January 20   Very cold. People are freezing because of the lack of fuel, like coal or wood. Along with this the typhus epidemic is on the increase. One person who came down with spotted typhus is Dr. Franciszka Standochowa, wife of a colonel from Cracow, also a physician who is now somewhere outside Poland. She had just arrived in the city.

Again we see more brutality against the Jews. During the last few days in Szczebrzeszyn several Jews were shot. Their crimes: leaving town without a permit, transporting a cow without a permit, hiding a fur coat, and walking without wearing the Star of David on the sleeve. Similar actions are occurring in other cities and villages.

Today I visited a sick old Jew named Winawer (brother of the well-known author Bruno Winawer). He lives in one small room divided by a wooden partition. He sleeps on a litter of straw on the floor, together with his wife and teenage daughter. The *Judenrat* refuses to help him because he is a convert to Christianity, and the Polish population is still not ready to accept him. I cannot take him to the hospital because I do not have any more space. All the beds and even the floor areas are being used. I feel very bad about this.

The lack of news is very depressing; we really do not know what is going on. We cannot trust the German-edited newspapers.

January 21   Today Dr. Stefan Matuszewski arrived from Warsaw. He will be working in my hospital. I hope this will give me more time for myself.

Today, along with a few others, I inspected an apartment house designated by the Germans as an isolation hospital for Jews who are sick with spotted typhus and typhoid fever. I can't visualize how it will help.

In Zwierzyniec part of the estate hospital will be converted into a typhus ward. From everywhere all you can hear is typhus, typhus.

The owner of the Alwa factory, Aleksander Waligora, was released from Auschwitz concentration camp. He wired his family from Cracow.

January 22 In Zamosc there are new victims of typhus: Dr. Jan Hauslinger, Dr. Domaradzki (director of the infectious ward at the hospital), and medic Krolikowski have come down with spotted typhus.

January 27 We are overworked with the spotted typhus epidemic. It is still on the increase, and during the last few days it has once again hit the Jewish inhabitants of Szczebrzeszyn. Never in my life have I seen such extreme poverty and uncleanliness. We are working in unbelievable conditions. We do not have enough bedding, shirts, or pots, and our help is not adequate. People are afraid of typhus, and even if we had good working conditions some would still not be willing to work at the hospital. I have other problems. The motor on the well pump gave out and all the water lines are frozen. I cannot hire a plumber because all the specialists have been taken by the Germans to Chelm to work on a military project. So we do not have water, and bathing the sick is impossible. Our supplies of coal and wood are almost exhausted; the same with food. Much of my time is spent keeping people calm. They come to me with even the smallest problems. No one seems to care that I have only limited ways of receiving help from the outside and that I too work in abnormal conditions. The whole day, from dawn until dusk, I am occupied with hospital business. For myself I have practically no time. I can write only before 6 A.M.; that way I get only an hour or so to write. My writing is going very slowly.

Freezing temperatures are holding. All trains are delayed, mail is very irregular, and sometimes days pass without any news. Even German papers are not delivered. So we do not have any news, again only rumors. I was told that close to Nielisz village a parachute was spotted hanging from a tree. The Germans searched the area without any result. All they have is a partly damaged parachute. Whether it is a British or Russian parachute, no one knows.

The Germans are now regulating with more and more ridiculous instructions. As an example, in Gorajec the Jews are prohibited from moving more than 10 m away from their houses. No one is allowed to walk down small trails. Every type of traffic, even foot traffic, must use the main highways and roads. In Chlopkowo the Germans killed a villager for walking on a small trail next to his own field. Jews seen on dirt roads are being shot.

Yesterday engineer Waligora came to see me. He doesn't look too bad on first impression, but after more careful observation you can notice that his body is swollen in several places. He is reluctant to talk about his experience in the concentration camp, and I did not ask him.

February

February 2   On Friday, January 30, the gestapo went to Zwierzyniec and arrested the surveyor Stanislaw Brandt. He was beaten during the arrest. His wife was hit so hard in the face by a German officer that she had a tooth knocked out. He was taken to a spot in the forest, already marked by the gestapo, where they dug up several machine guns. Besides Brandt the gestapo tried to arrest a young employee of the lumber mill, Swiatecki, but he escaped. The gestapo also searched a few other houses, but no one was there. I am sure that Brandt will be executed. He is a Polish reserve officer, around thirty years old, a very quiet man. He was married a few years before the war and has two small children. People in Zwierzyniec are very sad, but it seems that there is no way for him to be saved. We expect more arrests to come.

Yesterday the gestapo arrived in Szczebrzeszyn to arrest Stanislaw Rybicki, employee of a print shop, and Roman Kolodziejczyk, son of a local blacksmith. Both are members of the underground. The gestapo also came to arrest young Dolezal, not knowing that he had already been executed.

Because of these happenings the atmosphere in town is very tense.

Stefan Bauer, principal of the agricultural school in Janowice, was released from Oranienburg. He was arrested in June 1940. He had been in the concentration camp for 1½ years.

I see military traffic increasing on the highway. What the situation is on the Eastern Front nobody knows. We do not trust the newspapers.

February 4   Yesterday the gestapo came to town again. They were searching for two postal workers, Siciarz and Jozef Kolodziejczyk, who had already left town.

I learned some important details regarding the last series of arrests. I am sure that we can expect more.

Last year a young Polish officer came to the Zamosc region. He joined the underground and became a platoon leader. He was known as "Wisman" or "Rust." He came to Szczebrzeszyn occasionally and would spend the night at different people's homes, such as Kolodziejczyk's. He came often to visit hospital administrator Cichonski, and after Cichonski escaped he asked me for money for his organization.

Now he has appeared in a gestapo uniform and has begun arresting people. First was Brandt, with whom he hid machine guns. Now he is naming all his contacts in the underground.

Because of this, many people have left town, changing their names. Everyone is at a high level of panic. I myself do not feel too good, but I will not run. I have too much to do here. What will be, will be.

February 9 Yesterday, completely unexpected, Jerzy Plomienski showed up in my office, from a small forestry station in Hrubieszow County. We talked for two full days. We have much in common and can understand each other very well. He read to me a few chapters of his book on Edward Dembowski. In return I gave him a few chapters of my memoirs. He said that the writing is good and he thinks it will sell. Also he looked over my recently completed biography of Bohdanowicz from the Fifth Siberian Division in World War I. He liked it very much. So in general he gave me a boost to work even more. I am very pleased by his visit. When he left I promised to type his manuscript in two copies. My wife promised to type his manuscript about Dembowski.

For two days during his visit I completely forgot about the Germans, Auschwitz, and arrests. I lived in a different world.

Yesterday Michal Pawlik was released from Auschwitz. I have not seen him yet.

A few days ago the gestapo arrested forest ranger Wandycz. People are nervous. At night they listen for the gestapo. Most people are ready to escape at a minute's notice. We received news about new arrests in Krasnystaw, Chelm, and Krzeszowice.

Today I learned that Zygmunt Pomaranski was killed a few months ago in Auschwitz.

February 16 Today was a very nervous day. Around noon Rev. Kapalski came running to the hospital and without saying a word ran upstairs to hide in the attic. He finally told me that a few minutes ago the gestapo started a search in Guzowski's apartment house, where Rev. Kapalski lived. This made everyone here tense because Gozowski's apartments are across from the hospital.

I sent my son to find out what was happening and dressed myself in my white physician's coat, so in case of a gestapo visit I could quickly visit the typhus ward.

We received information from town that despite a search there were no arrests. The Germans were looking for something. They stayed for quite a while in Malinowski's restaurant.

After a few hours, when things calmed down, we learned the reason for the search. Several weeks ago the German military confiscated good furniture to be used in the officers' mess, which had been established in the parish hall. Some furniture was missing so the gestapo was ordered to find it. After searching the apartments for a couple of hours the gestapo left without anything.

During the events like this I stay calm and have a special urge to work, maybe because I am subconsciously counting my days. Today I spent several hours working and typing my manuscripts. This work soothes my nerves and relaxes me. But on the other hand, I am not alert to any outside activities, such as the Germans walking on the street next to the hospital or actually entering the building.

February 18 Last night the gestapo in Szczebrzeszyn again searched for furniture. They took some pieces from the Paprocki house. There is talk that they are opening some new quarters in Zamosc.

A couple of days ago gendarmes arrested a twenty-year-old Jewish girl for not wearing a Star of David. They took her outside the city, where she was shot.

February 19 In Zamosc eight young men were arrested: Tadeusz Bajkowski, two Wojtas brothers, and others. The morale of the city is low. People walking the city streets are always looking around, moving quickly, afraid that someone is watching them. Many do not sleep at home, and during the day they try to look very occupied with work. Without any news people are in a state of complete resignation, and many are close to acute nervous breakdown. I still have not lost my deepest conviction that, in the end, life will come back to normal and we will once again see an independent Poland.

I try not to waste any time. In the evening I spend several hours typing my memoirs and at least one hour a night, lying in bed, organizing my thoughts. This way I can keep my mental stability.

February 23 Robberies are again taking place. In Mokra Lipa Rev. Masztelarz was robbed; in Micholow, the Tomaszewski flour mill; and the Zwierzyniec railroad station was also hit.

Swista was arrested at the refinery, and in Szczebrzeszyn young Kafarski was taken.

Yesterday I visited Zwierzyniec. Here people are disturbed by the arrest of Brandt. They expect more searches. It is puzzling why only a few were arrested. "Wisman" knows of many people involved with the underground, but only a few were detained.

February 25 In Auschwitz concentration camp a young high school teacher, Cieslinski, was killed, and in Dachau, the banker Jan Kozlowski died. He had been arrested in June 1940.

A few German colonists from Brody who signed papers as *Volksdeutsch* were drafted into the German army. They left for training in Germany. Mayor Kraus, who is a German, faces the same situation.

March

March 4   For the past few days the gendarme company is on full alert. In town gendarmes and "blue police" walk with carbines. In Janow the gendarmerie post was attacked and a number of gendarmes were killed. In Izbica several telephone cables were cut and a few telephone poles destroyed.

Also a noon assault on a railroad train took place between Zwierzyniec and Bilgoraj. The robbers took over 100,000 zloty from the passengers. Probably events such as these are forcing the Germans to put more troops on patrol.

In Lublin prison, banker Kucharski died of spotted typhus. He was a very nice man with a very good reputation. Krzywdzinski from Szczebrzeszyn died in one of the concentration camps.

The lack of news keeps people in a bad mood. No one believes the newspapers. Yet the Jews I speak with tell me everything is fine.

March 5   Today I was called on a consultation to treat Pawlik. He is in very poor condition, almost critical. We had to pump almost three liters of fluid from his pleural cavity. He is swollen, especially in the feet and arms. Many thousands like him suffer and will die as a result of treatment in the concentration camps and prisons.

March 15   Life here is so monotonous that for the last ten days I have not written my diary. Here, briefly, are the events of the last few days. On March 8 Pawlik died. He was only thirty-seven years old. His funeral was on March 11, with hundreds of people attending, mostly women. In Auschwitz Roman Romanowski, a barber from Szczebrzeszyn died. In Zwierzyniec Mrs. Gulinska received a telegram from Auschwitz telling her that her second son, Marian, had died. In eight months she has lost two sons. As a mother she does not believe this and still has hope that it is a mistake, but we know the truth.

More and more people are being arrested during street raids and sent to labor camps. Already twice at the Zawada rail station all men without proof of employment were arrested and shipped off to an unknown place. What happened to them nobody knows.

Once again I became sick. In the evenings I have been suffering from a high fever and my heart has been troubling me also. A few times I was sure that I had reached the end. Today is the fourth day I have been in bed; my heart is still not functioning normally, but I have a feeling that again I will survive.

While lying in bed I write or I make corrections on my manuscript. My history of the Zamosc region has grown to the size of a large book. I am so involved in this that I pay little attention to the happenings on the outside, about hospital administration and rising prices.

March 25   Teacher Kilarski, arrested in June 1940, returned from the concentration camp. From all those taken captive at the same time only one, Wiktor Jozwiakowski, is still alive in the Oranienburg camp.

Life is passing us by in an atmosphere of death, violation of laws, and lawlessness. The population is terrorized more and more; the victims are countless.

A few days ago a special gestapo detachment arrived in the village of Deszkowice. The commune administrator escaped, but the village administrator, Wojciech Kobylarz, was shot as he attempted to run. His funeral was today. More than 1,000 people attended. This was a demonstration by the villagers against the atrocities of the Germans.

The same gestapo group began searches in Kulikowo and Rozlop. During the search the Germans stole many valuables. The teacher Padzinski was arrested.

During an escape from the Dyla camp in Bilgoraj, former hospital employee Jozef Okon was shot. He had been arrested at the Szczebrzeszyn railroad station for black marketeering.

Yesterday the gestapo spent several hours in Szczebrzeszyn searching for good furniture. They removed all window furnishings from the house of the Grochulski family, ordering that after it was cleaned and washed it must be delivered to the gestapo office.

More people are signing up for work with the German administration. In Szczebrzeszyn several young boys, including Wojtowicz and Byk, signed up as railroad guards. They received black uniforms similar to the ones used by railroad workers. Now they are trying to learn German.

Some people are signing up for labor in Germany: one was a young barber, Waclaw Zelazko. He was supposed to work as a barber in Germany, but instead he was assigned to farm work. In his letters he is crying that already he has two broken ribs.

The situation of the Jews is worsening. From different sources I have received information about the displacement of Jews. From Bilgoraj 250 Jews were moved to Tarnogrod. There are more and more cases of Jews being shot outside their own homes and also at the railroad stations.

On the highway we observe increasing traffic, practically all military vehicles.

Now the Germans are transporting entire trainloads, mostly Jews, but we do not know where, maybe closer to the front for hard labor. From all sides we experience danger. We do not know what to expect or when this will all end.

It is very difficult to buy food. There are more restrictions; even potatoes have been removed from the free market. Some prices are out of reach for the average person. For butter we pay 60 zloty, for bread, 8 zloty, and for bacon, 50 zloty. In Bilgoraj the Jews are allowed to buy only horsemeat. But the Jews are buying and selling everything possible. They are masters of the black market. Even though they are forbidden to travel, they have their own ways of organizing a very good supply system. Villagers sell to them freely, knowing that they will receive the highest possible price. From my window I can watch the exchanges.

At the Klemensow airfield new road work has begun.

March 26 The Jews are very disturbed about the forced movement of their population. From different areas we received information about actions against the Jews. Entire railroad trains loaded with Jews from Czechoslovakia, Germany, and, lately, Belgium passed through, possibly to Belzec, where a new large camp was just organized. I heard about what the Germans did to the Jews in Lublin. It is difficult to believe that it is true.

Today the evacuation of Jews from Izbica began. Many Jews were shot for no reason at all.

Today I noticed increasing air traffic, mostly transport planes. From the Russian front there is no real news, only that the fighting is very heavy.

March 29 In Auschwitz Jan Lazorczyk, a farmer from Kawenczyn, died. He was a solid and intelligent man.

Yesterday in Szczebrzeszyn police arrested a man named Szwed for the illegal sale of flour and the upholsterer Otlowski for the illegal butchering of a cow. Both were arrested because of denunciations by young Franczak. After the arrest, Franczak went to the police asking for a reward, but he was severely beaten and thrown out of the station. The commandant of gendarmes said that if he listened to all denunciations, half of Szczebrzeszyn would either be in jail or have been executed.

Jews now send Aryans as special messengers with different information. This way they can keep track of events around the area. A transport of 2,000 Jews from Czechoslovakia arrived in Izbica; some Jews were transported from Izbica to Belzec. Today another messenger was sent to Belzec for information about the new concentration camp.

Jews are staying in town. They do not venture out because the Germans will shoot them without asking any questions.

Our lives are filled with constant terror and it is very difficult to withstand it. You must have both physical and mental health to survive.

April

April 4   A few days ago the Germans decided to give St. Catherine's Catholic Church to the Orthodox church. Yesterday they took the keys to the church from the Catholic priest and today began moving in some Orthodox liturgical items. The population is boiling mad. This church, for the second time in its history, dating back to the seventeenth century, will be home to the Orthodox clergy. The first time was in 1883, when the Russians established an Orthodox parish with Orthodox priest Tracz as pastor. In 1917 the Catholic church regained it. History repeats itself. But people seem sure that the Orthodox won't be here too long and that they will leave the church in a hurry.

During some fighting in the forest in Zaklodzie a German gendarme, Himler, was killed. He will be buried in a local cemetery; the funeral will be tomorrow. City hall laid a large wreath on his coffin.

Today Mieczyslaw Kaminski, underground name "Miecz," was arrested. The gestapo had been looking for him for some time. He had always been able to escape. Really, this was his own fault. Instead of hiding quietly, he would walk through the town so everyone was able to see him.

I have new worries at the hospital. I received a copy of new regulations. Now, by order of the German administration, the hospital will not be given any food supply quota. Everyone will have to provide their own food, maybe through the black market. How can I provide my hospital with all of its food supplies? The German regulation states that at the time of admission to the hospital the patient must deposit their own food stamps with the hospital administration. That is fine. But who will feed sick farmers? They never received food stamps along with everyone else. When this question arose the answer was, "This is your problem. We will not give you any food."

April 8   On Saturday, April 4, the first services were held in the new Orthodox church. During Easter Sunday services typical Russian singing was heard. I was very upset seeing this old Catholic monastery once again become the object of political play.

On Easter Sunday, around 10 P.M., two young men armed with handguns entered the city jail. They forced the jailer to open the cell that held the young man Kaminski. After freeing Kaminski they locked the jailer in the cell, along with his wife. After some time the jailer's calls for help through a small window sent some passersby to inform the gendarmes. They arrived and started shooting, but no one was hit.

The jailer recognized both young men. He gave their names: Wejler and Marczewski, from the village of Brody. The gestapo searched the Wejler home and found two handguns. When young Wejler attempted to escape, policeman Gal shot him to death. Young Marczewski escaped, but his father was arrested. The same happened to Kaminski's wife, and his sister-in-law and twelve-year-old son were also arrested. His four-year-old daughter was left with neighbors.

On April 6 the funeral of gendarme Himler took place. On that day I was visiting in Zwierzyniec so I have only information from others. Most of the people attending the funeral were gendarmes, Germans in civilian clothing, and the entire city council. Flowers were sent by city hall, the "blue police," and the *Judenrat*. That same day the remains of Wejler were buried. The Germans were so brutal that they didn't allow his remains to be put in a casket. The public was kept away; only one priest was allowed.

In town we expect more arrests. The Jews are upset. We know for sure that every day two trains, consisting of twenty cars each, come to Belzec, one from Lublin, the other from Lwow. After being unloaded on separate tracks, all Jews are forced behind the barbed-wire enclosure. Some are killed with electricity, some with poison gases, and the bodies are burned.

On the way to Belzec the Jews experience many terrible things. They are aware of what will happen to them. Some try to fight back. At the railroad station in Szczebrzeszyn a young woman gave away a gold ring in exhange for a glass of water for her dying child. In Lublin people witnessed small children being thrown through the windows of speeding trains. Many people are shot before reaching Belzec.

April 11 Today the Jews received news that a trainload of people from Chelm was unloaded in Belzec and the empty train went on to Zamosc. I am sure that this is true because Jewish information is most reliable. This evening's news tells us that Zamosc is completely encircled and a so-called *Judenzug* (Jewish train) is waiting. Here in Szczebrzeszyn the atmosphere is very tense. Some Jews wait in complete resignation; others are running away to find places to hide. Many come to the hospital for help, but I have to refuse because of German orders. I admit only pregnant women and typhus cases.

April 12 The information from Zamosc is horrifying. Almost 2,500 Jews were evacuated. A few hundred were shot on the streets. Some men fought back. I do not have any details. Here in Szczebrzeszyn there is panic. Old

Jewish women spent the night in the Jewish cemetery, saying they would rather die here among the graves of their own families than be killed and burned in the concentration camps. Some are trying to escape from the city. Others are sending their small children to Warsaw to be placed with Polish families.

April 13   Last night passed quietly, but this morning panic among the Jewish population began again. They expect the gestapo and gendarmes to begin mass arrests at any time. Many Jews have left town already or hidden themselves, so only a few can be seen walking on the city streets. Some began moving big boxes and taking care of any personal business. In town a mob started assembling, waiting for the right moment to start removing everything from the Jewish homes. I have information that already some people are stealing whatever is possible to be carried from homes where the owners have been forced to move out. Lately the Jews have been giving goods for safekeeping to Aryans in towns or in the villages.

Jews are paying good money to be hidden. This is very dangerous because of regulations that state the punishment for hiding Jews is death. I know for certain that many children have been moved to Warsaw and other cities far away from Szczebrzeszyn.

In the afternoon the Jews disappeared from the streets. The black market reacted by lowering prices, because the best buyers were not available.

Most people are so tired they wish that any kind of end to this situation would come soon. The Jews' panic is also spreading to the Polish population.

April 15   Yesterday evening the situation improved because no trains arrived in Belzec and there has been no news from nearby villages of any arrests. The same today. Only a few Jews are on the streets, but the public phone near the post office is completely surrounded. It is impossible to get to the post office windows because of all the Jews standing there waiting to use the phone.

Yesterday someone from the Szczebrzeszyn railroad station called the gendarmes and informed them that several Jews were waiting in the crowd for the train to Warsaw. The gendarmes arrested eight Jews for illegal movement. Five of them have already been executed.

Yesterday the Orthodox priest came to me complaining that someone is breaking the windows in his church. He was sure that someone from the hospital was responsible. Later we learned that a group of small boys broke the windows by shooting stones with slings.

April 19   During the last few days there haven't been anymore trains to Belzec. The Jews hope that maybe the mass deportations have stopped. No one knows what caused this change in German behavior.

Former city translator Krol and Roman Waligora were released from Auschwitz. Waligora had been there for two years, and Krol for one.

At midnight, April 18, I was awakened by shots in the street, very close to the hospital. At first I was sure that new action against the Jews had begun, but later I learned that Gal, one of the "blue police," being completely drunk, began shooting out the windows in Jewish homes. The Jews were terrorized.

April 23   Yesterday I went to Bilgoraj to clear up some hospital business, particularly the problem of food supplies. No one knows a thing. The answer is the same: "You have to help yourself. Our hands are tied." I get the feeling that disorganization is growing now that the new *Kreishauptmann* has begun regulating everything possible.

There are very few people walking on the streets. A few days ago the Germans began the evacuation of Aryans. (This has now become the official designation for non-Jews.) Germans take the better houses for themselves. More gestapo troops with families are expected to arrive from Germany. Because of the heavy bombardments of German cities by British and American air forces, many Germans are trying to move their families to Polish cities, where so far no air raids have occurred or are expected.

I stopped in at Bilgoraj hospital. Administrator Pojasek was in Warsaw, so I spoke with the chief nurse. She refused to answer many questions, such as how much bread is given as a daily ration to the hospital patients and how much to the staff.

Today we had some real commotion in town, around 10 A.M. There was a big movement of police and gendarmes into town. They were after three bandits who were at the priest's house. One of the bandits started shooting. Very soon I received a wounded German soldier. As I learned, three soldiers were driving by in a truck when they saw gendarmes going after someone. They stopped the truck and the driver went with the gendarmes. He was ready to shoot when a bullet hit him in the leg. I gave him first aid, and because the bone was injured, I put him in a temporary cast. Before I even had time to finish, a German ambulance came and took him to a German hospital. In the meantime the gendarmes were chasing the bandits. One was killed, one escaped. Jewish police took part in the chase. This new police group was formed only a few days ago. Now eight young Jews are involved. They wear black caps with blue rims and carry rubber sticks.

A few minutes after the ambulance took the wounded soldier away I had a visit. Two armed officers and four armed soldiers entered the hospital and questioned me, asking several detailed questions and checking my ID papers.

In town people are afraid that reprisals can be expected. On the street I met Krol, who returned from Auschwitz a few days ago. So far he doesn't look too bad.

April 26   Today Mayor Kraus informed me that gendarmes questioned him on who gave me the order to treat a German soldier. He told them treatment was given under order of a German officer, since there are no German physicians around here. Today a German officer stopped at the hospital and gave me an affidavit that he was the one who ordered me to help, and he thanked me for it.

Since early morning many Jews have been in the area of city hall. From the labor bureau in Zamosc a German inspector came to take 350 Jews to a labor camp in Kulikowo, where roadwork is taking place. He ended up taking only 63 men, so the Jews expect more arrests. I also heard about the upcoming arrests from the mayor, who, since he is a German, is generally well informed.

April 28   I went on a visit to Zamosc. On the road between Szczebrze-szyn and Zamosc more German barracks were built. Around Janowice I noticed large brick buildings being constructed, maybe some big warehouses.

In Zamosc pedestrian traffic is almost nonexistent. Most Polish stores are closed, but new German ones are now open.

Last night several people were arrested. Practically all of them are factory workers who, during the short Soviet occupation of 1939, were members of the so-called Red Militia.

April 29   In Bilgoraj there are new regulations. Jews are not permitted to walk on Main Street. Today four Jews who disobeyed the new order were shot.

Even though mass deportations of Jews to the Belzec camp have stopped, the executions of Jews on the city streets are increasing. A few days ago in Zwierzyniec four members of the *Judenrat* were shot.

May

May 1   Yesterday, for the second time in less than a year, my eleven-year-old son, Tadeusz, left home. Late in the evening he returned. I had searched for him everywhere. After his return he told me he went to the forest to join the underground, but in Kosobudy he met a forest ranger who ordered him to return home.

May 5   For some time I have been receiving information about increasing underground activity. In the small forest hamlets several different groups are organizing resistance against the Germans. Besides fragments of the official Polish army still under the direction of the Polish government in London, the so-called Home Army, several political parties have begun to organize their own military units. Russian soldiers who escaped from German prisons are starting their own Soviet units with the help of local Communists. Sorry to say that some individuals form their own terror teams dedicated only to robbery for profit. Robberies are increasing, but no one knows for sure the motivation for the accompanying assaults or who is responsible for them. Lately a robbery occurred in the village of Chlopki, where one woman was wounded and brought to my hospital.

A few days ago Turobin was visited by a team of four gestapo officials. Within a few hours they killed 107 Jews. In Izbica two gestapo men were shot. Now the Germans are afraid of entering villages in small groups. The German headquarters in Szczebrzeszyn is now locked, even during daylight hours. Everyone having business there must call for an appointment and show an ID as they enter.

May 7 Today the "blue police," along with the Jewish police and with help from a few Polish civilians, arrested five Jews and eight women, including dentist Natan Bronsztein and his seventy-five-year-old father. First they were detained in the police jail but later were transferred to the city jail. No one knows the reason for these arrests.

As soon as I learned of Dr. Bronsztein's arrest I placed a call to the county doctor in Bilgoraj requesting his release, because he is the only dentist in the city.

In Zwierzyniec Edward Newlaczil and Swiatecki, a factory worker, were arrested.

May 8 Today we survived a terrible day. I still have not come to myself after this ordeal. Early yesterday evening seven Jews were taken from the city jail and moved to Zwierzyniec, two Jewish women and five Jewish men. Dr. Bronsztein and his father, old merchant Bronszpigel, young Ferszt, tailor Szer, and two women were loaded onto a truck. Young Ferszt jumped and started running, and a German guard killed him with one shot. People are sure that by now the others have all been executed.

Around 3 P.M. a real hell started in town. From Zamosc there arrived a group of gestapo. They ordered the *Judenrat* to provide 100 Jews for forced labor, giving only one hour for this to happen. After one hour passed the gestapo, with help from the gendarmes, started catching the Jews, but they really began a mass shooting. The shooting could be heard throughout the city. They shot people like ducks, killing them not only on the streets but also in their own houses—men, women, and children, indiscriminately. The number killed and wounded is hard to estimate. I will say that the number killed was over 100. At the time the first wounded were being counted. Jews came to me asking for help, so I dispatched a few crews with stretchers to pick up the wounded.

After a short while I began to think: I have had instructions from the German county administrator not to give any medical aid to Jews. So I called the police station and I was told that Jews are not my business. Then I called the county doctor in Bilgoraj. He told me the hospital has no right to give any help to the Jews since a Jewish doctor is in the city, and even more so during a mass action by the Germans. I posted a few people at the hospital entrance to explain that we are not allowed to admit any Jews.

I was lucky that I did so. There is no way I would have been able to save Jews, and certainly I would have been arrested and executed. Around 4 P.M. two gestapo men, one gendarme, and one member of the "blue police" entered the hospital lobby, all armed with machine guns, and asked if I had admitted or given help to any Jews. I told them no. They left after going through all the wards, but they came back through the wall and began looking again. Finally they took with them a young Jew who worked in the hospital as an orderly, a man who had all the necessary papers from the labor bureau. After a few hours he was released.

Around 5 P.M. the gestapo left Szczebrzeszyn. The Jews are terrified. Women are crying and tearing their clothes. Men went with shovels to dig graves in the cemetery, and the dead were transported there by horse-drawn wagon. Dr. Bolotny, the only Jewish physician in town, came to me begging for help. He could not do the work alone with so many wounded, some critically. I am saddened that I had to refuse to give any help at all. I did this only because of strict orders by the Germans. This was against my own feeling and against a physician's duties. With my eyes I can still see the wagons filled with the dead, one Jewish woman walking along with her dead child in her arms, and many wounded lying on the sidewalks across from my hospital, where I was forbidden to give them any help.

May 9   Today the only topic of discussion is yesterday's massacre. Several wounded were placed at the Jewish typhus isolation house. Some of them have already died. Dr. Bolotny again asked all Polish physicians for help. I agreed to help if he could provide some sort of release form from the Germans that would allow me to give medical assistance, but the release was never given.

This morning a number of Jews attempted to escape from the city, but they were stopped by other Jews who were afraid that a mass escape would give the Germans an excuse for more killing. At 8 A.M. sixty Jews were taken for labor in Kulikowo. We all feel that this is not yet the end.

I learned that yesterday's search of my hospital was because of a denunciation. A man named Wojtowicz told the Germans that I hid several Jews in the hospital. He even gave names.

The way some Poles behave is completely out of line. During the massacre some even laughed. Some went sneaking into Jewish houses from the back, searching for what could be stolen.

Here is something different: the gestapo ordered the *Judenrat* to pay 2,000 zloty and 3 lbs. of coffee for the ammunition used to kill Jews.

May 11 In Zwierzyniec the clerk of the Zamoyski estate, Miroslaw Rybicki, was arrested. Today at 8 A.M. the Jew Kligier, former owner of a publishing company, was executed in front of city hall.

May 13 There was a big sensation in town. A unit of 130 mounted gendarmes passed through. They rode in full military formation. They are probably going on a raid against a partisan unit in the forest.

I learned that in Josefow, on April 11, around noon, the gestapo killed some 150 people. This was horrifying to the point that even Becker, the German *Treuhander* of the Alwa plant, was completely terrified. He observed this while passing through Jozefow. Later he described the German action. He said that never in his life had he witnessed atrocities such as this. He said it was impossible to describe, and he himself had always said that all Jews should be exterminated.

May 15 More military columns are moving east through Szczebrzeszyn. It appears this is in connection with the German offensive on the Eastern Front.

Yesterday afternoon two German gendarmes and one member of the "blue police" went to the village of Gorajec to check on the Jews. A special messenger brought the information to us that fourteen Jews were killed.

May 16 Early today local gendarmes killed three Jews. Several Jews were locked in the local jail. When they were led outside to the waiting trucks, some started running. They would rather die in our city than be executed in Zamosc. One of those killed was the wife of Berger, former city councilman, who had left town along with the Russian army in 1939. Only one man, Dajles, escaped.

May 17 We learned about diversionary attacks from many different locations. A few days ago eight armed men attacked the Zamoyski palace in Zwierzyniec; with them was a Jew with a red band on his sleeve. At the same time an assault on the Susiec railroad station took place. Yesterday near Korytkowo some partisans shot at the county administrator in Bilgoraj as he drove by in his car. Throughout all the small villages partisans are taking food from the people. It is nearly impossible to find out who they are, Polish, Russian, even German deserters or plain bandits. The "blue police" don't even try to intervene. German gendarmes seem afraid to intervene, so this terrorist action continues throughout the county.

May 18 Yesterday on the road to Rozlopy German gendarmes shot to death two daughters of Jewish house painter Lemer.

May 19 Tonight the Jew Gelernter was killed next to city hall. He was being taken from city hall to Zwierzyniec for execution. He started to run and was shot. His body lay on the street for several hours.

Early this morning I received two wounded men. One, a peasant who saw two gendarmes approaching, started running and was shot. The other is the village administrator from Sasiadka, who was shot during a robbery.

This evening at 6 P.M. the new anti-aircraft alarm was sounded. This was another trial. It appears the Germans are counting on the possibility of Soviet air attacks. They are also afraid of partisans. Our own gendarmes are sitting in their quarters as if they were in a fortress. Even during the day it is impossible to enter.

May 21 Today I went to Zwierzyniec and had a few hours to stop in at the estate archives building. I am glad that the old collection of books is still intact. In charge is old Mr. Galinski. Two people work there full time. It seems as if work is much better organized than before when Potocki was in charge. Now the estate archives is under a German archivist from Lublin. Only a few old documents were removed, mostly regarding German craftsmen who moved to Zamosc in the seventeenth century from Germany. The old employees of the estate are worried because engineer Molinski, the new director of the sugar refinery in Klemensow, was named deputy director of the estate. He is disliked by everyone. It is possible that some personnel changes will be made.

In Szczebrzeszyn calm has still not returned after the robbery of Drozdzyk, the owner of the flour mill. A similar attack took place at the forest ranger station in Kosobudy, where rangers Kawka and Lot were robbed. The same thing occurred at the Korytkowo credit union and other locations. The attackers are laughing and telling people to notify the German police.

Yesterday in Zamosc some 200 people were taken from offices and factories. Most were sent to Germany; only a few were set free.

In Szczebrzeszyn a few hundred people received a summons for May 27 from the labor bureau. The young people are already hiding.

In the Krasnobrod monastery the Germans discovered arms and ammunition hidden there during September 1939. Several people were arrested.

May 22 Yesterday a well-armed group of partisans stopped two members of the "blue police" in the village of Podlesie. One escaped, but Soroka was wounded.

We are living during strange times. Now when people meet on the streets the normal way of greeting is, "Who was arrested? How many Jews were killed last night? Who was robbed?" These events are so common that, really, no one seems to care. Slowly you become accustomed to everything. Now people are afraid of what will happen during the upcoming Pentecost.

May 24 The first day of Pentecost. Last night around 11 P.M. I heard a very loud explosion. This morning I learned that someone had thrown a hand grenade behind the church. No one from the gendarmes or police went to investigate. The gendarme headquarters called the city telephone operator, asking if she by any chance knew anything about it. I received information about new action against Jews in Krasnobrod, Zamosc, and Tomaszow. Our own Jews are again in a state of shock.

Gestapo officials have arrived in the city. With them came the known *Volksdeutsch* Mazyrek and former Bernardin monk Maksymilian. People are leaving town. I wish I could go also, but with my obligation to the hospital this is impossible.

May 27 I went to Zamosc. Now, after visiting the local hospital, I can say that my hospital in Szczebrzeszyn is much better equipped. Here there is a complete lack of cotton, plaster and even injections. But they do not have any restrictions against Jews. They can be admitted for treatment. Only typhoid and typhus cases are isolated in a special Jewish ward.

In Zamosc people live in constant fear of robbery. Approximately thirty robberies take place each day. To retaliate, Germans kill hostages and burn houses. This also happens in the villages of Sitno, Horyszow, and others.

In Krasnobrod Dr. Lastawiecki was taken during a mass arrest.

May 28 At noon a robbery of the Klemensow sugar refinery took place. The employees were present. When the robbers left the factory some of the workers started after them, but a hand grenade stopped the effort to catch the robbers. Only three men were involved, but they took over 50,000 zloty. It appears this was a very well organized underground action.

Recently partisans entered the Paprocki farm in Florianka and the Zakrzewski farm in Gorecek. In both cases they were Russian, and they disappeared after taking food and supplies. We have so many similar cases now that I am not able to describe them all.

Jews are trying to find work because with labor cards they are safe. In my hospital I now employ fifteen Jews. They work in the kitchen and garden without any pay, and only a few receive food.

A very unpleasant event occurred a couple of days ago. Leopold Rytko, a former teacher, came to Mrs. Bronsztein, the wife of executed Dr. Natan Bronsztein, requesting 5,000 zloty. If she refused to pay he said she would be executed. Mrs. Bronsztein refused, so Rytko came down to 3,000 zloty, and then to 500.

June

June 1 A few days passed without any important events. We are still expecting more arrests, mostly among the young people. Not many people showed up for the May 27 transport to Germany.

As of today, one year has passed since the mass arrests in Szczebrzeszyn took place. I remember these dates and will never forget them as long as I live. Anyone who has not been personally abused by German brutality will not understand this feeling.

In Tomaszow Dr. Stefan Cybulski died of heart failure, just after his release from the prison in Lublin.

June 3 Last evening around 10 P.M. gendarmes brought a wounded Russian partisan to the hospital. He was shot as he passed through a village. Naturally his arrival was a big event in the hospital. I had a real problem providing security, because I was told that I was solely responsible for him. So, besides having a hospital helper sitting full time by his bed, I visited him every half hour. This morning a few gestapo men came and conducted an interrogation. One of them, named Mrozik, spoke very good Polish and also a little Ukrainian. All were armed with pistols and one with a machine gun. For tonight one member of the "blue police" was put on guard at the Russian's bedside. The "blue police" requested a list of hospital patients for review. They were looking for someone named Samborski, but they were not sure whether they sought a man or woman.

June 4 Yesterday gendarmes arrested Stanislaw Brylowski, a university student, a young boy named Kita, and a junior high school student named Lasocha. During a search of the Kita house a machine gun and ammunition were discovered.

June 5 This morning at 6 A.M gendarmes took the wounded Russian partisan from the hospital. He was executed outside the city.

The town is living in a state of deep depression. Young people received a second order to report to the labor bureau for work in Germany. The first time only a few people responded. We are afraid that mass arrests will follow soon. I was informed that the Germans brought in several plain-clothes agents to infiltrate the population. All signs point to us receiving some surprises.

During a search of the former monastery building in Krasnobrod the gestapo discovered weapons. Four people were arrested, but three have since been released: Dr. Lastowiecki, the commune administrator, and a member of the "blue police."

Robberies of offices, shops, and private houses are daily events. German gendarmes and "blue police" are completely helpless.

June 6   Yesterday Prokop, an employee of the brickyard, and his wife were arrested. During the search of their house the gestapo confiscated a handgun, a radio receiver, and the flag of the Szczebrzeszyn chapter of *Sokol*. Their young daughter escaped.

At the Alwa factory the young engineer Kazimierz Srodulski died. He had been drinking heavily lately. Yesterday around 4 P.M. he began complaining of a headache and pain in his eyeballs. He died of alcohol poisoning. Officially he died of acute uremia and swelling of the lungs. He was only thirty-seven years old, full of energy and very talented.

June 15   More than a whole week passed without any important occurrences. We all live thinking only about what the next day will bring and waiting for some unusual events.

Today we are seeing many arrests and searches. Yesterday around 10 P.M. the teacher Leopold Rytko was killed in his own home. He was known as a gestapo informer. Two men entered his house and shot him, then rode away on bicycles. Three young men were arrested and taken to jail: Leonard Jurczykowski, Czeslaw Kolodziejczyk, and Stanislaw Janicki. The whole day the gestapo have been snooping around. Other informants are scared to death. Nobody is sorry about the Rytko killing. He was known as an evil person. Tension in the city is growing as we wait for reprisals.

June 17   The last two days were very difficult. Gestapo agents went from house to house. They arrested three men: Jan Bac, young Antoni Franczak, son of the former mayor, and a city employee, Galant. People are very nervous.

During the afternoon a group of people went to see a performance of a small wandering circus that had just arrived in town. After the performance gendarmes and gestapo closed all exits, allowing only women and children to leave. All the men were searched. Approximately twenty were arrested, but no one knows the exact number.

At night nobody slept, my household included. From the street we heard the constant traffic of gendarmes and gestapo, and also shooting.

Around 2 A.M. my wife awakened me because of gunfire next to the hospital. I observed the street through the window. I noticed men standing near the hospital gate with flashlights, but they soon left. In half an hour they returned but went on past. In the morning I learned that Mr. and Mrs. Byk and old Karol Turowski had been shot.

The three young men arrested yesterday, Kolodziejczyk, Jurczykowski, and Janicki, tried to escape from jail. They began making a hole in the wall, but the gendarmes noticed something suspicious. They were executed on the street. This evening six others were killed.

Throughout the entire day I received information on searches and arrests.

In the afternoon the gendarmes removed twelve men from the jail. They were all tied to a long rope and forced to parade through town to a waiting truck. So far I know of Jan Bac, Antoni Franczak, restaurant owner Palikot, Kucharczyk, Wincenty Brylowski, railroad employee Jozef Okoniewski, Jan Kitowski, Galant, young Adamczyk, Leon Koczow, and the others. After being loaded onto the truck they left in the direction of Bilgoraj. What will happen to them nobody knows.

In the morning a Jew, Gelernter, who was cutting wood for the gendarmes, was shot. His brother had been shot previously.

All the stores in town are closed and practically no one in town is out walking. It looks as if all life has stopped. In my quarters one certain window is an observation point. The whole day my wife, my son, or I watch from there. We can see as far as the marketplace on one side and to the Zamosc highway on the other. The gestapo are still searching houses and checking the identification of everyone. Two old retirees, Maj. Malinowski and Col. Zielenski, were severely beaten.

Today was a terrifying day. My notes cannot in any way describe the horror of these last few hours.

Only because of my obligation to the hospital am I still here. Otherwise I would take my family and move away from Szczebrzeszyn. I have decided to stay and not leave my quarters overnight. Both of the other doctors in town, Jozwiakowski and Spoz, never stay in one place but constantly move around.

The general feeling is that last night's arrests were in retaliation for Rutka's killing. People are afraid to think of what might happen in the next few days.

June 18   The night was quiet. After the ordeal of the last few days we finally had a good night of rest and sleep. During the day things became normal again. Pedestrian traffic on the streets increased. Most stores and shops are open. The wives of the arrested went to Bilgoraj to check on their future. One thing is good: they are still alive. The mayor is attempting to secure the release of two city employees, Kitowski and Galant. This afternoon the funeral of young Janicki took place. The others were buried earlier. The commandant of the "blue police," Marunowski, told me that the night would be very quiet.

Around 9 P.M. this evening two truckloads of German air force men came to town and began a raid, looking for forced labor for the airfield. People began running and hiding. Two men, Spozowski and Nawrocki, came to my hospital to hide. I have never seen anything like this before.

I am trying to keep things at the hospital under control. I am particularly worried that personnel will begin escaping from the hospital. It is now 11 P.M. I checked to be sure that all the hospital doors are locked, and I went dead tired to my quarters. My wife is still sitting at the window, observing what is occurring outside.

June 19   Last night was finally a quiet one. I found out later about yesterday's affair with the German air force. They came to town for fun, and while walking around they found several young men who were grazing their horses and playing cards. When they saw the Germans they started running. Some of the Germans ran after them, shooting, but a few went to the gendarmes to report an illegal assembly of partisans. Of course the gendarmes conducted a search and arrested six people, but they were released shortly thereafter.

This morning I went to Zwierzyniec where Dr. Wroblewski had contracted spotted typhus. I called in a few of my friends for consultation. In a few hours Dr. Bogucki, Dr. Branicki, and Dr. Wieczorkiewicz came. Dr. Branicki brought with him his manuscript about his activities in the Fifth Siberian Division during World War I, where he was a physician. He began writing because of my insistence. Very soon I will begin to edit it.

June 20   Today there was no excitement. The day passed quietly.

June 22   Yesterday felt so normal that I decided to go to Zwierzyniec for a few hours. I was sure that after the last few hectic days we are faced with a relatively calm time.

As soon as I came back I was told that new arrests began around the Jewish housing area. The Germans were trying to take the Jews for labor at the airfield. Two old Jews were killed, a shoemaker whose name was not familiar to me and old Gelernter, whose two sons had been executed during the last few days. All those arrested were taken to Bilgoraj; in total, fifty-three Jews.

June 23 The night passed. Since early morning new actions against the Szczebrzeszyn population have been occurring. The gestapo have been walking the streets and checking IDs. How many people have been arrested, I don't know yet. So far it has been old, paralyzed Leonard Talanda and his son Aleksander, both active Ukrainians and members of the Orthodox church; Wladyslaw Chichocki, a court clerk; Hysa, owner of a soda stand; Czeslaw Trusz; Michal Jurczykowski, post office clerk; Piotr Rypinski, a butcher; Aleksander Michalski, a merchant; and a few others.

Around 3 P.M. more than twenty old Jews held in the city jail were taken to an empty lot on Frampolska Street and shot. The Jews in town are panicking.

In Bilgoraj Jan Prokop was executed. This is the ninth day of terrorist activities by the Germans in Szczebrzeszyn. The town is half dead. No one brings any food into the city, so our situation is really bad. We do not see an end to this. But we must withstand the pressure.

June 24 I learned some details about yesterday's execution of Jews at the empty lot. A big ditch had already been prepared a few days ago. When the Jews were brought for execution, they were told to lie down in the ditch. They were shot with machine guns. Then the next few were forced to lie down on top of the dead. They killed them all in three rows. All were very old men who prayed and begged for mercy.

July

July 3 Here in Szczebrzeszyn life has again become normal, but we do not know for how long.

We think a lot about the partisan activities, Polish or Russian, and the bandits. I do not know how it is in the other areas, but around the counties of Zamosc, Bilgoraj, Tomaszow, and also Hrubieszow some bizarre things are happening. I have information about some well-equipped forest units, some even mounted, about military exercises and even shooting ranges. We hear more and more news about armed assaults. A train traveling between Krasnobrod and Dlugi Kat was derailed, and an attack was mounted against the lumber mill in Dlugi Kat. This lumber mill is now owned by a German company and its director was killed during the assault. The main building was set on fire and the entire plant put out of commission. The same thing happened at a flour mill in Kawenczyn.

Soon after this many German military units began a search but with no results. They are supposed to destroy all partisan groups, but they are completely unprepared for fighting guerrilla warfare.

For a few days we have been hearing artillery fire. Lately the gendarmes have even been confiscating bicycles to be used as a means of transportation against the partisans. As an example, for a new bicycle Stanislaw Bohdanowicz received script for 1,400 zlotys.

Today I went to Zamosc specifically to see the home of the new city museum. When I looked at the old Jewish apartment house now completely renovated, I became very happy. The old building with the date of 1634 above the entry was completely restored to its original appearance. Renovation was under the guidance of architect Zaremba. He, along with museum director Kabat, moved all the pieces from the old building confiscated by the Germans to this new place. They added many items that had been stored in boxes, so as of now the museum looks much better than it did before. So far 60,000 zloty have been spent on the renovation of the building.

When I learned that the new mayor, Otto Werner, was not interested in this project, I decided to use my own psychology. I went to congratulate him on the contributions the city made in restoring the museum, and I invited him to come along with me and look at the newly opened display rooms. He agreed and we began walking and admiring the beautiful displays. After visiting several rooms he was so impressed that he congratulated architect Zaremba and director Kabat and then promised his and the city council's help in the further renovation of the museum.

After he left I pointed out to director Kabat that the more valuable items, such as very rare gold pieces, should be moved away for safekeeping. While looking at the museum I thought about my friend Rosinski, who did so much to help the museum start almost twenty years ago. He would be so happy to see it.

At the same time I was notified about the death of Stanislaw Przybylowicz in Oranienburg concentration camp. He was a natural-science teacher at the local high school who put together the first natural-science exhibition at the city museum.

July 4   This morning during a partisan raid on the furniture factory in Zwierzyniec a gestapo agent, Mrozik, was killed. He was a very dangerous man with good knowledge of the Polish language. He had on his conscience the murder of several people.

I do not know any details yet, but I expect more arrests in the Zwierzyniec area.

July 5   Now I have very limited information from Zwierzyniec. New gendarme and gestapo units arrived there, and sporadic action continues. Today the Polish underground and Soviet partisans attacked the railroad station and forestry station in Kawenczyn. They took only 500 zloty.

July 6   Today a fire occurred at the Turobin lumber mill and yesterday at the mill in Tereszpol. It appears that this was a well-organized action to destroy all sources of building materials necessary for new German military construction.

July 7   Tonight, for the second time in the last few days, the Szczebrzeszyn railroad station was attacked. More and more hold-ups are taking place, and the Germans are completely helpless. They have organized a special police, the so-called *Sonderdienst*, but this had not helped at all.

This afternoon I went to Zwierzyniec. There I learned that during a search of a nearby forest young Lokaj was killed, and a woman working in a field was shot. Yesterday Opila and Ciecko were arrested.

July 8   Last night around midnight a gendarme at the Szczebrzeszyn railroad station spotted several men standing outside the building. He called the gendarme post, and in a few minutes several soldiers with machine guns arrived. Naturally the "suspicious" characters disappeared. After walking around the soldiers returned to the barracks. As soon as they left the station was hit and all the money from the cashier's office was taken, approximately 2,000 zloty. This is the third assault on this station in four days.

Yesterday Piotr Rypin was released from the prison in Bilgoraj.

July 9   Around midnight a fire began in the village of Blonie. German police and gendarmes were stopping everyone on the streets, even firefighters.

New orders were posted regarding anti-aircraft shelters and trenches. The existing ones are to be renovated and more new ones installed.

Entering the nearby forest is prohibited for four days. It appears the Germans will try to search the forest looking for partisans.

July 11   Yesterday I went to Zwierzyniec to help with the delivery of a cousin of the Zamoyskis' child. There I was told about new arrests, a total of eleven people, including the building contractor Tadeusz Rugowski. I met Count Zoltowski, married to the daughter of Fudakowski from Krasnobrod. He told me that a few times Soviet partisans came there asking for food and that he was forced to play chess with an officer. The interesting thing about this: the officer held a handgun the whole time and even moved the chess piece with the gun barrel.

July 12   Today in Szczebrzeszyn a new detachment of gendarmes arrived. They will stay here until all of the partisans have been arrested or killed.

July 17   During the last few days nothing much has happened. Today in Hamernia engineer Kielczewski was killed. A large group of prisoners was moved from Bilgoraj to Lublin prison.

A few days ago in Jozefow the Germans began killing Jews. Around 1,500 people perished, mostly women and children. All the men were deported for labor to Germany.

For the last two days Jerzy Plomienski stayed with me. We spent several hours discussing the future of our literature. He was on his way to Uhrynow, at the invitation of Mr. and Mrs. Scibor-Rylski, carrying only one small briefcase and a small suitcase loaded with manuscripts.

July 18   Tonight in Szczebrzeszyn six Jews were executed. Jan Skora was arrested.

July 24   The week passed quietly. Today I am leaving on vacation.

August

August 4   I spent my vacation in Warsaw. I relaxed there in a completely different atmosphere. Once again I was able to contact people from the intellectual world. The war and the hard times that we live in do not have the strength to break their spirit. So I really relaxed. I took part in the usual Wednesday meeting at Rygiel's. This time Solecki talked about the collection of remembrance medals dated from the seventeenth century. He displayed several medals from his collection. From Rygiel I received a few very old drawings of Zamosc and a manuscript of Alexander Bruckner's about Krucygier from Szczebrzeszyn; it is a very short, one-page article written probably for some magazine. There I met Jan Pomorski, one of a new generation of collectors. I stopped by twice at his house to review his collection of Polish memoirs. He owns a beautiful collection of illustrations and etchings.

My overall impression from my stay in Warsaw this year is different from what I saw a year ago. I am used to the postwar ruins. I can see increasing selling activities. More stores are now open. The produce prices are high, but if you have money you can buy anything. The prices on suits or women's dresses are very high. But you can find all sorts of cheap, fake women's jewelry, crystals, and other types of women's items—bracelets, earrings, bags and such. Books are going up in price, but you can find used books in all the bookstores. It is possible to find some that were just printed, mostly children's books. In some bookstores you can even buy illegal editions of new books.

I purchased a copy of *Piesn Niepodlegla*, an anthology of poetry printed in 1942. Only 1,600 copies were printed. Good paper makes them look good, with even a multicolor title page. This book was sold out in a few days, all illegal transactions.

From printer Antoni Tropinski I received a copy of memoirs from the Majdanek concentration camp.

On the streets there is less traffic than before. Cars are used only by Germans. More Germans are seen on the streets than a year ago. You can hear the German language everywhere. Germans in civilian clothes can be seen. They wear a small swastika on their lapels. Signs are in two languages, German on top, Polish on the bottom. I noticed many more crippled, former soldiers with amputated arms and legs than I did last year. Occasionally a group of Jews who have been taken for labor can be seen.

No Jews are on the streets. I came to Warsaw at the time that mass murders of Jews in the ghetto began. I was told that about 5,000 people a day were being killed. At night I could hear machine-gun fire coming from the direction of the ghetto. The whole of Warsaw was in shock over the murder of a well-known physician.

By order of the German authorities, Raszej, a well-known surgeon from Poznan, along with Dr. Kazimierz Polak was consulting at the bedside of the publisher Gutmajer, a Jew. During the examination a few Lithuanian members of a special SS unit entered the room and shot all three of them dead. They had not even asked for identifications.

I heard many similar stories, but I am leaving them for Warsaw writers to describe.

Coming back I had no problems. I found out that even without any black market goods, and by paying a special fee to railroad workers, I was able to sit in a special car reserved for railroad personnel.

At home I learned that everything was in good order. Only once did German gendarmes search the hospital. They inspected the entire hospital including the typhus wards. They checked the kitchen, storage rooms, and private quarters. They spoke good Polish. They asked about a man with lung wounds.

Today new action began. In Szczebrzeszyn an attack on the office of the KKO-Credit Bank took place. The robbers forced the employees to open the safe. Sixty thousand zloty were taken.

It is interesting that Materna, the owner of the tobacco store next door, called the telephone operator to notify German gendarmes about the robbery. The operator was probably afraid of future consequences and ignored his call.

August 6   In the village of Turobin a gendarme was killed. The Germans arrested twenty-five men and executed them in public in the marketplace. The bodies were thrown into the septic tank behind city hall. The families were prohibited from removing the bodies.

August 8, 11 A.M.   In town the atmosphere is very tense. Last night it was clear that Jewish lives are in jeopardy. There is bad news from Bilgoraj and Zwierzyniec also.

German patrols increased throughout the night. Around 1 A.M. I was awakened by unusually loud noises on the street. I heard shouting in German, Polish, and Yiddish. A patrol stayed in one apartment for quite a while. In the second they merely forced the door open and left shortly after searching the inside. They never entered the attic area where a Jewish woman with four children was hiding.

In the morning I left the hospital to try and find out what had happened. All Jews must report at 8 A.M. across from the *Judenrat*. They are allowed to take 15 lbs. of baggage, food for five days, and 1,500 zloty per person. The mayor informed me the 2,000 Jews will be deported east to the Ukraine. Railroad workers said that a large train with fifty-five cars is ready at the station. So far there are no volunteers, so the Germans began mass arrests. I asked a gendarme what would happen if the Jews did not show up. His answer was, "We will kill them here."

It is 7 P.M. Without interruption, throughout the entire day, patrols of gestapo, gendarmes, *Sonderdienst*, "blue police," along with members of the *Judenrat* and the so-called Jewish Militia, patrolled the city. They searched houses, including basements and attics. Any Jews that were found were moved to the marketplace. Most Jewish houses are empty now, so city personnel began removing the belongings, loaded everything onto horse-drawn wagons, and took them for storage in warehouses around city hall. Most of the Jews are still hiding. Some Poles are helping the Germans search for Jews. In town the tension is growing.

August 8, 9 P.M.   Around 8 P.M. the Germans began moving the Jews from the marketplace. Some Jews attempted to escape, but the German police stopped them by shooting them. The shooting started a panic among the people standing near the streets, so everyone began running.

Several hundred Jews were taken to the railroad station. Some older men and women who were unable to walk quickly were beaten by the gendarmes.

I was able to observe this by standing on top of the hospital wall. It was so terrifying that I do not have the strength to describe it.

From Bilgoraj and a few surrounding villages around 1,000 Jews were taken to the railroad station. So far in Szczebrzeszyn thirteen Jews were killed. No one believes that the Jews will be moved to the Ukraine. They will all be killed.

After today's events it is difficult to gain control of myself, but I feel that this is not yet the end.

August 10 Yesterday no Jews were seen on the city streets. Late in the evening three more Jews were shot. I learned that the train carrying the Jews went to Belzec. They have probably been killed by now.

August 11 Today is a free market day but traffic is very light. Villagers are prohibited from selling anything to the Jews. City employees are going to Jewish houses and collecting all furniture, bedding, and household items and taking them to warehouses near city hall. In town only Jews with valid labor cards issued by the labor bureau can stay.

Now we are under so-called martial law. This allows the Germans to shoot anyone without any questions asked.

All food prices are up. The villagers have stopped deliveries to town.

August 12 Today a young Jewish woman with a small child and another Jew were shot. This afternoon county Dr. Snacki arrived from Bilgoraj, accompanied by a German official. They checked Dr. Sztreicher's dental equipment and also Dr. Bronsztein's cabinets. After taking some equipment they locked and sealed both offices. Dr. Bolotny's office was sealed. He is not allowed to help Jews anymore.

Both Dr. Snacki and the mayor told me that Jews in Szczebrzeszyn will be completely eliminated.

August 20 Every day a few Jews are shot. People are so used to it that it is no longer news. Every day a young Polish boy or a villager without a labor card is executed.

Almost everyone arrested lately has been moved from Lublin prison to Auschwitz concentration camp. Some of the prisoner's families have been evicted from their own homes, such as the Talanda family. Terror is increasing and it is difficult to withstand the pressure. People are asking if we can continue any longer. Some believe the war will end this year. Everyone awaits the creation of a second front in Europe.

We wait for good news from the Russian front. From every sign it appears that the coming fall and winter will be very severe. If so, our own situation doesn't look too bright. We live from day to day.

August 22 Today two gestapo agents from Zamosc began once again going through the list of people registered at city hall. After a few hours they went to the parish office to check the registration list of the parishioners. Later, one agent left but the other stayed in town. Some of the people are sure that tonight we will have more arrests, and some decided not to stay home.

August 26 Today, very early in the morning, Michalski and Kruk, former students at the University of Lublin, were arrested. Jan Bac was released from Lublin prison.

August 29 Since early morning, with the help of gestapo from Zamosc, new arrests took place. So far court clerk Niedzielski, organist Zlomanczuk, Bortkiewicz, Podsiadlowa, Kowalski, and a few others are being held. The wife of teacher Jozef Kollataj was severely beaten during an investigation but was later released.

Because of rumors that Szczebrzeszyn will be evacuated, people here are living under tremendous stress. I heard from Warsaw that the so-called general government will soon become part of Germany. So far there is no good news.

August 30 Today at the hospital we had some real excitement. Last night gendarmes brought to the hospital a young woman, Jadwiga Hornowska, from Szczebrzeszyn, with gunshot wounds to the head. A young man supposedly shot her when she opened the door to her apartment. Hornowska, the widow of an executed police officer, has been living with another man. He escaped a few days ago when the gestapo began looking for him. Card games took place in her house every day. Hornowska was interrogated at the hospital by the gestapo.

Tonight around 9 P.M. a man about thirty years of age entered the hospital. Holding a gun, he ordered that he be led to Hornowska's room. After checking everyone in the room with a flashlight, he stopped at her bed and shot her twice. He then ran from the hospital. I called the gendarmes and again an interrogation began. Both wounds were only superficial flesh wounds of the cheek. This is all very puzzling. Someone wants her dead, but who? I decided to move her into a separate room, and a policeman was posted at her door.

September

September 1 Today is the third anniversary of the war. This last year was much harder than the others. Terror is increasing, and we ask ourselves whether we will be able to survive to the end.

Almost every day brings something new. Today the Germans ordered a complete new census of everyone in town and the registration of all livestock. So city hall assigned two-man teams to go from house to house and begin the registration. One team just left the hospital. My wife, my son, and I are at the top of the list. What the reason is for the registration I do not know, but people speculate that this is probably the first step in the evacuation of the city. This type of news is very depressing. I myself am ready for the worst. The only thing I am worried about is my collection of books, prints, and particularly my own manuscripts. I put so much effort into these collections that losing them would be a terrible blow to my life. Most of my collection is supposed to go to libraries in Zamosc, Lublin, and Warsaw at the time of my death. This is depressing me more than the possibility of evacuation to an unknown location.

I write this and I am not sure why. If we must leave Szczebrzeszyn I will be unable to take all of the work with me. I have almost 800 handwritten pages covering the time since the beginning of the war until today. But I still hope to survive and keep my manuscript with me. Besides this I have over 600 pages of typewritten manuscripts of my memoirs, covering the period of 1918 until 1939, ready for publishing, and many smaller works also.

September 2 Today around noon a gestapo agent in uniform, accompanied by one in civilian clothing, visited the hospital. The civilian was Majewski, a Pole from Bilgoraj. They are gathering information about the Hornowska affair. As they left they said, "Being in Szczebrzeszyn is no good." I recognized through this statement that the gestapo are preparing some surprises for us.

A few days ago the Alwa plant was attacked. The robbers took 32,000 zloty.

September 3 We received alarming news about an air bombardment of Warsaw. I attempted to call, but all the telephone lines are reserved for the military.

In town more gestapo agents are snooping around. I have a feeling that this time new arrests will take place.

September 5   With memories still fresh I will try to describe the events of last night. Around 10 P.M. I heard the tremendous noise of high-flying heavy bombers. They flew in several groups, one after another. People who survived the bombardment of Warsaw in 1939 were terrified.

Around 11:30 P.M. a few gendarmes came to the hospital and ordered me to go with them and give first aid to their commandant, Lt. Foerster. I picked up my first-aid material and went with four gendarmes to their headquarters. I found the officer lying down with gunshot wounds to his side. He was hit while on patrol of the city. After administering first aid I requested an army ambulance to take him to the military hospital in Zamosc. I waited until 2 A.M. and sat by the wounded man. During the almost three-hour wait I was able to observe events taking place at the gendarme station.

At one point they received a call about a robbery of the local creamery. Several gendarmes and members of the "blue police" left to investigate, armed with handguns and carbines. After one hour they returned. On the table was a large bottle of vodka. Everyone had a drink from it; later they brought in some beer. They seemed very nervous. All around the room various guns, rifles, and hand grenades were scattered.

Finally the ambulance came. The orderlies moved the wounded officer so unprofessionally that they almost dropped him to the floor. After the ambulance left four armed gendarmes and one with a machine gun escorted me back to the hospital.

I am afraid that we will have some arrests in connection with the shooting of the gendarme officer.

September 5, 10 P.M.   So far the day has passed with no arrests. In town there has been an increased number of gestapo agents patrolling in civilian clothes. Many people are leaving town.

A few days ago several arrests took place in Turobin. Dr. Kwit and Dr. Bedalek were arrested, but Dr. Maczka escaped. So now Turobin has no physicians. Also three priests and a veterinarian, along with forty others, are being held. No one knows the reason for these arrests.

September 7   It is now two days after the shooting of Lt. Foerster, and still no reaction on the part of the Germans. This is very surprising. We still await reprisals.

September 9   Yesterday, since early morning, several arrests have taken place. Altogether twelve men, most of them unemployed and involved in the black market, were taken. Among them: Hojda, Czerwia, Wybacz, Wojtowicz, Kowalik, and old Misiarz, father of a known troublemaker. One peasant was killed. He was stopped on the street while trying to sell a load of lime. Without any kind of identification, he was transported to the city jail. He tried to escape and was shot.

In the evening a large truckload of gestapo agents arrived. This morning I learned that since 3 A.M. more arrests were made. Two prisoners, Zlomanczuk and Tykwinski, were brought in for interrogation from Lublin prison. The gestapo are trying to force them to reveal the names of other people involved in illegal activities. At the Klemensow refinery, Osicki and Cebrykowie were arrested. In Szczebrzeszyn, Bielecka and her daughter, the shoemaker Augustowski, and a few other people were taken.

The gestapo searched several houses, but most of the people they were looking for had moved out already. They went with Tykwinski to Szperowka, where they arrested Dzioch and Hadam. This time no professional people were arrested. Three times the gestapo searched the Firmanty store. No one was there, so the gendarmes removed all goods from the store and furniture from the house. This is supposed to be in direct connection to the shooting of Lt. Foerster, who died in Zamosc hospital.

Around 10 P.M. huge bombers flew over us. Gendarmes and police are talking confidentially about new arrests, so the atmosphere here in the city is gloomy.

September 10   Today was a quiet day. Tomorrow morning the funeral of Lt. Foerster will take place. We are sure that more arrests will follow, especially now that young Misiarz is walking around telling people that more gendarmes will be killed because of his father's arrest.

Tonight the flour mill belonging to Lysak in Kawenczyn was attacked again.

Wojdat, a former cadet of the sanitary military academy, was arrested yesterday in Bilgoraj. He had been working as a clerk. He was known for his heavy drinking. He had been advised not to come home but to escape. Instead of hiding he got drunk and began walking the streets, and finally he was arrested. This is not the first time that vodka has led people into gestapo hands.

We received information from Auschwitz that Franciszek Antczak had died. Before the war he was commandant of the police in Szczebrzeszyn.

This afternoon the city was hit with the news that 300 families will be evacuated soon. People are trying to guess who will be forced out.

September 15   A few days passed without any extraordinary events. So far, since the funeral of Foerster everything is quiet. But from the nearby villages and from Zamosc I received information about more arrests. People, particularly young ones, are trying to avoid travel by train.

On free market days the city is very quiet. The time for delivering grain quotas is at hand, so to avoid penalties everyone is taking grain to the collection stations. These stations are patrolled by armed guards.

I am having difficulty trying to find provisions for the hospital. Prices are rising. It is difficult to think about the upcoming winter.

September 17   Yesterday was a terrible day. Since midnight new arrests have taken place. On Zamojska Street all houses were searched. This action was concluded by noon. Many people were not home; some were able to escape at the last moment. Sometimes women were arrested instead of husbands and sons.

More than forty people were sent to prison in Bilgoraj. This list I made is not complete: Mrs. Jozwiakowska, wife of Antoni; mason Kolodziejczyk: Albin Grabowski; Zygmunt Grabowski; mason Czeslaw Biziorek; shoemaker Jan Kalinowski; Antoni Ostowicz; merchant Krzeszowski; Zlomaniec; Ksiazkowa; Stanislaw Hysa; Kryk; Trzcinska; Marszycki; Tadeusz Kot; Mikolaj Tymczak; attorney Wilk; Materna; Stanislaw Danieluk; chimney sweeper Gorniak; Antoni Stropek; Aleksander Stropek; Maria Pomianowska-Czernicka; Hasiec; miller Jan Bender; Kucharski; Lucja Swica; Rubaj; two Kowalik brothers; and Czerniakowski. Later two Jewish brothers, Sztreicher, one a barber, the other a dental technician, were arrested.

I was told that the "blue police" assisting the gendarmes in searching the houses helped some people to escape. The policemen tried to make plenty of noise by shouting on the streets and breaking doors to give enough time for some of the people to escape or hide.

I talked with the mayor. He is sure that this is not the end of the arrests. People here are so disturbed they are unable to work. Even Mayor Kraus seems very nervous. Here we are again fearing the upcoming days.

September 19   Yesterday two Grabowski brothers, also Gorniak and Kolodziejczyk, were released from Bilgoraj prison. Kalinowski and Hysa, both members of a civil defense unit, were transported to the labor bureau for disposition. The prison has such terrible living conditions that people are sleeping on the floors.

Yesterday the two Sztreicher brothers were executed. At night in cell no. 1 in Bilgoraj prison a mutiny took place. It is impossible to get any details. One guard was killed and a few prisoners escaped. But in the morning seventeen prisoners were executed, including three from Szczebrzeszyn: Kuczynski, Skora, and Biurko.

I try to note the exact account of all events. I try to gather all necessary details to show what is really occurring. But many times information received from eyewitnesses is not accurate. People are always adding something, so it is almost impossible to get to the truth. Even knowing that I sometimes fail to get the exact truth, I am sure that my notes give enough objective material to anyone who will be studying this period.

After the Bilgoraj mutiny we are expecting more arrests. People, in increasing numbers, spend the nights hiding out. No one walks the city streets. I now have fewer than twenty patients in the hospital. Most of the stores are closed. People are so nervous that some cannot even begin their normal workday.

The Germans posted big red announcements saying "German Patience Is *At An End*" and the only punishment for giving help to "*bandits and robbers*" will be death. Any villages hiding them will be burned down.

It so happens that the number of bandits and robbers is growing. Now with the autumn chill they come to the villages to stay overnight. It appears they are laughing at the gendarmes and police. Farmers and other villagers are caught between the very well armed underground and the gendarmes, with the "blue police." Their life is very difficult. The farmers try to help the partisans but they are afraid of German reprisals.

Living conditions are very difficult. Some of the people have already been broken and have lost their will to fight for survival. Everyone's hope is to survive until the end of the war.

September 22 Tonight a group of bandits attacked some farmers in Kawenczyn. A farmer, Wladyslaw Lazorczyk, and two evacuees, a mother and daughter, were killed. The bandits escaped, but the villagers were able to catch one, nineteen-year-old Leon Szpuga, from Topolcza. He was turned over to the gendarmes. Three women were released from prison: Jozwiakowska, Czernicka-Pomianowska, and Ksiazkowa.

Some prisoners were transported to Lublin, but no one knows what the Germans will do to them. Maybe they will be turned over to the labor bureau to be sent to labor camps in Germany, or maybe they will be shipped to concentration camps.

The last few days passed quietly. People are hoping that maybe the repression will end.

September 24 Yesterday morning young Januszewicz, the director of the brick kiln, was arrested.

I learned about an event that took place yesterday near Komarowa, in the county of Zamosc. Three people were riding together—Kosminski, road technician Szablinski, and a third one. They were stopped by some armed men in civilian clothing. The men inspected the identification papers of all three. Two were set free, but Szablinski, who carried a *Volksdeutsch* ID was shot. Because of this incident, all *Volksdeutsch* are very nervous.

September 30 Nothing much is happening. There are a few fires in the area, but that is all. Yesterday about 400 Jews from Radecznica and Goraj were brought to Szczebrzeszyn.

October 5 We are awaiting more deportations for labor in Germany. The streets are deserted; people, particularly youngsters, are avoiding walking, with good reason.

In Komorow, in direct connection with the shooting of Szablinski, fifty Poles and fifty Jews were arrested and executed. In Goraj a huge fire occurred at the grain-collecting station. Large warehouses full of grain were burned completely to the ground. One hundred people were arrested as hostages.

October 11 Januszewicz was released from Bilgoraj prison. In general last week was rather quiet. But yesterday, since early morning, the Germans began a roundup of young people. The "blue police" were checking houses with a list of names. They arrested several young girls; some were quickly released, but about fifteen girls are supposed to be transported to Szczebrzeszyn station. There are those who think their destination is Italy, where several girls who were taken a few weeks before ended up. All the new girls succeeded in escaping from the railroad station. People in town feel the Germans will try to hunt them down. Stores are closed, and we worry once again about the future of our youth.

The gendarmes are after the bandits. They have a free hand in killing people because of martial law, so they kill for no other reason than the urge to kill. Not one day passes without a few people being shot. Besides the gendarmes, people are afraid of the bandits. The October chill is forcing people to move from the forest to the villages. Mostly in Kawenczyn, real bandits are trying to avenge the killing of Szpuga. Two German teachers left Brody, afraid of partisan activities, so the school that was specially opened for the Germans and the *Volksdeutsch* was closed.

October 15 Yesterday I learned that the Germans are taking control of the county hospital in Zamosc. All hospital activities are supposed to cease in two weeks. The patients will either be released or transferred to my hospital in Szczebrzeszyn. Officially the hospital is to be used only for the German civilian population and *Volksdeutsch*.

We are shocked over the execution of Lejzor Zero. He was our hospital butcher who over the last twenty years delivered meat to the hospital. He leased an orchard from me and was a part of hospital life. Lately he was officially employed at the hospital with a work card from the labor bureau. He was a wonderful man; everyone liked him. During the last few years he helped me and I helped his family. Every evening he would stop at my office with the latest news. This morning gendarme Syring called him to report to the gendarme station. Zero went without any hesitation because he delivered meat to the gendarmes. After half an hour he left the station with three gendarmes, and they stopped by the city jail to pick up another Jew, Tuchszneider. On a horse-drawn wagon, under escort, they were driven to Michalow, where in a small forest they were executed. Just yesterday I talked with Lejzor about the outcome of the war. He told me he thought that the Germans had already lost the war, but he was not sure if we could survive. Everyone is very sad about his murder.

October 18   A few days ago the Germans finished off most of the Jews in Zamosc. Only twenty or so good mechanics are left. The old people were shot and the younger ones transported to Izbica. The same thing happened in Turobin. I am sure that the same fate awaits the Jews in Szczebrzeszyn.

A few days ago Maria Misiarzowa was executed. She was the mother of a known bandit who is the leader of a robber gang.

Lately the gendarmes and the "blue police" have been on full alert. At night they have increased their patrolling of the streets.

October 19   This morning I decided to go to Zamosc. I used a horse-drawn wagon on car wheels, a so-called horse bus. I tried to find out what had happened to Rosinski's collections, all supposedly stored in a safe place. I thought about moving and depositing them in the Zamoyski estate archives. I already had an agreement with Jan Zamoyski and the archive director, Galinski.

As we approached Zamosc I saw many people fleeing the city. Some tried to stop us. A young boy on a bicycle shouted to us that the Germans were trying to assemble everyone. The city is completely cut off. You are allowed to go in, but nobody can leave town. We went a few kilometers farther to Janowice, but there we received confirmation that it was very dangerous to continue. So after a few hours I returned home. I have not even tried to call my friends in Zamosc because all conversations are tapped.

In our town the atmosphere is very heavy. Jews are afraid of final extermination and we fear deportation to labor camps. Besides all of this we keep hearing about the increased activities of partisans, the underground army, and just plain bandits. These conditions make any kind of work effort worthless. We are still waiting for something to happen.

October 21 Today I planned to try to go to Zamosc again. I woke up very early to be ready, but around 6 A.M. I heard noise and through the window saw unusual movement. This was the beginning of the so-called German displacement of Jews, in reality a liquidation of the entire Jewish population in Szczebrzeszyn.

From early morning until late at night we witnessed indescribable events. Armed SS soldiers, gendarmes, and "blue police" ran through the city looking for Jews. Jews were assembled in the marketplace. The Jews were taken from their houses, barns, cellars, attics, and other hiding places. Pistol and gun shots were heard throughout the entire day. Sometimes hand grenades were thrown into the cellars. Jews were beaten and kicked; it made no difference whether they were men, women, or small children.

By 3 P.M. more than 900 Jews had been assembled. The Germans began moving them to the outskirts of the city. All had to walk except for members of the *Judenrat* and the Jewish police; they were allowed to use horse-drawn wagons. The action didn't stop even after they were taken out of town. The Germans still carried on the search for Jews. It was posted that the penalty for hiding Jews is death, but for showing their hiding places special rewards will be given.

All Jews will be shot. Between 400 and 500 have been killed. Poles were forced to begin digging graves in the Jewish cemetery. From information I received approximately 2,000 people are in hiding. The arrested Jews were loaded onto a train at the railroad station to be moved to an unknown location.

It was a terrifying day. I cannot describe everything that took place. You cannot even imagine the barbarism of the Germans. I am completely broken and cannot seem to find myself.

We received news of robberies increasing everywhere. During the last few weeks the incidence of rape has also increased. I have already examined many pregnancies. A few days ago the wife of a well-known farmer and later a young schoolteacher came in for examination.

October 22 The action against the Jews continues. The only difference is that the SS has moved out and the job is now in the hands of our own local gendarmes and the "blue police." They received orders to kill all the Jews, and they are obeying them. At the Jewish cemetery huge trenches are being dug and Jews are being shot while lying in them. The most brutal were two gendarmes, Pryczing and Syring.

The Jews that were moved yesterday out of Szczebrzeszyn were held at the Alwa plant. Around 9 P.M. another group of Jews from Zwierzyniec were brought in. Today around noon all were loaded into railroad cars, but by 4 P.M. the train had not moved. It is very cold and rainy. After the Jews were loaded into the cars, factory workers collected and brought to an assembly area money, gold, jewelry, and pearls.

In town some of the Jewish houses were sealed by the gendarmes, but others were left completely open, so robberies took place. It is a shame to say it but some Polish people took part in that crime. Some people even helped the gendarmes look for hidden Jews. The Germans even killed small Jewish children. It is hard to describe.

It is so terrible that it is almost impossible to comprehend. Legally the Jews don't exist in Szczebrzeszyn anymore, but still many Jews are in hiding. All will be killed sooner or later. I went to city hall today. The total number of Jews killed—they call them disabled—is unknown. Even the best specialists were exterminated. We can feel the shortage of good mechanics.

October 23   I went to Zamosc. There are only seven patients in the hospital. People there are cleaning and preparing for the transition of the hospital to German administration. No one knows what will really happen. So far the physicians and all hospital personnel must stay.

The general mood is bad. People live under the constant fear of deportation. Several stores were taken over by the Germans during the arrests on October 19. Approximately 3,000 were detained, including two physicians, Dr. Bogucki and Dr. Branicki. Half of those arrested were released the next day. Three hundred people were assigned to work on road repair as replacements for the liquidated Jews. There are practically no Jews in Zamosc. Maybe a few are still hiding.

Dr. Rosenbush-Szpiegelglass was transported along with other Jews to Izbica; the same with Dr. Roseman. But Dr. Skotnicki, an ophthalmologist, escaped. The streets are deserted. This is so depressing that I was glad to go home.

While I was gone, the gestapo, local gendarmes, "blue police," and some street people in Szczebrzeszyn again started the hunt for Jews. Particularly active was Matysiak, a policeman from Sulowo, and Skorzak, a city janitor. Skorzak had no gun, only an ax, and with the ax he killed several Jews. The whole day people hunted and killed Jews, while others brought corpses to the cemetery for burial.

October 24   In Szczebrzeszyn the hunt for Jews is still on. Additional gestapo agents came from Bilgoraj. With the help of gendarmes, "blue police," and some citizens they looked everywhere for Jews. All cellars, attics, and barns were searched. Most Jews were killed on the spot, but some were taken to the Jewish cemetery for public execution.

I witnessed a group of Jews being forced to march to the cemetery. On both sides of the prisoners marched gendarmes, "blue police," and so-called Polish guards dressed in black uniforms. To speed things up the Jews were beaten on their heads and backs with wooden sticks. This was a terrible picture.

Around noon the gestapo ordered that all men over the age of fifteen be ready by 2 P.M., with shovels, to start the burial of the Jews. The sale of alcohol to Polish people was stopped. All restaurants are now off limits.

I went to the gendarme post asking if hospital personnel would be excused from burial work. I was told that physicians would be but that all other personnel must report.

Without interruption, Jews from nearby villages are being transported to the cemetery. The dead were brought by horse-drawn wagons.

All furniture, bedding, and other goods were moved to the marketplace and stockpiled. Some townspeople tried to take advantage of poor security at the marketplace and stole the best pieces.

Most of the murdered Jews are old men, women, and small children. The younger men are in the forest. They are trying to organize and seek revenge. We are afraid that they will try to burn the city.

This is the fourth day like this. It is impossible to count the victims of this savage act of extermination by the Germans. It looks as if it is not over yet. By tomorrow more people must report to work at the cemetery.

October 26 Yesterday, on Sunday, the hunt for Jews was still on. Approximately fifty people were killed and their bodies transported to the cemetery. Approximately one hundred more were taken to the cemetery in two groups, women and children in one, men in another. All were killed.

I witnessed how Jews were removed from a hiding place in the ropemaker Dym's house. I counted approximately fifty Jews as they were taken to the jail. A crowd looked on, laughing and even beating the Jews; others searched homes for more victims.

One city hall employee, Kuczer, who took an active role in the killing, told me that two Jews ill with spotted typhus were shot and buried along with their beds and bedding in a four-meter-deep hole. He told me this and requested that I notify the county sanitary officer. He hopes for a reward for fighting the typhus epidemic.

What happened to Dr. Bolotny I do not know. Dentist Bronsztejnowa, along with her two young daughters, was transported to Belzec. Dr. Sztrejcherowa was shot in her own house.

I feel it is correct to give some names of the German gendarmes and members of the "blue police" who were very active in the killing of the Jews. Gendarmerie Commandant Meister Frymer; gendarmes Pryczing and Schult; Polish-speaking gendarmes Mendykowski, Wisenburg, Bot, Prestlaw, and Syring; and "blue police" Muranowski, Tatulinski, Hajduczak, and Jan Gal. The cruelest of all is Gal, who is even teaching his teenage son how to kill Jews.

October 26, 6 P.M.   People coming from town are talking about more German cruelties. My niece Zofia Karolakowa witnessed two gendarmes halt a young Jewish girl. She was beaten, kicked, and finally when she was unable to walk she was pulled by her hair to the cemetery and shot. Medic Matuszewski witnessed as Majewski, gestapo agent from Bilgoraj, shot five young Jewish girls.

On all sidewalks there are numerous blood stains. At the city jail every so often there are executions. No one works at city hall except the secretary, Babiarz, who in the absence of the mayor is running the city, and a few clerks who are directly involved in murdering the Jews. Some employees ran home, unable to stand it anymore, but others have become completely apathetic.

Now the robbery of Jewish homes is on the increase. To prevent this the "blue police" shot a young boy and a young woman, Felka Sawicowna. Throughout the entire day horse-drawn wagons hauled Jewish households to warehouses for storage.

This is so difficult to describe. I am making these notes on the spot, without any literary elaboration.

October 27   This is not the end. Action against the Jews continues, but there are not many Jews left. People walking on the street are so used to seeing corpses on the sidewalks that they pass by without any emotion. The body of a Polish boy, killed for robbery, lay on the street for more than twenty-four hours.

October 28   I went to town twice and both times I observed a group of Jews being taken to their death. I saw an old Jewish woman unable to walk anymore. A gestapo man shot her once but she was still alive; so he shot her again, then left. People see this now as a daily event and rarely react. I do not know why, but my reaction to these crimes is different from before.

October 29   No change. Horse-drawn wagons are still bringing Jewish goods to the marketplace. The gendarmes sort everything out. Some bedding and household items were given to the hospital; the same as in other cities. I am not at all pleased with this, but with a complete lack of supplies I decided to take them and register them into the hospital inventory.

October 30 Today there were still some more Jews executed at the cemetery, but most of them were from nearby villages. The gestapo arrived from Zamosc and brought with them a few trucks. They confiscated the best furniture from Polish apartments.

October 31 Still some Jews are hiding. Besides the gendarmes and the "blue police," four members of the Jewish police are very active in hunting the Jews. They know the hiding places, and they hope they will survive. One thing is sure: they will be the last ones shot.

In Zamosc engineer Braunsztein was executed. He had been in charge of all construction projects for the gestapo. From the police information center I learned that up until now around 3,000 Jews have been killed. The number of Jews who escaped or are still hiding is around 1,500.

November

November 2 Yesterday I went to Zwierzyniec. There the liquidation of the Jewish population has been completed. In Szczebrzeszyn the gendarmes still occasionally find hidden Jews. But in Zwierzyniec the gendarmes and the "blue police" now go to the forest to look for Jews. Several have been arrested and shot.

Jan Firmanty was arrested in a Lublin restaurant. The gestapo had been searching for him for some time.

November 4 The gendarmes and police have been bringing Jews they arrested in the forest to the city jail. Mayor Kraus informed me that, according to official statistics, 934 Jews have been deported recently. The number executed cannot be compiled exactly because no one was counting, but approximately 2,300 is the number used in official German correspondence.

In the forest the Jews live alone. Some bandits even take their clothing, leaving them naked. Occasionally partisans give them some help. Only the Russians force them to join the fighting with the underground.

Today the gestapo executed several Jews. The last to be shot were four young Jews who helped the Germans during the liquidation.

In the Jewish cemetery there are now three huge mass graves. One is still open. The dead lay there as if waiting for more victims to be brought.

From eye witnesses I have information that the Germans forced Jews to lie face down on top of the dead and then shot them with machine guns. Some did not die instantly but tried to stand up and cry for help.

During the last three days liquidation of Jews took place in Bilgoraj and Tarnogrod. In Tarnogrod Jews began fighting back. One gestapo agent was killed. Now the liquidation of Jews is taking place in Jozefow.

The entire highway from Bilgoraj to Zwierzyniec is littered with the bodies of Jews. It is impossible to accurately describe what has taken place during the last ten days.

Last Sunday in Krasnobrod, during Mass, the church was surrounded by gendarmes. All young people, boys and girls alike, were arrested and taken to prison in Zamosc. People suspect that after finishing the liquidation of the Jews the Germans will turn this violence against the Poles.

Robberies are daily events. There are people killed or wounded. The Germans take revenge for helping the partisans by killing entire families in the villages, as they did yesterday in Niedzielisko. Sometimes they are innocent victims. Three days ago the "blue police," by mistake, shot Aleksander Makara, from Sulow, and wounded Anna Siemczyk. She was brought to the hospital in very grave condition. To save her it was necessary to amputate her leg above the knee.

Even through these hard times we believe that the end of the war is near. The British offensive in Africa gives us a big morale boost.

November 10   Every now and then the gendarmes find Jews in their hideouts. Officially all Jews have been liquidated in the entire county of Bilgoraj. Only a small number still hide in the forest. Sometimes they come to town for food, but gendarme night patrols hunt for them.

November 14   The last few days passed quietly. Only once were the Germans able to find and execute a couple of Jews. The strange thing is that this is so common an event and the population is so used to it that it is no longer a shock.

People were sure that the Germans were only interested in the complete liquidation of the Jews, so the new wave of arrests in town came as a real surprise. Within a few hours several people were arrested, including former postmaster Jozef Kolodziejczyk, pharmacist Jan Szczyglowski, butcher Franciszek Rypin, Kitowski, barber Tadeusz Zelazko, Tadeusz Niedzwiecki, Zwycewicz, and, from Klemensow, Kukulowicz and Dwornik. During the arrests young Zbigniew Biedrzynski tried to escape and was shot, with five bullets to the head. The Germans prohibited a funeral; he was dumped in a grave without a casket. His father retrieved a few bones from the sidewalk and took them to the cemetery. Those arrested were held in the city jail but later were transported to prison in Bilgoraj.

A few days ago we received information that in Auschwitz the following people died: Okoniewski, Wincenty Brylowski, Zgnilec, and a handyman from the Baranski shop.

November 16   Yesterday and today the same type of news came in. I received information about mass arrests in Bilgoraj and Zamosc. From Zamosc I received information that high school custodian Tracz and a judge were killed. Drozdz, former instructor at the teacher's seminary, was arrested.

In one of the concentration camps Rev. Samolej, from Bilgoraj, was killed, and Michalski died in Auschwitz.

After the liquidation of Jews in Szczebrzeszyn the Germans assigned Jewish houses to Polish evacuees from western Poland. They pay a monthly rent to city hall. Today they received orders to vacate those houses by noon.

People now are very depressed. The general feeling is that with German failure on all fronts, terror will increase.

November 17   Szczyglowski, Rypin, and Zwycewicz were released from Bilgoraj prison. More teachers in nearby villages were arrested. Two of my former students, Klimak and Wejler, were among them.

I received information that in a few days we can expect more street roundups for the German labor camps.

Jews are continually hunted. Still they hide out.

During the past two years the household of the German gendarme post was managed by a thirty-year-old woman, Oberweis. She was a convert from Judaism and belonged to a very well known Jewish family from Goraj. She cooked for the gendarmes, and everyone was sure that she would survive, even after the complete liquidation of the Jews. Yesterday she was sent to buy something at the store. A gendarme followed her and shot her in the head. At least she was not expecting her death.

November 18   I learned that Judge Waclaw Trybalski, from Zamosc, was executed. Commune administrator Kaminski and Count Szeptycki, from Luban, were arrested.

Today again several Jews were executed. I was told that two young Jewish women with small children arrived at the gendarme post and asked to be shot. They had been in the forest for several days; the children were half-dead from starvation. They all were shot by the Germans.

From different sources I received news about increasing arrests. We are now sure that this is in connection with German defeats on all fronts.

November 19   I went to Zwierzyniec. Along the way I saw many gendarmes and SS troops on trucks and horse-drawn wagons. As soon as I arrived I was told that yesterday, during action against the partisans, the commandant of the local gendarmes, Meister Bauer, was killed and another gendarme wounded. Now the SS and gendarmes are beginning a large-scale operation against the forest people. After the killing of Bauer, people are terrified and expecting a good number of hostages to be taken. Again most men do not sleep at home.

In Zwierzyniec it has been ordered that everyone must stand at attention and greet the Germans when they pass on the streets.

November 20 Today Tadeusz Smola, a twenty-three-year-old man from Brody, was brought to the hospital with a gunshot wound to the face. He told me he was stopped on his way to work by a stranger who asked him if his name was Smola. When he answered "Yes," the man took out a gun and shot him. I learned that Smola is a registered *Volksdeutsch*. I moved him quickly to a German hospital in Zamosc. The gendarmes are beginning interrogations about the attempted murder. When I asked Smola's sister about the nationality of her brother, she answered, "German national, naturally."

Today I looked on as two Jews were forced to march to the cemetery to be shot. They were barely moving, looking terrible from starvation. It is a common occurrence that Jews come on their own to the gendarme post and ask to be shot.

November 21 From Krasnostaw County we learned of new arrests of large numbers of farmers and ranchers. A very good friend of mine, Witold Mogilnicki, a farmer from Bzowiec and collector of books, a very intelligent man, was arrested.

November 22 Last week in Zamosc forty people were arrested. I can name only a few: Wisniewski, Piotr, Starak, and Salomon. I do not know the other names.

I hope that in Zamosc someone is taking notes and the events taking place there will be put on paper, now, not in several months or years when our memories grow old. Even short notes giving names and details are very important for future historians. It is a sad fact that people are afraid to write any diaries now, hoping to write them after the war. I hope my diary will survive and Szczebrzeszyn will have a chronicled history of the last few years.

November 26 Yesterday I was called to see a sick gendarme. I met a few new gendarmes. They were all very polite. Next to each of the beds in the bedroom was a wooden stand holding a rifle. The Germans constantly move gendarmes from place to place, in this way making bribery practically impossible.

Now there are so many robberies occurring that it is impossible to count them all. Recently the Alwa factory was attacked again, as was a train near Belzec.

There are several Jews active with the bandits. The villages have turned against the Jews because of this and try to find them in the fields and forests. It is hard to believe but the attitude toward Jews is changing. There are many people who see the Jews not as human beings but as animals that must be destroyed.

November 27   This morning the Germans rounded up a group of young people for labor in Germany. Twenty-six were arrested, mostly girls; all were taken to the railroad station. Families were forbidden to give them even enough food for the journey. People here are very upset. There has been more news about upcoming arrests, particularly in Szczebrzeszyn.

November 30   Of the young people captured for labor in Germany several have escaped and are now walking on the city streets.

In Susiec, forest inspector Kazimierz Pozerski was arrested.

In Zamosc county a new evacuation action has begun. I do not have any details yet. Several villages around Skierbieszow, Zlojec, and Zarudzie were evacuated. From each village of the Nielisz commune twenty horse-drawn wagons must be delivered to help in the evacuation of other villages.

December

December 2   We ourselves live under the fear of evacuation. Since yesterday, without interruption, horse-drawn wagons have been moving from Zamosc in the direction of Zwierzyniec. People are fleeing the villages of Wielacza, Zawada, and others, leaving all their belongings behind, to escape the forced evacuation to German labor camps. In Zamosc evacuation of the city is expected to start at any time. Mrs. Bogucka called and asked if I can take some of her bedding, silver, and tableware for safekeeping.

Once again Poles are being admitted to the Zamosc hospital.

I went to treat a sick German gendarme, Kurtz. He has heart neurosis, cannot sleep, and is in very poor condition. He informed me that most of the gendarmes from Szczebrzeszyn have left the city to help in the evacuations. He personally has had enough of the war.

In Kawenczyn, by order of the German administration, even local firemen took part in rounding up young people. Approximately twenty were escorted to the police station for transport to Germany. I am noting this fact as characteristic of the situation in the villages.

It is so depressing now. I can still hear the noise of horse-drawn wagons going by. I think of all the thousands of people moving into the unknown. With the winter weather many will not survive, especially small children.

I try to work but it is not easy to force one's self to work under these conditions. I am not talking about my work as a physician, I mean my writing. I try to continue on my history of medicine at the Zamoyski estate. I leaf through four large packets containing all my notes and copies of old documents, but I cannot concentrate on serious work. The actual happenings in today's life are so far removed from those old histories written maybe 100 or more years ago that I am unable to do the logical work that is needed. Sometimes I can picture myself walking away, maybe with only one small suitcase, and leaving everything I have done for German destruction.

I went over a few documents that I had borrowed from the estate archive and decided to return them as soon as possible.

Today I received a letter from Stanislaw Dabrowski, who is still working on the origin of color-painted wedding chests in the region of Bilgoraj. He asked me to get him some pictures and also the text of songs that were sung during wedding ceremonies in the village of Wielacz, particularly when the chest was given to the bride.

It will be difficult to answer because the village of Wielacz was evacuated by the Germans. But I am glad that someone is still writing.

December 5 For the last two days the Germans were attempting to catch young people here. Firemen are being used for this dirty work. The firemen go from house to house checking everyone's ID, looking for people with labor bureau cards. So far about 50 people have been detained, but the quota is 250, so they still have far to go to fulfill it.

Today there was a raid against Pawlowski and Dawid in Brody. At the same time the German teacher was attacked. Increased gestapo action is a direct result of these incidents.

Today soldiers began evacuating the villages of Ploski and Zawada, and they finished Wielacz. People here are in a panic. They move from place to place, sleep completely clothed, and wait for the gendarmes to come. In Szczebrzeszyn the only topic of discussion is future evacuation.

A new announcement was posted in town regarding the sabotage of railroads. The railroad lines were divided into sectors. Each sector was given to a nearby village for security. If any sabotage takes place, the villages in charge of guarding that sector will be punished. In other words, several hostages will be executed.

Anyone who comes to our region must report to the police station no longer than twelve hours after arriving.

I received information that the medical board in Lublin assigned a physician to be my chief surgeon at the hospital. The mayor is positive that this will be a German who will replace me as hospital superintendent, but I am not worried. We feel very insecure. People are asking what the next day will bring.

December 6   This is the most difficult time of the last three years. People talk only about the evacuation of Szczebrzeszyn. They base their opinions on discussions overheard between gendarmes, some remarks made by the mayor, or the statements of drunken policemen. Many households are packing and leaving the city. Besides evacuation, the fear of deportation for forced labor in Germany is hanging over us. Ninety people have been deported, but another 140 more are due to leave. Throughout the city horse-drawn wagons carry people escaping the forced evacuation. This morning gendarmes have gathered a number of wagons at the marketplace, pending further instructions. The atmosphere is tiring and very depressing.

December 7   People live in panic. Some are packing and sending families to so-called safe places. Horse-drawn wagons continue to roll through the city loaded with household goods belonging to people escaping mostly from Zamosc County. Everyone talks about the evacuations but no one knows too much about them. People ask one another, Will we be evacuated, or maybe shot? No one knows anything for certain.

I myself do not believe the Germans will evacuate the entire city, so I have not packed and just await what will happen. I returned the manuscripts to the Zamoyski estate archives. I have not borrowed anymore, afraid that in case of evacuation they might be lost. In Zwierzyniec the people began talking about evacuation also, but not to the point of panic.

In the forests around us more and more people are trying to organize fighting units. Some former Polish officers are forming regular units for the Home Army (A.K.). Many villagers are forming their own units with only one goal, revenge. They are very well armed. Some try to burn down and completely destroy the evacuated villages before the new owners, mostly German settlers from eastern Europe, take possession of them.

I was informed that even in the very well organized and disciplined Home Army officers have a hard time holding down the growing urge for revenge. They wait for orders from the Polish government in London to tell them when to begin real action against the Germans. For now, uncoordinated action will only bring repressions against the civilian population. The situation here can become explosive. It cannot be avoided. Apathy is the worst thing possible. People must not be moved from place to place, evacuated and separated from their children.

December 8 I've received information from the evacuated villages. The Germans are bringing *Volksdeutsch* from Bessarabia who speak mainly Russian, but they are so afraid of staying that shortly after receiving their new houses they escape to the towns, particularly Zamosc. Many times the evacuees come back to burn down their own houses or kill the newcomers.

We ask ourselves, Where are the Germans taking the fully loaded trains of evacuees? We know that the general direction is west, so it is possible there is a special camp somewhere in Germany. If this is true, an uprising by the villagers will be difficult to contain. The time has not yet come for this. Any uprising should be coordinated.

Today the family of Jan Kitkowski received a telegram saying that he died at Auschwitz.

December 10 The day is coming to an end and so far has passed quietly. Nothing has been heard about new evacuations.

Everyone escaped from some of the villages. Zrebce is empty; no one stayed in that town. In Kitow all men between the ages of fifteen and thirty were taken by the Germans for shipment to labor camps in Germany.

It is sometimes difficult to believe what people are talking about. Some tell unbelievable stories, others just repeat them. I am noting this to show what conditions we are subjected to.

December 10 Today talk began again about the evacuation of Szczebrzeszyn. Tonight a raid by partisans took place in Nawoz. Five homes were burned down that were already inhabited by *Volksdeutsch*.

Some alarming news is also coming from Zamosc.

December 11 There is more information from the forest. The name Edward Misiarz is being repeated. He is supposed to be in charge of a large, well-equipped group of men. He is calling on all villagers to join him in the fight against the Germans, and he is offering help for women and children.

More and more villagers are escaping into the forest, joining existing groups or forming their own. They are seeking revenge, saying that they will destroy villages even prior to their evacuation. We talk less about the evacuation of Szczebrzeszyn now, but people are afraid that peasant action against the Germans will result in future German reaction.

Tonight a train around Dlugi Kat was derailed and railroad tracks at Susiec were destroyed.

December 13 For the last two days I was busy at the hospital, so I was unable to go to town. For that reason I have only limited information about happenings around us. The following events took place. At the Klemensow airfield three Polish guards in black uniforms disappeared, taking two rifles and a machine gun. In Kitow, in direct retaliation for the burning of houses in Nawoz, the Germans executed approximately 160 people. All were buried in a mass grave.

Yesterday a new doctor, assigned by the medical board of Lublin, reported to the hospital. He is Dr. Jerzy Jentys. He will be the new chief surgeon. Originally he is from Lukow, county of Radzyn. He left the local hospital there after the gestapo arrested his assistant, Dr. Szczerba.

December 14 I went to Zwierzyniec. There some people have radio information, but the news is always very short and doesn't give us much hope that the war will end soon. We are in a state of complete collapse. We do not have the strength to live under the same conditions as the last three years.

Only a quick end to the war can save us. It is particularly difficult to watch as all the villages are evacuated, how the Germans move people in carloads, separating men from women and children, how our intellectual world has been destroyed. We still as a group strongly believe in our final victory, but some of the people are breaking down. Their instinct for self-preservation takes priority over national pride.

The forests are full of people. Most are villagers who escaped evacuation. They are waiting for revenge against the Germans, but for now military action is impossible. This is a force ready to fight but knowing that they do not have much of a chance. From London we get only one answer on the Polish situation. We can't count on any help from the outside for four months, so wait and be patient. On the other hand, instructions from England are to destroy the villages prior to evacuation. The situation is becoming worse. Men who escape to the forest are in a better situation than women with children who attempt to flee. Now the Germans are prohibiting anyone from taking in people as guests, even their own families. So the escapees who wander aimlessly are finally arrested anyway and deported to Germany. In Udrycz one of the evacuees was Stefan Dybowski. He was a teacher and a well-known book collector who was active in the Friends of Books Association in Kalisz.

Forest ranger Ksiazek was killed near Zwierzyniec.

December 16 Today we had a visit from Mrs. Bogucka, from Zamosc. She is, as always, full of life, energy, and optimism. She informed me that Dr. Bogucki, superintendent of Zamosc hospital, has been demoted to the position of ward physician. The new superintendent is a German, Breitfus, an old surgeon born in Petersburg who lived in Russia for years. Many people have fled from Zamosc fearing arrest.

In Szczebrzeszyn the gendarmes and "blue police" searched for people who were afraid of evacuation of their own villages and came here. They came to the hospital and arrested two young nurse's aides. Finally when I explained to them that professional help is difficult to find today, they gave up. It was easier for me because two of the gendarmes were patients of mine. The only one I had trouble with was a policeman, Tatulinski, who insisted that the law forbids the hiring of escapees. But he was told by one of the gendarmes to shut up.

December 25, Christmas Day   More than a week ago I stopped my diary. I am tired of writing the same stories again and again. Nothing much has happened. People are nervous, as always. The evacuation of the villages has stopped. Some villagers are beginning to move back to the empty villages. In Wielacza more than one-third of the people returned, so the Germans surrounded the village and arrested more people than the first time.

There is something wrong with German planning. Now they are even moving their own *Volksdeutsch* from one village to the next.

December 29   Today, since early morning, we have heard artillery fire coming from the direction of Niedzielisko and the nearby forest. We have received information about fighting between the Germans and partisans around Komorow.

In the forest, around ranger posts and some small settlements, peasants are trying to organize themselves. Their numbers are growing. They are forming so-called peasant battalions and trying to collect arms and ammunition. I listen to all the rumors, but it is difficult to come up with the right conclusions, so I do not write about them all.

In Auschwitz the following people died: young Kafarski, Stanislaw Rybicki, and Roman Kolodziejczyk (Warta), all active members of the underground, all from Szczebrzeszyn.

December 30   German terror is growing, but partisan action is also. Yesterday Zloje was burned down. The village had already been evacuated and the Germans had moved in many new settlers, all *Volksdeutsch*. The same thing occurred in Kawenczyn. Near Zwierzyniec thirty horse-drawn wagons loaded with lumber for airfield work were attacked. In Zwierzyniec gestapo informer Kulik and his wife were shot. He had taken part in the Jewish liquidation. Yesterday in Kosobudy the Germans executed six men, and they threatened to burn down the village for giving help to the underground. Now in many of the villages you can see young people wearing Polish eagles on their hats.

Late in the evening merchant Grodzicki was arrested here in Szczebrze-szyn. At the Klemensow sugar refinery the Germans confiscated the entire coal supply.

We expect there will be action in our area. We live from day to day. Shooting, which we hear constantly, is now a normal occurrence. People can get used to everything.

December 31   Grodzicki was released after one day in jail. Around 2 P.M. I was called to attend a sick gendarme. As I walked to the gendarme post a soldier told me about a battle between gendarmes and the SS against a peasant battalion near Wojda. He said that twenty-four peasants were killed and forty wagons were captured. The Germans lost one SS agent and had four wounded. The battle is still going on.

We Have Begun to Fight Back

January

January 1 The public mood is finally better. People feel sure that with the new year beginning the war will finally end. Last night at midnight, as the beginning of organized action against the German occupation, a strike against the Szczebrzeszyn railroad station took place. Approximately sixty armed men surrounded the station; they threw six hand grenades. The passengers were ordered to lie flat on the floor. They were assured that nothing would happen to them. All the money was taken from the station office, and several cans of gasoline were removed from the supply room. The water tower was set on fire. While the tower was burning the partisans asked the people in the station to go out and "admire" the fireworks. Everything went smoothly. The German *Treuhänder* Baker, from the Alwa plant, saw the fire and called the gendarme post in Szczebrzeszyn, but without any result. As I learned the gendarmes were completely drunk and ignored all calls.

We fear possible German retaliation against the neighboring villages.

At the same time the railroad bridge between Izbica and Ruskie Piaski was blown up. To confirm this I called the railroad station to find out what time the train from Belzec would arrive. I was told that the train would only go as far as Zawada. The connection from Zawada will be restored in three to four days. We do not know what retaliation the Germans will take because of these acts of sabotage. But if they do, we can expect more action from the underground.

All of this happened on New Year's Eve. Also two other bridges were blown up, a small one in Minkowice, another in Ruskie Piaski. There the passengers had to walk on narrow planks to get to the other train waiting on the opposite side of the bridge. This way Dr. Matuszewski, who was on vacation in Warsaw, was able to reach Szczebrzeszyn. I was told that a man in command of a group of partisans wears the *Virtuti Militar* cross on his lapel and is addressed by the others as captain.

January 5 As I thought, the attacks have not ended. More and more attacks on the railroad are taking place in different locations. The trains between Dlugi Kat and Krasnobrod are under constant machine gun fire. Trains were blown up near Krasnik and Trawniki. In Zaburz the German informer Koperski was shot.

Both yesterday and today, in revenge, the Germans sent gendarmes and SS units to the following villages: Staw Ujazdowski, Krzak, Nielisz, and Deszkowice. Many people were killed. Now it is time for the partisans to strike back. The Germans are fearful of actions by the underground, particularly the *Volksdeutsch*.

The gendarme quarters in Szczebrzeszyn are preparing for the worst. Even the second floor iron bars have been installed in all the windows. Last night the gendarmes ordered from the blacksmith shop special iron bars to protect doors.

Mayor Kraus is planning to send his wife and children to Lubaczow and is thinking about what he will do if "the card will change."

More people arrive in the forest every day. They are being well organized under military discipline. Seeing this, I am reminded of the so-called January Uprising of 1863, against the Russian occupation. Many men, especially young ones, escaped Russian deportation to Siberia by joining the partisans in the forest. Today history repeats itself. More people are organizing military units than ever before.

I was sure that this type of warfare had ended with the First World War, during the Bolshevik revolution. But now it has been revived.

From the forest we receive information about the leaders of the underground troops, about "Podkowa," "Grom," and others. They are growing in stature in the eyes of the people as heroes of the modern war. The result of this is the mass escape of young people to the forest. With the coming spring probably all the youth will be fighting.

In Szczebrzeszyn people await mass arrests. They are afraid that city employee Kuczer, now a German informer and candidate for gestapo service, will begin giving names of people who support the underground movement. He had been temporarily transferred to Lublin, but as he left the city he vowed that he would return in gestapo uniform and then "half of Szczebrzeszyn would go to jail." How much of this is true I do not know. Even Mayor Kraus told me to be very cautious when speaking with Kuczer.

From a gendarme I learned that two Jews found hiding in a cellar were shot.

January 6 In Nielisz the Germans executed approximately fifty people. Tonight the gendarmes searched the Kolodziejczyk farm. In the attic they found five Jews. Kolodziejczyk had fed them and hidden them for several months. All were shot.

From Auschwitz telegrams arrived with the news of the deaths of surveyor Stanislaw Brandt and ranger Wandycz.

January 10 I am disturbed about the incident that concerned Dr. Jerzy Jentys, now a surgeon in my hospital. Yesterday two Germans in civilian clothing, in company with Kuczer, stopped at his house. They told him he was in the house illegally, because the house belongs to one Okoniewska. They beat him on the face and took him to see the mayor. The mayor explained that Okoniewska was moved to another apartment and her house had been allocated to Dr. Jentys, and that the doctor had nothing to do with this decision. As soon as I learned about this I visited Dr. Jentys to give him my sympathy. His face is badly bruised and his nose is broken. I note this as an example of the never-ending brutality of the Germans.

January 16 Yesterday I went to Zwierzyniec. I borrowed several folders from the estate archives for research. There I met a young, very nice man who is very much interested in memoirs. I promised to give him several interesting items. He is Tadeusz Kuncewicz, known in the underground as "Podkowa," a staff officer from the commandant of the Lublin region of the Home Army. The meeting took place in the home of Waclaw Skuratowicz. We talked about medical help for the fighting units. I agreed to help them with the necessary surgical and first-aid equipment, including the material that I've had in my possession since 1939.

The overall situation in Zwierzyniec is not too bad, although people still fear partisan raids and German retaliation.

Forest ranger Pozerski was released from prison. Yesterday at the Zawada railroad station all male passengers from three different trains were arrested, including Kalita, owner of a small market in Szczebrzeszyn.

January 18 Yesterday in Szczebrzeszyn several people, mostly supporters of the communist system, were arrested, including Hysa and Zankin.

A few months ago I made a list of people who had been arrested by the gestapo. By mistake I omitted the name of Edward Otlowski, from Szczebrzeszyn. Yesterday I learned that he was killed in the Majdanek concentration camp.

In town people are nervous again. Talk of new arrests is the main topic of conversation. As always, most men do not stay home at night.

January 19   More arrests. We received information about people who have just disappeared. From Szczebrzeszyn approximately ten people vanished. Besides them Kalita, Florkiewicz, Gaska, and Kraus were detained. They all were on their way from Warsaw with goods for their stores.

This morning three horse-drawn wagons brought several people to Szczebrzeszyn; all had been arrested at the railroad station. On the outskirts of town Drabik was arrested, but he escaped. His wife and daughter are being held.

We worry about what is going on around us, but we are happy about the world news. On the Eastern Front the Germans are retreating; the very severe winter, with temperatures below $-20°F$, is helping the Russians. Air attacks on Berlin and new British action in Africa please us.

Today I went to see young Kucharski, who was released a few weeks ago from Majdanek. He is still in very poor health. Today old Materna returned from Lublin prison; he was arrested during the summer of last year. Hysa and Koscik, from Przedmiescie, and a few people in Szperowka were arrested.

January 20   In Lublin prison the old medic from Szczebrzeszyn, Leonard Talanda, died. He had been arrested last year, along with his son. This morning the gendarmes arrested three people in the railroad station who were train passengers.

January 21   Tonight the gendarmes and the "blue police" arrested young people, mostly young girls, for the labor camps in Germany.

January 22   There is once again a feeling of deep depression in town. Most men are not staying home but hiding. Only older women move about on the streets. Around the city jail many people stand and wait for news of the prisoners. Approximately twenty-eight people are inside, all arrested at the railroad station.

Yesterday the gendarmes brought three elderly women to the hospital; two were very ill and had been arrested for black marketeering. They come from Lwow and Zolkwia.

January 23   Today I am fifty-eight years old. I still hope to survive until the end of the war.

This afternoon the gendarmes took all the prisoners from the city jail, including the three sick women, to an undisclosed destination. There is news coming in from many locations about mass arrests. The situation is very tense. No one knows exactly what is going on. During the last arrests the firemen were very active. Mayor Kraus visited me after Molinski, the director of the Klemensow refinery, had come to him with a complaint. He explained that the firemen went to the refinery with a list of employees to be arrested. They were ready to destroy the list for a liter of vodka per head.

Today I received two wounded men who had been shot by the Germans. In Szperowka a young boy, Tadeusz Strzalkowski, was killed by the gendarmes. It is impossible to count all the casualties. We received news that the prisoners who had been transported from Szczebrzeszyn to the railroad station had escaped.

January 26   Last night around midnight, from the direction of Zamosc, we heard explosions. Today railroad workers told us that some bombings took place, but nobody knows who and where. It is interesting to note that tonight none of the street lights were on.

January 28   Real excitement occurred during the last two days. Yesterday morning two soldiers from *Sonderdienst* came into the local pharmacy with new registration forms. On special forms they registered all the employees and then ordered them to sign. Some people signed without checking the forms. Among the physicians, Dr. Spoz was first. He looked at the form and realized that it was a request for identification papers for people claiming German nationality. At first he refused to sign, but after being pressured he did. Very shortly thereafter he came to the hospital, very nervous and informed me of what had happened, and he asked how he could get his form back. I called all the physicians together to discuss the matter. As I found out, all physicians, pharmacists, veterinarians, dentists, and nurses must fill out the registration forms. During the meeting it was decided that everyone had to make their own decision, whether or not to sign the form or refuse.

Today a uniformed German visited Dr. Warchalowska. She and her husband agreed to sign the forms if they were allowed to cross out the title statement, the part that said this was a request for a German ID card. The Germans said it was illegal to make any changes in the form, so Dr. Wachalowska and her husband refused to sign.

This afternoon a German came to the hospital. Besides me, Dr. Jentys, Dr. Matuszewski, and Dr. Spoz were present. The German requested that my wife be present during the meeting. He began by filling out my questionnaire. The heading in German read, *"Antrag auf Erleitung eines Ausweiss für Deutschstämmige,"* and below that in Polish, "Request for Issuance of an Identification Card to Persons of German Origin." The form contained a long list of questions including personal data of not only the person listed but also the name, religion, and occupation of his or her parents and grandparents. Once I gave this information I was asked to sign the questionnaire. I first asked the German what the purpose of this inquiry was. The German answered that the army needs physicians and this census will give a general count of the number of available doctors. He is using this form because the others have not yet been printed, but the heading is not binding. I told him that I would not sign, but after crossing out the heading with red ink I decided to sign. Under my signature I added "Polish National." My wife signed and added, "I am not asking for any identification."

Dr. Matuszewski did the same, but Dr. Jentys signed without any question. Dr. Spoz requested that the questionnaire he signed a few days before be returned to him for additional comments, but the German refused. During the entire time Mayor Kraus was present.

I learned that many people in Zamosc signed this questionnaire without any reservations. This was stated also in the underground press. Now we ask ourselves what kind, if any, repressions we will face.

Today there was an inspection conducted by *Kreishauptmann* from Bilgoraj. Last night all the prisoners in the Zwierzyniec city jail were freed by partisans and the guards were locked in. Also, 30,000 zloty were taken. Commune administrator Paszkowski was locked in the jail. Before being locked up the prison guards were forced to carry all items confiscated by the partisans to Bialy Stup.

January 29 I went to Zwierzyniec. The underground received instructions to prevent the signing of the German questionnaires. Today the Germans talked to more people about the forms. In Zwierzyniec the following people refused to sign: Dr. Wroblewski, Dr. Saciuk, dentist Kira Wroblewska, and dentist Smieciuszewska. But in Szczebrzeszyn the following people did sign the form: veterinarian Cebula, nurse Slomska, and nurse Nowinska.

While in Zwierzyniec I was able to give information to the official of the Home Army about the stand taken by the physicians in Szczebrzeszyn with regard to the German questionnaire. I signed an affidavit that Dr. Spoz was forced by the Germans to sign, that he was the first physician interrogated, and that very soon after he gave me a full report, which enabled me and the other doctors to take a stand regarding the German questionnaire. This affidavit was put into a bottle and buried in the hospital garden.

We received news about an assault on the German sector of Zamosc. There was much shooting, but we do not have any details.

The mayor informed Dr. Matuszewski that he received 142 petitions from applicants applying for *Volksdeutsch* status. He said that some of the names would be surprising. How much truth is in this I do not know. I am noting this to help remind myself to check on this matter in the future.

Today I had some doubts whether signing the questionnaire was correct, even after crossing out some words. I pointed out my nationality quite clearly, but the Polish government is asking us not to sign at all.

January 30 Last night the Germans went to see dentist Zielinski. He refused to sign. During a long discussion one of the Germans said that he could see an organized action against signing the forms and that he was sure the "old goat" from the hospital was behind this. Finally Zielinski and his technician, Szafranski, signed, but they crossed out the heading. The same with Dr. Jozwiakowski. But nurses Borowiczowa and Szewczykowna signed. Szewczykowna added by her signature "Signed as requested."

Some people have been telling me to leave the city for a few weeks, but I have decided to stay. I am in a state of confusion. On the one hand I do not want to leave my home. On the other hand I would not like to be arrested by the gestapo. But after weighing the considerations in favor of my duties as a physician, I have decided to stay.

February

February 1 Today the local commandant of the Home Army, "Piotr" (later "Adam"), stopped in to see me. He advised me to stay home and not to move. So I am still here. He told me how the former hospital administrator, Cichonski, died. As I pointed out previously, during the mass arrests in Szczebrzeszyn of June 1941, Cichonski escaped through the window. He hid in several different locations, but in Labunie the gestapo arrested him along with the brothers Maszadro. While they were being transported one of the brothers jumped from the car. The Germans killed him at once. The Germans put him and the other Maszadro in handcuffs and took both of them to Zamosc prison. Cichonski was afraid of torture during gestapo interrogation so he took poison, a capsule of potassium cyanide, and killed himself.

He carried the capsule of potassium cyanide with him. I prepared it for him some time ago. While he was in prison he conspired with Dr. Jozwiakowski for more potassium cyanide and a dose of luminal. I am very depressed about this. Of course now I see Cichowski very differently. Some time ago I was very negative about his behavior, and I previously noted these feelings. But I am not changing any of this in my diary, so my notes will reflect whatever I see at the time. I do see him in a different light now. He died on November 15, 1942.

February 2 Last night a group of "blue police" was on its way to investigate a robbery. At the Klemensow railroad station they stopped a few men. They were part of a regular Home Army unit. During a short fight three policemen were killed: Antoni Kletowski and Antoni Szczygielski, from Zwierzyniec, and Stanislaw Cedler, from Szczebrzeszyn. Wounded were policemen Matysiak, from Sulow, and the German gendarme in charge of the entire operation. A young man, Jozef Kirylo, from Bodaczow, was brought to the hospital with wounds to the stomach and chest. He died a few hours after admission. He was the driver of the police wagon.

All the dead policemen were taken to the county morgue and I was called to perform the autopsies. That is how I know their names. During the autopsies I was able to observe how this depressed the German gendarmes and Polish policemen.

February 3 Today robbers attacked the house of butcher Dworniczak and took all his meat together with his money. In Topolcza farmer Jozef Swistka was beaten during a robbery on his farm. He was taken to the hospital in very serious condition.

People are talking about a battle between Russian partisans and Germans around Skierbieszow. Several German gendarmes have supposedly been killed.

February 4 At night several German military units passed through our town in the direction of Krasnobrod and Tomaszow. From rumors I know about fighting in that area. I do not have any details yet.

The same German who was taking statements from the physicians is now going around to other people requesting they sign. Today he went to the flour mill owner, Lenart, in Kawenczyn. Whether he signed or not I do not know. I heard many rumors, but I feel that they are not important.

February 6 This is the third day of fighting in the area between Krasnobrod, Jozefow, and Bondyrz. Military vehicles carrying soldiers and gendarmes travel through Szczebrzeszyn in one direction, while military ambulances with wounded go in the other.

People have mentioned Russian paratrooper action in support of Russian partisan units. Those units are thought to be very well equipped. The Germans are supposed to have sustained heavy casualties, both killed and wounded. All civilian traffic on the highways has stopped. The Germans are checking the ID's of everyone walking on the city streets. Many men have been arrested and moved to the Zamosc prison. In Krasnobrod many people have been arrested, including Dr. Konstanty Lastawiecki. I just received a phone call that he has been released. We live in suspense awaiting whatever will happen.

February 7   The fighting continues. Motorized traffic is still heavy. People coming from Krasnobrod and Jozefow are telling horror stories. Most of the village men were arrested. A while later the older ones and those having steady employment were released. Dr. Lastawiecki and many others were executed, mainly those who had no identification.

February 8   The military traffic is very light now. From conversations with the Germans it appears that the fighting has stopped. The Russian partisans and other units moved deeper into the forest past Jozefow. In Szczebrzeszyn the Germans are trying to register as many people as they can by having them sign the *Volksdeutsch* list. I hope that sooner or later we will be able to read the list.

February 12   We have been observing an increase in the traffic of military vehicles. Mostly at night long columns of trucks move in the direction of Zamosc, the same as before the war with Russia. Yesterday ten trucks carrying civilians passed through Szczebrzeszyn, probably people taken from nearby villages for labor in Germany.

From a reliable source I learned that the gestapo requested from city hall the dimensions of the city marketplace. The market will be completely cleared and not used until further notice. Now the question is, what for? The other unknown German activity is the digging of large holes and trenches in the Brodzki forest.

The registration for German identification cards is going strong. Now the Germans are calling on women with maiden names of German origin. They are asking about their children. One woman was dismissed when she stated that her son is a Polish officer abroad; another one told them she had four daughters and the Germans told her they do not need them. In Klemensow, Zieleniewski refused to sign the questionnaire. This was a surprise because some people thought he was a collaborator. The German hit him in the face for refusing.

February 14   In Bilgoraj a county driver, Holowinski, escaped into the forest in a car with additional canisters of gasoline, guns, and ammunition. I learned he was a former pilot in the Polish air force. No one knows where he went, but the consensus is that he went to the partisans.

Last evening I received a call from the station master in Zawada. He requested the names and phone numbers of all hospital physicians and what type of vehicles we have to transport the wounded. I am puzzled about this request. Yesterday the gestapo searched several houses looking for good carpets. Finally they took two old carpets from Judge Mazurkiewicz's home.

I had a visit from Miss Teresa Szalska and farmer Jarocinski. I received from them a very old clay statuette of Christ, broken into several pieces. I am sure it can be restored. I am very pleased with this gift. Clay statuettes are almost nonexistent in our region. Mr. Jarocinski promised me two very old glass paintings.

February 22   More than a week has passed. Nothing that happened was really worth writing about. We are living and awaiting news from the Russian front. In front of the Michalska store, where German newspapers are sold, people stand and wait. The news from the front is good. The Russians are moving west; now Kijew is in their hands. I am looking at a map and it makes me very happy. Evacuees from the east are passing through, mostly officials escaping the Russians, such as the mayor of Charkow, and some ranchers from Poltawa.

In view of what is occurring on the Russian front our own situation is not so important. But to people directly involved it is a tragedy. Yesterday the village of Grabowiec was evacuated and German colonists moved in. The registration for *Volksdeutsch* status is still going on. Dr. Zawrotniak signed the questionnaire after crossing out the heading and some other wording.

Many people were released from the Majdanek concentration camp. It is difficult to say if this is a change in policy or if the Germans are preparing some new tricks.

Robbery is on the increase and with it the rape of women and teenage girls. I have much work just checking for pregnancy and venereal diseases. Because of the fear of revenge by the bandits, the villagers are not notifying the German gendarmes or Polish police about robberies or rapes.

People are waiting for some big events, not doing much, just waiting. On the other hand I started working hard on my memoirs and other works. I am concentrating on the history of medicine in Zamosc. This project takes up all my free time.

February 25   During the registration of people with German surnames an employee of the Zamoyski estate, Milbrandt, refused to sign the questionnaire and was severely beaten.

In Bilgoraj four people were arrested, including county inspector Ziemba.

Yesterday I was called on to perform a physical examination on a young man who was just released from the Majdanek camp. He was there for only two months. He left in very good physical condition, but now he is a complete wreck of a man.

I admitted a young woman to the hospital. A few weeks ago she, her husband, and five children were evacuated from the village of Katy. Her husband was sent to Auschwitz, she was kept in Zamosc, and the children were sent to the children's camp in Garwolin. Eventually she was sent for labor in Germany. Around Warsaw she escaped from the train. In Garwolin she found all her children. She was lucky to place them at the nearby farms, and then she returned to see what she could save in her own village. But all this caused a miscarriage. She was in her fourth month of pregnancy.

Yesterday Mrs. Podolinska, a bookkeeper in Bilgoraj who speaks German very well, told me that armed robbery is on the increase, particularly of flour mills, lumber mills, and other establishments producing goods for German use. This action is very well organized. At the Iwanczyk flour mill (4 km from Bilgoraj), all of the equipment was destroyed. This was done by a squad of twenty men, all Russian, who were well equipped, in helmets and military uniforms. She told me that the Germans are really worried. They are afraid of the Russians coming here.

February 27 In Jozefow many people were arrested. In Bilgoraj the Germans surrounded a high school and arrested the students, boys and girls, beginning with the thirteen year olds. They took them to the railroad station for deportation to labor camps in Germany, but some escaped.

In Zamosc a drunk SS soldier, Binkowski, shot a teacher, Wladyslaw Roman Trzeciak. He mistook him for a Jew. There was some shooting in Kulikowo; a few people were killed. In Klemensow the Germans killed a man without identification papers. And so every day we have some killing or other crimes. Every day it is the same—murder, arrest, robbery, and other crimes. Even with the good news about the German retreat on the Eastern Front we do not see any end to this situation.

A few days ago the director of forestry, Stanislaw Kostecki, was driving in a truck with a German forest inspector. Around Jozefow the truck was stopped by some armed men. After a search they took all the money, papers, and clothing from Kostecki and the German, leaving them in their underwear, but the driver was not searched. He was able to repair the truck and return to Bilgoraj.

March

March 2 I was told about an occurrence in Jozefow. A young man, Konrad Bartozewski, an officer of the Home Army known as "Wir," was arrested along with another officer, Hieronim Miac ("Korsarz"). Young

Bartozewski, the son of a veterinary doctor, was put in jail. But after a few hours people from the forest came and liberated both of them. After this happened a detachment of German gendarmes came to Jozefow and arrested the entire Bartozewski family. The Germans assembled them near city hall, then in full view of thousands of people, the old veterinarian, his wife, and daughter were executed. Sixty more people were jailed.

I was told by Mayor Kraus that during his visit to Bilgoraj he learned about a partisan raid in Huta Krzeszowska, where four policemen were killed and one was wounded in the head.

In Szczebrzeszyn it was announced by the Germans that all traffic on the highway to Zwierzyniec will stop for three days because of military exercises in the nearby forest. People are now fearing new arrests and deportations to Germany.

March 8   A few days ago Zienkiewicz, the director of the brewery in Zwierzyniec, was robbed. In retaliation the Germans arrested several people, but after a short investigation most were released. In Stawy Noakowskie an evacuee from western Poland, Stefaniak, who was employed as a translator, and in Staw Ujazdowski a young man, Jan Balicki, were killed. Balicki had been in the German labor camps. He signed an application volunteering to join the German army and fight against the Russians. The news of his death spread quickly throughout the entire region. It is proof that the Germans will never have the chance to form a Polish unit to fight the Soviets because of a negative and firm stand by the entire population.

The Germans are calling more people for labor camps. Yesterday only three old men reported. It is spring and young people are moving into the forest. I was told that many people are ready to escape and move into the forest as soon as the Germans begin new mass arrests.

March 11   A few days ago in Topolcza the Germans arrested the Panas family. They lined up all six members by the barn and executed them.

In the *Information Bulletin of the Home Army, No. 9*, dated March 4, 1943, the following information was printed: "During the first few days of February, in the region of Krasnobrod, the Germans began an action against partisan units. To help the partisans a company of the Home Army was assigned. In heavy fighting from the 4th to the 12th of February, twenty Home Army soldiers were killed. German casualties are unknown but are thought to be heavy. Signed on February 26, 1943, by the commandant of the region." On page 5 of the same bulletin a more detailed account of the fighting near Krasnobrod is available.

During the last few weeks prices have been going up. People do not trust the Polish zloty, being printed by the millions by the German-controlled bank, the Bank Emisyjny. They will buy anything just to spend the unstable money. On the other hand, merchants are not willing to sell for normal prices, so the prices on everything are going up. Warsaw has the same situation. For example, I purchased a Waterman fountain pen in Warsaw for 1,500 zloty.

March 14   Stanislaw Adamczyk, sanitation inspector from Szczebrzeszyn, died in Auschwitz. He was arrested in June 1941. In Majdanek, Adolf Stanislaw Zlomaniec, a well-known civic leader, was killed.

Last night during an attack on the lumber mill in Dlugi Kat several Germans were killed. People around here are expecting German retaliation and executions, so many families are leaving their villages.

March 20   On Monday, March 15, during late evening, between 7 P.M. and 8 P.M., a raid at Rapy took place. The lumber mill and railroad station were burned down. The car of *Treuhander* Becker was shot at. In Rozaniec the new owner of a large farm, a German, was killed. The military barracks were burned down. In retaliation the Germans set the entire village of Rozaniec on fire. More than 800 people were arrested and taken to the barracks in Zwierzyniec, mostly women and children. There is talk of the possibility of freeing those jailed by armed action. We are sure the Germans will begin evacuation action against other villages very soon.

The information from the Eastern Front does not give us too much hope for a quick end to the war. Tension is mounting, particularly among the young people.

March 22   At the hospital I admitted a villager from Gruszka Zaporska. He had been hiding six Jews from Radecznica in his barn, giving them not only shelter but also food for several weeks. When the Germans began searching his farm he attempted to escape and was wounded. He died a few hours after his admission to the hospital. The Germans ordered that he be buried in the cemetery as a bandit, which means without a casket in an unmarked grave. The next day this man's wife, his eight-year-old son, and his three-year-old daughter were executed, along with the six Jews.

During a raid on the gendarme post in Lukowa, several German gendarmes, "blue police," and Russians in German service were taken prisoner and moved into the forest. This action was conducted by a platoon of the Home Army, with Lt. Zbigniew Rzewski in command.

Yesterday *Volksdeutsch* Mart and two women were killed.

March 26   Today during a raid against the railroad station in Bialy Slup a transport of pigs was captured. During the fighting two *Volksdeutsch* were killed.

March 29 Last week Mrs. Kowerska, one of the most popular people in Zamosc, was arrested.

On Saturday, March 27, around 11 A.M., two armed men entered the Commune Credit Union in Zwierzyniec and took 53,000 zloty.

Somewhere between Zwierzyniec and Krasnobrod a train was derailed.

March 30 I received information about yesterday's train derailment. Tracks were damaged and two engines, with six cars, were thrown from the tracks. In retaliation several forest rangers were killed. Today at the railroad station in Krasnobrod several bodies were brought in. Some were in forest service uniforms.

March 31 Yesterday the Germans started fires in the following villages: Pardysowka Duza, Wywloczka, and part of Bagno. In Turzyniec and Topolcza people are fleeing, expecting the same, mostly women and children. The men are still waiting to fight back or escape into the forest.

The German excuse for burning the villages: they were headquarters of different partisan groups.

April

April 1 Tonight in Zwierzyniec the brothers Skuratowicz, Jozef and Waclaw, were arrested. I am particularly sorry for Waclaw Skuratowicz, a young teacher of natural science. He is a very talented man and has already published a few books. Last week he brought me his latest work about mammals and asked for advice and corrections. He is a man who offers great talent to any field of study.

April 5 I have no more details about the arrests in Zwierzyniec, only sketchy information. Besides the Skuratowicz brothers, two Rzeszutkos, two sisters Krasulanka, Mrs. Krasula, and a few employees of the post office were arrested. I was told by eye witnesses that all prisoners were tortured, especially Waclaw Skuratowicz. It is difficult for me to think about this.

On Saturday, April 3, the partisans shot down a German plane. It came down and crashed near the school building. I learned this from the school principal.

April 8 Today a special group of Germans, including gestapo and gendarmes, searched all the stores in town. Fourteen stores were closed and the owners arrested. They are to be sent to labor camps. Last night firemen searched for young people to be sent for labor in Germany.

This is the fourth day I am in bed. I came down with a slight flu but now I am lying here with heart problems, which is usual for me after a high fever. I am very depressed. I can see the amount of work ahead of me, yet I feel that my strength is quickly disappearing. It is difficult for me to realize that maybe my life will end before the war ends. At this time I have several thousand pages written on subjects close to my heart—the history of Poland and particularly the Zamosc region. I do not know if it will all survive the war, but I hope that maybe someday someone will benefit from it.

April 11   On April 10 in Zwierzyniec a German collaborator, Tudorowski, was shot. Today I received information on the way Waclaw Skuratowicz was tortured. He was beaten until he lost consciousness, then while lying on the floor the gendarmes poured buckets of ice cold water over him and the beating began again.

All arrestees from Zwierzyniec were held for a week in Zamosc gestapo headquarters. Just yesterday they were all moved to the barracks, not to the main prison. Of all the women, Maria Krasulanka received the worst punishment.

April 18   Yesterday on the highway to Bilgoraj, near Panasowka, a German car came under machine gun fire. Two gestapo men were wounded. A few days ago, on the same highway, gendarmes ambushed and killed seven soldiers of the Home Army. Again we have been hearing rumors about the evacuation of the population around Lublin.

We have been receiving good news about German losses in Africa, so the overall feeling is good.

April 18   Today a tax collector from Zamosc came to the hospital. He was in civilian clothing wearing a swastika on his lapel. He greeted me in German style, saying "Heil Hitler." After this greeting he spoke Polish. After finishing his official business he began talking about himself and about the occurrences in Zamosc and Tomaszow. He told me he is the brother of Dr. Borzecki, from Zamosc. After his departure I tried to obtain some information about him. I learned that he is very close to the gestapo.

Marcin Krzeszowski and Jozef Kolodziejczyk died in Majdanek.

April 21   Last night, from her apartment in Bilgoraj, Jadwiga Mozdzenska, a known gestapo informer, was kidnapped by a Home Army unit. During interrogation she gave much important information. Then after a short time she was executed.

April 22   Yesterday a fire broke out in a Bodaczowo barn during illegal distillation of moonshine. By 5 P.M. the village of Zurawica was on fire.

April 23   Yesterday at noon, in Susiec, an attack on a train took place. A tanker loaded with gasoline was set on fire. Train traffic was interrupted for several hours.

I was told today that Jan Tyszka, who was wounded during his arrest, was taken from the hospital in Bilgoraj by the Germans and shot. In Zamosc, Jozef Skuratowicz, ill with pneumonia, was transferred from the prison to the hospital. He is to be released. Mrs. Skuratowicz hopes that maybe she will be able to save her second son, Waclaw. So far, using bribes of vodka, she has held off any more torture.

May

May 2   The last few days passed without any major events taking place. Occasionally military vehicles carrying German soldiers passed through. Somewhere around Susiec another fire destroyed a large section of forest. Tonight a raid on the Klemensow railroad station took place. The station was burned down.

Cebrykow, Osicki, and Zietek were released from Lublin prison. I was told the situation in prison has improved—less beating.

Around Szczebrzeszyn, during the evacuation of Wielacza, the Germans began restoring a damaged church. This is in direct connection with the German plans to begin recruitment of Poles into military units to fight the Soviets.

May 6   On Sunday, May 2, around 11 P.M., flour mill inspector Jan Fleisner was walking along with a man named Nahajka. They were walking through the park in Zwierzyniec, but they never reached their homes. Yesterday someone found a hat and Nahajka's handkerchief, but Fleisner has disappeared completely. For some time he had been working in Szczebrzeszyn with his brother-in-law. Lately he had taken up a position as inspector of flour mill production and had moved to Zwierzyniec. I was told that he signed a *Volksdeutsch* list, but I cannot prove it. There were complaints that he took bribes of money and vodka. (Later I learned he was working with the gestapo and was executed after a verdict was reached by a Home Army tribunal.) Naturally this incident was a blow to several German collaborators.

On May 3 ranger Klemens Nazarewicz and his wife, Zofia, were killed. This was a case of common robbery, because both were known as very good people.

In Szczebrzeszyn things are quiet. It is a very unusual feeling. We still await a wave of new arrests.

During the last few days electricians have been removing copper conductors and replacing them with iron ones. I am not sure if this will work.

Last night I learned a few details about a Russian air raid on Lublin and Chelm.

Behind what appears to be a relatively calm atmosphere, you can feel the underlying tension, mainly because of the alarming news coming from city hall.

A few days ago the Germans requested from several villages the names of all young males. They are to be forced to join the *Todt* organization, paramilitary labor units. Now with good weather young people are preparing themselves for escape into the forest.

Jozef Skuratowicz was released from Zamosc prison.

May 7   Last night in Zwierzyniec a German was wounded. In connection with this incident several people, including a drugstore clerk, Fela Piorowna, were arrested.

May 8   Last night several trucks carrying gendarmes came to Szczebrzeszyn. From here they went on horse-drawn wagons in the direction of Blonie. This morning eleven trucks full of soldiers, three scout cars, and eight empty trucks went in the same direction. A few hours later they all came back carrying soldiers. Later, twenty men were brought to the city jail, all villagers from Kawenczyn.

The village had been completely surrounded by gendarmes. The men were forced to assemble next to city hall and some were arrested. The entire family of ranger Jan Gumieniak was executed; both of his parents, very old people, his wife, and two children. He himself was arrested and sent to Zamosc.

Most of the gendarmes spent the night in town. Now people are worried and have begun talking about the possibility of more arrests. During the night we heard shooting.

May 9   I went to Zwierzyniec. There I visited Jozef Skuratowicz. He is still in bed and looks awful. Fela Piorowna is still in prison in Bilgoraj. Fleisner is still missing, and people are sure that he is dead. More and more men are escaping into the forest.

Many Armenians who decided to join the Germans in the fight against the Russians are also escaping into the forest. They are joining the Soviet partisan groups or forming their own robber bands.

I was told that in Kitowo the Germans began the exhumation of villagers killed and buried in a mass grave, a total of 165 persons. They will be buried in individual graves. The same is being done in the Zamosc Rotunda, where all those executed were buried in a mass grave. The work of exhumation is being done by a small group of Jews.

I was unable to check on this, but with the discovery of a mass grave of Polish officers in the Katyn forest, this is a very logical move by the Germans. I am noting this for my own use so I will be able to check on it in the future.

May 12   Many young people received notices to report to the labor bureau for deportation for labor in Germany. Most are fourteen-year-old teenagers. Of course everyone in town is upset over this. I am sure that only a few will report, so the Germans will start a new roundup.

Young Michal Jurczykowski, from Szczebrzeszyn, died in Auschwitz.

May 13   The news about British and American successes in Africa, and particularly the occupation of Tunis, was a big event. People drank a lot of vodka, named for this occasion "Tunisowka."

This morning the gestapo took some very expensive furniture from the home of Judge Mazurkiewicz.

Wisniewski and Salomon, from Zamosc, were released from Lublin prison, but an accountant of the country printhouse, Jan Siedlecki, was arrested.

May 14   Last night on the Bilgoraj highway several German trucks and cars were shot at and burned. Mayor Kraus informed me that from Bilgoraj, in the direction of Zwierzyniec and Szczebrzeszyn, a large group of partisans, more than 300 strong, is moving. This unit is traveling slowly through the forest and is destroying everything that is German.

The mayor is planning to go to Bilgoraj for a few days, along with refinery director Molinski, but he is afraid to go by car. Mayor Kraus is afraid to leave town because the only identification he has is a *Volksdeutsch* passbook. The employees of the county offices in Bilgoraj are not traveling at all but try to do all their work by mail or phone.

In some factories, such as sugar refineries, armed guards from *Sonderdienst* are posted. As I was told, in the forest there are many different groups—the well-disciplined units of the Home Army, well-armed Soviet partisans, people's battalions, and even small independent groups—all fighting against the Germans and sometimes even among themselves. The staff of the Home Army is trying to coordinate the movement of all units, but sometimes with no result. Because everyone has to eat, robberies take place. It is a normal, daily event for food to be stolen from the farms. The Germans are fearful of walking through villages; even in small groups they are attacked and killed.

In our area the Germans are drinking heavily. Mayor Kraus showed me how he is trying to secure the door to his apartment. This is proof that we are coming to the last days of the occupation.

We just received news about a Soviet bombardment of Warsaw.

May 15 Last night near Susiec a German armored train was blown up, and today near Tereszpol a train was derailed. On the Tanwa River in Bilgoraj County a bridge was destroyed. The Germans are very nervous about this. They are unable to control travel routes. Traveling on highways and railroads is now very dangerous.

In the forest the so-called forest people are now in charge. Lumber is not being taken to the lumber mills. This is slowing German military construction. On the highways traffic is now in many cases being controlled by partisans.

Nothing like this has happened before. People are not complaining at all. The people feel that the worse the situation gets, the better it really is.

May 16 A postal employee, Kapusniak, showed me an anonymous letter addressed to the gestapo in Bilgoraj, which was signed only "X.Y." It was addressed to gestapo agent Majewski. The letter is handwritten with many misspellings. It is really an accusation against me. First the author states that I am a Communist, that before the war I was in charge of Communist propaganda at the teacher's seminary and that I even helped a former student, Eugeniusz Kowalik, escape to Russia from prison in Zamosc. In 1939 I was supposed to have given help to Soviet authorities. At the end the author writes that I am a Jew and my real name is Kluk, not Klukowski. The letter names a few other Communists, such as Goleniak and Gaska. After reading the letter, on the one hand I was amused, particularly about my Jewish origin, but on the other hand I am really upset about the meanness of some people.

We do have many dedicated and honest people. The mother of Waclaw Skuratowicz, who was tortured by the gestapo, never complained. She was so determined to help her son that she sent to the prison some of his clothing, in which she sewed a potassium cyanide capsule.

May 17 Along with Dr. Snacki I visited Zamosc. (It is interesting to note that upon leaving his home he took with him two personal first-aid kits.) We drove there in a county car, passing through the evacuated villages of Wieloncza and Zawada. Some houses are completely destroyed. German settlers are moving in. Everywhere you can see young German boys in *Hitlerjugend* uniforms.

Zamosc looks completely different from before. Very few people walk around. Most of the stores are owned by Germans and have German signs. I stopped in at the print shop. The printers are still working. They asked me when we will start printing in Polish again. Museum director Kabat told me the Germans closed the city museum and took all the keys to the building. I am very disturbed by this because a few weeks ago thirteen big boxes containing the collections of the late notary Rosinski were deposited at the museum. I hope they will survive.

While walking on the street I was stopped by a uniformed gestapo man. He greeted me very warmly: "Hallo, a doctor from Szczebrzeszyn. How are you? You do not recognize me? I am Mazuryk." He then reminded me that when I was arrested in 1941 he, Mazuryk, tried to get me released at once and, really, I am alive only because of him. I was completely surprised, because at first I had not recognized him. After a short talk he left. I was very happy that no one saw me taking with him. I learned that Mazuryk is a different person now. Once a killer and a sadist, he has become a very gentle person, trying to help everyone. It looks as if he is thinking about his own future.

During the past few days several evacuated villages have been burned down by the partisans. Some were already occupied by German settlers, such as Labunie.

May 18   At the railroad stations in Krasnobrod and Dlugi Kat, Armenian guards killed several German soldiers and members of the "blue police" and escaped into the forest to join Russian partisan units. The gendarme post in Tarnogrod came under machine gun fire. In Zolkiewice, Turobin, and Wysokie all registration books were destroyed. Assaults on German military vehicles are common events.

Everyone asks the same question, What will tomorrow bring?

May 20   I have a few items of news to write about. At night on May 19 a train coming from Lwow was held up in Susiec. Several German soldiers were killed. Tarnogrod was completely surrounded by partisans. All roads were guarded with machine guns; from the stores all the food was taken. The partisans searched for police commandant Darmochwal, a Ukrainian, who is known for his cooperation with the Germans, but it so happens that he was not at home. He was in Warsaw. His home was badly damaged.

In Korytkowo all the lumber stacked for delivery to the German airfields was set on fire. The Germans do not feel safe. They are even afraid of using the trains.

May 21   The twenty villagers from Kawenczyn were released from Zamosc prison. Only ranger Gumieniak is still there.

May 23   Because of Mrs. Bogucka's birthday I went to visit her in Zamosc. Several people were there also. I was surprised how much older everyone looked. Some people are now completely gray; some look twenty years older. I am sure that in the eyes of others I look like an old man. During this visit I heard a lot of gossip.

Restaurant owner Pawel Kudyk, his wife, and daughter were shot for closely collaborating with the Germans. I was told about several people who signed up for *Volksdeutsch* status and now are saying that they are German. Among others, former judge Stanislaw Cybulski, engineer Sekutowicz, pharmacist Suchanski, and Leon Czernicki, who is a member of an old and very rich Polish family in Zamosc.

Most of the talk was about Mrs. Irena Kuncewiczowa, the former wife of an attorney. She is now a *Volksdeutsch*. Her very young son attends a German school and is a member of the *Hitlerjugend*. People such as she, with Polish names, were never forced to change nationality. So it is pleasant to see others, including Prof. Otto Werner, who is of German origin, refuse to change their nationality. Several times he was threatened and arrested.

Among the physicians in Zamosc the following are now *Volksdeutsch:* Dr. Rytter, Dr. Hauslinger, Dr. Lorens, Dr. Guminski, and old Dr. Korczak. Dr. Hauslinger signed the *Volksdeutsch* list with the approval of the Home Army staff. At his house the underground has a safe headquarters. He is still a very active member of the resistance.

May 24   Today I went on business to city hall. All the employees are very nervous. In speaking with them I learned that in the county of Krasnystaw the registration books for fourteen communes and several parishes were destroyed. Registration books are now being locked in a steel safe. Guards are posted even at night. New alarm systems have been installed in all the offices so in case of any disturbance the police and Armenian units can be called on quickly. In Bilgoraj the Germans are digging shelters and trenches around the area occupied by German families.

People talk about a partisan group a few thousand strong moving toward Bilgoraj.

The underground military court has sentenced several Germans and informants to death. Some verdicts have already been executed. The Germans are terrified. We now live in a war of nerves. No one believes the Germans will be able to control this situation. It appears the end of the war is near. But we still face very hard times ahead of us.

May 26 Last night in Zamosc, by order of the underground court, Kuncewiczowa was executed in her own apartment. People are very glad that once again another person who collaborated with the enemy has been liquidated. During the morning hours more arrests took place. Yesterday on a street in Szczebrzeszyn I saw the brother of teacher Lodzia Hascowna walking along in the German uniform of the *Schutz Polizei*. He is here on vacation from France where he is serving.

May 27 Again in Zamosc the underground tried to liquidate an informer, Karolkowa. Her behavior and contact with German agents has for some time been on people's minds. At the last moment she was able to escape through the window. Last week in Topolnica, Genowefa Bebenek-Swistkowa was killed.

May 28 At 7 A.M. five wounded Armenians were brought to the hospital by German gendarmes. One Armenian is very badly wounded and was immediately operated on; he stayed in the hospital. The other four were moved to the hospital in Zamosc. Around noon the morgue received two Germans and four Armenians who were killed in a battle near Sulow. During the fight a well-organized mounted unit took part on the side of the underground. At the time of the assault two Germans and fourteen Armenians were inside one of the commune buildings. It was made of brick and proved impossible to burn down. Partisan Marcin Paprocki ("Wilk"), from Sulow, was killed. A second assault took place in Radecznica; a third in Nielisz. Both of those commune buildings were burned down.

Many gendarmes and Armenians were there to fight and burn down the villages. During the assault a very well organized partisan group took part in the fighting. One of the gendarmes looked at a dead Armenian and said, "I can expect the same."

For some time now we have had no information at all concerning Jews in our region. But now again a long train loaded with Jews passed through the railroad station in Szczebrzeszyn, in the direction of Chelm. The Jews are being transported totally naked. During the journey some of the Jews try to escape by jumping from the train, but guards shoot them to death. A few days ago a young Jewish woman attempted to escape with her seven-year-old child. She was killed by the guards but the child was not harmed. Workers at the Alwa factory gave the child food, but when the Germans learned of this a gendarme went there and killed the youngster.

May 29 In Bilgoraj the Germans are so fearful of new attacks that they ordered a high brick wall to be constructed around the gestapo office. A few days ago in Bilgoraj an employee of the criminal section of the police, Mrozik, was arrested. He is the brother of a gestapo agent who was killed in Zwierzyniec.

In Goraj teacher Pajaczkowa was liquidated as a German informer. Registration books in the communes of Goraj, Kocuda, and Frampol were destroyed.

May 30 Last night between Susiec and Mazila a passenger train was derailed. The repair work is still continuing. The derailed trains are mostly the work of Soviet group actions. Polish units are not taking part in the derailment of passenger trains. At this time underground activities are concentrated at destroying all registration books and liquidating informers.

Antoni Stropka and Czeslaw Biziorek, both from Szczebrzeszyn, died in Majdanek. Fela Piorowna was moved from Bilgoraj to Lublin prison. Still no one knows why she was arrested.

The spirit of the Germans is very low. Practically none of them believe in victory. Gestapo agent Mazuryk, from Zamosc, brought a very old violin to Zwierzyniec, asking his former teacher Splewinski to keep the instrument. He is sure that he will not survive, but he would like the violin for his young son.

Between 7 and 8 P.M. we heard shooting from the direction of Brody. In our town people are counting on an assault on our city hall very soon. Everyone is waiting for it.

When I compare today's situation with a year ago I can see a big difference. Last year only the Polish population lived under the constant fear of arrest, deportation, evacuation, or execution. Now both Poles and Germans alike live in fear of the future. We are still afraid of the Germans, but now the Germans are afraid of us. This is a nerve-shattering situation, a real war of nerves. But we are sure to win this war.

In Sulow, in connection with the killing of Germans and Armenians, more than sixty men were arrested and moved to Zamosc prison. In a group of prisoners who were liberated during transport from Lublin to Warsaw, near Celestyn, two men from Szczebrzeszyn were freed, Bortkiewicz and Tykwinski.

June

June 1, 3 P.M. A few days ago the police hours were set from 4 A.M. until 10 P.M. Today around noon the police hours were changed. You can walk on the streets only from 5 A.M. until 8 P.M. Now, in summer, those hours are hard to live with. One hour after the new regulations were posted a panic began. Within a few minutes all the horse-drawn wagons assembled for the free market had disappeared and city traffic stopped. No one has an explanation and people are panicking.

Since early morning the Germans have been burning the village of Suchy. Even German airplanes were involved.

Tension grows day by day. People wait for something to happen. Many different kinds of rumors are spreading.

June 1, 8 P.M. I learned what caused this morning's panic. A truck carrying gendarmes arrived, and because there was no space to park a gendarme began shouting *"Weg, Weg"* (out, out) to clear a space. The first horse-drawn wagon moved, and within a few minutes others began leaving.

An aircraft destroyed the village of Jozefow, which for a few days was occupied by partisan units.

Last night in Bilgoraj two gestapo agents were killed. Probably because of the killings police hours have been changed.

June 2 Besides the two gestapo agents who were killed, gestapo chief Kolb from Bilgoraj was wounded in the leg.

The wife of a pharmacist in Jozefow was brought to the hospital with wounds received during the air bombardment. In that town many people were killed or wounded. Only a few people are still there; the rest have left.

I heard terrifying stories from Suchy. The village was first completely surrounded by German soldiers and subjected to machine gun fire. Then the Germans started fires in several places around the town's perimeter. Lastly several airplanes dropped bombs on the burning village. Almost 200 people were killed. Jan Zamoyski confirmed this during a conversation.

During our talk I asked Jan Zamoyski if he still drives his car and if he has been attacked at any time. He said no because he drives himself and his chauffeur sits next to him holding a red and white Polish national flag.

I was told that in Zamosc several Germans and German informers who received death sentences by the underground courts were liquidated.

June 4 Jozef Hasiec and Aleksander Stropek, both from Szczebrzeszyn, were killed in Majdanek. People still talk about the events in Suchy. By order of the German authorities all those killed were buried in a mass grave outside the town, not in the cemetery. More than 180 persons were buried.

June 6 Today the village of Siedlisko, near Zamosc, was burned down. In the past the inhabitants were mainly Orthodox, having their own nice church, a very well organized parish, but in 1942 all were evacuated and German settlers took over. The assault on the village was coordinated by a unit of the Home Army in retaliation for the slaughter in Suchy. Several

Germans were killed. From the village some livestock and produce were taken to supply the forest kitchens.

Tonight in Topolcza informer Leon Niechaj, from Blonie, was liquidated.

June 6, 8 P.M.   In the surrounding villages there is absolute panic. From Topolcza and others people are fleeing their homes. They are afraid that a liquidation such as at Suchy will be repeated. This is in connection with flights of several bombers over the village. They then flew over Kosobudzki forest, probably to bomb a village.

People coming from the east tell us horror stories. As soon as German troops are pulled back, even before the Russians take over administration, very well armed Ukrainians are murdering the Poles. The Polish population there has begun fighting back. The rule "An eye for an eye, a tooth for a tooth" is now the new law. In our town people are very excited. They await what the next day will bring and wonder if by chance our own town will be subject to any unusual events.

June 7   Today near Szczebrzeszyn the Germans killed a young man, Zdzislaw Jozwiakowski ("Huzar"), and after a long hunt they wounded young Gdula. Both were members of the underground and both were armed. In town when people heard the shooting and saw armed Armenians running into positions a panic started. All city employees, including the mayor, ran away, leaving customers in unattended offices.

In Jozefow there is a very interesting situation. All German gendarmes, "blue police," and Armenians fled from the town. Even the priest left the parish hall. Now the only authorities are the partisans. Nobody knows exactly who, because members of the Home Army, peasant battalions, and Russian partisans are all mixed together. In a fight near Jozefow a very popular Russian commander, "Miszka," was killed. Yesterday his funeral took place at the Hamernia cemetery. Yesterday the police hours were changed again. Now we can walk until 8 P.M.

German informer and *Volksdeutsch* Edward Motte was liquidated in Abramow. Police hours have been changed again—you can walk until 9 P.M.

Yesterday in Kosobudy, during a Mass in the Catholic church, several men were arrested.

June 9   In retaliation for the attack on Siedlisko the Germans arrested most of the men in Wieprzyc and Szewnia. Some escaped into the forest and joined partisan groups. In this way the underground received more recruits.

June 10   Leaflets were dropped from German planes. The German-edited newspaper, printed in Polish, *Nowy Glos Lubelski*, printed the text of the leaflet. It states that German authorities are outraged about the assault on Siedlisko and talk about retaliation. As a penalty for the destruction of German homes, ten Polish homes will be destroyed for every one German home. For every one German killed, ten Poles will be executed. This announcement was taken seriously by everyone, but we do not know how the underground, particularly the Soviets, will react to it. This morning the Germans called a meeting in Bilgoraj of all Polish officials, including mayors, commune secretaries, and even priests. The Germans stated that the new restrictions will be very severe. Some of the priests told me that the people left the meeting feeling very depressed.

June 14   For the two days of Pentecost I stayed in Zwierzyniec. I tried to relax a little and take a break from the Szczebrzeszyn atmosphere. Even life in Zwierzyniec is not too safe. The few days passed quickly and quietly.

On Saturday Fela Piorowna was finally released from prison. She was greeted by the townspeople with enthusiasm. Kozlowski, who was arrested along with her, was also released. Two workers, Opila and Ciecko, were released from the camp in Debica.

The family of Dr. Wroblewski had a little excitement when his fifteen-year-old daughter, Lilka, and a friend ran away to join the partisans in the forest. After a few days Mrs. Wroblewska found both girls in Bondyrz and persuaded them to return home. During my stay I learned many facts and also heard many rumors that are not fit to be repeated.

June 15   The following story is very characteristic of the mentality of some people. Today a woman, widow of the former postmaster killed a few months ago in Majdanek, came to see me asking for a very confidential interview. After I agreed she told me that her young daughter is dating an Armenian soldier. He is supposed to be a student at a medical school and now works as a medic in an Armenian unit. He wants to marry her daughter. The loving mother came asking for advice. She wants to know if I know anything about him. She worries if he is an honest man. I was not able to tell the loving mother everything I know about him, so I mentioned only that he has proposed to two nurses and even to my own secretary.

June 16   Medic Wojdatt was released from the prison in Lublin.

June 17   In Hrubieszow Dr. Paszkiewicz was arrested. In Wysokie a physician disappeared. In Lezajsk several people were executed, including a physician.

In town new rumors are growing about upcoming mass arrests and that people below the age of sixty will be deported. This is preventing people from doing any normal work.

June 18 Lucjan Wawryka, from Szczebrzeszyn, was arrested yesterday in Bilgoraj. Lately he lived in Gorajec and came to Bilgoraj asking for permission to travel to Warsaw. During the filing of the necessary papers he was arrested by the gestapo and taken to prison.

June 19 Last night many things happened. We learned about them this morning. A unit of the Home Army attacked the Alwa factory. German *Treuhander* Becker escaped, but his house was demolished. The office and telephone equipment were destroyed. At the railroad station the telephone equipment was destroyed. In Brody *Volksdeutsch* Michal Harkot was shot and taken to the hospital. In Staw Noakowski an evacuee from Poznan, Lemanski, was shot; his wife, Bronislawa, was wounded. In Susiec partisans took control of the entire stock of a grain warehouse.

Kwapisz was killed in Staw Ujazdowski. All of the forests are now in the hands of the underground. It is impossible to take any wood to the lumber mills. No one drives in the forest. Yesterday the Germans, by force, mobilized more than forty horse-drawn wagons to start hauling lumber to the mills, but this morning the wagons had disappeared.

Last night the office of the commune in Tereszpol was burned down.

June 21 Yesterday only a few people came to the free market. People are fearful of mass arrests similar to those in Kosobudy and Krasnobrod, but the day passed quietly. Two old beggars were arrested near the church and shot. Last night several trucks carrying gendarmes passed through town in the direction of Zwierzyniec. On Rozlopska highway the gendarmes checked all IDs. They even stopped Dr. Warchalowska. Now only police and military telephone calls can be placed to Zamosc.

June 21, 2 P.M. In town tension is mounting. Gendarmes and Polish police are checking the identification of anyone passing by. They are even stopping cars.

Around 11 A.M., at the post office, the Germans confiscated all postage stamps and money, saying that the postal service is closed. Telephones can now only be used for military purposes. We are trying to figure out what it all means. No one is walking the streets.

June 22 Today was a quiet day. The only topic of conversation was the closing of the post office. Now we are completely isolated from the world, the same as in September and October 1939.

Last night I received a copy of an underground paper, *Echa Lesne* (no. 3). It is machine printed in small type on very thin paper with a very good-looking, colorful first page. I was promised nos. 1 and 2 for my collection.

June 24 Throughout the night military transports passed through the city in the direction of Zwierzyniec. For quite a while I had not seen such a large movement. This morning we learned that most of the gendarmes and "blue police" left for special assignment. Only the youngest gendarme, Bot, and the oldest policeman, Hajduczak, are still here. They told me the others are searching for bandits.

The gestapo ordered for tomorrow morning several horse-drawn wagons to haul to the train station the furniture and other belongings confiscated during the liquidation of the Jews. From the county doctor I received a warning not to leave the hospital, even for a short time, and to stay in my quarters.

Several villages such as Stalowa Wola, Rzeszow, and others are now in the hands of the underground. Underground units are moving closer to our city. The situation is very tense. Now a list must be posted on each house giving the names of people living there.

Telephone service for gendarmes and police has been cut off.

June 25 Last night around 10 P.M. a gendarme, Brok, for no reason, shot down fireman Leopold Gaska. His brother, Boleslaw Gaska, is known for his pro-Communist actions. The Germans dug more trenches along the highways and set up machine gun posts.

We heard about the evacuation of villages around Zwierzyniec and Bilgoraj. So far only the evacuation of Bukownica has been confirmed.

This type of news, even though it is unconfirmed, makes the people very tense and nervous, particularly in the small villages. Many women are moving into town with their young children. They feel more secure here.

June 26 A train with ten cars of evacuees came through the Szczebrzeszyn railroad station, supposedly bound for Zamosc. The phones are still not working. The wife of commandant of the "blue police" told me the reason for this is a simple one: the bandits can easily plug into the lines and overhear all conversations. Also she told me that the order for the gendarmes and police to move out into the field brought them almost to the panic stage. The old gendarme Kurtz asked for a small Our Lady medal to wear around his neck. He hopes this medal will save him in case he is captured by the partisans.

First-class mail is now being delivered along with newspapers.

June 28 I received a short note from a good friend of mine, Tadeusz Guminski, who is in charge of a Polish relief committee in Jozefow. He is asking for help in getting his wife and fifteen-month-old daughter released (they were arrested in Aleksandrow). I went to see Jan Zamoyski, who is president of the Polish relief committee in this region. He promised help. As we learned, both the mother and daughter are in prison.

In the new series of evacuations the following villages were affected: Aleksandrow, Gorecko Koscielne, Bukownica, Hedwizyna, Majdan, and Wola. Temporarily, all evacuees were moved to Zamosc and put into a camp behind barbed wire.

Last night several gendarmes returned. Today more troops moved through Szczebrzeszyn. In Bilgoraj there are also many troops. People are afraid of evacuation. The news about the possibility of evacuation spreads quickly and it makes people very nervous. No one seems able to follow their normal routine. People's attention is focused on the possibility of evacuation.

Today the remaining Jewish furniture was moved from the warehouses to the railroad station. A few people attempted to steal some of it. In direct connection with this a woman and a man were shot when they were caught trying to move furniture over the Wieprz River.

All houses have a list of inhabitants posted. At the hospital we have two lists, one of hospital personnel and one of patients. We expect the SS to begin checking the lists. We are nervous. I am unable to concentrate and work. For relaxation I play cards. Some people cannot withstand the pressure anymore and show symptoms of nervous breakdown.

June 29   Early this morning I learned about the nerve-shattering night that the townspeople experienced. Most inhabitants did not sleep at all while waiting for evacuations to begin and at the same time packing and preparing. This morning tension has increased even more because the Germans are not allowing anyone to enter the city. Also the employees of the refinery and workers at the airfield were not permitted to leave the city.

Last night Romanowska and her two children were arrested. Talanda was also arrested. He had for some time now been in the mentally disturbed ward of the Chelm hospital.

Yesterday the seventh-grade students received draft cards for the labor camps in Germany. They are only thirteen and fourteen years old. People do not know what to do. The stronger ones are escaping into the forest.

June 30   The night passed. Military traffic is rather heavy. Some military units have been moving toward Zwierzyniec. Cars and motorcycles seem to be traveling in different directions. This is typical of a prefront area.

Because of the lack of communication we do not know what is happening in the nearby villages. Naturally there is plenty of gossip. City hall expects new arrests and searches.

June 30, 7 P.M. I started my work again and am writing about medicine in the Zamosc region.

Today the post office was reopened but the phones are still out of order.

July

July 1 Last night, because of the news that Tarnogrod was evacuated and because a new group of gestapo arrived, people reached the hysteria stage. But the night passed quietly.

July 1, 11 A.M. A new action has begun. Many arrests have created a tense situation in town.

July 2 Yesterday around 4 P.M., the town filled with soldiers, *Schutz Polizei,* and gendarmes. Outside the city several trucks with benches were assembled. The first group of arrested was brought by highway from the direction of Brodzka Gora. Later more men were brought from Brody. Several railroad workers were bunched into a special group. The Germans were not sure where to assemble everyone. First they were taken to the Pereta flour mill; later they were moved to the old, partially destroyed synagogue. Men from our city were arrested also. The Germans arrested men under sixty years of age from stores, offices, and private home. A few priests and three physicians, Dr. Jentys, Dr. Spoz, and Dr. Jozwiakowski, were arrested.

In front of the synagogue the gestapo set up two large tables and began the interrogation. IDs were checked and so on. Some people were released, such as the physicians, workers from the sugar refinery, and airfield workers. Some tried to escape, but this was impossible. The entire town was surrounded by soldiers armed with machine guns. The gendarmes and soldiers continued searching private homes.

Only a small number of people were able to hide. We observed all of this quietly and were ready to be evacuated also. I was dressed and had my rucksack packed and ready with important items.

At the hospital we prepared ourselves for the worst. Because of a warning, "*Achtung! Fleckfieber,*" no one entered the hospital. The local gendarmes kept some of the arrested men for work at the gendarme post. Three millers, Filipkowski, Lysak, and Koszel, two mechanics, the brothers Budzynski, two butchers, the brothers Rypina, and a few bakers were put to work cutting firewood. Women were left alone. They walked around the town cursing the Germans.

The gestapo removed eleven men from those arrested and marked a big letter "W" on their foreheads. They were Dominik Amborski, former high school teacher; Tadeusz Postulski, postal clerk; Wit Naszynski, book-keeper; Dworniczak, butcher; Jan Dolezal, retired ranger; Adolf Cichocki, clerk; Feliks Krukowski, driver; Marion Fedorowicz and Kazimierz Wawrz-kowicz, employees of Alwa; Glowacki; and another man I do not know. These men were placed under special guard. All others were taken inside the synagogue and into the partially destroyed Orthodox church.

At the hospital, after locking the doors, I decided to assign the personnel to special duty. My time would be 4 A.M. A few minutes after 5 A.M. the Germans formed a marching unit with the eleven men with "W" marks being closely guarded by the *Schutz Polizei.* Around 1,500 men were assembled. All of them looked healthy. As they passed I tried to recognize friends. I stood behind the hospital wall and had a good view of the street. In the last group I recognized a few priests: old Rev. Maslowski, Rev. Kowalczyk, and Rev. Winnicki, from Mokra Lipa. A large group of women stood on both sides of the street, cursing the Germans and crying.

Seeing this I was reminded of the Jews marching prior to their liquidation. Everything looked the same, except for one thing: the big difference was attitude. The Jews marched in complete resignation, guarded only by a few gendarmes. Here these marching men showed hatred toward Germans and were being guarded by hundreds of soldiers carrying machine guns.

I am completely exhausted. I am also angry that two hospital workers, farm helpers, were arrested. At 8 A.M. I went to the gendarme post requesting their release. I was very much surprised that the lieutenant in charge agreed to help. All arrestees were put behind barbed wire in Zwierzyniec. Requests for their release were taken to Zwierzyniec by Deputy City Mayor Babiarz.

Around 1 P.M. all the priests and the two hospital workers were released. For several hours townswomen waited on the highway leading to Zwierzyniec for any men who might be released. So far a few hundred have been freed.

The eleven marked men were held in separate barracks. During interrogation they were severely beaten. Rev. Winnicki witnessed these brutalities. We hope that more people will be released.

This morning the city looked as if it had been struck by some major catastrophe. Stores were closed; people were hiding. This afternoon the city began to breathe again. The city is still depressed.

July 3   Today no one was released. City hall secretary Babiarz, acting as mayor during the absence of Kraus, went to Zwierzyniec trying to secure the release of the city firemen. Many trucks carrying women and children evacuated from other villages passed through town. The barracks in

Zwierzyniec are full, as are those in Zamosc. From various sources we have received information of the evacuation of entire villages or sometimes individual families, as in Bilgoraj and Tarnogrod.

People tell unbelievable stories. In Zamosc the situation is the worst because many evacuees have been moved there. It is a very grave situation. Most men have either been arrested or have escaped into the forest. So all the field work is left in the hands of women and children. This is summer, the time when most of the field work is done.

I cannot foresee the end of German action against the entire Lublin region. The gestapo are everywhere. They drive through the cities, towns, and villages in open scout cars with machine guns. People are so nervously exhausted that they shake whenever they see a German. I try to force myself to work. Today I was able to work for maybe one hour.

We are living in a difficult time period. People are being killed by the thousands. Sometimes we feel that holding out against this is beyond our strength. But we still fight, believing that our nation cannot be destroyed. Personally, I am sure that we will restore our lives back to normal soon after the end of the war, but we will still suffer heavy casualties until then.

July 4   The traffic on the highway is heavy. Trucks carrying evacuees move in the direction of Zamosc, and the empty ones come back and go in the direction of Bilgoraj. Several prisoners were released from the barracks in Zwierzyniec. Mayor Kraus, now back from vacation, went to Zwierzyniec to try to secure the release of more prisoners. There are again rumors about the pending evacuation of our city and all the nearby villages.

I have had enough of this. I finally forced myself to begin some serious work. I am now sitting in my quiet study working on a description of the first operation performed by using ether as a source of anesthesia. This operation was performed in 1847 by Dr. Wieniawski, in Szczebrzeszyn. I am so involved in this work that I can forget what is occurring on the outside. A few hours of intensive work has changed my nervous system completely. Now I feel completely calm and am able to control myself.

July 5   The day passed quietly, but the rumor of evacuation is still going strong. People talk only about it.

July 6   Since early morning the situation in the city has been very tense. Even though this is a free market day the streets are empty. Only a few women walk around. The Alwa factory was surrounded by gendarmes and several employees were arrested. In Brody there were heavy patrols.

July 6, 3 P.M.   The gestapo, accompanied by Mayor Kraus, went to an apartment occupied by a few priests. They were looking for Rev. Kapalski, but he was not at home.

July 6, 10 P.M.   We have a very mysterious situation. A gestapo agent arrived at the parish hall and ordered Rev. Kowalczyk to call a meeting of all the town's priests at the Krol Restaurant, near the hospital, but not one priest showed up. Then the gestapo, along with Mayor Kraus, returned to see Rev. Kowalczyk, and all of them went to talk to the Orthodox priest. While the gestapo agents were inside the house, Rev. Kowalczyk jumped over the fence and escaped. Mayor Kraus did not try to stop him but only warned the gestapo. By then the priest was gone and the gestapo were furious. They went off trying to find Rev. Kapalski, who at the time was hiding in my hospital, but instead they arrested Rev. Maslowski and took him to Zwierzyniec. People from Zwierzyniec said that both Rev. Maslowski and Mayor Kraus were put behind barbed wire. The mayor's wife went to Zwierzyniec to learn of any news of her husband. She was told that no one had been brought from Szczebrzeszyn and no one knew anything about Mayor Kraus.

July 7, 10 A.M.   Still there is no news of Mayor Kraus. The gendarme post has no information about him. This is causing a big sensation in the city. People talk only about this event. They ask, "Why are the gestapo searching for priests? Why did Rev. Kowalczyk escape?" and so on. The situation appears strange. Why do the gestapo need the priests? If they are to be arrested, why call a meeting? Maybe it would be different if Rev. Kowalczyk had not escaped.

July 7, 10 P.M.   Now, officially, Mayor Kraus has been arrested. He is in Zwierzyniec, isolated from the other prisoners. He has no right to receive any food parcels.

Traffic on the highways is slowing down. The German military staff from Klemensow has moved out. Troops involved in the evacuations have moved farther past Janow.

Today Dr. Bienkowski, from Zamosc, told me that around that area approximately 12,000 people were arrested.

Today we received the tragic news about the death of Gen. Wladyslaw Sikorski, in Gibraltar.

July 8   Last night, just before midnight, the Germans executed Chrzanowa, an old woman known for cussing. She was not quite a normal woman. Lately she was saying that during the last arrests in Szczebrzeszyn the gendarmes hid people in their own quarters. Finally the gendarmes had enough of her.

The mayor is still in jail. So far all intervention from the county administration has been without result.

In Zwierzyniec the building of the forestry inspectorate was converted into a gestapo office. Mr. Pruszkowski, who occupied two of the rooms, was evicted. Now the gestapo uses them for interrogation and torture. This morning Postulski was carried off to jail, beaten and bloody.

The two priests who are still free in Szczebrzeszyn, Rev. Kapalski and Rev. Przysucha, are hiding, but this morning they celebrated Mass. Rev. Kowalczyk is probably somewhere in the forest, and Rev. Maslowski is in jail.

July 10, 9 P.M.   I do not know how to start. I am sure that I am not ready to describe the events of this terrible day. My pen cannot describe all that was happening.

Before 6 A.M. the Germans began announcing that something important was about to happen. As we learned, it was an order for all people—men, women, and children—to assemble as soon as possible at the marketplace ready for departure. At once the streets emptied. Many people began packing or hiding; some did nothing. Many were prepared because of the evacuation rumors that have been circulating for the past few days. I dressed myself as quickly as possible and ran to the gendarme post. Since I knew the man in charge, I went directly to him. I asked the lieutenant what I was supposed to do with the patients, particularly those with spotted typhus. After talking with gestapo agents the lieutenant told me that hospital personnel and all patients will stay. We do not have to move.

I ran back as quickly as possible to give the good news to the hospital. I told all personnel that it would be a normal workday. I also went through the wards and spread the news.

Residents began leaving their rooms. I told the janitors to lock all the doors, knowing from previous experience that people will come and try to hide at the hospital. I only made exceptions for the families of personnel and patients. All others were sent away. I admitted a few pregnant women. We already had a good number of people staying in the hospital.

I had to refuse admission to many people. It was a difficult thing to do, but I had to in order to keep the hospital personnel and patients safe. Up to now I have been able to save 150 people. We still do not feel safe. My wife and son prepared for a journey in the event of trouble, and they waited quietly.

The population began assembling at the marketplace. I was surprised that the number of soldiers and gendarmes present was very low. Our own gendarmes from the Szczebrzeszyn post behaved rather well, no shouting, kicking, or beating. On the other hand, the few from other areas were very brutal.

After a few hours almost everyone was at the marketplace. Dr. Warchalowska with her husband, Dr. Spoz and his entire family, dentists, city employees were all there. The verification of identification began. All physicians, dentists, workers at the Alwa plant, and some mechanics, and their families, were sent home. All people without labor cards were sent to Zwierzyniec and put behind wire, mostly small farmers, owners of small shops, and the unemployed, along with their families. How many people were taken it is difficult to say. Even the city does not have any count. It appears that between 300 and 400 people were arrested. All Ukrainians are staying.

This evening one carload of people was released, all workers at the Alwa factory. This was accomplished through the intervention of *Treuhander* Becker.

People stayed fairly calm, at least as calm as possible in a situation such as this. A few tried to hide or escape, but most of the population did assemble at the marketplace.

Now the new development. Since early morning several new people have arrived in town—men armed with guns, and women and children, all speaking German. They were looking for better houses to occupy. Later gendarmes moved them off to an unknown location.

People here are exhausted. It is impossible for whole families to escape. Single men can go to fight in the forest, but most must do what the Germans tell them.

July 11   Throughout the night, people were busy packing and moving. Much luggage was delivered to the hospital and stored. Today the special German housing commission began working.

Several houses have already been taken. To be prepared for any event I began packing. In one large suitcase I packed my printed work, one copy each. Because of security reasons I am not taking my manuscripts.

Around us the following villages have been completely evacuated: Bodaczow, Deszkowice, Rozlopy, Sulow, and Kolonia Sulowska. Evacuation has begun in Turobin. It is impossible to evaluate this action. Definitely, it is a terrible blow to our economy, let alone the loss of our national heritage.

Those arrested in Szczebrzeszyn are all now in the Zwierzyniec barracks. The Germans reason for this: supposedly our city is under Communist influence. The Germans are questioning these prisoners from Szczebrzeszyn, and during interrogation they are beating and kicking them and pulling out their fingernails. Former school principal Stanislaw Wegierski was killed.

July 11, 10 p.m.   Around 5 p.m. the Germans began moving people from their homes. One of the first, Dr. Jozwiakowski, was forced to move out with his entire family. He was allowed to take his medical equipment and only personal items, such as clothing. The furniture and bedding for four people had to stay.

Several houses on Zamojska Street were confiscated. Tomorrow more of the same will follow. Some people are moving their luggage into the hospital. Around noon many horse-drawn wagons carrying new settlers arrived in town. They are from the Tomaszow area, the village of Sabaudia.

These events are rapidly lowering resistance in many people. It is difficult to keep people in line, requesting that they work normally. Many hospital personnel have family members behind barbed wire. Today the hospital administrator went to Zwierzyniec to try to gain the release of two young kitchen helpers. Not obeying my orders, they went to see their families and were arrested along with them.

Completely exhausted, physically and mentally, I went to bed. I try to concentrate to remember the events of the last few days. I have tried to note the most important items. I am so exhausted that while lying down I think that only death will give me full peace. At the same time it feels so good to lie down in my own bed. While lying in bed I read *The Lives of the Martyrs*, by Duhamel.

July 12, 7 A.M.   Last night I slept well. I feel good and relaxed. I am starting my workday full of energy.

July 12, 10 P.M.   The special housing commission began assigning apartments to new German settlers. Not too many settlers are in the downtown area, but many have already received houses in the suburbs. They are not even waiting for people to move out and are taking furniture and household goods from loaded wagons. They get extremely upset when they find that people have taken the bedding.

We have a very peculiar situation. Only Polish people, mostly Catholics, are being forced to move out. Ukrainians and Orthodox are being allowed to stay. Because of this, many people are congregating across from the Orthodox parish, requesting applications for changing their religion from Catholic to Orthodox.

I was told by Rev. Szepietowski, from Zwierzyniec, that this is a common trend. He mentioned the names of villages where almost all the inhabitants have changed their religion. In Kosobudy the Catholic priest does not have one parishioner left. I compare this situation with one from a hundred years ago, when the Russians forced the population to change their religion from Greco-Catholic to Orthodox, against a strong peasant protest.

It is difficult to understand this, particularly when remembering the first stage of the war, when it seemed that all the people attended every Catholic service. This is a very poor method of self-preservation and shows that maybe the bond between people and the Church is superficial. I will try to find out the number of people asking for a change of religion.

The overall atmosphere in town is now much more pleasant. People seem friendly and calm. The reason for this: American and British forces took Sicily and the Soviets are advancing on the Eastern Front. We see now that military action against the Germans is in full swing and events are occurring that will speed up the defeat of our enemies.

July 13 A bricklayer from Szczebrzeszyn, Menderski, died in Zwierzyniec prison. In the same prison eighty-year-old Barbara Waszczuk, who was partly paralyzed, passed away. She had been arrested a few months before. Some people from Szczebrzeszyn were moved from Zwierzyniec prison to Zamosc.

July 14 The new German settlers are beginning to organize. In suburban Przedmiescie they have a new village administrator. In town, several changes in administration are expected.

I finally received more information about the changing of religion. So far 552 people have signed up as Orthodox. But as fast as this trend began, it is ending, and some people are trying to withdraw their applications. It has been learned that the change of religion has no relation to deportation, except that the Orthodox will be evacuated to Ukrainian regions.

In the village of Sola, where many people signed up for *Volksdeutsch* status, practically all the men were drafted into the German army, but this has not stopped the evacuation of their families.

Last night twenty-two men who were arrested on July 1 were released from Zwierzyniec. Now they must report for labor at the airfield. Their release was so late that I was unable to speak with any of them.

July 15 Finally this morning I spoke to one of the released men. Just before his release he was questioned and beaten by the gestapo. I examined his buttocks. He was bruised to the color of a blue plum.

I spoke with the mayor. Szczebrzeszyn is considered legally evacuated. The newcomers will be Germans. The administration of the city will change and will be completely in German hands. Szczebrzeszyn has been downgraded from city status to that of a village. The official name will be Dorf Szczebrzeszyn, Kreis Zamosc. So we will be back in Zamosc County. Poles will be tolerated only as a labor force. We are not sure of the future.

July 16 In town everything is quiet. A poster signed by the deputy mayor proclaims that the evacuation is finally complete. People have begun working normally, particularly those involved in agriculture. If anyone stops working they face deportation to concentration camps. The situation is made worse because German settlers are taking—or, it is better to say, stealing—everything from hand tools to wagons. In Mokra Lipa Rev. Przysucha was arrested and transported in handcuffs to Zamosc prison.

Today some women were released from Zamosc prison.

July 17   Life seems to be stabilizing. People are beginning to work again, making up for lost time.

An article by the commandant of the SS in the Lublin Region was printed in the newspaper *Nowy Glos Lubeski*. This article states that because of increasing activity by Soviet underground units, some villages close to the forest will be evacuated. Anyone who returns to their own home will not be harmed, but those who are now hiding and have not returned by July 31 will be handled as "Soviet bandits." This article was copied at city hall and posted in town.

July 18   Our town is practically deserted. The church is closed; there is not even one priest left. The Germans took the church vestments, chalices, monstrances, and books for shipment to German churches that were destroyed during air raids.

Today a gendarme came to the hospital asking for a secure storage space where, in case of emergency, all surgical equipment, drugs, and dressing can be stored. He showed me orders the gendarme post received concerning this. This is the first time in many months the Germans have shown any interest in hospital affairs. Maybe they are expecting some air action.

July 19   Today new regulations regarding the hours of window blackout were posted. Again the civil defense units were activated. Cichocki, one of the eleven men marked with the letter "W," was released from Zwierzyniec.

July 21   Yesterday in Szczebrzeszyn a new detachment of gendarmes arrived. They took over several private apartments for their quarters, including the entire second floor of the pharmacy building. Dr. Jozwiakowski's apartment was returned to him. This was probably the result of an interview with Bunsch, the German administrator of the Zamoyski estate.

This morning all Ukrainians were moved from Szczebrzeszyn and other villages to Tarnogrod. This was done in a completely different manner from the evacuation of the Poles. Each Ukrainian received a horse-drawn wagon and was allowed to take as much of the household as he or she wished. This was an official action. Anyone registered as Ukrainian had to go. So two of my women orderlies were forced to go, even though I tried to keep them at the hospital.

This morning another group of gendarmes arrived. It is being said that they are organizing a special action against the forest. Lately, new raids have begun which are aimed at the German administration and the German economy.

In Tereszpol a large wholesale market was robbed and a German was wounded. In Zurawnica and Kawenczyn cows were stolen from a central assembly point; in Zawada, two Germans and three Armenians were killed. It appears previous German actions did not get good results at all. The people still left in Szczebrzeszyn do not feel very good about this. They are sure that new retaliatory action by the Germans will begin soon.

July 23 On Monday, July 19, the Ukrainian mayor of Zolkiewka and Fik, the village administrator of Turobin, were assassinated. Two hand grenades were thrown as they drove along in an official car, killing both instantly. The killing of Fik was a mistake; he was a very good man. On the other hand, the Ukrainian was already the subject of many actions, but he always escaped injury.

Today in town the Germans ordered all the wives of people arrested and held in Zamosc to join them in order to be evacuated together.

Today city hall is beginning the registration of all inhabitants. I do not know how many times this has already been done.

July 26 Yesterday around noon people began talking about the possibility of a new evacuation of Poles from Szczebrzeszyn. People began packing and preparing for the worst. But the night passed quietly. Only a few drunk gendarmes and policemen began very noisy arguments and then started shooting.

This morning the news about the fall of Mussolini spread quickly. People feel this is the beginning of the end for Germany and that the war will finish soon. People feel really good; they smile as they walk.

July 27 This morning *Armarzt*, from Zamosc, carried out an inspection of the hospital. He was dressed in civilian clothes but carried a carbine and was accompanied by two armed soldiers. After a very careful inspection he told me I had to admit any Germans to the hospital who required hospitalization. For this I had to reserve two large rooms. A separate room was to be reserved for women with venereal disease.

By 7 A.M. tomorrow, at the offices of the *Arbeitsamt*, everyone, men and women, must assembly and be ready for special assignments, mostly to help with farm work. After intervening I received permission to report a list of my personnel. Anyone working at the hospital will be excused automatically.

From Bilgoraj we received news of new assassinations. Near Krasnik *Kreishauptmann* Adam and *Kreislandwirt* Geier were killed. Along with them my former driver Leon Brutt, lately employed as county chauffeur, was shot. *Kreishauptmann* Adams was a rather good man. I was informed that he had opposed the evacuation of Poles and also the brutality that was involved.

July 28 Today I learned about the existence in Zamosc of two very peculiar institutions. By German order I admitted two prostitutes, one with a letter from the "Armenian Bordel" and the second with a letter from the "Wermacht Bordel." So far, in Szczebrzeszyn, we do not have any similar houses. Armenians have no complaints because some of the townswomen are very friendly toward them.

July 29 According to new regulations, German soldiers are not allowed on the streets after 9 P.M. Also, soldiers must walk in pairs, not alone. When I asked a German officer the reason for this, his answer was that in our city the soldiers are not safe.

July 31 Two days ago a train between Susiec and Krasnobrod was derailed, and yesterday a train near Bukownica was blown up. Ten Armenians and two Germans were killed.

Yesterday the funerals of Adam and Geier took place in Bilgoraj. In the county offices there is complete chaos.

August

August 1 Today I went to Zwierzyniec. I was able to see for myself the terrible situation of people being held in isolation camps. On the highway, near the barracks, only German cars are allowed to drive; all other vehicles must drive on the other side of the camp, along the forest. Behind the barbed wire I was able to see some people who were barely moving, looking terrible. Some tried to wave to me, but because the sun was in my eyes I could not recognize anyone. Any kind of waving or greeting could provoke shooting by the German guards and also beating of the prisoners. At the pharmacy I met a good friend, Mr. Smutek, a teacher from Tarnogrod. He and his wife and daughter are being held at the camp, behind barbed wire. He now works in the camp sickroom, so he is able to get out and walk to the pharmacy for medicine. He looks terrible, dirty, skinny, and in torn clothing, but he is better off than the others because people on the outside try to help him.

But the worst for me was the visit to the estate hospital where about forty children, up to the age of five, were being kept. They are ill, mostly with dysentery and measles. They lay in small wooden beds, two together because of lack of space. They look terrible, like skeletons. Some of the stronger ones are lying outside in the shade of some trees. Some are still at the estate orphanage. A total of 214 children were taken from the camp, all under five years of age. The general supervision is being done by young Mrs. Zamoyska, but many women and teenage girls from the neighborhood are helping. They sit there for hours; they feed and wash them. I was ready to take some children with me to Szczebrzeszyn, but the Germans would not allow them to leave Zwierzyniec.

When I saw the small dying children I thought of the 10,000 Polish officers killed in Katyn. Today behind bars in Zwierzyniec are more than 3,000 people, some who are in jail and some who are only evacuees. Yesterday several men were moved to prison in Lublin.

You can see that the Germans do not feel safe. At the barracks and gendarme posts they are preparing themselves for an attack by the partisans. They are even placing sacks filled with sand around the doors and windows.

As I learned, our forest is preparing for more fighting. The last few weeks created some confusion and disorganization, but now because more young people are joining the underground units they are stronger than before. It appears new action against the Germans will begin any day. It depends on the news from both the Eastern and Western fronts. The Germans understand this situation very well. They are depressed and drinking more than before.

August 2   In the forest near Bilgoraj, German forest inspector Knisling was killed. At the same time a forest ranger, Sikorski, perished. He was a very good man who was just in the wrong place at the wrong time.

August 3   I was called to see a sick gendarme. At the gendarme post I noticed that all windows were covered with wire mesh. When I asked why, I was told that this was protection against hand grenades.

August 7   Many people were transferred from the camp in Zwierzyniec to prisons in Zamosc and Lublin, but some were released and returned to Szczebrzeszyn, including Dolezal, Dworniczak, and Amborski. Some signed the *Volksdeutsch* list, including Amborski and Dworniczak.

The Germans are working on construction of buildings at two airfields, Mokre and Labunie. The work is progressing very quickly. They are using prisoners and additional manpower from the labor bureau. I have come to the conclusion that because of the situation on the Eastern Front, they have begun to prepare new airfields inside their own territory.

August 9   Today I was told by the administrator of German settlers that all livestock and inventory belonging to the hospital would be confiscated and given to them. Taking from me all my horses, cows, pigs, and chickens would be a disaster for the hospital. I decided to go tomorrow morning to complain at the county office in Bilgoraj, but I am not sure if this will help. The new Germans in town are already beginning to take over stores and shops and also are taking furniture from people still living in Szczebrzeszyn. I met with the new so-called *Hauptdorfführer*, Lt. Maier. He is an arrogant young man, a typical German. His wife is a witch. She goes through any apartments she wants to and takes what she wants, mostly good carpets.

August 10   I went to Bilgoraj with a few pounds of good sausage and a few liters of vodka, as gifts for the German officials. I was still surprised at how easily I was able to solve everything. The new *Kreislandwirt* to whom Inspector Furman (one sausage and a liter of vodka) explained the situation, signed papers stating that nothing can be taken from the hospital and that items already removed must be returned as soon as possible.

There was complete chaos in the Bilgoraj county offices. The new county administrator had not yet arrived. So on everyone's desk there is a folder entitled "For Further Action," and no one does anything except file all the papers into those folders.

On the way back I stopped at Zwierzyniec. The hospital is full of patients. Finally the camp has been closed. There are approximately 150 sick people still there. Some will stay but most will be transported to hospitals in Bilgoraj and Szczebrzeszyn.

I was able to read a communiqué from the Polish relief committee concerning an audience with Gov. Gen. Frank in Cracow. He received a delegation from the Polish relief committee headed by Pres. Roniker. The reason for the meeting was the pacification of the Zamosc Region. I was completely shocked when I read the statements of the German officials, including Gov. Frank. He explained that several low-ranking German officials made big mistakes by enforcing evacuations and that some will be removed from their posts, including Lublin chief of police Globotznik. Then he promised a complete change in the method of administration.

When I came back to Szczebrzeszyn I was told that Stanislaw Radwan Gluchowski had been killed. He was a very fat, big man who worked with livestock and was very well known for his brutality. He forced villagers to pay him up to 500 zloty per head for undeclared cattle. In a short time he became a very rich man.

August 11 Late in the evening I received a transport of patients from the hospital in Zwierzyniec. All were very acute cases of dysentery. A special couple are the Sienkas; she is seventy years old and blind, he is seventy-eight. They are both trying to hide their terrible condition from each other.

Seeing these people in stages of complete exhaustion, unable to even move, makes the hatred of the Germans grow, so that we are ready to kill them with our bare hands. Now that we can foresee the end of the war, we are sure that our time for revenge will come.

August 12 Yesterday and today many internees from Zamosc were released. On the streets you can recognize them by their very pale complexions, swelling of all joints, and slow movement.

August 13 Several people released from the Zwierzyniec camp were brought to my hospital. One of them was Feliks Krukowski, a driver, who was arrested on July 1, in Szczebrzeszyn, and marked with a letter "W" on his forehead. He was badly beaten during interrogation. It is hard to recognize this thirty-eight-year-old man who had been very well built and in excellent physical condition. Now he has a yellow complexion and must lay on his side or stomach. His back is black from beatings. He has several open wounds, almost to the bone.

The entire camp in Zwierzyniec is closed. Some people were released, some were transferred to other camps. The gestapo and SS soldiers from the camp were relocated. Approximately 600 former inmates are now in Zamosc. Others were released to work on the airfields.

After the very tiring events of July our town is returning to normal. Many people have come back. Almost everyone has adjusted themselves to the living conditions forced upon us because of the presence of the new German settlers.

Good news from both fronts is giving the people new strength to live.

August 14 Today in Brody high school student Stanislawa Pilatowna was arrested. It is possible that a few other high school girls will be detained, particularly those who had visited her frequently.

August 18 The last few days passed very quietly. The problem of returning Szczebrzeszyn back to Zamosc County still has not been solved. On the city streets you can see many Germans in civilian clothing, mostly women and children, all new settlers. The Germans organized for the children a new preschool, taking for this purpose a parish hall.

On August 15, on Polish National Day, partisans in the forest celebrated with a special Mass.

In Tereszpol the Germans killed Czeslaw Jozwiakowski, a professional sergeant of the Polish army, very active in the underground, who was known as "Most." A few months ago his brother Zdzislaw was killed in Szczebrzeszyn.

August 19   From Frampol I admitted fourteen cases of spotted typhus. They all were in the Zwierzyniec camp previously. Rev. Maslowski, just released from Zamosc prison, visited the hospital. He told me about people who were broken during interrogation and who told the Germans everything. He was able to hear their "confessions" through the very thin walls. In particular he mentioned Mr. D. from Szczebrzeszyn.

August 21   Last night a loud explosion was heard from the direction of Zamosc. A Russian aircraft supposedly dropped a bomb in Hrubieszow. As a result, window blackouts are being checked again.

August 22   Around noon the deputy *Kreishauptmann* from Zamosc, along with the county physician, arrived at the hospital. During the inspection Dr. Snacki, the county physician from Bilgoraj, was also present. After the inspection the German physician from Zamosc said that in a few days he will be here again to officially register my hospital as a county hospital. So now it is official, we are again part of Zamosc County.

I went to Zwierzyniec. The camp is empty. Builder Rogowski returned from Lublin prison.

People are talking about fighting around Krzeszowo, where a large Soviet group is involved.

Last evening, around 7 P.M., a Russian group, 500 men strong, entered Tereszpol and took provisions. People say the soldiers addressed their leader as "Comrade Major." During the day in Tereszpol two "civilians" killed farmer Swacha.

August 27   Today we are disturbed about a new German atrocity. This morning an eight-year-old boy, Miko Bugala, was found lying in an orchard with gunshot wounds. He was taken to the hospital where he died. We learned the boy went there for apples. The new owner, a German locksmith, shot him and left him to die, without telling anyone. This German will surely be liquidated very soon.

The epidemic of spotted typhus is spreading mostly among people released from the Zwierzyniec camp. The number of cases in my hospital is over one hundred. This is even higher than the epidemic of the years 1919–21. Today I was told that the former administrator of Zamosc hospital, Siedlecki, was killed during a gestapo interrogation.

August 30   This morning a drunk farmer from Kawenczyn brought to the hospital a wounded young man. He told me the man had hurt himself with a pitchfork while mowing hay, but the wound was from a gunshot. Naturally I acted as if I believed him. He insisted that after first aid he would take the wounded man home. He signed the registration form with a false name. I recognized the young man. He was nineteen-year-old Tadeusz Jozwiakowski, brother of Zdzislaw and Czeslaw, who were killed by the Germans. Everyone knew that the Jozwiakowski brothers had been active in the underground. All physicians are required to report gunshot wounds to the police. But I have never obeyed this order. In this case I wrote in the books that the wound was an accident caused by a hay fork. I hope that everyone on the hospital staff will be quiet about this, otherwise I face arrest and transport to a concentration camp.

August 31   Today Szczebrzeszyn officially changed its designation. First the name was changed; second, we are now again in Zamosc County. Our official name is Dorfgemeine Szczebrzeszyn, Kreis Zamosc. From a city we have been demoted to a commune. Commune Szczebrzeszyn now includes twenty-five villages, such as Brody Male, Brody Duze, Kawenczyn, Kawenczynek, and Sulow. The mayor was told to prepare a reception for approximately 150 people. This afternoon administration officials from Zamosc and Bilgoraj counties and all village administrators assembled in Krzeszowski hall. But no one from the Polish community was invited. I will try to find out how the reception went. At any rate it was a historical event for Szczebrzeszyn.

It is now the end of the fourth year of the war. I am trying to evaluate the events of these four years, all of our miseries and defeats, both national and personal. Every year has been different. From year to year German terror increases.

Our only good luck was that, from the beginning of the war, we have believed in our final victory and the quick end of the war. Without this it would have been difficult to survive. If in the first year of the war people knew that it would last so long, many surely would have broken completely and begun collaborating with the enemy. Now events point to a quick end to the war. The urge for revenge is growing.

It is difficult to describe the destruction of our land and the sacrifices of our populations, the evacuation, deportation, and murder of thousands of people. In Zamosc, where before the war intellectual life flourished, now only a few intellectuals survive. Some were murdered and others are dying in concentration camps. But even if German repression increases, they will not keep our nation from revenge. We will survive until the end of the war.

September

September 1 Today, to resolve several hospital affairs, I went to the county offices in Zamosc. The last time I visited the city was in May. Since then Zamosc has changed again. The number of Germans is constantly growing. On the streets most people are Germans. Eighty percent of the shops are German. German is now the official language. Children run carrying swastikas, and this is in front of the beautiful Zamosc city hall on the marketplace. The street names have been changed. Ulica Swietego Mikolaja is now Robert Koch Strasse.

The SS rules the city and is trying to Germanize it as quickly as possible. Mayor Werner informed me that the population of Zamosc dropped from 28,000 before the war to about 21,000 as of now. Several thousand Jews were killed. Out of the 21,000 around 3,000 declared themselves *Reichdeutsche*, *Volksdeutsch*, or *Stammdeutsche*. Those newly created Germans are in for a big surprise. On September 4 all men must register to form some sort of military unit to fight the oncoming Soviet troops.

September 3 This afternoon the new German *Dorfführer*, on order of the *Reichskommissar*, arrived at the hospital with papers stating that all our properties are confiscated. All hospital wagons, horses, cows, all our farm equipment, and, what is worse, all our food supplies were taken. In a few hours we lost everything. I was almost crying as I supervised this giveaway.

September 4 Today I learned that Waclaw Skuratowicz returned to Zwierzyniec. I went to see him, but when I arrived in Zwierzyniec he was not at home. From Zamosc prison he had been transferred to Majdanek concentration camp and then finally released.

September 9 This morning we received news about the capitulation of Italy. Everyone is happy, saying this is the end of Germany. The younger and more aggressive people now talk about active defiance against the occupants.

More people are coming to the hospital asking for help. Besides those ill with spotted typhus, I am receiving cases of acute malnutrition among the people released from concentration camps and prisons. A forty-nine-year-old farmer, Jakub Mogilnicki, from Kosobudy, who spent only three months in Majdanek, died after a few hours' stay in the hospital.

September 12   People are so happy because of Italy's capitulation that the consumption of alcohol tripled, not only in our town, but also in all the nearby villages. We await more good news. Without radios it is impossible to follow world events, so we must rely on rumors and gossip, such as "One woman told another . . ."

September 14   I do not know why people are afraid of September 15. Some expect new mass arrests, some new evacuations; so many people have moved out to spend the night in the nearby villages. It is possible that this situation was created by the news of new arrests in Zamosc. So far I learned about the arrests of retired music teacher Bryk and milkman Hajduk.

September 15   The night passed quietly. Now we await what the next day will bring. The town is still very tense.

September 20   Even though September 15 passed without any events occurring, there is a depressed atmosphere in town. Lately people seem more nervous again; young people and former soldiers are not staying home at night. This might be because of what happened near Krasnobrod. Home Army officer Capt. "Bartosz" Staszewski was arrested. During interrogation in Zamosc, where he was beaten and tortured, he agreed to show where in the forest weapons were buried and where he hid his daily reports. He did this hoping that he would be rescued by the underground on the way there, but that never happened. Now we are afraid that under torture he might give more information concerning the underground organization, and that would be disastrous.

From Zamosc there is more information concerning current arrests. Mrs. Hrebieniukowa-Jacewiczowa, a former high school teacher, and several others are being held. Sorry, but I do not know their names.

Last night in Krasnystaw an assault on the prison took place. It was a complete success. Supposedly around 500 people were freed. Personally I think that number is too high.

Already the third month has passed since the Catholic church in Szczebrzeszyn has been closed; still there is not one priest living in town. For religious services people must travel to Topolcza. It is interesting that the Orthodox church is still open, and the Orthodox priest can celebrate Mass, even though the number of parishioners has declined.

We are positive that we are seeing the last stages of our war and that the Germans are very exhausted. Their might is crumbling. This is evident because of their defeats on all fronts. We hope that by the end of the year we will be liberated by the Soviet army with the help of our own underground.

September 25 A few days ago a commission composed of gestapo agents arrived in town and again began checking the list of people who signed *Volksdeutsch* and *Stammdeutsch* papers. First they went to Brody for two days; now they are in Szczebrzeszyn. They are issuing special summonses to appear in Hrubieszow on a certain date. People who are involved fear that this is in relation to the news that new *Volksdeutsch* will be shipped to Germany for further Germanization. In Szczebrzeszyn the commission is still working.

This afternoon sensational news spread throughout the town. Last night in Bilgoraj a very well organized assault on the prison took place. All prisoners were freed and the sick ones were taken away by horse-drawn wagons. During this action the entire city was surrounded by soldiers of the Home Army. It was done very professionally, quickly, and they were in complete control.

September 28 Slowly I am receiving information about the assault on the prison in Bilgoraj. I have decided not to give too many details because I am sure participants in this incident will later give me very specific information. Seventy people were freed, including forest ranger Boleslaw Usow and university professor Ludwik Ehrlich ("Farley").

Boguslaw Hertz hung himself this morning in Zamosc. Already in 1939 he had signed up as a *Volksdeutsch*, and for four years he acted against the Poles. His suicide caused a big sensation in Zamosc because of an open letter he had written just before his death, addressed to the German authorities. The letter started with S.O.B. and stated that in three weeks every German will be hanging just as he is now.

September 29 Last night two men with gunshot wounds were brought to the hospital. Both were very popular in Zamosc and Zwierzyniec: Jacek Jakimowicz, co-owner of a lumber yard, and Adam Wyczolkowski, former university student now working as a clerk. The shooting occurred during a party at Kalweit's in Zwierzyniec. Two armed men entered the house and told everyone to lie down on the floor. Jakimowicz jumped on one of the men and Wyczolkowski hit him with a chair. The second man shot twice, then both left. The owner called the police. Shortly after the German gendarmes, "blue police," and Armenians arrived, a robbery of the brewery in

Zwierzyniec took place; 10,000 zloty were taken. At the same time railroad tracks near Susiec were destroyed. I now feel that we are coming to a time when these types of events will increase. It proves to me that the war is coming to an end.

October

October 1 Last night a fire broke out at the Klemensow sugar refinery. The local fire brigade began fighting the fire when the gendarmes and police arrived, totally drunk, and began shooting the firefighters. One fireman, eighteen-year-old Tadeusz Pulikowski, was shot while handling a fire hose. This morning his parents brought him to the hospital.

Bank director Tadeusz Ossowski was killed near Krasnik. He was from a well-known family. After the Russian revolution he came to work at the Zamoyski estate before joining the Farmer's Bank.

The special gestapo commission left Szczebrzeszyn. From among the physicians only Dr. Spoz and the veterinarian, Dr. Cebula, were called to report to Hrubieszow, but they decided not to appear. I am trying to establish the number of people who did go to Hrubieszow. So far as I see it, the number is very small.

October 2 A few days ago someone shot at the *Dorfführer* in Rozlupy. He was only slightly wounded in the hand and chest. But today his deputy, a German settler, was killed by a single shot from a carbine. He died on arrival at the hospital. People are so full of hatred against the Germans that the crying of his mother and wife caused no reaction among the people who watched.

October 3 Every day what we see around us are assaults, robberies, and killing. A few days ago in Kosobudy, and also in Tereszpol, all money collected for taxes was taken. In Florin the flour dryer was destroyed by hand grenades. At the Alwa factory the warehouse was robbed and all the food was taken from the kitchen. Not only the factory but also the entire village of Brody was surrounded by partisans. Photographer Cichocki was taken and later executed.

"Bartosz" Staszewski committed suicide. After he had been taken to the third floor of the gestapo building, he jumped through the window and was killed instantly.

As I mentioned before, one of the people freed from Bilgoraj prison was Prof. Ludwik Ehrlich, from Lwow, who has been living in our area lately. As always he has been gathering historical materials, this time about German atrocities.

October 10   On October 4 I was able to transport the wounded Jacek Jakimowicz to Warsaw in a German Red Cross ambulance. The drive was very quick; it took us only five and a half hours. Passing through Lublin I was able to see the camp at Majdanek. It was impossible to see individual prisoners from the quickly moving car. I did notice a few groups of people working on assignments. Looking at this camp it was difficult to comprehend just how many people had been killed there.

I spent three days in Warsaw. There seemed to me to be much more excitement than last year. On the second day after my arrival the Germans tried to remove the monument of the aviator at Unia Lubelska Place. When they approached the monument machine gun fire held them back, so they were forced to retreat. On Aleja Szucha a gestapo inspector was gunned down. There is much shooting on the streets. German gendarmes cruise the streets in open cars, carrying carbines and machine guns. Some houses are surrounded by gendarmes and "blue police." You can see this several times a day. Once, while I was riding the streetcar on Narutowicz Place, a shot was fired. Immediately all passengers lay down on the floor. It appears this is a daily routine and people are prepared for it.

I was able to see that underground activities are very well organized. But I was really impressed with the preparation for new publications. It has been decided that a new publishing house, Wisla, will start up as soon as the war is over. The organizers have already collected new literary works of the best-known Polish writers. This publication will be known as *First Book* and will be printed as soon as the Germans retreat from Warsaw. It will contain short stories and articles of surviving authors. I was able to inspect the graphic art for this publication, compiled by my first cousin Eryk Lipinski, a very well known graphic artist. Many university professors and scientists are working on new books. Prof. Antoniewicz is working on a new edition of his *History Of Culture*. Prof. Dr. Orlowski is finishing his second volume of *Internal Medicine*. Again I went to a meeting at Stefan Rygiel's, where I met many friends. There I learned details about new illegal publications.

After living so long under the daily pressure of surviving at my hospital, those three days in Warsaw were a real pleasure. I left Warsaw physically very tired but full of hope for a better future.

I came back by train. This was a terrifying experience. I was at the station by 8 P.M. and had to wait three hours for departure. We were enroute the full night. We arrived at Rejowiec very late and I had to wait for a train to Chelm-Lwow. Finally I arrived at Szczebrzeszyn at 8 P.M. The complete trip took twenty-four hours.

As soon as I set foot in the Szczebrzeszyn station I was told what had occurred during my absence. In Tereszpol the Germans arrested a Catholic priest and many other men. Forest ranger Piatkowski and several other rangers were detained in Panasowka. From Majdanek, Naszynski, Cwik, Pilip, and Franciszek Glowacki all those arrested on July 1 were released.

Today, after more than three months, a Mass celebrated by Rev. Kapalski took place, not in the parish church, but in the small St. Leonard Chapel at the cemetery.

October 14 Piatkowski and the other forest rangers were released. The situation in Zwierzyniec is still very tense. Here in our town the German settlers organized themselves by taking over Polish stores, shops, and other businesses. Every day the number of Polish possessions shrinks and German ones grow.

The new commune of Szczebrzeszyn is officially on the map. The new name is Hauptdorf Szcz, or Stadtgemeine Szcz. It consists of a total of thirty-one villages and colonies, thirteen German and eighteen Polish.

Deutsche Dörfer (German Villages)

1. Szczebrzeszyn	8. Bodaczow
2. Rozlopy	9. Wieloncza
3. Colony Sulow	10. Zawada
4. Zrebce	11. Gross Brody
5. Tworyczow	12. Sulow
6. Kitowo	13. Colony Zamojska
7. Deszkowice	

Polnische Dörfer (Polish Villages)

1. Marynowka	10. Sulowek
2. Katy I	11. Kulikow
3. Katy II	12. Michalow
4. Niedzielsko	13. Szperowka
5. Klemensow	14. Sasiadka
6. Brody Male	15. Mokre Lipie
7. Kawenczyn	16. Blonie
8. Kawenczynek	17. Colony Kawenizyn
9. Sulowiec	18. Colony Rozlopy

Today I received a sick woman from Deszkowice who had special papers signed by the *Dorfführer*. The papers had many stamps. Next to the signature of the SS *Dorfführer* was a long stamp, "Hauptdorf Szczebrzeszyn, Kreis Zamosc, G.G." This paper with all the signatures and stamps is now in my collection of war documents.

From all the signs I can feel that the Germans are not sure of themselves. The so-called *Dorfführer* are afraid to stay home at night. The settlers say they will be glad to go home. The Polish *Volksdeutsch* are afraid not only of the approaching Russians but also of their own neighbors. Some are looking at the possibility of moving to Warsaw and other Western cities.

October 17 I met former Polish capt. Eberhardt, who now works as a clerk at the German Mokre airfield. He informed me that approximately 1,400 people work there, including 800 Jews from Poniatowka, near Warsaw. The work is split into two shifts and goes on twenty-four hours a day. They are building new asphalt runways. At the Klemensow airfield work is going full speed. From Zamosc the Germans are starting to evacuate large warehouses full of military equipment. Events point to the Russian front quickly moving toward us.

October 19 Last night a group of underground soldiers surrounded the village of Duze Brody. This is a German village occupied by German settlers and *Volksdeutsch*. From already prepared lists the partisans called for the gathering of all horses, cows, and pigs. All were taken to the forest. The livestock of the few remaining Poles was not touched. Some of the Germans who protested received severe beatings. While leaving the village the commanding officer, Lt. "Dolina," told the Germans that any German retaliation will result in the execution of all Germans in Brody.

October 20 This morning Jerzy Plomienski came by to see me. For some time he was a guest at the Scibor-Rylski estate in Uhrynow, county of Hrubieszow. But after Ukrainians burned the mansion he escaped, and now he is going back to Warsaw. He told me of the Ukrainian terror in the eastern provinces. This is occurring even in Hrubieszow County, where Ukrainian peasants are killing Poles. People are trying to escape to the west. Even in Szczebrzeszyn we can see a few horse-drawn wagons with escapees from Sokal.

October 27 The entire day was very quiet. In the nearby villages there is always shooting, which seems normal now.

Today my twelve-year-old son Tadeusz was sworn in as a member of the Home Army. The swearing in was performed by Tadeusz Guminski ("Lowicki" or "Szyszka"). This was my attempt to start him in conspiracy work, in the type of work permitted at his young age. During the entire ceremony, which took place in my private office, I was present. But at the one moment when I looked into the face of my boy, I felt so moved that to avoid crying I left the room.

Fifty months of war and slavery have made us emotionally nervous. I personally can feel this more and more with every passing day.

October 28 Yesterday in Rozlupy a seventeen-year-old German settler on guard duty was wounded. He was brought to the hospital. In retaliation the Germans arrested ten men, but after several hours they were all released.

The entire day gendarmes checked the identification of everyone entering our town.

October 29   Today a secretary from Zamosc County visited me in my office. He gave me some details of life in Zamosc. People there feel the Russian front is moving quickly toward us. The Germans, mainly gestapo agents, are sending their families back to Germany. Through our town, in a westerly direction, trains and convoys loaded with equipment travel rapidly. The airfield in Mokre is complete. A new airfield is being constructed in Labunie. The airfield at home has been moved to Klemensow. Forty-five cars loaded with military personnel and laborers were transported there also. The task of enlarging the airfield is moving along rapidly. In Count Szeptycki's palace, in Labunie, a new military hospital has been established. The military hospital in Zamosc is now full of wounded.

Here in Szczebrzeszyn the German spirit is very low. I learned this during a talk with *Dorfführer* Steinher.

November

November 5   Tonight an assault took place on the village of Ploskie, near Zamosc. This village is now inhabited by German settlers. Only horses, cows, and pigs were taken. A German guard who began shooting was killed. The partisans were very polite toward any Germans who did not protest, but those who did received beatings. This action took the Germans by surprise.

Today at the hospital we had a big surprise. This afternoon horse-drawn wagons full of agricultural equipment began arriving at the hospital, followed by horses, cows, pigs, and more wagons. We finally got back everything that was taken from us weeks ago. The German county administrator from Zamosc personally checked the list of confiscated items.

November 10   I visited Naszynski. It has been more than a month since he was released from Majdanek. He looks terrible. He is so ill that he cannot feed himself. Yesterday Gwiazdowski, Glowacki, and Pilip came back from Majdanek. They were taken there on July 1, but they look much better.

In our town lately you can feel that something is coming. People are again nervous and expect more arrests. It is possible that a new contingent of men will be taken to work on the Klemensow airfield. The work there is in full swing. In our town, particularly on Sunday, many German airmen walk around. Many of them are totally drunk.

At Mokre airfield 150 Jews were killed. The work there is finished, so it is unnecessary to feed so many people. This is typical of the German mentality. From each direction I receive information about the final liquidation of the remaining Jews.

Everyone's attention is on the progress on the Eastern Front. People watch the events and count when we can see the Russian troops. Some are afraid and say this will be another occupation, but others hope that the Soviet troops will arrive soon.

November 16   The entire week I did not make any notations in my diary, but nothing important has happened. Only in the last few days have I felt that something is going wrong with the Germans on the Eastern Front and that the front is coming closer and closer to our town. A few days ago an official German communiqué gave information about the evacuation of Kiev. Today there is news that fighting is taking place on the streets of Zytomierz. The people are very nervous, asking each other when the Red Army will be here and what to do when the Germans begin retreating from our area. This is the period people fear most. We receive news that the Germans are forcing people to move out along with the German army. We are told that those who refuse to move out are being shot. Many people are now moving to isolated places to escape being in the large cities, towns, or villages at the time of the German retreat.

As far as the Germans are concerned, for the last few days we have been in a war zone. We await new German guidelines. Now, as always, during the time of important events we can feel the lack of salt. All salt supplies have been sold out, and now it is impossible to buy even a few grams.

We await the moment when German settlers begin to move out. More trains with evacuees from the east pass through the Szczebrzeszyn railroad station.

I personally have resumed work on my history of medicine in the Zamosc Region. I am now working on the eighteenth chapter. Only two more remain unfinished. I am trying to speed up this work and have it finished in the next few weeks. I know that a time will come when I will be unable even to hold a pen in my hand. I do not know what to do with the manuscripts. I have no time to type them.

November 23   A new German counteroffensive has begun. So we must wait a while longer for the arrival of Russian troops. Again we fear new German repression, evacuation of villages, deportations, and executions. People again started packing to be ready for any event. We are all under constant pressure and almost at the nerve-breaking point.

On Sunday, November 21, two German sergeants near Bialy Slup were killed. People are afraid that the Germans will retaliate.

November 25 Szczebrzeszyn experienced something unexpected. At the railroad station, on his way to Warsaw, postmaster Pazdziora was arrested.

November 28 The situation seems stalemated. Newspapers are not giving any information about the Allied forces on either front. People have stopped dreaming about the end of the war in 1943. Only a few weeks remain until the end of the year. The same feeling prevails in Zwierzyniec, but there people drink more than in Szczebrzeszyn.

We are worried about new German methods of securing themselves against assault. They take hostages and put them in prison in Zamosc. Occasionally they post lists containing names of the hostages to be killed. Every few days the list of executed persons is posted, with a note that this is in retaliation for the killing of a German or an assault on a village. Any one of us can be taken as hostage.

In Szczebrzeszyn the Germans are trying to take over all Polish establishments. Stores are run by Germans; we have German barbers, tailors, shoemakers, bakers, butchers, and mechanics. A new restaurant was opened with the name Neue Heimat. I worry that soon I will have a German hospital administrator and a German head nurse.

December

December 2 I went to Zamosc. Accidentally I met a few people, old friends, whom I had not seen for quite some time. I noticed how much they had aged. It is as if the period of war shows even on people's faces. The overall feeling in Zamosc is not good. People still talk about what is facing us when the Russian army takes over the city. They are afraid that the retreating German army will not stop at destroying buildings, bridges, highways, and other objects of military value but will also begin killing or deporting the intellectuals still living in the city. Because of this people are drinking. Wherever I stopped to talk, first it is vodka. People are drinking not only in restaurants but also in every office, shop, and store. In the print shop everyone was drinking. Instead of shot glasses they used new ink pots. At the print shop I received, as a gift, a copy of the first book printed in Polish. Up until now no Polish books have been printed since the beginning of the war. This book by Prof. Galczynski, from Lublin, entitled *Food Products*, was printed on good paper using characters I selected when we were publishing *Teka Zamojska*, before the war. It totaled 270 pages.

This morning the new commandant of the gendarme post in Szczebrzeszyn inspected the hospital for readiness in case of air attack. He told me I was to provide a civil defense squad. This squad of twenty must be composed of hospital personnel only, and I will be in charge. It appears the Germans are counting on air attacks.

Postmaster Pazdziora was released from Lublin prison. With the "new Germans" there are many problems. I am trying to learn who out of Szcze-brzeszyn's citizens are now German and who are still Poles. Little by little it is possible to come to some conclusions. First, all the children from *Volks-deutsch* families were removed from Polish schools and placed in German ones. The new *Volksdeutsch* must stand night guard duty. They finally received German food stamps.

It is hard to believe that practically every one of those people volunteered for this, without any pressure from the Germans. Among these "new Germans" are Polish army officers and Polish government employees, all with typical Polish names: Stanislaw Kiszka, Jan Flak, Ostrowski, Bielecki, and others. I hope to finally have a full list of those people, but it will be hard work to determine who signed the *Volksdeutsch* petition voluntarily and who was forced to sign it. An example is Dr. Hauslinger in Zamosc.

December 4 I am noting and will try to describe a very interesting situation. Several German settlers are Catholic, but they have no right to go to Polish Catholic church. (The parish church is still closed, so the priest holds services in St. Leonard's Chapel at the cemetery.) The priests were told by the German authorities they have no right to give any religious sacraments to German settlers, such as baptisms, confessions, communion, or marriage. In spite of these restrictions the settlers are going to church. The new regulations now also include all of the *Volksdeutsch*. I had an example of this today. A woman, her maiden name was Rybicka, her married name Kucharska, gave birth to a girl. Her brother was killed. Her husband is in the Majdanek concentration camp. She had signed the *Volksdeutsch* list, so to baptize the girl she had to go to Zamosc.

December 6 Tonight Wit Naszynski died after his return from the Majdanek camp. We had done everything possible to keep him alive. He was a very good man.

Yesterday in Zrebice three Germans were killed. I do not have any details yet, but we are afraid of reprisals, particularly the taking of hostages. The Germans began activating civil defense procedures. New shelters are being built.

December 8 I have a big headache. The Germans in Zamosc refused to give my hospital any produce. They say the hospital must be self-supporting. They forget that German settlers took all our supplies. How can I support one hundred people, patients and personnel? Only for a few weeks, maybe a month, that's all.

In Zwierzyniec several factory workers were arrested. The Germans confiscated a large amount of guns and ammunition.

A very well organized assault took place in Suchowola, a village of mostly German settlers. The partisans took everything—livestock, equipment, and even personal possessions. The Germans were moved several kilometers and released on the highway.

In Zamosc four men were executed in front of the high school. We are counting on more reprisals.

December 10   This morning a special detachment of gendarmes went to Zrebice. Later a few trucks carrying soldiers drove past Szczebrzeszyn on the road to Kawenczyn and Topolcza. The picture of armed, helmeted gendarmes going by in fast trucks is depressing. We know by now that this is a special mission of execution or other bloody work.

On Sunday, November 28, a young woman, Maria Piasecka ("Zar"), was arrested in Pulawy. She was arrested carrying illegal literature. She worked as a secretary for the Polish relief committee, first in Jozefow and later in Sol, near Bilgoraj. She had been arrested once before and spent half a year in prison in Cracow.

December 11   Early yesterday morning some Germans came to Zrebice. They assembled several people at the old blacksmith shop and executed twenty of the men they had brought from Zamosc. They were removed from the trucks while wearing only underwear and tied with barbed wire. From Zrebice the Germans went to Topolcza, where they executed more men, some very young boys and very old men.

December 14   I went again to Zamosc. On my way I noticed new highway signs with the name Krzeszow and also the distance in kilometers. Krzeszow is west of here on the road to Cracow. I get the feeling this is in preparation for retreat.

All of Zamosc feels the terror of new executions. On December 11 the Germans posted a list of twenty-nine people who were executed in retaliation for the assaults on Zrebice and Ciechanow. All of the executed were from Bilgoraj and Zamosc counties. One of them was Stefan Kozlowski, clerk in the law office of attorney Zielinski, in Zamosc. Next to his name was a notation that he was executed for belonging to an illegal organization. Yesterday his wife was arrested. On the same poster another thirty names were listed. They will be executed if the assaults on German villages do not stop. The last name on the list is Zygmunt Arentowicz, from Zamosc.

In Zamosc there is very heavy traffic. You can hear the German language everywhere. For the first time I noticed the presence of Ukrainians, very tall men dressed in dark blue-green uniforms with sheepskin hats. They are from Poltawa. The Germans organized them into a Ukrainian SS unit.

December 17   Piasecka ("Zar") was moved from the prison in Lublin to Bilgoraj. From Bilgoraj she sent a message, "Send me poison. What I went through in Lublin I will not be able to withstand a second time." The underground sent her poison. We do not know if she is still alive. Four people from the office of the Polish relief committee are being held in connection with her arrest. One man, Mr. Markiewicz, died during interrogation. The others are in prison.

Today I received a series of photographs from the "Grom" unit of the Home Army. These pictures show partisan life in the forest and have a special charm for young people.

In Bilgoraj a change took place in the gestapo. Chief Kolb was replaced by Capt. Waldemar Trautwein. On the outside he appears very cultured. He has a university education, but he can torture people just like the notorious Kolb.

December 19   Today around 6 P.M. a baker from a German bakery, twenty-one-year-old Boguslaw Niezgoda, was shot. He was a gestapo informer. He was wounded in the stomach, at the apartment of the bakery owner, a German settler, in the presence of several Germans. The execution was accomplished by one man who was very well dressed and calm. After the shooting he simply left. Niezgoda was brought to the hospital, where he died during surgery. It is clear that he was executed as a result of a verdict by the underground tribunal of justice. His death made the Germans in town very nervous, particularly the informers.

December 23   Jaworski was arrested a few weeks ago in Brody, and in Szczebrzeszyn, Kolcunowa was arrested. Jaworski butchered a pig and Kolcunowa tried to sell meat and bacon. On Monday, December 20, both were shot. Because many people are involved in the black market sale of meat, it is impossible to buy any now.

Again today I hear a rumor that several people had been freed from Bilgoraj prison.

December 25   Today is the fifth Christmas of the war. Before noon more than 5,000 people went to hear Mass at the small chapel at the cemetery.

Nothing but drinking from noon until late evening. The Germans allowed three liters of vodka per person for all settlers and *Volksdeutsch*, so some people are jealous.

In Zamosc several people were executed.

December 26   Without even one shot a platoon of the Home Army, under the leadership of "Grom," entered the prison in Bilgoraj. All prisoners were freed. Among them was Piasecka, who was just prevented from taking poison.

In Potok a Ukrainian, Byk, was liquidated. In retaliation the Ukrainians killed several people, including Rev. Nowosad and the daughter of Polish *Sejm* member Kondysar, who is in the Oranienburg concentration camp.

I received more photos from the forest and several issues of an underground newspaper, *Powstaniec*, 200 copies of which are printed every week. The publisher is "Lowicki." During the last few weeks my collection has grown rapidly.

December 28   Last night in Zwierzyniec the gestapo arrested Adam Karpinski, former officer Gasiorowski, along with his wife, and two Jasin brothers from the brewery. Neither Karpinski nor Gasiorowski had been involved in any underground activities. Also Czernicka, daughter of a policeman who died recently in Auschwitz, was arrested.

December 31   Today I met the very popular Lt. "Woyna." He came along with other Home Army officers. I like him very much.

Karpinski and Gasiorowski were released. Gasiorowska is still in prison. Czernicka was moved to Zamosc.

The Days of Our Slavery
Are Numbered

January

January 2 Yesterday we began a new year. Everyone is sure that this will be the last year of the war. The last two days, yesterday and today, I spent in Zwierzyniec. Many people were enjoying themselves drinking and talking, but some pessimists just said, "Something is in the air."

The last arrests (Czernicka and Jasinow) occurred while a search was being conducted for someone else (Praschilowa), and it clearly shows that the gestapo are lurking around once again. Many people do not stay home at night.

A few days ago a group of twelve Turkmenian soldiers, part of a company of SS stationed in Zwierzyniec, escaped into the forest.

January 6 Yesterday the forest people abducted a policeman, Tatulinski, from Zwierzyniec; he is the son of a policeman from Szczebrzeszyn. Young Tatulinski had a very poor reputation and for some time had been on a list of dangerous people.

Today we had a few guests from Zwierzyniec. They brought with them area commandant "Adam" and a cavalry platoon leader, "Sep." This type of visit is very good for morale.

Yesterday in Szczebrzeszyn, former court usher Niedzielski was arrested. This was the second time. He has already been in Majdanek once.

January 7   This morning the warehouse in Zwierzyniec that stored tobacco products and vodka was set on fire.

Postulski, who was arrested in July 1943, was released from Majdanek. He was the last of the eleven men marked with a "W" by the Germans.

Tension is growing in relation to the new Soviet offensive and the crossing of Russian troops at the Polish border. The possibility of air strikes has increased, and because of this the city is now divided into three main civil defense areas. People are curious what position those in the forest will take when the German troops begin retreating and the Russians come.

January 9   A few days ago the administrator of the commune of Jozefow, Gielczyk, was kidnapped. In Blonie ranger Surmacz was killed. He was known as a German spy. He expected this and never stayed in the same place at night. The general topic of conversation is the Soviet offensive. The storm from the east is moving quickly toward us.

January 10   I went to Zwierzyniec and met two officers of the Home Army, Capt. "Zegota" (Tadeusz Szturberk-Rychter) and Capt. "Miecz" (Mieczyslaw Rakoczy), deputy to inspector Kalina.

I spend three hours going over various papers at the Zamoyski archive, necessary information for my work.

January 12   Today an official German communiqué gave some details about the Eastern Front. Soviet troops are now west of the San River. Rumors from Zamosc state that Pinsk has been taken by Russian troops and Kowel has been bombarded and burned. More and more evacuees from the east are passing through. Every one of them has a different story. It is impossible to evaluate whether the Germans are evacuating all the people or the people are escaping on their own. It is just as difficult to learn what the Germans are doing to the people who refuse to move out and, more important, how the Russians are behaving in the occupied areas. The overall feeling is very tense. The talk is of the front lines being very close to us and also of the possibility of being under Russian occupation.

The Germans are trying to act calm about this situation and are trying to behave normally. Arrests still continue; last night Czeslaw Guzowski was arrested in Szczebrzeszyn, and in Zwierzyniec six people were arrested.

January 14   Today at the hospital an old nurse, Sr. Zofia Klimczuk, died. She had been an Orthodox nun at the monastery in Kawenczyn, but even before World War I she was assigned to the Szczebrzeszyn hospital. She was the most dedicated nurse I had ever met. She worked until 1931, when she became paralyzed. She stayed in bed for the last thirteen years of her life. During this time she dictated to me memoirs of her life at the Orthodox monastery in Radecznica and also of her work in the Szczebrzeszyn hospital during World War I. There are some very interesting stories. I have the manuscript ready for publication.

January 15 Throughout the villages the Germans have begun new mass arrests. Last night they came for teacher Bohun in Czarnystok. He started a fight and wounded a gendarme, but then he was killed. Some people say he killed himself; others, that the gendarme shot him.

More people are fleeing from the east. I talked with a clerk from the county office in Ostrog. He arrived in Szczebrzeszyn this morning. He gave me more details about the situation. The Russians are only 200 km away from us, in a straight line. For the motorized units this is only a few hours. All cities in the Wolyn region are in a state of evacuation, but so far most of the Polish population has decided to stay. Only employees of city offices, policemen, and particularly *Volksdeutsch* are moving out quickly. Also doing the same are people who are known as German sympathizers and informers, all the people who are afraid of the future, when the Russians will arrive.

The overall feeling is that this time the Germans are unable to stop the Russian offensive. In the German administration and also the German military you can see complete chaos. Germany is already finished. Their might is breaking apart and the time for the end is near. This is an all-embracing feeling, but the people who are more realistic are still counting on very difficult days.

I myself feel and hope that Germany will capitulate before the Russian armies arrive in our area, and in this way we will be spared street fighting.

In my hospital no one is planning to evacuate and go west with the Germans. From experience I am sure that during the critical time some will escape, but the majority will stay on the job. In case of bombardment and street fighting, the most difficult task will be keeping everyone in line. This is the time I am most afraid of. In our commune, all *Dorfführers* drafted a detailed list of all *Volksdeutsch*, including ages, for city hall. I am sure it was prepared in connection with drafting all Germans into the military service. The gendarmes are working on a list of Polish men.

January 19 Here in our town it is not possible to feel the front coming closer. Highway traffic is normal. The escapees staying with friends or relatives are very quiet. In Zamosc many vehicles pass through in the direction of Lublin and Lwow. These are cars loaded with civilians, women and children and their luggage, and also military vehicles. Sometimes one car pulls a few others. This is a typical picture of retreat. It is exactly the same as in September 1939.

We await the main events that should happen soon. We count on the people in the forest to begin a major action. Some people still talk about upcoming arrests. For now there is only sporadic action.

January 20   Today for the first time wagons carrying German evacuees passed through Szczebrzeszyn. Now even our own *Volksdeutsch* are not so sure of themselves.

In town the big news item that has become the subject of discussion is the breakdown of the talks between the Polish government in London and the Soviets.

January 21   There are new restrictions on the railroad. Poles are prohibited from using the so-called fast trains. The use of normal trains is dangerous, however. Today during the morning hours in Zawada the gestapo stopped three trains. Everyone, including *Volksdeutsch*, were checked for identification. After personal searches only a few people were released. Others were loaded onto trucks and moved to undisclosed locations, supposedly near Zamosc. The trains now all carry military personnel. More evacuees from the east are passing through Zamosc. In our town everything seems normal.

January 23   I must note a few events. In Krasnobrod a horse-drawn wagon carrying a few German civilians and a gendarme was ambushed. During the shooting the gendarme was killed, but also a young, very good ranger, Podobinski, was shot.

Last night from Klemensow airfield 26 young Jews out of a total of 400 still working there escaped into the forest. Yesterday evening between 6 P.M. and 7 P.M. an assault took place on a warehouse in Zwierzyniec. The warehouse is located very near both a gendarme post and a "blue police" station. Many goods were taken, including 700 liters of vodka. At the time of the action a platoon of *Schutz Polizei* was also in town. The underground used the horse-drawn wagons that were to be used to evacuate some of the Germans as the means of transporting the loot. The work was done very professionally.

January 28   Yesterday the gestapo again arrested Postulski, who was released only a few weeks ago from Majdanek. In town there is a new flu epidemic. At the hospital, in one week, fourteen of the personnel became ill. I am in bed for the sixth day.

February

February 5   Slowly I have been recuperating from the flu, but I am still not in good condition yet. For almost two weeks I was unable to leave my quarters, so I had to learn about current events from others.

On Wednesday, February 2, a new German criminal action took place in Zwierzyniec. The Germans brought twenty prisoners from Zamosc, all from Zwierzyniec or the nearby villages. Employees from businesses around the marketplace were assembled to witness the public execution. Just before the execution a gestapo officer read, in good Polish, the verdict that all twenty will be shot in retaliation for the killing of the gestapo informer Ostaszewski, a former high school student from Szczebrzeszyn, and lately a driver in Bilgoraj.

Among the executed were three workers from the Alwa plant, Jozef Skiba and two Pietruszkas, father and son, from Tereszpol; two Wolanins, father and son, from Bagno; two Kierszowskis; and so on. During the execution a few of the prisoners began singing a Polish song from World War I, "In a Dark Grave." I was told about this and I am trying to get the exact events from an eye witness.

On Thursday, February 3, the local gendarme post ordered me to prepare space for fifteen wounded in case of air attacks. The space is to be in a separate room on the main floor, not on the second or third floor. From this it is plain to see the Germans are preparing for air raids.

Today's communiqué brought the news that Rowno and Luck have been taken by Soviet troops. From other sources I learned that Soviet troops are already near Wlodzimierz. The Germans around here are extremely nervous. They were called together for a special meeting. Tomorrow I will know what it concerned. If the Russians continue at the same pace, Szczebrzeszyn can be in their hands in a few days. Everything depends on how they decide to act. They can stop along the Bug River to reorganize their troops or they can move west as quickly as possible. We will have to wait a few days to see what will finally happen. So far no one is planning to leave town, except for the *Volksdeutsch*, who are already packed.

In the forest all the necessary preparations for quick action are underway. In some villages, and especially Zwierzyniec, officers of the Home Army and other underground units are daily guests. They even take part in the social life.

February 7   We do not yet have any news about the situation on the Eastern Front along the Bug River. It is certain that Soviet troops were very close to Wlodzimierz, but we do not know if it was taken. Yesterday many horse-drawn wagons passed through Szczebrzeszyn carrying a variety of military and civilians, with luggage and many household items also. These people spoke only among themselves, German, Ukrainian, and even Polish, so we were unable to really learn who they were.

From Labun and also the entire commune of Krasnobrod all the "Blacks" (*Volksdeutsch*) left. Each family was given six horse-drawn wagons to move their belongings. Some even took pieces of sheet metal from the roofs and tiles from the stoves. Hrubieszow is being evacuated and the post office is not accepting any mail.

Since Monday we have not had any news. Tomorrow we are supposed to receive an edition of the Lublin *Nowy Glos Lubelski*, hopefully with German communiqués from the last two days.

Our *Volksdeutsch* are in a state of breakdown, but they are still here. At the last meeting they discussed night guard duty. The Polish people would like to see this all end. Russian troops are only 100 km from us, in a straight line. As of now we still do not see any of the German troops pulling back.

People are very worried about the breakdown of discussions between the Polish Government in London and the Soviets. There are many rumors, but so far nothing positive. This can be a big turning point in our future.

Practically all my free time is spent at the typewriter, working on all my projects.

Yesterday I received a nice gift—a small, pocket-size 1944 calendar, bound in white linen, with nice drawings, all handmade. This gift was sent by Warsaw to our fighting Home Army.

February 8 Last night all postal and telephone communication with Hrubieszow was disrupted. Today the same situation occurred with Lwow. Where the Russian troops are fighting we really do not know. During the last several hours many horse-drawn wagon passed through. Each group was escorted by motorcycles and light tanks. Last night the *Sonderdienst* guards were removed from Klemensow. Now plant workers are guarding the factory; soon they are to receive arms. In the last few days an army hospital was established at the Zamoyski palace in Klemensow. The wounded were moved there from the railroad station, not in ambulances, but on sleds.

German settlers are very nervous and disturbed.

February 9 In Zamosc there have been more arrests. At this time I know that the two young brothers Fenc, both high school students, are being held. Their father, a high school teacher, has already been in Oranienburg concentration camp for four years.

Last night Russian troops took Wlodzimierz.

The convoys passing through Szczebrzeszyn are really a mixture of military and civilian vehicles, carrying women and children, military equipment, and household items. The Hrubieszow highway is completely blocked by escapees from the east. We have not seen any regular German units yet. People say the Soviets are taking villages without one shot being fired, and the Germans are retreating without a fight. Our own Germans are awaiting the orders to evacuate. The situation is very tense. We do not know what will happen during the next few days.

February 11 In Zamosc more than twenty people were arrested. Besides the two young Fencs, high school teacher Bojarczuk, teacher Begiella, former military man Kozlowski, merchant Kruk, Miss Jaworska, and several others were arrested. Bojarczuk, who taught Polish, was recently employed as a night guard. He particularly wanted that kind of work so he would not have to stay home at night. In addition, eight people from the co-op Snop and a few laborers were also arrested. It is impossible to establish how many people were arrested and who they are. It is hard to say what the reason for the arrests was. It is thought that they were taken as hostages to be shot in retaliation for terrorist assaults on Germans.

Yesterday the flow of escapees began slowing down. It appears the Russian offensive has stalled somewhere.

Yesterday the Germans called special meetings in Bilgoraj and Zamosc, including all commune and village administrators and even clergy. They talked about the dangers of Russian invasion, then asked if we would rather be under German or Russian administration. Naturally no one answered. A petition was sent to Gov. Gen. Frank asking that the Lublin region be defended against Russian aggression. Some people fear this is the first step in the direction of mobilizing Poles into fighting units.

February 13 A few days ago German planes dropped bombs on several villages of the commune of Lipy, in Bilgoraj County. I learned that there were many casualties. A large group of Russian cavalry broke through Kamionka Strumilowa and Zolkiew in the direction of Jaroslaw. Soviet partisan units from our own forests are moving toward Rawa Ruska. Early this morning a Russian patrol arrived in Florianki, only 5 km from Zwierzyniec. What all this is supposed to prove I don't know. Yesterday I spoke with a few high-ranking officers from the Home Army; they do not know either. We are now in the process of teaching a special fighting course and a sanitation course. The sanitation course is being conducted by a young physician from Starachowice.

February 14   The situation is very tense. Everyone talks about the Soviet troops and their progress, and the fact that they are not coming from the east, the Bug River, but from the south. People who arrived here from Belzec say that Russian troops took over Cieszanow and are moving toward Bilgoraj. Some even say they personally heard artillery detonations. People seem so nervous that any kind of noise is thought to be bombardment. I myself cannot detect anything.

From Zamosc comes good news. The gestapo have started packing and are ready to move out.

February 15   From day to day the situation becomes more tense. Tonight two bridges were blown up, one at Susiec, one at Dlugi Kat. This morning a train consisting of a locomotive and only three cars, coming from Rejowice, stopped at Zwierzyniec. No trains can go any farther. The railroad stations, where just a few days ago up to forty trains passed through every twenty-four hours, is now completely dead.

Today no mail or newspapers were delivered from Lublin. During the day more news arrived. Russian troops supposedly took Jozefow, and later Lukowa and Osuchy. The afternoon news has them already in Tarnogrod and very close to Bilgoraj.

Between 4 P.M. and 5 P.M. several cars, trucks, and ambulances, came through Szczebrzeszyn carrying German physicians and nurses in the direction of Zamosc. Later we saw cars with gendarmes, "blue police," and German county employees all taking their families away from Bilgoraj. Now we are sure Bilgoraj is being evacuated. Our "own" German settlers and *Volksdeutsch* are just waiting to move out, but so far German authorities are trying to force them to stay. They are under constant surveillance. They cannot leave their homes without written permission.

The Russian troops are very close now, mostly partisan or paratrooper units, but there are regular army units also. No German troops are seen. The Polish population has quieted down and calmly waits for new events. The only thing people want to know is what the next day will bring. Some people are waiting anxiously to start fighting the Germans.

February 16   Last night around 10 P.M. a bridge over the Tanwia River, between Bilgoraj and Tarnogrod, was blown. Aside from that, nothing else occurred. Since Sunday we have not had any newspaper, and we do not know what is going on in the outside world.

February 17   Last night the train station in Susiec burned down. This morning around 10 A.M. we heard a very loud explosion. This evening we still do not know what it was. There is no mail or newspaper, so we are completely out of touch with the world. Even information from the nearby villages is not arriving. We do not know what is occurring in Bilgoraj, Tarnogrod, Jozefow, or even the forests around us. We have not even seen our own underground people since Sunday. I myself have been busy the entire day typing.

February 18 Yesterday near the Mokre airfield a German bomber crashed. That was the cause of the explosion we heard. Nothing happened all day, except finally we received mail and newspapers.

February 19 Around us it appears the Soviet troops have halted or moved off in another direction. The situation is very calm. Some German county offices began an almost normal workday. In Zamosc there is no excitement. It is the same in our town.

February 20 Yesterday four German planes dropped bombs on the village of Osuchy, near Jozefow, and later on the forest. A large number of German gendarmes began an action against the Russian partisans. At the same time our own units of the Home Army were in a very difficult situation. The headquarters in Zwierzyniec has not received any news for quite some time and "Adam" is very nervous. Zwierzyniec is full of gendarmes. The police hours have been changed again. You can drive your horse-drawn wagon until 5 P.M. and walk until 7 P.M. But after 5 P.M. everyone is searched.

Last night the railroad bridge over the highway between Izbica and Krasnystaw was destroyed. Traffic will be stopped for several days.

Soviet troops are now moving from Tarnogrod toward the county of Janow.

February 21 We finally received information from the forest: our units are safe. I do not have any details yet, only that the situation is very grave. Some soldiers have frostbitten feet. Several were taken for treatment to the villages surrounding Szczebrzeszyn. I sent a nurse to provide first aid. One man will be brought to the hospital tomorrow.

Tonight in Zwierzyniec the grandmother, mother, and sister of slain German informant Ostaszewski were executed. In Zwierzyniec the atmosphere is very tense. People feel the Germans will retaliate with more executions. The Germans are threatening to kill every tenth person.

February 22 Now in Bilgoraj County you can walk around until 6 P.M. All bridges are heavily guarded. At the hospital near the Wieprz River, guard duty is handled by Russian SS units, formed from Russian POW. Again there is no mail or newspaper.

February 23   Mayor Kraus, of Tarnogrod, a known Ukrainian activist and enemy of the Poles, was killed. He was a brother of Szczebrzeszyn mayor Andreas Kraus, a Ukrainian *Volksdeutsch*. He attempted to escape from the Russians but was captured before he fled.

February 25   Overall, yesterday was very quiet, but today was full of excitement. First we learned that the Russians took Susiec, passed through Bialy Slup, were on the outskirts of Zwierzyniec, and finally moved off toward Kosobudy. Zwierzyniec was still surrounded by Germans who did not allow anyone to leave the town. This afternoon a railroad worker was brought to the hospital with leg wounds. He was passing through Dlugi Kat when a road mine exploded. One man was killed and another slightly wounded. The poor man's wounds were so bad that we had to amputate his leg above the knee. Toward evening the hospital administrator returned with more news: this morning around 10 A.M. Soviet troops took control of several villages around Zamosc, including Kosobudy, Wieprzec, Wychody, Bialowola, Zarzecze, and Lipsko. The Bilgoraj county offices were moved to Zamosc. The railroad tracks between Rawa Ruska and Szczebrzeszyn have been destroyed in three places. From here trains go only to Zawada. A few German military units were moved in the direction of Bilgoraj, but three tanks were destroyed by mines. Because of the many rumors, I am only noting the facts that I am sure of.

Here, we are very nervous. Kosobudy is only 12 km from Szczebrzeszyn. Tonight underground units passed through Rozlopy (only 3 km from us). The Soviet presence in villages so close to us is a big surprise to everyone.

February 27   Yesterday a brief fight took place between Germans and Russians in Lipsko, but no details yet.

Today "Grom" came to the hospital with wounds to his right arm. He was brought from the forest near Kawenczyn by a few officers, all in uniform and armed.

February 28   "Grom" is so popular in the Home Army units that news about his being wounded spread quickly. To be on the safe side we moved him from the hospital to a nearby village.

Today "Podkowa" and "Sep," armed with guns and grenades, visited us. They are wonderful men, especially "Podkowa." Two of my nurses were sworn into the Home Army.

As is normal in the underground, friction among the leaders is increasing. Most officers are now against "Adam," while the popularity of "Grom" and "Podkowa" grows.

From Tarnogrod comes news about the murder of Poles by Ukrainian partisans. Dr. Kryszkiewicz was killed. This is supposed to be retaliation in connection with the execution of Mayor Kraus.

March

March 2   The news about the murder of Poles by Ukrainians in Tarnogrod is true. Among them was Dr. Kryszkiewicz, a young physician totally dedicated to medicine and never involved in politics. I am sure that now from the Polish side some form of retaliation will take place.

Soviet troops took several villages around Tarnogrod and Jozefow. It appears as if a formation is moving toward Bilgoraj. The area around Janow and Krasnik is in Russian hands. Around Hrubieszow the Russian partisans are moving quickly. The Germans now have only one way to retreat, through Lublin.

Today I received a visit in my quarters from my former seminary student, teacher Antoni Radzik ("Orkisz"), currently an aide to inspector "Kalina."

March 4   Around Tarnogrod and Bilgoraj, Ukrainian SS units are still fighting and killing Poles.

Rail traffic has been restored. Trains now travel in both directions, but only during daylight; there are no night trains. Around 2 P.M. artillery fire was heard. It was impossible to figure out from which direction it came. The only fact we are sure of is that Russian troops are not too far away from us and they are constantly changing locations. The Germans feel very unsafe. Two Germans from the Zamoyski estate, Bunsch and Grossemik, do not stay home at night but go to the gendarme station.

Constantly we hear of assaults, robberies, and murders. Some are organized by different partisan units, but some are carried out by individuals for their own profit. The command of the Home Army is trying to fight this, but without much success.

March 5   Today was filled with emotion. My wife took my son to Kawenczyn to see "Grom." My son came back soon; my wife was supposed to come back by horse-drawn wagon, together with nurse Michalina Wosinska, who was specially assigned to the care of "Grom." Around noon the nurse arrived, but my wife decided to stay for a few more hours. In the meantime we learned of a strange man who had been asking around if an officer named "Grom" was in the hospital. An hour later six gendarmes, along with the post commander, went to Kawenczyn. All were armed with machine guns. I was sure that they went to capture "Grom," so I sent my son again to Kawenczyn for details. One hour later my wife and son returned. It so happened that the gendarmes stopped at the house where "Grom" was staying. My wife first spotted the gendarmes. "Grom" started to put his shoes on and called one of his men. He reported that approximately thirty partisans were ready for action. "Grom" relaxed knowing that none of the gendarmes would leave alive. During this time the gendarmes turned around and left. They stayed in the village only a short while and returned to Szczebrzeszyn. We are all glad it came to a good end.

I went myself to change the dressings on "Grom's" wounds. Dr. Jentys and Dr. Matuszewski had done this previously. As we traveled through the village we saw many villagers stopping to talk to each other. The driver, Martyn, explained to me that these villagers really are soldiers who are very well armed and trained.

Finally we stopped at a house. After going through a living room full of village women, we entered a bedroom where "Grom," "Sep," and "Kawka" sat. "Grom's" wound is healing very well. I came back home filled with hope for the future.

I am sure the gendarmes knew about "Grom" and where he was staying. They recognized that there was no chance to start anything against thirty well-armed men.

It still is a problem. The Germans can mobilize a strong assault unit to take "Grom." Now "Grom" will be moved to another location. He will not be taken alive, but the village will suffer, and it will be an easy connection to make between the hospital, hospital physician, and underground.

March 6 Around noon "Adam" arrived. From him I learned that small Russian units and their patrols took several villages around Zwierzyniec, including Bondyrz, Guclow, Obrocz, Tereszpol, Panasowka, Czarnystok, Lipowiec, Gorajec, and the villages of the commune of Radecznica. Some troops passed through Zurawnica and Kawenczyn at night. In Radecznica the Soviets took over the police station. During the day they passed through Kawenczynek. Since early morning fighting has been going on around Obrocz. The entire day we've heard artillery and machine gun fire. During the evening the fighting increased. Phosphorous shells can be seen lighting up the area near Zwierzyniec. Phosphorous tracers have been shot in the direction of Kawenczyn, Topolcza, and the forest. Around 10 P.M. the shooting continued. We were able to observe the firing, probably coming from Zurawica. We can hear machine gun fire nearby.

At the hospital everyone is excited. People stay outside to observe the battles. I went through all the hospital wards to calm down the patients.

I am sure that the fighting will stop soon and the Soviets will move quickly to another location, and not come to Szczebrzeszyn now. We are worried about our own units in the forest.

"Adam" stayed overnight. He is rather nervous also.

March 7 We have some details about yesterday's fighting. One large Soviet unit was trying to reach Kawenczyn along the Brodzki forest. To accomplish this they had to cross the railroad tracks and highway from Szczebrzeszyn to Zwierzyniec, right next to the Alwa plant. At the same time a military train was coming from Zwierzyniec. Russian engineers planted a mine, but the explosion was not strong enough to cause any damage. The Soviets began shooting from both sides. The Germans left the train and took positions in the ditches along the tracks. The fighting went on for some time. As a result the train engineer and conductor were wounded. Several Germans were killed or wounded. Russian casualties are unknown because, as always, they took their wounded and dead with them. Only a few dead horses and horse-drawn wagons were left behind.

More fighting between the Soviets and the Germans took place at the following villages: Obrocz, Kosobudy, Zarzecze, Wieprzecz, and Topornica. These villages came under artillery fire.

The night passed. For a long while there was no traffic. Around 4 A.M. a German column with tanks, armored cars, and other motorized vehicles arrived in town from Zamosc. The Germans began procuring horse-drawn wagons from the nearby villages. Around 9 A.M. the motorized column left town, but this time approximately twenty horse-drawn wagons were sent ahead of the military vehicles. The column moved rather slowly. It is clear that the Germans were using the horse-drawn wagons and Polish drivers to check for land mines, and mines were there. From Brody Male five young men were brought to the hospital, all wounded by a mine explosion on the highway. One person died at the site, one lost both legs, and four others were slightly wounded. A few hours later more casualties from Kosobudy arrived.

I tried to call Zwierzyniec, but telephone communication has been shut down since yesterday.

Russian units are concentrating on the commune of Radecznica. Telephone communication there is not functioning. From my viewpoint I have come to the conclusion that the Germans will try to eradicate the local Russian units around us. More and more German military units are moving through our town toward Radecznica, Bilgoraj, and Tarnogrod.

Everyone asks, "What will happen now?" But people are so used to news of the fighting around us that no one is particularly nervous. Yesterday's battle was only 3 km from town. Our life-style has not changed at all, except for the Germans and *Volksdeutsch* feeling terrorized.

March 8   More German units than before are passing through town, including army, gendarmes, and *Schutz Polizei*. Some go toward Zwierzyniec, others toward Radecznica and Gorajec, but some have stayed in Szczebrzeszyn. Some of the soldiers, especially from the *Schutz Polizei* speak Polish among themselves.

Russian partisans who are now in several villages of the commune of Radecznica destroyed bridges and set land mines, so traffic on the roads is very slow. From news out of that area it is certain that the Russians are very well organized, with good military equipment, including artillery. The Germans really are afraid of fighting; land mines scare them the most. Yesterday a mine exploded near Topolcza, killing one man and wounding another. At night heavy patrols move throughout the city. It is possible to walk on the city streets only until 7 P.M.

March 9   Tonight a group of Polish partisans attacked the village of Tworyczow, killing ten German settlers, including a known SS man, Kitzman, who before the war was a teacher in Brody. Two wounded, one a German teacher, were brought to the hospital for treatment. Kitzman's wife of only two weeks was also killed. The news about the death of Kitzman was a good surprise for the Polish people everywhere. German settlers and *Volksdeutsch* are finally beginning to realize they can be killed also.

More German troops keep moving through Szczebrzeszyn. From Zamosc prison the older Fenc was released. His younger brother, "Wir," was beaten very severely by the gestapo and finally thrown into a cellar, where he died from hunger.

March 10   A unit of Ukrainian SS arrived in Zwierzyniec. Today they began patrolling some of the nearby villages. This unit is supposed to be used against the Home Army platoons of "Grom" and "Podkowa." Villagers fear that during this action many people will be killed because Ukrainian SS troops are known for their cruelty.

The news spread quickly of Russian army units taking Tarnopol and Zloczow; Lwow is the next logical target. Other news has it that one Russian motorized unit broke through German defenses and is moving quickly west, toward our area. We are now closer than before to seeing the Red Army in our city. As a result the tension in town is growing.

Today the ten Germans who were killed in Tworyczow were brought to the hospital morgue; four men, three women, and three boys. They were laid out in one row, alongside Kitzman. German settlers passed through to identify the bodies.

At night there were again many vehicles moving through town from the direction of Zwierzyniec and Zamosc. It is difficult to figure out exactly where they are coming from and where they are traveling to.

March 11   The day passed with no special events. The military moved out, the town is empty, only German settlers are left and they move only in heavily armed groups. Everything points to the Germans being afraid to stay here. All Germans have moved out of Tworyczow.

March 12   Today the funeral of the ten Germans killed in Tworyczow took place. They were placed in wooden caskets, without being washed, exactly like they were brought in. They had been robbed completely. Kitzman was covered in an old woman's dress. The caskets, covered with red flags and black swastikas, were transported to the cemetery on ten horse-drawn wagons. Approximately 300 to 400 Germans were present. You can feel the hostile attitude of the Germans toward the Poles.

Yesterday we heard artillery fire to the north, but today we heard it to the south.

The railroad can now be used without special passes. It seems the Germans are sure that when more Poles use the trains, there is less likelihood of derailment, because the partisans try not to kill their own people.

March 15   With everything happening now you can feel the Russian troops coming. The German settlers received instructions to be ready for evacuation. They are supposed to supply their own food for a few days and also to have feed for their livestock. Yesterday a meeting of all Germans took place, but *Volksdeutsch* were excluded. More and more Germans are leaving the villages and coming to town. They feel safer in larger groups. Polish people observe very carefully what is going on in German circles and are awaiting their departure.

I went to Kawenczyn to see "Sep," who is ill.

March 16   I met the commandant of the Bilgoraj Home Army, "Bojar" (or "Orsza"). He visited the hospital. We discussed my collection of historical materials. During our conversation I learned that the news about the beating of Dr. Pojaskowa in Bilgoraj, by the Ukrainian SS, was not true. Nothing like this occurred at all. I am noting this fact to prove how careful you must be when writing down what people say. You can really only be sure of what you witness yourself.

In our town things are quiet. I received information that Russian patrols are close to Susiec and paratroopers have been dropped elsewhere.

March 17   Two days ago the gestapo in Zwierzyniec arrested Andrzej Kostecki and a young woman Podczaska. The arrest of Kostecki was a real surprise because of his previous behavior. He had been very close to some of the Germans, and for a time his name was on the list of people to be liquidated. But for some reason the execution was postponed. Then he ended up in "Grom's" underground unit, but after a few weeks he was dismissed. Now people are afraid that during the investigation he could reveal details of underground activities.

Today, Rabinski and Klemens Hysa, both known as Communist sympathizers, were arrested in Szczebrzeszyn.

Today I went to Zamosc. For some time I stood at a window observing traffic. It is true that you can see more Germans than Poles walking around. It makes a very unpleasant picture. I only hope that soon this will change and that hope keeps us going. I was told about terrible things taking place in Hrubieszow County. Ukrainian nationalists are torturing and murdering Poles, singling out large farmers and ranchers. In retaliation the Polish underground is killing Ukrainians. Many people are fleeing that area.

Today around 3 P.M. an alarm sounded in Szczebrzeszyn. Somewhere close by Soviet planes flew.

March 18   Around 3 P.M. all Germans in town received instructions to pack and be ready to move out. Naturally all the settlers and *Volksdeutsch* are in a panic. They are trying to sell whatever they can—crying, cursing, shouting, and running around without any purpose. No one has any real information about what is happening and what is behind the sudden German evacuation.

Dr. Warnowsky, a German born in St. Petersburg, came by the hospital and tried to call the Zamosc hospital, but all lines are dead. He doesn't know for sure, but he thinks that probably the Russians broke through German defenses. As he left the hospital he said, "This is the penalty for our stupidity. First you must win the war, then you can begin pacification."

At 9 P.M. the situation is still very tense. The first horse-drawn wagons loaded with household items, bedding, luggage, and even furniture began arriving from Brody. Some Germans are not even waiting for instructions but are moving out on their own, most of them going in the direction of Zamosc. The Germans are afraid that they are already surrounded by Russian troops, especially now, since all telephone communication with Lublin and Zamosc has been cut off.

In Zamosc there is complete chaos. Here our *Volksdeutsch* and *Stamm-deutsch* face a dilemma: What to do? To escape or stay? Where to go? How to provide for one's self?

Some Poles are fearful of the time between the German pullout and the arrival of Russian troops or the Home Army because they think the Ukrainians will start a massacre.

Overall there is a happy feeling here. The days of our slavery are now numbered. We see Germans escaping. This is the day we have been waiting for years to see.

March 19   Since early morning the traffic in town has been heavy. From every direction horse-drawn wagons carrying German settlers have been arriving. Here in town Germans are looking for wagons and horses. To save the hospital horses from being requisitioned, I had the hospital administrator take them to Brody, with the hope that his family can take care of them. But around 6 P.M. the *Dorfführer* arrived requesting the horses for German physicians. When he learned that our horses were gone, he told me I had one hour to provide him with horses, otherwise I would be shot. There was nothing else to do but bring the horses back and give them to the German physician. Now, another problem: who would drive the wagon and horses? Finally hospital foreman Gurski agreed to go. I told him I would pay 1,000 zloty if he would bring the horses back to the hospital.

Loaded wagons were staged on both sides of Zamojska Street and also in the marketplace. Yesterday the Germans were sure that they would go to Zamosc, but earlier today it appeared that Bilgoraj and Zwierzyniec would be their destination. Now the situation has changed once again. The road to Zamosc and Lublin is cut off, as is the road to Bilgoraj. Mayor Kraus left town this morning, with his family, by train to either Lubaczow or Jaroslaw.

The Germans are burning the files at city hall. The local *Volksdeutsch* have not yet been ordered to move out. If they decide to escape on their own, they must supply horses and wagons. So far only a few have begun packing. The Germans are selling their belongings, even cows and pigs, for very low prices. Our own people are busily buying. I am sure the Germans will not survive the road without big surprises. Now they are to travel to Radom, and later to Lodz. Today's picture of German misery makes us all feel good. We have come to the day when we can see Germans escaping from Neue Deutsche Stadt Szczebrzeszyn (new German city of Szczebrzeszyn).

March 20   The Germans are still here. Loaded wagons sit in the streets, ready to move on a moment's notice. No one knows when this will happen. Some Germans are even returning to their houses. In the late evening the news began circulating that evacuation has begun at the Klemensow airfield. Their hospital and wounded have already left. Our own boys in the forest are waiting to attack German evacuees and take from them their weapons, wagons, and horses. The Germans fear this. Some *Volksdeutsch* fled to the forest to join the partisans.

March 21   Last night a *Volksdeutsch* shoemaker, Franciszek Borowinski, was killed. Who is responsible is unknown. This morning a gendarme shot Andrzej Kurzawski, from Zurawnica, who was mentally ill.

Since early morning the Germans have been preparing to evacuate. Poles have been standing around watching. Around 9 A.M. the first wagons left. German women and children, up to the age of fourteen, are leaving by train for Zamosc, and from there to Lodz. Men are going with their weapons. This family separation has the Germans very upset. They are also afraid of the partisans. Some of them even say that before their final departure they will burn the town.

The German air force is ready for evacuation. From very reliable sources we received information that the Germans have gathered enough explosives at the airfield to blow up the Alwa plant and the Klemensow sugar refinery.

German Zamosc is fleeing. All offices are closed. Trains are loaded with escapees. There is very heavy traffic on the highway. We still are waiting for all the Germans to leave town. From the east we hear artillery fire. Our people fear the coming night.

March 22   Today I received a notice from the county administration. It states that Germans have no right to confiscate from the Poles any horses or wagons, and those already taken must be returned.

Mayor Kraus is back in Szczebrzeszyn and began working again in city hall. It appears things are coming back to normal. The Alwa plant, which was ready for demolition a few days ago, began normal production. Evacuation of the airfield is still in progress, and the Germans are planting land mines there.

Today I went to Kawenczyn to speak with "Grom." From "Kawka" I learned that fifteen platoons of the Home Army were ready to help us in case the Germans in Szczebrzeszyn began any kind of action against the Poles.

March 23   Some Germans are returning and starting work as normal, but others are still preparing for evacuation. Hepp, the owner of the German restaurant, reopened his business. City employees were called back for work. The news from the front tells us that Soviet troops are crossing the Bug River and are moving quickly toward the west. The post office is not accepting any parcels or certified mail; only postcards are allowed. The same situation is occurring in Zamosc.

March 24   Today *Volksdeutsch* families are to move out. Approximately forty horse-drawn wagons were assembled, but nothing happened. The offices in Zamosc and Szczebrzeszyn are trying to work as normal.

Guzowski and Niedzielski were released from the prison in Zamosc. The townspeople are terribly disappointed that the Germans are still here.

March 25   Some German men are still here. They are seen on the streets and as of yet have not moved out. Their wagons, loaded and waiting, are now covered with snow. Yesterday there was a snowstorm. Evacuation preparations are still in progress. In Szczebrzeszyn all telephone receivers, even the one in the hospital, were removed. The city offices are working normally, and all employees received advance pay for April.

March 26   The German settlers from Hrubieszow County refused to evacuate. They fear being sent to evacuation camps in Lodz. They are concentrating in Przedmiescie and waiting. Yesterday gendarmes surrounded them and took their horses. In this way they forced the settlers to move out. Today I received news from Zamosc that the Germans returned a closed cathedral for religious use. This was an unexpected move.

March 28   Nothing much has happened during the last two days. The evacuation of settlers is progressing very slowly. It is more visible in Zamosc than here. The "Blacks" are arriving in Zamosc and being loaded onto trains. It is very quiet here, but we know that our boys from the forest have something in mind.

March 31   A few days passed without much excitement. Today evacuation activities are increasing. More *Volksdeutsch* are leaving. In Zamosc there is complete chaos, but the evacuation is progressing rapidly.

Today an unexpected event occurred. Jerzy Palmowski ("Beck"), who was in charge of company supplies, left the "Podkowa" unit. Last month I brought him into the underground. After he left his unit he stopped by the hospital to give his sister, the hospital secretary, some money for the company and asked her to return it to "Podkowa."

In Zwierzyniec Mr. and Mrs. Podczaski and their maid were arrested. They supposedly urged members of an Armenian SS company to escape into the forest.

April

April 2   Yesterday near Panasowka a truck carrying gendarmes came under attack. Eight gendarmes were killed; the rest were kidnapped into the forest. In Blonie, a confidant of the gestapo, Jan Trusz, was liquidated.

April 3   Since early morning "Blacks" have been moved out. They went to Zawada with all their belongings to be loaded onto a train. All of the men returned, probably to help guard the town. The remaining *Volksdeutsch* are scared to death. They fear the unknowns of an evacuation similar to the one in Zamosc.

April 4   Yesterday there was shooting from the direction of Blonie. The gendarmes and police went there but returned in a very short time. Today I learned that a small partisan unit attacked Hartman, the German owner of the old Pereta flour mill. He was able to phone for help. During the fighting a German officer was killed. We are afraid of reprisals, particularly the taking of hostages.

At night many planes flew over the city and supposedly dropped some paratroopers. Again it looks as if the Russian front is coming closer.

April 6   This morning, around 7 A.M., very well armed units of the German army, including tanks and artillery, arrived in Szczebrzeszyn. They quickly moved through the city. At first everyone was sure this was the beginning of retaliatory action because of the officer's killing. It soon became clear that this action was directed against Russian cavalry patrols entering Radecznica. Some patrols are near Zdzielce, so the German units were sent to destroy them. Outside the city the Germans have begun digging defense trenches. The German soldiers look terrible; they are all very tired, unshaven, dirty, and hungry. Some were limping. After a few hours they left town. Information received from Zamosc tells us that some Soviet units are now in Izbica and that fighting is still occurring. We observe these events with mounting interest.

April 7   Everything is quiet again. We have no German troops, or Russians. Again in Panasowka a German car was attacked. A known gestapo agent, Majewski, was mortally wounded. He was taken to the hospital in Zwierzyniec. He was known for his brutality and had murdered hundreds of Jews and several Poles. People are happy that he is practically out of circulation.

April 8   Majewski is still alive. He received several lung wounds and is now in the hospital in Zamosc.

Our situation hasn't changed. Some settlers returned to the villages. They have been ordered to begin field work. On the other hand they are to be ready to move out again on a half-hour's notice. This contradictory situation is typical of German logic today.

April 11 Today is the third day of Easter, the fifth Easter of the war. Instead of the traditional "Happy Easter," people greet each other with "Safe Easter." Even though we have high prices and a difficult situation, the Easter food is as good as always. There may be fewer cakes, tortes, and cookies because of the lack of nuts, raisins, chocolate, and almonds.

Majewski died at the Zamosc hospital. He was conscious to the last moment. He talked about God and what would happen to his children.

After the incident with Majewski the highway to Bilgoraj was declared very dangerous. In Zwierzyniec, where the highway turns toward Bilgoraj, a new German sign is posted, *"Bandengefahr."* All vehicles now move in convoys.

From Bilgoraj I received information that Podczaski died during the investigation and that his wife is very sick from the beatings. Two of their sons are in partisan units. The older one, age nineteen, swears that he will kill the responsible Germans, even if he must do it alone.

The situation has become tense once again. Someone spread the news that we can expect mass arrests tonight.

April 13 Yesterday around 3 P.M., near Tereszpol, a patrol of twelve men under the leadership of "Selim" and his fiancée, "Zar," attacked a train. Eight prisoners were freed and approximately 15 tons of grain were taken. Everyone was checked for identification, a few members of the "blue police" were left unharmed, but the Ukrainians were taken into the forest.

This afternoon I spoke with "Podkowa." He gave me the details of the assault on Majewski. For some time the underground had been trying to kill him, but with no luck. The last time, in Panasowka, the car in which he was riding sped up and escaped when the shooting started. This time Majewski was mortally wounded.

April 14 Tonight two Ukrainian women where shot near the Szczebrzeszyn train station. Also, three Ukrainian newcomers, supposedly very important persons, were taken into the forest and liquidated.

April 15 Today a Russian platoon destroyed a German convoy on the highway between Zwierzyniec and Panasowka. This is the first time they used electrically controlled mines. Several German gendarmes were killed and wounded. (As I learned later, this was done not by the Russians but by a training unit of the Home Army.)

One large detachment of Russians is moving from Osuchy and Debica in the direction of Tereszpol. The leaders of Polish units are in contact with the Soviets, and Polish officers have even been assigned as guides. I received several notes and memos, written by the Russians, to Polish units. I am keeping them as part of my collection.

Our troops in the forest are on full alert. Training is in full swing; military exercises, including shooting practice, are taking place. People are not paying attention to the danger; they just want to become involved. The Germans, through their brutal handling of villagers, make people strong and wanting revenge. No one can travel through the villages without being searched by our side. If someone doesn't have proper identification, he is taken to the village commandant and then into the forest. In this way many gestapo agents, even those speaking fluent Polish, have been eliminated.

April 16   Last night, somewhere around Susiec, two trains were blown up. One was an armored train, the other a rescue train. Rail traffic is almost nonexistent. Trains can travel only as far as Zwierzyniec.

Russian patrols have been seen in Marynowka, Katy, and Kosobudy. I would love to see a Russian patrol come through our town at night, or even in the daytime. The Germans are so nervous, they will probably die from fear.

April 17   Last night many Russian planes flew over. It is possible that a paratrooper unit was dropped behind German lines.

Today I received a surprise visit from two Jews. I had not seen them for quite a while. I spoke with one of them, young Wagner, son of a rich merchant from Zamosc. He is now working at the Klemensow airfield. He came here with a sick friend and was escorted by a German airman who stayed outside the hospital. We were able to talk without any witness. I knew the Wagners very well. He is the only one from the entire family who survived. Originally, 250 Jews worked at the Klemensow airfield; now there are only 95. The rest died or were killed. Young Wagner looked very good. He was well dressed and appeared to be fed properly. He seems sure of himself, like a man who has a good amount of money.

April 18   During the entire day horse-drawn wagons passed through carrying Polish evacuees from around Hrubieszow. We received information about what is occurring in the area of Hrubieszow, Tomaszow, and Sokal. Ukrainian nationalists are murdering Poles and singling out large farmers and ranchers. Then Polish units kill the Ukrainians. Thousands of people have perished on both sides.

It appears the Germans' situation has improved. Yesterday the Germans brought new settlers from Suchowola and Lipsk and placed them in Rozlop and Tworyczow. Now, because of spring, field work has resumed. At the Alwa plant, equipment and machinery has been inspected, and they are ready to begin production.

April 19 Last evening, around 6 P.M., Jozef Felendzer, from Brody, was shot. He was of a German family who had settled here before World War I. During recent years as a *Volksdeutsch* he had taken part in activities against the Poles. He was a friend of Kitzman. The underground tried to kill him a few times before. Once he stayed in the hospital a few weeks because of chest wounds. Some of the local *Volksdeutsch* were still afraid of being shot. For some it will be a just punishment.

Last night the railroad station in Susiec and tracks in Tworyczow were destroyed.

April 20 Tonight an armored train was blown up between Susiec and Zwierzyniec. Trains can only travel as far as Zawada.

Today two men, Tadeusz Lewicki ("Rogala") and "Lasocki" stopped by to visit. Both were sent here from Warsaw to organize a special underground information service. "Rogal" is a university professor from Lwow.

April 21 Around noon the Germans began an air bombardment of the forests around Jozefow, where there is supposed to be a large concentration of Soviet troops. I admitted some wounded villagers from Turzyniec and Brzeziny.

Tonight in Zwierzyniec the partisans kidnapped three people known to be German informers: Zdanowski, owner of a restaurant; Kowalko, a sheet metal worker; and Klimaczynska, owner of a small bar.

April 23 During the last two days I visited Zwierzyniec twice. People there are still talking about the kidnapping. More people were supposed to be taken, but they escaped. These include the translator from the lumber mill, Schilke, and a very popular person in Zwierzyniec, Adam Karpinski.

I visited a cemetery in Zwierzyniec. On the right side, near the fence, is a long row of graves of people who died in prison or during evacuation and pacification, or were killed by the gestapo. On many graves a small engraving noted "Died Tragically." I asked one of the local women if she could make a list of all the dead, beginning with soldiers from 1939.

I forgot to note that a few days ago a robbery took place on Tomaszewski's farm, in Michalow. Several horses, cows, and pigs were taken. This is peculiar because Tomaszewski is a very good and honest man.

During the Easter holidays ranger Kielczewski, from Frampol, was liquidated. (He was not related to the very well known Kilczewski family from Sola.)

April 24   The underground movement is growing rapidly. Yesterday, on Sunday, men from all the local villages departed for military exercises. Women went to the forest to prepare food. All units had very active training. The "Norbert" company, along with several Russian soldiers, went to fight the Ukrainian nationalists. Last night a special assembly of officers took place. It is obvious that preparation for action against German troops is taking place.

At the present there is little actual fighting, but every day a bridge or railroad station is blown up. Last night a train was destroyed at Krasnobrod. The trains must travel slowly. As a rule, in front of the engine there are two and sometimes three empty cars hooked up, so in case of mines they will be destroyed first.

This evening, around 6 P.M., two German planes bombarded the village of Szperowka, where a class for officer training was taking place. As of now I do not have any other details.

April 26   Around midnight the railroad bridge over the Wieprz River, near Zwierzyniec, was blown up. Among the underground units there are very intense activities. The concentration of strength is as never before. The troops are ready to move in the direction of Tomaszow and Rawa Ruska. The long-awaited fight against Ukrainian nationalists is ready to start. In our area a small group of Ukrainians, twenty men strong, has begun operations. Soon they will be liquidated. Now there is no other way to survive. The fight is for life or death. Today many people left for a military assembly. Some physicians volunteered—Dr. Jozwiakowski was the first. I am the next in line. Today I volunteered. I am worried if my heart will allow me to go. Today I began physical exercises, like walking in long boots. There is only one thing I would like to do before going and that is to finish some of my work. It looks as if I will be able to.

For four days we have been without any news. Even rumors are coming slowly, and they are not very reliable.

April 28   Yesterday the exercises near Guciow and Krasnobrod were a big success. Almost 1,000 people were involved, all from Zamosc County.

During one and a half days they marched over 80 km. Along with Dr. Jozwiakowski, two nurses were involved.

Dr. Jablonski, from Tomaszow, and five nurses took part in action at Laszczow. On the way back they came across a gendarme patrol and one nurse was killed as she began to flee. A physician and the other nurses were arrested and later released. Dr. Jablonski told the gendarmes that he was going to deliver a baby.

In Szczebrzeszyn many new people are arriving, particularly from Belzec and Rawa Ruska. People are saying that several Ukrainians carrying Polish identification papers arrived also.

Today I received information that a few weeks ago the so-called peasant battalions were planning an assault against my hospital. Their objective was to take money and supplies, but when this came to the attention of the Home Army the peasants decided to forego the project.

I am very eager to learn if this is in fact true.

April 29   The commandant of the local gendarme post received a warning from the Home Army. If he will stay quiet, he will survive; but if he tries to involve himself and his men in actions against the partisans, he will be liquidated.

Our units returned from Rawa Ruska. We expect action soon from "Podkowa," who is somewhere in the area of Szczebrzeszyn.

In town there are more unknown faces. More Ukrainians are coming in. Our people watch them very closely. It is difficult to recognize them because many hold Polish identification cards.

May

May 1   This morning, around 8 A.M., a robbery of credit union Rolnik, in Szczebrzeszyn, took place. Seventy thousand zloty were taken, along with food stamps worth 100,000 zloty. This was accomplished very quietly by a group under Lt. "Gruda."

Yesterday a train between Krasnobrod and Dlugi Kat was blown up. In Ruskie Piaski two gendarmes were killed. Besides these events, people are preparing for something big to happen soon.

May 2   Yesterday in Sasiadka two gendarmes were killed and one wounded. Last night an assault on the sugar refinery in Klemensow took place. Nineteen soldiers of the Home Army were involved. Five train cars of sugar ready for shipment to the German army supply depot were taken. The sugar was loaded onto seventy-eight horse-drawn wagons that had been assembled. Telephone installations at the Klemensow and

Szczebrzeszyn railroad stations were destroyed. At the same time four partisans, working on their own, robbed the refinery office of 38,000 zloty. This action was not prepared by the Home Army and was done without their approval, but after the soldiers returned the money they were only reprimanded.

A second assault took place in Michalow, where fourteen horses, ten cows, and several large pigs were taken. The horses and cows were taken because they were to be shipped to Germany the next day. Some horses had already been shipped the day before. In Ruskie Piaski a train was derailed.

There has been plenty of excitement. Together with the air activities the day has been full. In Zamosc, for several nights now, the air alarms have sounded.

Around 8 P.M. a young man with head wounds was brought in. He had no documents; the only items in his pockets were ammunition clips.

Today I finished my work about sanitary services at the Zamoyski estate, established 400 years ago. It is more than 300 pages in length. It took me eighteen months. I reviewed several documents from the Estate archives. Some materials I compiled as long ago as 1936. I was so afraid that I would not finish it. I now have the complete satisfaction that during this very difficult time I was able to start and finish this historical work. I dedicated it to Prof. Wrzosek, the best-known historian of medicine in our time.

A few days ago a small group of partisans under the command of a young man named "Lanca" came into our area. He recently led an assault on the farm of Stefan Huskowski, in Sulowiec. This was an independent group, but now they have joined the Home Army.

May 3 May 3, a Polish national holiday. Around 10 A.M. "Wyrwa" (Stanislaw Ksiazek, a teacher and former student of mine), the commandant of our district Home Army, invited me, by special messenger, to take part in holiday festivities at the camp. Without second thoughts I took a small horse coach and drove alone to Brody and then to Kawenczyn. There I left my horses and along with Rev. Waclaw Plonka (Czarny), a Bernardin monk from Radecznica and chaplain of the Ninth Infantry Regiment, rode on a peasant wagon into the forest. Lt. "Sep" rode on horseback. His orderly, a very smart young man from Szczebrzeszyn, Bogus Lepionko, rode with us on the wagon. It was not very far to the camp, only a few kilometers. The camp is located in a ravine near Lukaszowiec.

As soon as we entered the forest a soldier carrying a rifle, ready to shoot, confronted us. He asked for a password, and after Lt. "Sep" identified himself, he let us pass. This first encounter with a soldier of our Home Army (so-called A.K.) was for me a very emotional event. After a couple hundred meters we stopped. I was sure that we had to walk a few more kilometers, but after a few minutes we entered the camp. I was greeted by a young lieutenant with a familiar face. His name is Lt. "Beton" and he was my student at the teacher's seminary in Szczebrzeszyn.

A couple minutes later we were in the center of the camp. I looked around. Among the trees stood small groups of people, guests and soldiers. I knew many of the faces. Lt. "Wyrwa" acted as host. With him were other officers and sergeants, including Lt. "Gruda" (Stefan Krzaczek, a teacher and former student of mine), Cpl. "Mlot" (Aleksander Lysak), and Sgt. "Kawka" (Kowalczyk).

Many guests and soldiers were known to me but I cannot remember all the names. Besides the ones already mentioned, the following were present:

1. Jan Guzowski ("Blyskavica")
2. Marian Kleban ("Cezary," teacher)
3. Marian Ksiazek ("Nieuchwytny")
4. Lt. Zeleznicki ("Sikora")
5. Krawczyk (school principal)
6. Mazurek ("Zagloba")
7. Mikolaj Kapsalski
8. "Orzech" (quartermaster)
9. Czerwieniec
10. Niechaj (tailor, from Blonie)
11. Flis ("Jablko")
12. "Prom"
13. Adam ("Rusa")
14. "Gwiazdor"
15. Michalska ("Chlopczysko")
16. Fela Sankowska ("Kozak")

I was guided through the entire camp. First we went to the bunker. Though a very narrow doorway we entered a small but very clean cellar with bunk beds on both sides and an emergency exit. Then we went to the kitchen. Here the head person was "Stary" (Antoni Jozwiakowski). In large pots good Polish *bigos* and borscht had been prepared. A few young girls from Szczebrzeszyn were helping cut pieces of meat. We walked through the entire camp.

In a clearing among the trees a field altar with a cross and candles had been built. On the ground below an eagle had been made out of pine branches. Next to it stood a heavy machine gun.

All the soldiers wore similar hats, made from linen. The officers wore old military uniforms. On all the hats was a Polish eagle, and everyone was armed with guns, rifles, and grenades.

Among the soldiers walked a boy, maybe sixteen years old, named "Antalek." He is from Kawenczyn. For some time he walked with Lt. "Kawka," carrying a bag full of miscellaneous items. He would stop and hand out pistols or hand grenades. The young boy kept begging to be admitted to the underground. Finally "Kawka" took him into his platoon. His stepmother, afraid that something terrible could happen to him, took his shoes. "Antalek" used a rifle to force her to give the shoes back. So from now on he is a soldier.

Everything I observed made a great impression on me. It was all so realistic, yet at the same time romantic. This was the remnant of the Polish army, survivors of the September fight, and next to them stood very young boys, full of energy and enthusiasm. This small platoon of volunteers was the beginning of the future restored Polish army. This camp looked as if it had been taken from the uprising of 1863.

Commandant Wyrwa took me aside and asked if I could say a few words to the soldiers after Mass. I am trained in public speaking and under normal conditions I would be glad to do it, but today I was too tense, too nervous, with a frog in my throat, so I refused. Almost five years of war has had a tremendous effect on our thinking and behavior. I personally was ready to cry a few times, so I knew that if I spoke I would not be able to control myself.

The current war and terror of the Germans trying to destroy everything that is Polish made a big change in our thinking. Our national pride and urge for revenge brought the nation together once again. The hatred of the Germans, even among the most unconcerned people, started a love of anything Polish. Now the Polish army, always the pride of the nation, shows itself for the first time in almost five years in this small group of forest soldiers. As I looked at the faces of all those assembled, I was not surprised to see tears in some of their eyes.

For a long while we waited for the arrival of Inspector "Kalina," the highest-ranking officer of the Home Army in this region, but he was unable to attend. Also unable to attend were "Grom" and "Podkowa," who were engaged in action in Hrubieszow County.

Around 2 P.M. the Mass began. The celebrant was Rev. Waclaw. Everyone took a place around the altar. A total of forty-one soldiers and many civilian guests had assembled. During the service the thirty-man-strong platoon of Lt. Kawka arrived.

After the Mass "Wyrwa" made a short speech and invited everyone to lunch. Large tables full of good Polish *bigos* and borscht were provided.

Quartermaster "Stary" gave out the drinks. Young women from Szczebrze-szyn provided cakes.

I left the camp around 5 P.M. because of my duties at the hospital. The other guests stayed long into the night. From the camp I was escorted by Bogus Lepionko, armed with a Russian carbine.

I was very happy that "Wyrwa" had invited me to his camp. For a few hours I again felt that I was a citizen of the free Poland. I came home in the best of physical and mental condition.

May 4   A few days ago on the highway near Hedwizyn a German truck was ambushed and 2,000 l of vodka were taken. Last night in Zwierzyniec a German informer, Lesniewski, was killed.

May 5   A large detachment of partisans came to Kosobudy from Wolyn for a rest. The underground movement is growing.

Today Dr. Stefan Jozwiakowski ("Jaga"), now our underground sanitary chief, came by to discuss sanitary services in the partisan units. All physicians, even some who have never served in the military, will be placed under the county sanitary chief. No one can leave without special permission. The physicians must, at their own expense, have all necessary instruments and drugs assembled to provide first aid in case of emergency, and each will be required to account for one hundred wounded. We are to be ready at a minute's notice. I personally have to train several nurses for this emergency work.

May 7   A couple of days ago a woman, Podiasowa, and later her husband, a shoemaker from Szczebrzeszyn, were killed. Both signed a *Volksdeutsch* list and were known as German confidants.

On the Zwierzyniec railroad tracks a train was destroyed. After more than fifteen hours traffic was restored.

May 8   Tonight a pump supplying water to the railroad tower at the Szcze-brzeszyn station was completely destroyed. Also the station telephone and semaphores were damaged. This morning a train from Zwierzyniec was derailed. Around 11 A.M. an armored train coming from Zwierzyniec was destroyed. For a small railroad station it was certainly enough excitement for one day.

I am noting all railroad events taking place in our section just to show what is occurring toward the direction of Lwow. As of now there is no direct communication with Lwow at all. Some people are trying to reach the city, but that is very dangerous.

Now between Zwierzyniec and Rawa Ruska all passengers are searched by partisans. All *Volksdeutsch* and Ukrainians are taken to the forest for further interrogation.

May 9   In our town you can feel excitement. It is a sign of new, upcoming events. The Germans are restarting the Klemensow airfield once again, even confiscating private houses for the soon to be arriving German pilots. All Jewish workers were moved away from the airfield. Several Jews escaped, but many were killed. They knew this was their last chance before final liquidation.

Yesterday and today many Polish escapees from Rawa Ruska arrived in our town. There the Ukrainians are the law. Ukrainians set May 10 as the day by which all Polish families must leave. Seventeen families came to Szczebrzeszyn, but they will eventually travel farther, to Krasnystaw County.

Today new orders: all Polish men between the ages of eighteen and sixty-five must report for guard duty, to be doubled with German soldiers. Ukrainians who recently arrived in town must move out.

Lately many people have left and gone west. First Grabowski, then the wife of mill owner Tomaszewski, who took with her several horse-drawn wagons full of belongings, and lastly Mrs. Zamoyski, with her children, all left Michalow because of their fear of the Soviets. They call them Bolsheviks. The Alwa plant is closed and all workers were dismissed. Spirits are very low in town. People wait for something coming from the east.

May 10   Last night near Zwierzyniec the "Podkowa" group blew up a train. Smaller assaults are daily events, so I do not note all of them.

Near Florianka British airplanes have been dropping weapons and ammunition for the Home Army. In the forest instructions in shooting and other types of warfare are in full swing. Underground activities are increasing. Throughout the day we could hear artillery fire, but very far off in the distance. Escapees from the Ukrainian terror are still arriving from Rawa Ruska.

May 13   Last night we were awakened by explosions coming from the direction of Zwierzyniec. Later, for more than an hour, machine gun fire, rifle fire, and grenades were heard. This morning we learned that this was an action of the "Podkowa" unit. They blew up a bridge over the Wieprz River. For certain, railroad communication is cut off for several days. At the same time our people fought an Azerbejdzan unit. It was formed from captive soldiers of the Soviet army who agreed to serve in the German army.

May 16 I visited Zwierzyniec. At the headquarters of the Home Army there is some uneasiness because of a large German operation that began infiltrating the Zamosc region forest from the south and west.

For several days we have been without newpapers, so we do not know what is going on around the world. Radio news does not give us any firm information either.

I finished work on how to record daily events. The title is *Information for People Writing Daily Diaries in Partisan Units*. I typed over twenty sets and delivered them to "Adam" for distribution.

May 17 I went to Zamosc. Everyone there is very tired because last night three air alarms were called and people spent much of their time in the shelters. People expect more air strikes at any time now. News about the air bombardment of Lublin and Chelm is spreading.

In Zamosc there is unusually heavy traffic. There are cars and horse-drawn wagons everywhere. The different offices began evacuation and took with them their files, beginning with the year 1939. A similar situation is taking place in most warehouses. On the highway there are many motor-ized vehicles loaded with luggage and furniture (mostly antiques). Also the Germans are shipping grain, butter, and eggs all the way to Germany.

It appears they are moving out for good. As I passed the old academy building I noticed that the 300-year-old bronze plaque had been removed by the Germans. A few weeks ago it was still there.

I stopped in at a print shop. We talked about a few items, in particular about a songbook containing songs of the underground units in the Zamosc region. I was pleasantly surprised that the print shop agreed to print it without any reservations at all.

From my friends I learned that Dr. Szpringer, a well-known physician, was killed. He had signed the *Volksdeutsch* list.

On the streets I met a gendarme from Zwierzyniec. At first I was un-able to recognize him, because he wore a fine civilian suit. He was walking along with a woman who cooked for the gendarmes in Zwierzyniec. She was a patient of mine, and she told me that all gendarmes received orders to buy civilian clothing for after-duty hours, as a safety measure.

At the Mokre airfield there are now more than thirty planes. Pilot train-ing goes on constantly. Every few minutes a plane takes off and shortly thereafter lands. This type of exercise continues for hours. Around the air-field many underground shelters are being built.

The Germans are to defend Zamosc. This is very bad news because this beautiful city can be easily destroyed. This has already happened to too many Polish cities.

May 18   At this time we are completely cut off from the rest of the country. There is no rail traffic. Between Lublin and Warsaw two large bridges, one in Pulawy and another in Deblin, were completely destroyed. Last night an armored train was blown up around Ploski, near Zamosc. A passenger train was destroyed near Izbica. So there is no rail traffic in either direction. It is dangerous to travel on the highway. This morning a peasant was blown to pieces by a mine as he rode on a horse-drawn wagon. The Germans are even using automobiles in convoys, but they still do not have enough equipment to evacuate all the warehouses. The stores of grain, sugar, flour, vodka, and other commodities will finally end up in our hands. It is clear that in today's war, sabotage and diversion play a very important role, and they are being carried out by partisan groups of the Home Army.

May 19   Last night again there was rifle and machine gun fire, for about one hour. I later learned that this was an assault against the *Volksdeutsch*. At the Bendera flour mill the machinery was destroyed, and the wife of Hajer, owner of the Sulowka flour mill, was killed. At 11 P.M. an air alarm roused people from their beds, but it was a false alarm.

I went to Radecznica. I breathed more freely there than in our town. You do not feel the German presence there anymore. I met with many young people. I talked with "Grom," of the "Grom" unit. At the monastery I learned that their print shop is intact and we can use it. We can easily move the small hand printing machine to the forest camp. I already have plans in my head on what to print.

May 20   At noon a train consisting of a locomotive and two cars was blown up in Zurawnica. Even small incidents such as this one disrupt the normal railroad schedule.

The highway between Zwierzyniec and Bilgoraj is now open, but old Piatkowski drove over a land mine and was severely wounded. The railroad between Zwierzyniec and Bilgoraj is again not functioning.

Here, around us, assaults on *Volksdeutsch* are events that are constantly repeated. Robbers are taking everything from livestock to household items. So far the families of Kraus, Wildhirt, Wojtowicz, "Siegmunt" Bielecki, and Paul were robbed. These men had not been staying at home at night, so they are still alive.

May 21   Today again I went to Zamosc. The city has certainly changed during the past year. You see fewer Germans than before. The cathedral is back to being a church (before it was used as a grain warehouse for the Germans). Now, after a floor cleaning, regular services have begun. Many people attended the first service. The church was packed, so many people stood out in the cemetery surrounding the church. At the marketplace only a few Germans in uniform were seen. At city hall and also the academy building the German flags were removed. Looking down on the marketplace from the second floor of Bogucki's house, I had the feeling of being in a free Zamosc once again. But the overall mood of the people here is different from what we have in Szczebrzeszyn. In Zamosc we do not feel the nearness of the forest, as in Zwierzyniec or Szczebrzeszyn. The people here are not in contact with those in the forest, and they are not involved in underground actions as we are. This can explain the resignation here, which we do not have in our town. People here talk only about air attacks and evacuation. The evacuation of the offices is going on at full speed. All bank records have already been moved west to Ostrow Mazowiecki.

The news about the slaughter of Poles by Ukrainians around Tyszowiec came as a shock. Many Polish families are fleeing from that area; they are moving west, farther into the unknown.

When I returned home I was told about more casualties on the highway. Between Zwierzyniec and Bilgoraj several people were killed by land mines; four Germans were among them.

May 22   I received two visitors from Zamosc, both German, the *Amtarzt* Dr. Zimmer and chief sanitary officer Dr. Steinherr. They supposedly came on an inspection, but the real purpose of their visit was to force bribes from us. Without any hesitation they told me that because Dr. Zimmer is going on vacation he needs food. They gave me a paper (so-called *Bezugschein*) ordering us to butcher a pig.

Yesterday in Zwierzyniec, around 4 P.M., two Azerbejdzans were killed during the shooting and one German was wounded. In retaliation the Azerbejdzans began shooting at anyone nearby. A few wounded were brought to the hospital in Szczebrzeszyn.

May 23   Just before noon three Germans came to inspect the hospital. The chief sanitary officer of the district, from Lublin, was accompanied by Dr. Zimmer and Dr. Steinherr. As a result of this inspection each of them received 6 kg of bacon and a loaf of bread. Besides this the chief received a large sack of potatoes. Yesterday the doctors received 3 kg of sugar each. I am noting this to show how bribes are spreading even into professions such as physicians. Sorry to say that bribes on the part of the Germans are even being given to Polish office clerks. The situation now is that to be heard in the office you must give a bribe.

During the afternoon I went to Zwierzyniec. There Azerbejdzans are afraid of an attack on their quarters, so they transformed them into a fortress, as did the gendarmes to their post. Instead of a fence they built a thick wall out of heavy timber, with small openings in place of windows, from which they could shoot.

During action at Susiec young Podczaski, from Zwierzyniec, was killed. He was in the "Podkowa" platoon.

May 24 Today "Wyrwa" stopped by to talk about my publication efforts. Soon we will be able to start the printing machine and we will be printing a short weekly bulletin.

May 25 Today Lt. Jan Kryk ("Topola"), a former teacher, brought me some music he had composed. It will be added to the songs I received previously from "Adam." I am beginning to edit the songs. All of them will be printed at the Zamosc print shop. From "Topola" I learned that his brother Leonard Kryk, also a teacher, was killed in Auschwitz.

May 26 In town a rumor began because of an overheard telephone conversation: before Sunday several villages will be pacified, including Blonie, Kawenczyn, Topolcza, and Szperowka. This caused much tension.

This morning gendarmes began loading their belongings and moved them to an unknown location. In Zamosc evacuation is proceeding at full speed. I learned that Szczebrzeszyn will soon host a large army group. In town the Germans are taking houses as quarters. Some people are saying that a battalion of Ukrainian SS will be here soon. This is what people fear the most.

May 27 In Lublin a list of hostages was published. Those people will be shot in case of any action against the Germans. One person on the list is Postulski, from Szczebrzeszyn. A few days ago the administrator of the Alwa plant, a German named Becker, was killed in Lublin. A time bomb exploded in his own house.

Here in our town much is happening. The Germans are preparing quarters for a large detachment. The high school is now empty and ready to receive troops. On the highway there are many trucks carrying soldiers toward Zwierzyniec.

Last night in Brody Duze several villagers were arrested; among them was Czuk and his seventeen-year-old son. People are talking about the upcoming pacification and are very nervous.

The forest units are now moving farther from the villages. I must note one event. As I mentioned before, a few days ago I had a sanitary inspection. All three German physicians, just before their departure, began complaining that they were hungry and would like to eat lunch. I ordered lunch. They especially liked the rye bread, so I sent to baker Basajewski for an additional three loaves.

Today before noon I received a note from the gendarme post that someone from a German office in Zamosc would like to talk with me. As I learned, the sanitation chief took one loaf of bread with him to Lublin. He invited the local governor to lunch and served Basajewski's bread. The governor liked it so much that from now on I have to send fives loaves of rye bread twice a week to the *Amtarzt* in Zamosc and he will make arrangements for delivery to Lublin. I am noting this minor, comical event to illustrate how the Germans force people to please them and how arrogant they are in demanding personal services.

May 29   Monday is the second day of Pentecost. Today I have many events to describe, but because of my emotional feelings I am not sure that I will be able to do it. This year the commandant of the peasant battalions decided to celebrate the second day of Pentecost as the traditional working-class holiday. For this event Home Army units were also invited. A special shooting training class will be conducted by "Wyrwa." He, on his side, invited Dr. Jozwiakowski and me. At 8 A.M., along with Dr. Jozwiakowski, we went by horse-drawn wagon to Szperowka and later on foot through the forest until we came to the meadow where the ceremony was to be performed. When we arrived at the camp the military units were already assembled. The first platoon, a unit of the Home Army shooting training class, was placed under the command of "Nieuchwytny." I saw many familiar faces from Szczebrzeszyn, including Mroczkowski, director of the labor bureau; Pic, contractor; Rzepecki; Kapec; and Jerzy Jozwiakowski, son of a physician. On the left side were eleven young girls with Michalowa Radzikowna. Other units included the special training platoon of Lt. "Beton," peasant battalion officer training, and others.

More people began arriving—officers in old uniforms carrying sidearms, many soldiers also in old military uniforms. Some without uniforms wore red and white arm bands on their left sleeve. The civilian public was well dressed, particularly the young girls. Many dignitaries arrived also. The commandant of all peasant battalions, Maj. Kaminski, and the delegate of the Polish government in London, Judge Witoszka ("Marek"), were there. After all the assembled units were counted, the total number of soldiers was 782. Of the civilians assembled there, I counted over 2,000 strong.

Rev. Waclaw, from Radecznica, celebrated a field Mass. During the ceremony a beautiful folk choir sang. After the Mass there were short speeches by several people. In the name of the Home Army, Inspector "Kalina," Mr. Jaworski, and "Czeremcha," from Klemensow, greeted those present. Very good speakers were Maj. Kaminski and later Judge Witoszek. He pointed out that in the future Poland the working classes will have more say and that the future Poland can only be a "People Poland." After one minute of silence for all the soldiers killed in the struggle against the Germans, the Polish national anthem was sung by the assembled crowd.

A half hour later a parade of all military units began. A group of several people were assembled to review the parade, including the honored guests. I was invited also. The parade began with an honor guard, commanded by "Rolicz," which carried a Polish red and white flag. Then came the platoon of the officer training class, and finally all the others. The presentation was very good. Most soldiers were armed with old Polish rifles, others with hand machine guns. In the last unit we were able to see soldiers in old police, fire department, and forest ranger uniforms, and civilian jackets. Many soldiers wore white and red arm bands with different letters on them, such as "W.P." (*Wojsko Polskie*, Polish army), "Ch.S." (*Chlopska Straz*, peasant guards), "L.S.B." (*Ludowa Straz Bezpieczenstwa*, People's Intelligence Service), and others. Many soldiers carried hand grenades.

A special camera team filmed all the activities. After the parade a lunch of good bean soup and *bigos*, prepared by "Stary," was served. There were some interesting moments I will never forget, including the face of a young woman, cashier at Rolnik, in Szczebrzeszyn, when she was introduced to Lt. "Gruda." It so happens that a few weeks ago "Gruda" led an assault on Rolnik where several thousand zloty were taken.

People finally began departing. During the festivities German planes flew over four times. As this occurred the crowd flattened out on their stomachs among the trees. Once the religious services were interrupted. Around 6 P.M., along with Dr. Jozwiakowski, we said good-bye and left for home.

Today was a special day. I was impressed with the look of the peasant battalions, composed of strong, older villagers and youth, all trying to do their best, marching together as one unit. Today's activities had a "people's" character to them. It was obvious to everyone that the mass of peasants, and in the city the mass of workers, would be the most powerful element in the rebuilding of a future Poland.

We were able to see the results of our underground work—that despite the German repressions, terror, and pacification, it was possible to build the cadres of the future Polish army. To this army the population looks as the only source of might in the struggle against the German occupation.

May 30   Yesterday's activities were the topic of conversation everywhere, especially in Szczebrzeszyn. Some people fear that a few German informers were there also. There is talk that the gestapo have a list of over 150 people who are to be arrested shortly in Szczebrzeszyn. So far this is only gossip. But the fact is that the gestapo took the registration list of inhabitants from city hall, and that is especially alarming.

May 31 A few events took place recently. On May 29 two young boys from Szczebrzeszyn left their homes. One was the son of a shoemaker, Augustowski, who was evacuated from Poznan four years ago; the other was Rytko, son of a teacher killed a few years ago. Young Rytko was known as a German confidant. To this day neither has returned. From various sources I learned that Rytko was liquidated and Augustowski was forced to join an underground unit in the forest.

Yesterday in Szczebrzeszyn a Jew, Miller, was killed. In Kitow, on May 29, a gendarme was killed. Today in Brody Duze two *Volksdeutsch* were liquidated, Wladyslaw Matej and Piotr Paszt. Both of the bodies were brought to the hospital morgue where in the presence of gendarmes I was forced to do an autopsy. During the shooting two villagers were wounded, both Poles.

Near Panasowka a few horse-drawn wagons coming from the festivities and carrying underground soldiers were involved in a battle with Germans. One wagon was missing. The rumor is spreading that the missing wagon carried the film crew and the films are now in German hands. If this is true, and if the films were taken by the Germans, then we are facing terrible days.

By evening several arrests were made in Szczebrzeszyn. Several horse-drawn wagons carrying *Volksdeutsch* from Brody Duze passed through.

June

June 1 A *Volksdeutsch*, Teofil Lembryk, from Brody Duze, disappeared. I know that he was liquidated.

In the afternoon a long convoy of empty horse-drawn wagons went to Brody; they were guarded by gendarmes armed with rifles. They are supposed to evacuate all the Germans. This evening they returned carrying *Volksdeutsch* evacuees and stopped at Przedmiescie Zamojskie; later they are to be moved by train to Lodz. The Polish population escaped quickly into the forest. So now the very prosperous village of Brody Duze is completely empty.

We have received news about fighting between the villagers and Germans in Wysokie, near Turobin, and in Bzowiec. We fear that because of this the Germans will begin a new action of pacification.

June 2 Around 8 P.M. German troops set up machine gun emplacements around the city. I received information that the Germans have now surrounded the city from all sides. On the streets, patrols of armed, helmeted soldiers are moving about. Many military vehicles are passing through, some on caterpillar tracks. In town tension is growing. There are some people who arrived at the hospital just before the police curfew. They feel safer there than in their own private homes. We are puzzled because of this unusual action. We can hear explosions in the distance.

It is now 11 P.M. Normally at this time I am already in bed, but tonight I am waiting. Nothing happened until around midnight, when three color rockets were seen from the direction of Klemensow.

June 3   The night passed. There are no airplanes now, no traffic, no shooting, everything is very quiet. We learned of the German exercises that were to familiarize their soldiers in surrounding tactics. The exercises stopped after the shooting of the three rockets. Now only patrols consisting of one gendarme and four soldiers move about the streets.

I received news that a large Russian unit, 1,000 men strong, arrived in the so-called Cetnarz, a forest near Kawenczyn. It is possible that the Germans are preparing themselves in case of an attack.

Our underground obtained a list from the gestapo of fifty people who are supposed to be arrested. They have all been notified.

June 4   Tomorrow all *Volksdeutsch* and *Stammdeutsch* women and their children, up to the age of sixteen, are to move out. Most of the families have a real problem. To move to camps without the head of the family is very difficult. You cannot stay because the Germans will not allow it, and you cannot escape into the forest because you are a renegade. It is a dilemma.

June 5   Early this morning the *Volksdeutsch* from Brody Duze, who were temporarily staying in Przedmiescie, moved out. Now our own *Volksdeutsch* families are supposed to be ready to move. Several horse-drawn wagons were waiting to take them. Of the fifty-four registered families, only six showed up (Menderski, Wildhirt, Paul, and three others). All others disappeared. They are afraid of the camp in Lodz because of the news that quickly spread of a raid by British bombers that killed Krol, from Szczebrzeszyn, the owner of a restaurant, along with his two sons. (Later I learned that this information was false.)

June 6   Around noon we received good news, that this morning the Allied forces landed in France, the beginning of the invasion. The news electrified everyone. Within a few hours the entire city was talking exclusively about the invasion. The overall mood is demonstrated by the amount of vodka consumed. Even "Leszcz" showed up and stayed overnight.

June 7   Yesterday the local gendarmes in Brody arrested Strzygon, who was in charge of an underground radio station located in the forest, only 7 km from Szczebrzeszyn. Everything possible was done to force his release. Today he is free, even though the gendarmes were aware that he is a man of the forest. Near the gendarme post a special detachment of the Home Army waited to free him.

June 8   The only topic of conversation is the invasion of France. This is a very emotional subject for Poles, and for Germans also, but the reaction is completely different.

Again the airfield at Klemensow has been reopened. Yesterday several transports of bombs were delivered there. Flight activities are on the increase.

Today the gestapo began interviewing *Volksdeutsch* to learn why they are still in town. Some were beaten, such as the barber Gortner.

June 9   All *Volksdeutsch* were supposed to be gone by this morning. Only four families left—Stanislaw Kiszka, Czochra, Pilip, and Kolodziejczyk. The rest tried to escape. They are in real trouble. During the interrogation of those captured, the Germans took their ID cards. Without identification they are bandits.

From Krasnystaw County comes bad news. The Germans began action against the villages. They are taking the livestock while people try to escape. So far there is nothing about murders, which has been a common occurrence during evacuations.

June 10   I went to Zwierzyniec. From the new front in the west comes news about the successes of the Allied forces.

I have to note a very sad fact. A young man, Zbigniew Cichowicz, former high school student and son of an accountant from Zamosc, was liquidated. His mother still works at the Zamoyski estate. He had joined the "Lanca" underground unit, but he was watched very carefully. After a long investigation it became clear that he was a gestapo informer in Bilgoraj.

More German troops are concentrating in Szczebrzeszyn and Zwierzyniec. On the highway there is increased traffic. Most of the military vehicles are traveling in the direction of Bilgoraj. Four *Volksdeutsch* families who left yesterday returned to Szczebrzeszyn from the Zawada train station. Only a few other families showed up there, so the transport was delayed. They are supposed to go back to the railroad station on June 19.

June 12   Last night near Kawenczynek a barber, Waclaw Zelazko, from Szczebrzeszyn, was liquidated.

I learned that the notorious gestapo agent Boleslaw Mazurek was transferred from Zamosc to Chelm.

Today I had a pleasant surprise. On their way from Zwierzyniec to Zamosc, four members of the underground school examination team, Tadeusz Gajewski, Stanislawa Zochowska, Wozniakowna, and Kucharska, stopped by to visit. They were in Zwierzyniec conducting high school final examinations. It is interesting to mention that our underground schooling is very well organized and young people can finish not only elementary but also high school.

From the nearby villages I received rumors about upcoming events. In Zwierzyniec the people await mass arrests.

Here we are observing German preparations for the defense of the city. Machine guns and antitank guns have been placed around the city and also along the Wieprz River. One heavy machine gun has been set up near the hospital. It appears the Germans have decided to fight here.

June 14   In Zwierzyniec there is an even more tense situation. The people there fear arrests. Almost all the men without labor cards have escaped. Kalwejt is staying overnight at my place.

June 16   Last night, around 11 P.M., there was an alarm. After one hour it was called off. Nobody really paid any attention to it, and no one went to the shelters.

Today the Germans finally forced the *Volksdeutsch* to move out. Approximately fifteen horse-drawn wagons left. I do not know all the names, only a few. Included were the families of Hausner, Kucharski, Kiszka, Czochra, Menderski, and Pilip.

From Zwierzyniec comes bad news. The village is surrounded by Germans. On the roads and streets, even in Szczebrzeszyn, the gendarmes are searching everyone. Some people are trying to escape from Zwierzyniec. Many of them have come to Szczebrzeszyn. At the hospital there is much coming and going. Several people have come by to see me: "Leszcz," "Cezary," Rev. Waclaw, "Czarny," and Kalwejt ("Borowka"). They talked about life in the forest. It is a very interesting life. There are so many people in the forest that local village women walk there with baskets loaded with cigarettes, matches, beer, lemonade, and sandwiches, and sell them for high prices, almost resembling the free market.

In the forest there are many different types of people assembled, even deserters from the German army. A few days ago an officer observed a German soldier with hand grenades and a pistol in his belt and a rifle in his hands. He walked along slowly, looking around constantly. But there was one strange thing: he held the rifle so the barrel was directed at himself.

Every now and then he stopped to rest and then whistled loudly. He would point the rifle at the ground and hold his hands up. Then he would begin walking again. When he finally saw our soldiers he threw down his rifle and shouted in broken Polish, "I want to be a Polish soldier." When he was finally taken to headquarters it was learned that he was from German Silesia and spoke only a few words of Polish. He was enlisted as a private in one of the platoons.

"Cezary," an aide to "Adam," told me another story. One day the chaplain was conducting a field Mass in Latin. While he was saying *"Dominus Vobiscum,"* he spotted a German plane. Without thinking he shouted, "Boys, this S.O.B. is looking for us. Take cover."

Sorry to say, but I learned that a very popular Szczebrzeszyn high school student, Misiarz, went to the forest and organized his own small group, including Jews, but was active in common robberies. Finally he was killed during a fight with the Germans.

A few weeks ago near Zwierzyniec young Ziminski, a partisan and at the same time a German informer, was liquidated. It is sad that these liquidations are very common in our area. They are carried out because it is necessary to rid our area of German informers. It is impossible to note them all.

I hope that after the war we will have enough material from the underground prosecutor's office to review all these cases.

June 16 Today Lt. "Rosa," a judge from Wilno and an officer involved in sabotage activities, visited me. With interest I listened to his stories about several assaults in which he played a major role. Occasionally I had the feeling that he politely exaggerated some events. I explained to him how important eye witness reports are and urged him to start putting his stories on paper. During our conversations we talked about a *Volksdeutsch* from Szczebrzeszyn, Julius Maks, a well-known gestapo informer. He has already been sentenced to death by a military tribunal but has always been able to escape. I said that liquidating him in his own house was no good, because it is too close to the hospital and the Germans might retaliate against the patients.

Besides "Rosa" I spoke today with Rev. Waclaw, "Cezary," and "Borowka." During their visit two of my nurses were sworn in as military nurses.

June 17 Around 8 A.M. I was informed that Maks was kidnapped in Blonie, where he went to buy milk and produce. He was handcuffed and taken to Kawenczyn by horse-drawn wagon and from there on foot to the camp. A preliminary investigation began. From Lt. Kollataj ("Ikar"), my former student, I learned some details. He was pleased that in one week the underground was able to liquidate four German confidants—Zelazko, mother and daughter Majchrzak, and a woman I do not know—and now they arrested Maks. He is still alive, but only because he tells some interesting stories. He will be liquidated soon.

I forgot to note that a few days ago several prisoners were freed from Zamosc prison. Lt. "Rosa" was sure that this was not an organized action. We learned that one of the prisoners, young Lt. "Lis," was able to disarm one of the guards. Then, armed with a rifle and pistol, he disarmed more guards and freed several prisoners. He was unable to free any women from the women's ward. I am trying to contact Lt. "Lis" to obtain more information from him.

This morning I admitted to the hospital Lucjan Rekas ("Udrycki") with chest wounds. He died a few hours later. He was a very brave young man. He was wounded in action against the Germans somewhere near Zamosc. Because of gendarme patrols he was not admitted to the Zamosc hospital, but after thirty hours of suffering he was brought to my hospital, already in critical condition.

June 19   Yesterday in Bondyrz a very important meeting was to take place. Almost all the high-ranking officers were present. Just before the meeting was to begin a large detachment of Germans, including tanks, arrived and took over the village. Where they were going was unknown, but our own units were forced to move to the locality of Krzywe, between Kosobudy and Szczebrzeszyn.

In Zwierzyniec there are many German troops—people say the headquarters of two divisions. Those troops are all fighting units. So far there has been no pacification action, but the units are on alert. Soldiers search all passersby. In Zwierzyniec an aide to inspector "Kalina," "Orkisz," was stopped but somehow escaped, leaving all his documents in German hands.

Around 9 A.M. the Szczebrzeszyn railroad station was warned about a Russian air attack. The everyday activities of preparing for defense, the digging of more trenches and shelters, preparing machine gun and antitank weapon positions, is beginning to have an effect on the population. The news that the Russians made a breakthrough near Sokal, and their quick advance toward the west, came to us as a big surprise. We fear that our city will be the scene of bloody fighting, which can lead to a devastating situation.

June 20   Our troops, commanded by "Adam," were able to cross the highway near Zwierzyniec and the Wieprz River, and now they are passing through Kawenczyn and Turzyniec.

Yesterday Maks was liquidated.

Here on the highway the traffic is very heavy. Every minute convoys of military equipment or soldiers are on the move. I observe many empty ambulances going in the direction of Zamosc and then returning with wounded. We really do not know where the Russian-German battles are taking place. We do not know if the Russians have the support of the underground units. Last night the Germans were engaged in an action somewhere near Blizowie, where they burned an entire village. Now we await what the next day will bring.

June 21 We have more information from the forest. The Home Army unit commanded by "Woyna," a few others, and "Kalina" and his deputy "Miecz" were encircled in the Jozefow forest by German forces. We do not know what is occurring there, but I myself am very worried, because "Kalina" was carrying some of the underground archives.

In Bondyrz the Germans discovered a large supply of uniforms and shoes and took them to Zwierzyniec. At the same time the banner of the Ninth Infantry Regiment was lost.

The Germans arrested many people in the vicinity of Zwierzyniec. Some were moved to a camp in Bilgoraj, but the rest were placed in a camp in Zwierzyniec. We are afraid of some arrests. People are not staying home at night. "Borowka" and "Cezary" are spending the night in my quarters.

June 22 Our own underground administration is working out very well and becoming more authoritative. I have received information that in many cases people are not going to German authorities but are trying to solve disputes with the help of the village or region commandant. Today I did the same thing. The hospital received 81 tons of coal. It was mandatory to unload the railroad cars as soon as possible. Our own hospital horses and wagons, moving four times a day, would take three weeks. I was aware that city hall would not help; the Germans would not either. Private wagons would charge 100 zloty per trip. So I sent a request to Commandant "Wyrwa." He ordered four villages, Blonie, Kawenczyn, Topoloza, and Brody, to help. On his order several horse-drawn wagons arrived at the railroad station and in few hours the coal was unloaded at the hospital. I could not believe it; if the Germans had given such an order no one would have showed up.

Along with the coal for the hospital I received from "Wyrwa" one hundredweight of sugar and two hundredweight of grain.

June 23 Today I went to Zwierzyniec. In the barracks and behind the barbed wire there were 200 children and 700 adults, mostly women. These people had been brought from Jozefow, Aleksandrow, Pardysowka, Bondyrz, Tereszpol, and Bukownica. In Jozefow even priests were taken. Everyone who stayed home was arrested. The action has not stopped. Some army units have moved out though. But people in Zwierzyniec are still afraid to return to their houses.

June 24 All *Volksdeutsch* received orders to report on July 1, in Zamosc, for a special investigation. More than likely they will be drafted into the *Sonderdienst*.

June 25 Operations near here are coming to an end. People from the Zwierzyniec camp have been moved to Lublin's Krochmalna Street *Arbeitsamt*. There have been no new transports, but the memories of the last few days are still very strong. Villagers are disappointed that their leaders deserted them, moving into secure places. In particular people from the peasant battalions are disturbed. They are extremely upset about the warehouses full of uniforms, shoes, and arms in Bondyrz and Trzepieciny that were taken by the Germans. As far as I know the Home Army refused to distribute these good to the peasant battalions. Some fighting among underground units began as a result. On Friday, June 23, near Krzywe, peasants killed Wal ("Msciwy"), from Wielacza, and shot at Lt. Stefan Pozdzik ("Wrzos"), but he survived. The upset peasants swear to kill the leaders of the Home Army.

The population is mentally exhausted and people's emotions break for no apparent reason. This is the result of today's war, along with the constant fear for one's own safety and the lack of discipline, so important in conspiracy work. Almost the entire population is involved in one way or another in an anti-German stance. But there is much proof that the German gendarmes, and especially the gestapo, are very well informed about what is really occurring in our society. If they begin new mass retaliations, most of the valuable people would end up in prison or concentration camps, and only the people in the forest would be able to survive. Not everyone can go to the forest; someone must stay and do the daily work.

June 27 I went to Zwierzyniec. The situation involving our troops in the Jozefow forest is still not clear. We know that casualties are high. Units commanded by "Podkowa" and "Dolina" went to help.

I was told that recently a Russian colonel, Michal Rodzki, fifty-two years of age, who was in the "Grom" battalion, defected to the Germans along with his wife and is now giving the enemy important information.

Quartermaster Przyczynek ("Bor") was captured by the Germans, with 80,000 zloty in cash.

Behind the wires in Zwierzyniec I noticed only a few old men. The rest have been evacuated.

June 28   At 6 P.M. "Reczyc" and "Cezary" arrived with a request that physicians, nurses, and their medical equipment be dispatched to the Jozefow forest. There is still no detailed information about the fighting there. The feeling is that our troops were beaten and then lost all contact with the leadership. From several sources I learned about heavy casualties. Many wounded have been left without any medical help at all. Two physicians have been wounded also; one is Dr. Lucjan Kopec ("Radwan"), from Bilgoraj hospital.

After a confrontation with Dr. "Jaga," a hospital surgeon, Dr. Jerzy Jentys ("Kamil") and nurse Michalina went to help. Hopefully by tomorrow we will have information about the situation in the forest.

Last night on the highway near Rap four gendarmes were killed.

June 29   This morning I went to Kawenczyn. I met with "Wyrwa," "Wrzos," "Grom," and others, but the information about our troops near Jozefow is still very sketchy.

Around noon several people assembled in my quarters: "Komar," "Mlot," "Cezary," Szymanski ("Siwek"), Suchodolski ("Dniestr"), "Orlicz," Huskowski ("Harlej"). We discussed the situation. Clearly the leadership lost contact with all the units and what we have is complete disorganization. Even contact with Commandant "Adam" has been lost. His aide "Cezary" has been unable to make contact with him for several days.

Late in the afternoon Dr. Jentys returned. He was able to go only as far as Goreck. The area beyond is under German control. He was only able to see one wounded soldier, Tadeusz Szanojca ("Sum"), who was brought to the hospital in critical condition by nurse Michalina.

Around 5 P.M. I met again with "Borowka" and "Cezary." This time Capt. "Adam," who had just arrived, participated in the discussion. We again discussed medical help. One physician was to go immediately. After a short discussion I decided to go. I began preparing myself for the journey when "Adam" changed his mind. I was told to stay home and await further instructions. He sent out patrols to find out when the roads would be clear.

We are puzzled as to why he is willing to send physicians from Szczebrzeszyn when in Kawenczyn there are two physicians who are ready to go at any time, Dr. Alapin ("Kwiatkowski") and Dr. Poradowska ("Helena").

"Adam" left me a long list of drugs and first-aid supplies prepared by one of the Home Army physicians, with an order that I supply them. I know that these necessary supplies have been parachuted several times

already by British airplanes, all packed in neat leather pouches. Several
times I was told about this by partisan officers who then asked me what the
uses were for several of the individual items. (Naturally the instructions
were all in English, not in Polish.) I am puzzled as to where it has all
disappeared.

From "Adam" I cannot get any information about the fighting.

At about 10 P.M. German soldiers with full equipment and helmets
broke down the fences around the hospital. Some went with guns ready in
the direction of Blonie; some stayed. Our entire city is encircled by German
soldiers. We do not know if this is a real action or again just an exercise. At
first the hospital personnel were nervous, but when, after some time, nothing happened, they calmed down. Around 11:20 P.M. we went to sleep.

June 30   The night passed very quietly. From the Jozefow forest deputy
inspector Capt. Rakoczy ("Miecz") arrived in Zwierzyniec. He is very
tired and unable to talk. What happened to inspector "Kalina" is unknown.
Some say that he was captured by the Germans, others that he was killed.
We know for certain that the commanding officer of a special company,
Lt. "Woyna," a very popular man and one of the bravest officers, who had
already earned the *Krzyz Walecznych* (Cross of Valour), was killed. I knew
him well because he visited us several times and was a frequent visitor
at Kalwejt's, in Zwierzyniec. Also killed was Lt. Kryk ("Topola"). Not
long ago he gave me music that he had written, new songs for the underground.

The number of names of the dead are unknown. The officers seem to
have decided not to talk about it. We feel that approximately 5,000 men
were involved in the battle against the Germans: some 3,000 Russians,
1,000 PPR (Polish Workers party), and 1,000 of the Home Army and peasant battalions.

Today our military leaders received information about the possibility of
new German actions, this time to include Lipowiec, Frampol, Radecznica,
and Szczebrzeszyn. It is not pleasant news, but it cannot be helped. We
must wait and see. Some people are leaving. Today at the hospital I received a wounded sergeant, "Dziewiatka," from the Ninth Infantry Regiment, in Zamosc.

"Adam" informed me that it is impossible to drive to Jozefow, so I must
still wait. Nurse Kazia Osiecka, who just arrived from the Warsaw hospital, was sent to duty with the "Wrzos" unit.

Our relations with the officers and soldiers of the different underground
units are from day to day becoming closer than ever before. It seems as if
everyone wants to take part in the goings-on. Even my young son Tadeusz

is serving as a messenger, riding his bicycle from one place to another. He is particularly well known in Kawenczyn.

During the last few days I was able to supply our units with plastic map covers. They are difficult to obtain, but I learned that by washing clean the X-ray films I could produce good-quality plastic sheets.

July

July 1 "Grom's" wounded brother was admitted to the hospital. He had taken part in the heavy fighting at Osuchy, near Jozefow. He was wounded seven days ago by one of his own soldiers who became mentally ill. I am receiving much information about this fight. Some say that inspector "Kalina" was guilty of negligence, some that Capt. "Adam" was at fault because he left his units without any command. It is very difficult to fairly judge the situation. Hopefully, in the future, some historian will be able to assemble all the facts.

Today I had a long conversation with "Grom's" brother. He lays complete blame for the defeat on inspector "Kalina," who was in command of all the units. He disappeared and was unable to command. He seems to have lost his head. He was unable to command as large a unit as a regiment (Ninth Infantry Regiment). Up until now in the history of this regiment this was the worst defeat.

I am trying to work out the details of events of the past few weeks. I began collecting every bit of information from people who witnessed the events of those days. I hope that after the war I will maybe also be able to review information from the German side.

Tonight "Szum" died. He was a very brave soldier. He took part in the assassination attempt on gestapo chief Kolb. For his actions he received the *Krzyz Walecznych.* He had been wounded in the bladder and lay in a field for four days. He was transported to the hospital on the seventh day in critical condition, with urine poisoning. His family is in Jozefow.

July 2 The entire day I spent in Sulowiec visiting Stefan Huskowski. There I met Boncza-Pioro, "Colt," "Leszcz," Cadet "Korczak," from the "Podkowa" units, and young Jurek Zochowski, also from "Podkowa." "Korczak" took part in the Jozefow battle and together with several other soldiers succeeded in breaking through German lines. He outlined the battle on a map, which showed the day-by-day fighting and movement of the units.

We passed through the village of Rozlopy. The houses are all empty. The *Volksdeutsch* have already gone, but the former owners have not yet returned. They are still afraid. Everywhere you look you see total devastation. No livestock; the village looks dead.

July 3 Today three gendarmes came to the hospital and searched it, beginning in the spotted typhus ward. They stopped at every bed and looked at the illness cards and asked questions. Before they left they checked to see if we had any wounded. In some of the hospitals, such as Tomaszow, the wounded were kept in the spotted typhus ward. I am sure they came here because of somebody's report that we are treating the wounded. This is a warning for us that we must be very careful.

Today in Kawenczyn, the sister-in-law of Maks ("Waskowna") was liquidated.

July 4 I went to Kawenczyn to meet with "Adam." I brought him back to stay in my quarters overnight. He talked constantly about the defeat at Osuchy. Besides "Woyna" and "Topola," inspector "Kalina" was killed as well as physician Tadeusz Blachta ("Oldan"). He had worked in my hospital for almost a year and later in Bilgoraj. For some time he had been a member of the underground. Not long ago he was married. While he was at my hospital in Szczebrzeszyn I talked him into writing stories about his service in the sanitary cadet corp in Warsaw. He began a few chapters but was unable to finish.

Quartermaster "Bor" (Przyczynek) was killed also. What happened to his fifteen-year-old daughter is unknown. Also missing are forest ranger Makuch ("Kruk") and his wife, and a nurse from Jozefow, Aniela Nowakowna. Lt. Golebiowski ("Irka") was wounded in the leg and transported to Kawenczyn. He was in command of the Hrubieszow region and had taken part in the Jozefow battle.

Sanitary patrols are working now, so practically all the wounded are receiving medical treatment.

I spoke with "Adam" about the events of the last few weeks, how to start writing a history of each unit, and finally about the publication of a songbook.

July 5 This morning a messenger on his way to see "Lowicki" (Guminski), in Korytrowo, county of Bilgoraj, was arrested by the Germans. She had with her 30 lbs. of printing paper and several sheets of information. The information included names, such as Janislawski ("Mruk"), from Zwierzyniec. We notified him right away. Now everything depends on her behavior during the investigation.

A young soldier in very grave condition, Jakubik ("Marek"), from "Wir's" unit, was brought to the hospital. He lay in a field without any medical attention for four days. Some other lightly wounded men were taken to the village of Kawenczyn.

July 6   Around 2 P.M. a gendarme lieutenant escorted by two gendarmes arrived at the hospital and requested a private conversation with me. I was positive that this visit was in direct relation to the treatment of wounded the hospital has been providing. I was right. The gendarmes first asked if I had admitted four bandits for treatment recently. I strongly denied this. The gendarmes searched the hospital beginning at the large men's ward. They checked the identification of all patients. During this entire time our wounded boys and all the nurses prayed. But no one was found. The gendarmes then searched private quarters, kitchens, and storage spaces. They omitted only my apartment. The gendarmes interrogated all the patients. I was worried that some of the boys would sleep and not be on guard, but things went smoothly. Not one of the wounded was discovered. After the search the lieutenant said to me, "We know that you are treating wounded, but we cannot prove it. Be careful because this means your life." The search took more than one hour.

Today in Brody two soldiers from the "Wrzos" unit were arrested by the gendarmes. During interrogation they were tortured. I learned that a rescue team has been organized.

July 7   The attempt to free the two soldiers of the "Wrzos" unit was a fiasco. Under heavy guard they were moved to Zamosc. "Wrzos" informed his sister who works in the hospital to warn us, because one of the soldiers knows about our activities and supposedly is giving this information to the Germans. Tension has built up in the hospital as a result.

Today I received a "confidential" stamped envelope from the German *Amtarzt* in Zamosc. Its contents were simple: in case of a general evacuation all German patients are to be moved to the German hospital in Lublin. Polish patients can stay, or if they so wish can be moved to Tomaszow Mazowiecki.

From Zamosc comes news that evacuation of the city will be ordered soon. Yesterday the Germans began removing furniture from city hall. The Russian troops' front line is once again supposed to be along the Bug River.

July 8   I went to Kawenczyn to meet with "Norbert" since he cannot be seen in Szczebrzeszyn. He is now an aide to the Ninth Infantry Regiment. The first battalion is under the command of "Dolina." During our meeting "Podkowa" made an appearance. We went through the partisan song material, which is ready for printing. I also tried to encourage them to start writing their own memoirs, or at least to make daily notes of their activities. It is sad that our underground leaders do not see the importance of historical material. Maybe "Norbert" is different. "Podkowa" completely disdains the importance of history. "Norbert" agreed to write about the "Weisman affair." He was very close to him and was the one who finally carried out the liquidation.

"Adam" stopped in Szczebrzeszyn for a brief time. He said that he is so busy he has no time to even think. After talking with him I got the feeling that he was right.

Mrs. Janislawska arrived from Zamosc and asked us to notify her husband that he can safely return home. The messenger girl supposedly arrested by the Germans arrived safely and gave her papers to "Lowicki." This was an alarm without any proof; one woman was simply told by another that a girl had been arrested.

July 9   From our area comes sad news. Sixty soldiers of the underground were executed by the Germans. They had been captured during the fighting in the Jozefow forest. Some officers, including "Adam," were sure that the Germans would recognize the soldiers of the Home Army and give them POW status. Several others have been arrested also. One of them was a baker who supplied bread to the troops.

I went to Zwierzyniec to discuss printing the songbook. We also discussed a front page carrying the symbol of the Ninth Infantry Regiment.

July 10   While in Zamosc I visited the print shop and gave them the manuscript of the songbook. I do not know if it will be possible to print it here. Printers in Lublin were arrested and people here are afraid.

On the highway there is very heavy traffic. Military convoys move constantly from Zamosc toward Bilgoraj. Here in Szczebrzeszyn we hear artillery explosions.

The daughter of quartermaster Bor is now in the Majdanek concentration camp.

July 12   I went to Zurawica to see "Waligora," who had been wounded and now also has the flu. He was in the "Woyna" unit. I learned more details about the fighting near Osuchy.

July 13   Recently we heard the rumor that the Germans are planning to open the graves of the murdered Jews, remove the bodies, and burn them. The Niechaj family, who lived next to the Jewish cemetery, was evacuated. Yesterday the Germans closed the small church in the Catholic cemetery, and today all the streets around both cemeteries were closed to traffic.

After several requests the Germans returned the key to the parish church and allowed Mass to be held there, but this is only for a few days. The news about the opening of the church spread quickly and many people came to the first service, mostly women. I went myself. I was curious as to how the church looked after being closed for more than two years. I noticed dirty floors and walls but no drastic vandalism. This afternoon the Germans ordered the church closed again.

Strange things are going on in the Jewish cemetery. No one is allowed to enter. The cemetery is surrounded by military guards armed with rifles. Warning signs stating that anyone entering will be shot were posted. Many cars and trucks come and go. A large group of prisoners was brought from Zamosc. The cemetery has been divided into sections; then the Germans built fences covered with tarps, so no one can observe what is taking place.

July 14   Since early morning, with his usual energy, Rev. Kapalski began doing everything in his power to reopen the church. As a result the lieutenant of gendarmes gave him permission to hold only one Mass, and then he closed the church again. On Sundays the priests will be allowed to hold Mass in the small cemetery church, without the public.

We learned that the Germans are moving Jewish bodies to be burned at the Rotunda. No bodies were burned at the cemetery.

Since yesterday we have heard artillery fire. It appears as if the Russians are attempting to force their way across the Bug River and take Sokal and Wlodzimierz.

In Zamosc the gestapo tried to arrest young Stanislaw Zminda, the son of a very well known watchmaker. He escaped through the attic and jumped to the roof of the next house, but he touched the high voltage line and was electrocuted. He fell dead. He had been very active in underground activities.

July 15   Sometimes, with heavy wind, you can smell the odor of decomposed bodies from the Jewish cemetery.

We can hear artillery firing without interruption, but we have been unable to learn many details. There is a rumor that around Sokal there is heavy fighting.

Last night in Kawenczyn the Germans arrested Judge Witoszka, "Marek," aide to the regional commandant "Lys" (or "Norweg"), and also, from Zwierzyniec, "Wilczek," commune administrator Cwik, and the Panas family, a total of fifteen people. Of course, people here are nervous. All the arrested are very well known but we do not know how they will behave during interrogation. My hospital is in danger also. One of them, Mrs. Ponas, worked for some time as a hospital helper; she married only a few weeks ago. She knew about every hospital activity. She met several underground leaders at the hospital, and later in Kawenczyn she saw them in Polish uniforms and carrying arms. I personally do not feel very good about this. Now, today, a German gendarme, unknown to me (not from our post), arrived at the hospital asking about me. In his notebook my name was underlined. I cannot understand why he would want me.

July 16 Today around 10 A.M. the Germans completed their work in the cemetery and left. The roads are all open. The church is open also. The Germans did a lot of digging; they did move something, but it is impossible for them to have removed thousands of badly decomposed bodies in only a few days.

The artillery fire is closer. It is said that Sokal has been taken by Soviet troops.

The people who were arrested yesterday were moved first to the Cetnar jail, but now they are in Zwierzyniec, in the "blue police" jail. It appears they may go free.

"Adam" is spending the night. He has just returned from Lublin. After "Kalina's" death he is taking over the duties of inspector of the Zamosc region. There are definitely some personnel changes in leadership pending. For several hours we discussed the history of the underground. He read a portion of my diary. He also gave me to read several orders from the inspectorate to the units and their replies to the inspectorate. I am sorry to say that today's situation does not permit me to keep those documents. They had to be destroyed. During the last action, through the last days of June, most of the inspectorate's documents were destroyed. It will be very difficult to reconstruct those events.

"Adam" complained about the very poor organization of sanitary operations. The chief physician, Dr. Tyczkowski, was dismissed because of it. "Adam" must now appoint a new chief physician. I hope this will be Dr. Jozwiakowski ("Jaga"). I know all the physicians in the surrounding counties and I feel he is the best choice. I told this to "Adam." "Adam" mentioned to me that Dr. Bienkowski, from Zamosc, cannot be used in any underground activities because he signed the *Volksdeutsch* list. I was very much surprised to hear this because a few weeks earlier Dr. Bienkowski was in Szczebrzeszyn and Radecznica to organize special courses for the training of medics and field nurses.

"Adam" is positive that Russian troops will be here within three weeks.

July 17 Today Judge Witoszka and the others were released from jail. Only the commune administrator, Cwik, and messenger Swistek are still being held. They should be freed soon.

Today the first roll call of physicians took place in the hospital. Present were "Wyrwa" and "Komar." The topic was organization of sanitary services. From the radio news it is clear that German troops are on the retreat. The Germans do not have any more strength to stop Russian troops who are now entering East Prussia.

It appears as if the Germans are preparing themselves for gas warfare. In Zamosc and Zwierzyniec we observed German infantry exercises with gas masks. In Zamosc even horses had special gas masks over their mouths. After putting together the information concerning the German military on all fronts, it is clear that we are close to the final stages of this war.

July 18   The main topic of conversation is the Eastern Front, about Wlodzimierz, Hrubieszow, Sokal, and Belzec.

Late this evening the remaining *Volksdeutsch* began packing again and are to move on a minute's notice. The situation is the same at city hall. By order of the German administration in Zamosc the new mayor is a minor clerk, Sygit, and the city secretary, Skorczynski, is the former secretary of the commune of Sulow. The final evacuation of the Germans is tied to the situation at the Front. We know that last night Sokal was taken by the Soviets.

The Russian deserters who have been serving in different SS units are escaping en masse and joining the partisans. Last night thirty of them escaped. The Germans are searching for them, but with no result. People are nervously awaiting the upcoming events.

July 19   At 4 A.M. the labor bureau, *Arbeitsamt*, was evacuated. The post office is closed. The Germans removed all signs and even mail boxes. Only the telephone exchange is still operating.

German files in city hall are being readied for transport. Night clerks have been waiting by the telephones for final evacuation notice. The new mayor signed the papers that made the change in administration legal. The gendarmes have already shipped their files and heavy luggage. They now have only small hand bags to carry.

Around noon the news spread that the Germans had begun a counteroffensive and the evacuations were put on hold for a few days. People began worrying again, but this afternoon all the German civil employees left town. They and the *Volksdeutsch* had been drinking heavily and shooting, but so far there have been no accidents. The gendarmes are still here. The county administration has left Zamosc. The Zamosc evacuation is in full operation.

Highway traffic is heavy but not at all organized. Some vehicles travel toward Zamosc-Lublin, some toward Bilgoraj-Krzeszow. The Germans say the road to Bilgoraj is very dangerous because of bandit activities. There are many military convoys, but all the vehicles are loaded with private luggage. This time the scene of a typical retreat is good for our eyes.

Several times today I walked through the city streets to see for myself what was going on. While walking you must be careful not to show your delight at the German departure. One of the hospital helpers was almost arrested because she smiled as the Germans were moving out. In spite of the German departure the situation in town is still not clear. We do not know what the future will bring.

Despite the happiness caused by the Germans' departure people are still very tense. Some tell rumors about forced evacuations and the arrests of all men. Some people are trying to hide their valuables because of rumors about robberies in the so called no-man's-land. Here at the hospital I am trying to keep everything normal. We are seeking out hiding places for male patients, in case the Germans begin an evacuation of the male population.

July 20   The German military headquarters, *Ortskommandantur*, moved into town. They took over the city hall.

Traffic on the highway is increasing. Tanks and other vehicles on caterpillar tracks, as well as cars and other vehicles, are traveling mainly toward the west. In town the people are nervous and some are packing again.

Underground activities are increasing. In Zamosc it was ordered that underground members and their families leave the city. It appears as if the general mobilization is coming. It is clear that our troops will be involved in fighting very soon.

July 21   Throughout the entire night there was heavy traffic.

Today the Germans are leaving for good, mostly in the direction of Bilgoraj. Once in a while a car is seen speeding toward Zamosc. There are motor vehicle convoys, long lines of horse-drawn wagons, but you can see people on foot also. It looks as if this is a smooth retreat, but in reality the Germans are very nervous. It is possible that this is because of the rumored assassination attempt on Hitler and that he has been wounded, with the government now being in the hands of Goering and Himmler.

Some prisoners were released from Zamosc prison, but others were executed.

At noon the traffic became so heavy that some cars had to use the side roads leading to Blonie and Topolcza.

At 4 P.M. I went to Kawenczyn. Germans are everywhere. I met with "Wyrwa," ("Lys" Norweg), and others. Home Army headquarters had to find another location. The advice is for people to leave the big cities, but the physicians must stay. Different units arrived and prepared to spend the night. But around 8 P.M. the situation changed. All units received orders to move out. From Zamosc there have been more convoys coming in, but around 10 P.M. the direction of the movement changed. More convoys now are coming from Zwierzyniec and Kawenczyn. Officers have come by the hospital asking for directions to Frampol-Janow or Turobin-Lublin.

In town traffic is so heavy that practically all the vehicles are standing still. It seems the Germans do not know where to go because the roads have been closed.

At the hospital all our horses were confiscated. The "well-organized retreat" is turning into flight. Because of this the young helpers at the Cwik bakery removed the German sign *"Bäckerei."* It was the first German sign removed in the city. People who saw this felt happiness.

July 22 We experienced a bad night, no sleep. Motor vehicles passed by constantly, now from Bilgoraj. At the hospital no one went to bed. All the personnel were on alert and in place, except Dr. Matuszewski, who left the hospital to move his family to a village. He returned at 10 A.M.

Around 2 A.M. our own gendarme post moved out.

Last night the Germans killed Konstanty Jozwiakowski, brother of Dr. Jozwiakowski, and also Stanislaw Michalski.

Early this morning motorized convoys still moved along, together with slow-moving horse-drawn wagons. The drivers of the wagons who were forced to go told us they had to turn around by Hedwizyn and Rop, near Bilgoraj. By 10 A.M. the traffic became practically nonexistent. Everything is calm, but we can hear artillery fire.

Telephone communication with Zamosc is dead. The last call was at 3 A.M., when the telephone operator simply said "Good-bye."

In the hospital attic the Germans installed an observation post to check on the highway between Szczebrzeszyn and Zwierzyniec. But at 5 A.M. they moved out. The Germans suggested that all patients be moved to the first floor. At the same time we were able to hear artillery fire from the direction of Zwierzyniec and Brodzka Gora.

The Germans began blowing up railroad tracks. At the hospital we began work very early. Some patients were moved to the first floor; some were moved away from windows into the corridors.

July 22, 8 P.M. The artillery fire has been increasing. The railroad station in Klemensow is on fire. We can still hear loud explosions. The Germans are blowing up the bridges.

July 22, 9 P.M. A young, very energetic German physician visited the hospital. He ordered us to move all patients up from the first floor. Now it is forbidden to remove anything from the hospital. In case of disobedience the penalty is death. For himself he took a room in my quarters. We must comply with his orders and finish by 11 P.M.

We started work and we really had to rush because military vehicles began arriving and parking on the hospital grounds. I was forced to move all our medical supplies from the first floor. Some of them I placed in my quarters and others in the nurses quarters. By 11 P.M. we had finished. The patients were moved and the first floor was empty. At the same time the artillery fire increased. Some explosions were very close. Fires raged close by; buildings were burning.

The military moved in; they even took over our kitchen. German wounded began arriving. The slightly wounded were placed in St. Catherine's Church, on the floor, the others in the hospital beds or mattresses on the floor. Every now and then Russian planes flew over. Even though they did not drop any bombs, the Germans stopped work and hid in the shelters.

The constant explosions, the movement of German soldiers, and heavy military traffic put us into a different mood. Many people moved into the cellar, and not only hospital employees. Some sat on benches; some tried to sleep on the floor. The nurses stayed on the upper floor with our patients. I myself moved from station to station. Around 1 A.M. I decided to lie down, completely dressed.

July 23 I awoke around 4 A.M. and, as always, went on my hospital rounds. More and more German wounded arrived. A long row of ambulances waited by the hospital. Besides the first floor of the hospital the church was also crowded with wounded. Around 6 A.M. the Germans began moving the lightly wounded in the direction of Gorajec-Frampol-Janow, but they were not sure if it was even possible.

Wounded arrived all day. Some were transported farther on. The first wounded came from the Zamosc hospital and later others were brought directly from the battlefield. Their condition was very poor. They were all dirty, unshaven, with just first-aid dressing. Not much medical treatment could be seen. There was only one physician in charge, and he was involved with administration. The two medics were unable to give any aid and instead only administered injections of morphine.

The young physician was rather nice now. He spoke to us in French. From him I learned that the German situation is very bad. Chelm and Rejowiec have been taken by the Russians. The highway to Lublin is in Russian hands, so there is no way to escape.

Around 3 P.M. the Soviets began a bombardment of Zamosc. The bombs were dropped in the vicinity of the zoo. Shortly after the bombardment the traffic on the highway from Zamosc increased.

Here in our town there is no one on the streets. Many people have fled already. Dr. Jentys, his family, Dr. Spoz, and Dr. Warchalowska are now in Szperowka. Besides myself there are only two physicians still here, Dr. Matuszewski and Dr. Jozwiakowski.

The German physician had taken a room in my quarters and installed a radio in our sitting room. So after almost five years we were able to listen to radio news. The German physician asked where he could buy a civilian suit. One of his nurses had already purchased a dress and escaped.

July 24   Last night I went to sleep early, finally undressed. After two sleepless nights, eight hours of sleep made me feel good. I awoke full of energy.

During the night the Germans moved out their wounded. All convoys are now going in the direction of Frampol. On Brodzka Hill anti-aircraft guns were installed. We can see them clearly.

July 24, 10 A.M.   The Germans are extremely nervous. They talk openly about their situation. All roads are now cut off by Russian or Home Army units. They are trying to get to Frampol, hoping that there they can force their way through. Zurawica is burning.

At noon the last Germans left the hospital, except one medic, who is in charge of the first-aid station. Electrical service from Zamosc has been cut off.

Around 1 P.M. a fire broke out in Kawenczyn.

July 24, 2 P.M.   Several German tanks, including "Tigers," traveled on the road toward Kawenczyn. At the hospital we began moving our patients back to the first floor.

July 24, 3 P.M.   There is news that a Home Army unit was destroyed by the Germans, somewhere near Szperowka.

Now only a few cars pass through town. The streets are completely deserted. German soldiers are on the move and are destroying shops and stores. Some local people are also taking part in the robberies.

Around 4 P.M. the last German sanitary unit moved out. They left some dead soldiers. There are no German soldiers at the hospital. This is not as good as it seems, because we can be subject to robberies by various kinds of deserters. Late this evening we could observe the glow of fires. Around 11 P.M. there was a very loud explosion.

July 25   It was a very tiring night. I was sure that the Germans had already gone, but new units began arriving. In a very short time the town was again filled with trucks, tanks, guns, and horse-drawn wagons. No one was able to sleep. There was tremendous noise everywhere. We didn't even undress. I could only sleep for a couple hours.

Since early morning the streets have been crowded with soldiers, typical front-line units. They talk with the civilians. They say that if the Russians begin an air bombardment the entire city will be destroyed in no time. People are very tired and nervous. At the hospital I had a hard time forcing the help to do any work at all. The floors were covered with debris and there was complete disorganization. Everyone is depressed.

At noon traffic increased, but it was completely disorganized. Many cars stopped at the hospital asking for directions to Frampol. That seems to be the only escape from here. Many heavy tanks are moving through. The anti-aircraft guns were removed.

At noon German officers inspected our shelter. They said that soon German planes would begin bombarding the town. On the roof of the hospital they placed a large red flag with a black swastika. They stated that in case of a bombardment we must move out of the shelter, which can only be occupied by Germans.

From Dr. Spoz, who just returned from Szperowka, I learned that around that town the Germans installed many red flags. More people are now returning from Szperowka.

Zwierzyniec has been taken by Soviet units. Around 5 P.M. a fire broke out in Szperowka.

The Germans killed Piotr Niechaj ("Szpak"), a tailor from Blonie, and Talanda, a baker from Szczebrzeszyn. Wladislaw Samulak, from Kawenczyn, was wounded in the stomach and brought to the hospital.

Last night, in a fight near Szperowka, Cwik, from Kawenczyn, and Zbyszek ("Sas") Jaworski were killed. Lt. Sikora was in command of that particular platoon of the Home Army. People are saying that this defeat was a result of his mistakes.

July 26   I was told that just after the destruction of the bridge the Home Army will enter the city.

At 3 A.M. I sat on the hospital wall observing all the roads leading into town.

Around 4 A.M. there was great noise from the direction of Zwierzyniec, but it turned out to be a false alarm. So far our boys have not come. People began coming out onto the streets to have a look around. But we are still waiting to see some of our soldiers.

At 4:30 A.M. I was notified that four soldiers were seen near the destroyed bridge. Through my field glasses I recognized them as Russian soldiers. They came as far as the river bank and then turned away. I still have hope that our own soldiers will be the first ones into town.

I ordered the removal of the German hospital sign and the installation of the old Polish one, which I had kept hidden.

We went to inspect the destroyed bridge. It was sad to see this practically new bridge destroyed. I still remember the opening of the bridge and the ribbon cutting by the county administrator, Sochanski, shortly before the war began.

Shortly after 6 A.M. four Russian soldiers crossed the river and are now sitting and talking with a group of people.

Around 7:30 A.M., from the direction of the bridge, a small group of Soviet soldiers came walking toward town.

At 8 A.M. a Russian officer arrived at the hospital. While talking with him I heard the cry, "Our boys are coming!" I left everything and ran to see for myself. From the direction of Blonie a group of approximately twenty young men approached; all were armed, in uniform, with red scarves around their necks and red and white arm bands on their left sleeves. The people went wild. They were crying, shouting, and throwing flowers.

I first went to the marketplace. There I saw "Podkowa" on horseback, along with his aide, "Korczak" (Siwinski), both in uniforms covered with flowers. I greeted "Podkowa" warmly, holding back my emotions as well as I could.

There was a red and white flag flying over city hall. I ordered our old flag to be flown over the hospital. I had hidden this flag for almost five years. After a short while "Podkowa" arrived at the hospital and decided to organize his headquarters in the hospital office.

We went to inspect the partisans, particularly the wounded soldiers. We were walking through one of the wards when "Podkowa" received information that the Russian colonel to whom "Podkowa" was to report, had arrived. When we went outside we found the colonel standing by his car. After a short introduction he began a speech. He talked about the Germans, brothers, and the independence of Poland. He assured us that the Russians are our friends and the Russian military will give the Poles the complete freedom to organize our own administration, but it must be democratic. He was a very good speaker.

At the same time more platoons of the Home Army and other underground organizations began arriving in town. More Russian troops, along with tanks and artillery, arrived also.

"Podkowa" went to Klemensow while we waited for the large military group commanded by Capt. "Waclaw."

Around 10:30 A.M. practically the entire town population assembled in the marketplace, mostly women, children, and old men. Then down Frampolska Street came a well-equipped battalion of the Home Army. In the lead was Capt. "Waclaw." With their own platoons were "Sanok,"

"Sikora," "Komar," "Nieuchwytny," "Kawka," and others. So many faces I knew well, and now, officially, they were soldiers. A town delegation led by teacher Glowacki greeted Capt. "Waclaw" with the traditional bread and salt. People shouted, cried, and threw flowers. The entire day passed in this way. In town, every flower was used.

Around lunchtime "Waclaw," "Wyrwa," "Sanok," "Gruda," "Kawka," and others came to visit me at the hospital. We began receiving many wounded soldiers, who up until this time had been kept in the nearby villages. It is difficult to describe what I was going through. Never in my life have I been so happy. Sometimes I was unable to control myself.

By nightfall we were completely exhausted, but very happy. Today our slavery ended. Almost five years of German occupation, along with its terror, is over. In spite of the arrests, torture, evacuations, and murders, we survived.

Appendix

1. Cybulski (judge)
2. Leonowicz (judge)
3. Laparewicz (judge)
4. Trybalski (judge)
5. Bajkowski (lawyer)
6. Czernicki, Tomasz (lawyer, member of Parliament)
7. Sikorski, Stanislaw (lawyer)
8. Legiec, Antoni (lawyer)
9. Mroczek (lawyer)
10. Rosinski, Henryk (notary)
11. Bielawski, Andrzej (civil engineer)
12. Klimek, Adam (architect)
13. Tyczkowski, Julian (physician)
14. Werner, Otto (professor)
15. Szczepaniec, Jan (school inspector)
16. Fenc, Pawel (teacher)
17. Zajlich, Stanislaw (teacher)
18. Przybylowicz, Stanislaw (school principal)
19. Wisniewski (director of co-op "Snop")
20. Lipczynski (farmer)
21. Zawisza, Franciszek (priest)
22. Staniszewski, Waclaw (priest)
23. Trochonowicz, Franciszek (priest)
24. Kazanecki (merchant)
25. Bauer, Stefan (school principal)

26. Molicki, Stanislaw (civil engineer)
27. Wiecowski (clerk)
28. Dziemski (translator)
29. Zietek (clerk)
30. Turzanski
31. Lyp (barber)
32. Kowalski, Jan (bricklayer)
33. Margules (architect; only Jew)
34. Kowalski (clerk)
35. Bialkowski (electrical engineer)
36. Dziuba, Waclaw
37. Kozlowski, Jan (banker)
38. Podwinski, Henryk (banker)
39. Czerski, Stanislaw (industrialist)
40. Jakimowicz, Jacek (industrialist)
41. Rauch, Herman (lawyer)
42. Szeptycki, Aleksander (Count)
43. Los, Adam (Count)
44. Dobrzanski (clerk)
45. Sozanski
46. Wytrzeszczewski, Jozef (farmer)
47. Plocharz, Tadeusz (clerk)
48. Debczynski, Stanislaw (administrator, Zamojski estates)
49. Kostecki, Stanislaw (forestry ranger)
50. Kiciak (teacher)
51. Cieslicki, Jozef (priest)
52. Szczyglowski, Jan (pharmacist)
53. Szczyglowski, Czeslaw (pharmacist)
54. Kafarski, Michal (merchant)
55. Kilarski, Stefan (teacher)
56. Przysada, Andrzej (farmer)
57. Franczak, Jan (city mayor)
58. Jazwiakowski, Wiktor (high school principal)
59. Wysocki (teacher)
60. Czekanski, Kazimierz (priest)
61. Gunia (teacher)
62. Sierkowski, Franciszer (farmer)
63. Kolinski (forestry ranger)
64. Wolowski (former ambassador)
65. Wojcikowski, Wojciech (priest)
66. Fudakowski, Kazimierz (senator)
67. Lastowiecki, Konstanty (physician)
68. Stanko, Feliks (lumber mill owner)
69. Bardel, Marcin (priest)
70. Gasior, Wladyslaw (teacher)
71. Cybulski, Stefan (physician)

72. Koziolkiewicz, Czeslaw (priest)
73. Chmielewski, Jozef (priest)
74. Guranowski (physician)
75. Ruszel (school inspector)
76. Ordyczynski (school inspector)
77. Lagowski (school principal)
78. Janiuk (teacher)
79. Pajak (teacher)
80. Krynski (city mayor)
81. Karbonowski (clerk)
82. Lisek (clerk)
83. Michno (judge)
84. Seneszyn (merchant)
85. Kostrzewa, Mikolaj (priest)
86. Diduch (farmer, member of Parliament)
87. Wasko (school principal)
88. Ossowski, Tadeusz (banker)
89. Klos, Wladyslaw (priest)
90. Chroscinski, Leon (priest)
91. Bargiel, Wladyslaw (priest)
92. Liwerski, Jozef (priest)
93. Maj, Dominik (priest)
94. Orzel, Jan (priest)
95. Swistowski, Michal (farmer)
96. Kociuba, Jan (farmer)
97. Jozwiak (farmer)
98. Starowiejski (farmer)
99. Beldowski, Czeslaw (farmer)
100. Beldowski, Mieczyslaw (farmer)
101. Bramski, Jan (university student)
102. Rozmus, Stanislaw (judge)
103. Andrzejewski (banker)
104. Andrzejewski (secretary)
105. Gajewski (lumber mill owner)
106. Czeczukowicz
107. Truchonowicz (county administrator)
108. Martyni, Marian (lawyer)
109. Kuszel, Antoni (court clerk)
110. Bukietynski (electrical engineer)
111. Tokarczuk (teacher)
112. Klukowski, Zygmunt (physician)

Index